The Music of Pavel Haas

The Czech composer Pavel Haas (1899–1944) is commonly positioned in the history of twentieth-century music as a representative of Leoš Janáček's compositional school and as one of the Jewish composers imprisoned by the Nazis in the concentration camp of Terezín (Theresienstadt). However, the nature of Janáček's influence remains largely unexplained and the focus on the context of the Holocaust tends to yield a one-sided view of Haas's oeuvre. The existing scholarship offers limited insight into Haas's compositional idiom and does not sufficiently explain the composer's position with respect to broader aesthetic trends and artistic networks in inter-war Czechoslovakia and beyond. This book is the first attempt to provide a comprehensive (albeit necessarily selective) discussion of Haas's music since the publication of Lubomír Peduzzi's 'life and work' monograph in 1993. It provides the reader with an enhanced understanding of Haas's music through analytical and hermeneutical interpretation as well as cultural and aesthetic contextualisation, and thus reveals the rich nuances of Haas's multi-faceted work which have not been sufficiently recognised so far.

Martin Čurda completed his Ph.D. studies at Cardiff University, School of Music in 2017. He is currently employed as a lecturer in musicology at the Faculty of Fine Arts and Music of the University of Ostrava (Czech Republic), teaching courses related to music analysis and semiotics, music history since 1900, and performance practice. His research into the music of Pavel Haas has so far led to the publication of several journal articles and book chapters, as well as to the organisation of the first international academic conference focusing specifically on this composer (Pavel Haas Study Day, 2016). His research combines musical-analytical methods with hermeneutic enquiry rooted in semiotics, cultural critique, and discourse analysis, revealing the interaction of music, culture and politics.

Ashgate Studies in Theory and Analysis of Music After 1900

Series Editor:
Judy Lochhead, Stony Brook University, USA

The *Ashgate Studies in Theory and Analysis of Music After 1900* series celebrates and interrogates the diversity of music composed since 1900, and embraces innovative and interdisciplinary approaches to this repertoire. A recent resurgence of interest in theoretical and analytical readings of music comes in the wake of, and as a response to, the great successes of musicological approaches informed by cultural studies at the turn of the century. This interest builds upon the considerable insights of cultural studies while also recognizing the importance of critical and speculative approaches to music theory and the knowledge-producing potentials of analytical close readings. Proposals for monographs and essay collections are welcomed on music in the classical tradition created after 1900 to the present through the lens of theory and analysis. The series particularly encourages interdisciplinary studies that combine theory and/or analysis with such topical areas as gender and sexuality, post-colonial and migration studies, voice and text, philosophy, technology, politics, and sound studies, to name a few.

György Ligeti's *Le Grand Macabre*: Postmodernism, Musico-Dramatic Form and the Grotesque
Peter Edwards

The Musical Thought and Spiritual Lives of Heinrich Schenker and Arnold Schoenberg
Matthew Arndt

Michael Finnissy at 70: Bright Futures, Dark Pasts
Edited by Ian Pace and Nigel McBride

Compositional Process in Elliott Carter's String Quartets: A Study in Sketches
Laura Emmery

The Music of Pavel Haas: Analytical and Hermeneutical Studies
Martin Čurda

For more information about this series, please visit: www.routledge.com/music/series/ASTAMN

The Music of Pavel Haas
Analytical and Hermeneutical Studies

Martin Čurda

Routledge
Taylor & Francis Group

LONDON AND NEW YORK

First published 2020
by Routledge
2 Park Square, Milton Park, Abingdon, Oxon OX14 4RN

and by Routledge
52 Vanderbilt Avenue, New York, NY 10017

Routledge is an imprint of the Taylor & Francis Group, an informa business

British Library Cataloguing-in-Publication Data
A catalogue record for this book is available from the British Library

Library of Congress Cataloging-in-Publication Data
Names: Čurda, Martin, author.
Title: The music of Pavel Haas : analytical and hermeneutical studies /
    Martin Čurda.
Description: New York : Routledge, 2020. | Series: Ashgate studies in theory
    and analysis of music after 1900 | Includes bibliographical references
    and index. |
Identifiers: LCCN 2019055680 (print) | LCCN 2019055681 (ebook) |
    ISBN 9781138360013 (hardback) | ISBN 9780429433351 (ebook)
Subjects: LCSH: Haas, Pavel—Criticism and interpretation. | Music—
    Czechoslovakia—20th century—History and criticism. | Concentration
    camp inmates as musicians—Czech Republic—Terezín (Ústecký kraj) |
    Janáček, Leoš, 1854–1928—Influence.
Classification: LCC ML410.H1001 C87 2020 (print) | LCC ML410.H1001
    (ebook) | DDC 780.92—dc23
LC record available at https://lccn.loc.gov/2019055680
LC ebook record available at https://lccn.loc.gov/2019055681

ISBN: 978-1-138-36001-3 (hbk)
ISBN: 978-0-429-43335-1 (ebk)

Typeset in Times New Roman
by Apex CoVantage, LLC

Contents

Illustrations

Figures

Musical examples

Tables

Introduction

Introduction

In the case of Pavel Haas (1899–1944), a number of factors have conspired to push the music of a highly accomplished composer to the verge of oblivion. As a student of Leoš Janáček and a life-long resident of Brno (Moravia), Haas had limited opportunities to have his music performed in the Czechoslovak capital Prague (Bohemia) or abroad and thus build a reputation on a national or even international level. During the Nazi occupation of Czechoslovakia, the composer was banned from performance, imprisoned in Terezín (Theresienstadt) and eventually killed in Auschwitz due to his Jewish origins.[1] Little was done in the following Communist era to revive his musical legacy.[2] It was not until the 1990s that Haas's works became more broadly available to scholars, performers, and audiences. Although Czech composer and musicologist Lubomír Peduzzi had continuously published academic articles on various aspects of Haas's work since the late 1940s, his seminal 'life and work' monograph on the composer only appeared in 1993.[3] Most of Haas's works only survived in manuscripts until 1991, when the publishing house Tempo Praha (in collaboration with Bote & Bock Berlin) started producing modern editions revised by Peduzzi.[4] CD recordings of Haas's music were first distributed internationally by Channel Classics ('Composers from Theresienstadt', 1991), Decca Records ('Entartete Musik' series, 1994), and Koch Schwann ('Böhmen & Mähren: Musik Jüdischer Komponisten', 1994). In the present day, most of Haas's major works are available in the form of printed editions and CD recordings. New recordings and concert performances (mostly of chamber pieces and songs) continue to emerge and Haas's music is no longer as one-sidedly associated with Terezín and Jewishness as it was in the 1990s.

However, despite these continuing efforts, much remains to be done in terms of deepening and broadening the critical understanding of Haas's work. Very few substantial pieces of academic research have appeared since the publication of Peduzzi's monograph. On the whole, the vast majority of available scholarship focuses on the works Haas composed during the Second World War. In Anglophone academic literature, Haas is mentioned almost exclusively in the context of music in Terezín (a selective overview of the relevant literature will be presented below). Arguably, the traumatic and tragic shadow of the Holocaust threatens to obscure the rich nuances of Haas's multi-faceted work. It is one of the objectives of this book to offer a more balanced view of Haas's work and draw attention to aspects that have been overlooked so far.

Peduzzi positioned Haas in the history of twentieth-century music as a composer whose stylistic development was informed by Janáček on the one hand and Stravinsky on the other.[5] In other words, Peduzzi argued that Haas achieved a synthesis between Janáček's idiosyncratic style, rooted in the local folk-music tradition, and the Stravinskian strand of international ('Western') musical modernism. While this assessment is essentially correct, it does not take into account the 'middle-ground' context of Czechoslovak music, arts, and culture of the time. In order to fill this gap, Chapter 1 contains a survey of avant-garde movements, discourse platforms, ideas, and networks in inter-war Czechoslovakia, with regard to contemporary developments in other national contexts.

Chapter 2 demonstrates that the Czech avant-garde movement known as Poetism, which itself drew on the contemporary Parisian avant-garde, was a major influence on Haas's works from the 1920s. The examination of Haas's String Quartet No. 2 'From the Monkey Mountains', Op. 7 (1925) and other relevant pieces shows that Haas engaged with the characteristic topoi of Poetism and that there is a strong affinity between the composer's predilection for rhythmic vitality, humour, caricature, and the grotesque and Poetism's emphasis on physicality, sensuality, and 'everyday' art (from fairground, circus, and carnival to jazz-band music and silent-film slapsticks).

Some of the key features of Haas's style, already observed in his 1925 string quartet (ambiguous play with meaning, grotesque and caricature-like exaggeration and distortion, and collage-like juxtaposition of incongruous elements) reappear in the Suite for Piano, Op. 13 (1935). The discussion of the latter work in Chapter 3 demonstrates the continuity of these features in Haas's work and explains their development over time. Since the suite is also representative of Neoclassical tendencies, which became increasingly apparent in Haas's music from the 1930s onward, this chapter also explains how the perceived Neoclassical virtues (previously discussed in Chapter 1), such as economy of means, concision, clarity of line and contour, diatonicism, and rhythmic vitality, manifest themselves in this piece.

Chapter 4 examines the importance of rhythmic and metric procedures in Haas's music with reference to Janáček's theory and compositional practice of *sčasování* ('metro-rhythmics'). It will be observed that Haas's use of Janáčekian techniques (such as repetition, superimposition, and montage) raises questions of fragmentation, discontinuity, development, and stasis, which have been discussed mostly in the area of Stravinsky studies. Case studies used to illustrate these issues include the first movement of String Quartet No. 2 (1925), the one-movement Study for Strings (1943), and the first movement of String Quartet No. 3, Op. 15 (1937–38). Although the analyses of these works focus primarily on the relationship between rhythm and form, attention is also paid to issues of pitch structure (especially the duality of diatonicism and pitch symmetry). This chapter thus provides a comprehensive discussion of Haas's compositional technique with regard to the broader problems of early twentieth-century modernist musical syntax.

Chapter 5 contains a critical reading of Haas's opera *Charlatan* (1934–37), which is one of the composer's key works. While the themes of fairground and carnival, which feature prominently in the opera, provide continuity with Haas's earlier works, *Charlatan* places greater emphasis on the terrifying aspect of the grotesque and on uncanny imagery suggestive of internal conflicts within human subjectivity, thus anticipating features that would appear in some of Haas's later works. Particularly fascinating (and highly characteristic of the composer's lifelong fascination with semantic ambiguity) is the opera's tragi-comical genre, which combines elements of farce, tragedy, and horror. This chapter also sheds new light on the idea (originally proposed by Michael Beckerman) that *Charlatan*, because of its dark undertones, is a kind of commentary on the historical context of the late 1930s, marked by the rising threat of Nazism.[6]

Haas's Four Songs on Chinese Poetry (1944) contain a poignant reflection of the composer's experience of incarceration in the concentration camp of Terezín. Chapter 6 explores the meanings encoded in the piece, the strategies of signification employed to convey them, and the relationship between the author and the protagonist of his work. The analysis demonstrates how psychological phenomena such as trauma, grief, and melancholy are portrayed in Haas's music through patterns of declamation and expressive gestures. The related notion of agency is used to discuss the significance of linear motion, circular motion, and stasis in the piece. The preceding analysis of *Charlatan* is of immediate relevance to the discussion of uncanny imagery (symmetrical 'mirrors', parallel 'shadows', enharmonic 'doubles') in the Four Songs. Finally, this chapter offers an explanation of the semantic ambiguity that arises from cyclic alternation between oppositional images and moods throughout the cycle (day/night; light/darkness; motion/stasis; and so on).

The works studied here are selected in such a way as to reflect most of the chronological stages of Haas's career from 1925 to 1944, to represent a variety of different genres, and to address as many of the issues raised by Haas's music as possible. However, a number of works and thematic areas will inevitably be left unaddressed. Future research may shed more light on Haas's studies with Janáček through the study of archival sources (lecture notes and study pieces), and his early compositions such as *Čínské písně* (*Chinese Songs*), Op. 4 (1919–21),[7] and *Zesmutnělé scherzo* (*Saddened Scherzo*), Op. 5 (1921).[8] Of particular interest among Haas's early works is his song cycle *Fata Morgana*, Op. 6 (1923) for tenor, piano, and string quartet, which combines in a fascinating way Janáčekian compositional idiom with the eroticism, exoticism, and mysticism of poetry by Rabindranath Tagore. Haas's predilection for unusual instrumental combinations also manifests itself in his song cycle *Vyvolená* (*The Chosen One*), Op. 8 (1927), for tenor, flute, violin, French horn, and piano on the words of Jiří Wolker. A potential study focusing specifically on Haas's song cycles should also consider the *Sedm písní v lidovém tónu* (*Seven Songs in Folk Tone*), Op. 18 (1939–40), for tenor/soprano and piano, a piece of masterful and witty folkloric stylisation, based on poems by František Ladislav Čelakovský.

Still awaiting critical examination is Haas's music for theatre and film (detailed further on in this chapter). The present discussion of Haas's engagement with the themes of the Czech avant-garde would find a logical continuation in an analysis of *Předehra pro Rozhlas* (*Overture for Radio*), Op. 11 (1930–31), a humorous, quasi-Futurist celebration of the new technological medium, scored for a small orchestra and a quartet of male voices.[9] The study of Haas's Psalm 29, Op. 12 (1931–32) for organ, baritone, female choir, and a small orchestra (a contemporary sacred counterpart of the Overture) might bring insight into Haas's attitude towards religion. Haas's Suite for Oboe and Piano, Op. 17 (1939) and his unfinished Symphony (1940–41), both composed during the Nazi occupation but before his deportation to Terezín, are relatively well known as poignant manifestations of patriotism and have received some attention in the existing scholarship, which, however, does not exhaust the possibilities of critical interpretation.[10] It will have to be left to future research to fill these (and other) gaps in the knowledge of Haas's music.

This book aspires to enhance the knowledge and understanding of Haas's music through analytical and hermeneutical interpretation, as well as cultural and aesthetic contextualisation, rather than heuristic and historiographical documentation. In this respect, it will contribute relatively little to the foundational work of Peduzzi. Most of the chapters are based on close reading of the musical score, using a variety of methodologies from the fields of music analysis and semiotics (including theoretical approaches to semantic ambiguity, musical topics, markedness and correlation, gesture and agency, and so on).[11] In most cases, however, analysis is in the service of a broader, hermeneutical enquiry, which interprets the work in question through a specifically designed conceptual, contextual, and/ or intertextual framework. The focus on the text of Haas's works is determined partly by personal preference and partly by the fact that there is very little archival material other than musical scores and drafts.[12] Moreover, virtually no personal or business correspondence, diaries, or other documents are extant that might bring insight into Haas's personality, intellectual outlook, socio-cultural affiliations, and so on.

Biographical and historiographical information relevant to discussions of particular works will be provided in the corresponding chapters of this study. However, since there is no comprehensive historiographical account of Haas's life and work available in English, it seems pertinent to include a brief summary of Haas's personal background and his professional affiliations.[13]

Haas's social, national, and ethnic background

Pavel Haas came from a lower-middle-class 'assimilated' Jewish family of mixed (Czech and Russian) national background with few artistic and intellectual affiliations. According to Peduzzi, Pavel Haas and his younger brother Hugo (a popular Czech actor in the inter-war era and a successful Hollywood director after the war)[14] were sons of Zikmund Haas, a shoe seller who came to Brno in the 1890s from dominantly Czech rural regions of eastern Bohemia, and his Russian wife Olga Epsteinová, who was 'the daughter of a steam navigation company clerk from Odessa'.[15] Before the First World War, the majority of Brno's population was German. This situation changed with the foundation of the independent Czechoslovak state in 1918, although there was a strong German minority in Brno throughout the inter-war era.[16] The family spoke Czech in private; Pavel and Hugo were sent to German primary school due to the political circumstances of the Austro-Hungarian Empire, which required knowledge of German, but both continued their studies in Czech secondary schools. Thus, unlike many Jewish artists and intellectuals of the time, Haas and his brother were unambiguously Czech (rather than German) in terms of language, as well as social and professional affiliations (as will be seen).[17] It should also be noted that Brno, as the urban centre of Moravia, is a geographical and cultural counterpart of Prague, the capital of Bohemia, as well as the Czech (previously Czechoslovak) state as a whole. In this sense, Haas was a Moravian (as opposed to Bohemian) composer.

Little can be established with certainty about Haas's attitude to his Jewish origins. However, he did not come from a family of active worshippers and there is little evidence to suggest that he maintained particularly close contact (prior to his imprisonment in Terezín, where this was not a matter of choice) with Jewish culture, religion, or music, apart from his connection to his uncle Richard Reichner, a cantor in a synagogue in Kolín nad Labem (a city relatively distant from Brno). Peduzzi provided the following assessment of Reichner's influence:

> The boys [Pavel and Hugo] often spent their vacations with Reichner's family and Pavel was apparently strongly engaged by what Hugo did not particularly care about: the synagogal chants. The plaintive and yet passionate Jewish songs sung by uncle Reichner in the synagogue influenced the perceptive boy for life.[18]

Peduzzi suggests that these visits may have inspired the young composer to engage with Biblical themes in some of his early (mostly unfinished) works, such as *Jonah* (*Jonáš*, 1914), *Exodus of the Israelites from Egypt* (*Odchod Izraele z Egypta*, 1915), or Psalm 19 (1916).[19] He also points out that, when searching for suitable material for an opera, Haas considered works by Jewish writers, including Solomon An-sky's *The Dybbuk* and Stanislav Lom's *Penitent Venus*.[20] Peduzzi concludes the following:

> Without completing any of these projects (except for Psalm 19), Haas later (roughly in the mid-1920s) arrived at a purely musical solution: he assimilated the specifics of Hebrew melodies into [the range of] his own expressive means and used them to personalise his musical language.[21]

Peduzzi refers particularly to 'Preghiera' and 'Epilogo' from Haas's Wind Quintet, Op. 10 (1929), to which one may add the first movement of the unfinished Symphony (1940–41).[22] In these pieces, melodic elements which may be perceived as 'Jewish' (melismatic delivery, ornamentation, modality) are combined with ritualistic, quasi-religious character (call and response patterns, slow pacing, chant-like unisons).

However, it is noteworthy that references to Jewishness with regard to Haas and/or his music were extremely rare in contemporary newspaper articles and concert reviews. Out of more than 150 clippings from Czech and German newspapers (published between 1920 and 1938) which the composer himself compiled in a notebook entitled 'Moje úspěchy a ne-úspěchy' ('My Successes and Non-successes')[23] only four concert reviews contain a reference to 'Jewish' or, more obliquely, 'racial' elements in Haas's music; Haas himself is always presented as a Moravian composer of Czech nationality and/or a student of Janáček's – never as a Jewish composer.[24]

Further discussion of these issues might also take into account Haas's Psalm 29, Op.12 (1931–32) for organ, baritone, female choir, and small orchestra, which is the composer's only (complete) piece of sacred music; his male choir *Al S'fod* (Terezín, 1942), which is Haas's only work on a Hebrew text; and his incidental music for Samson Raphaelson's play *The Jazz Singer* (produced in Brno in 1928 under the title *Černý troubadour/The Black Troubadour*), which tells the story of a synagogue cantor's son who leaves the Jewish community to become a jazz singer.[25]

Haas's above-mentioned interest in An-Sky's *The Dybbuk*, a play based on Jewish folk tales and customs and informed by the writer's own ethnographic research,[26] may be suggestive of the composer's will to explore his Jewish origins. However, Haas arguably had other reasons to engage with this particular piece, too. *The Dybbuk* became widely known following its 1922 production, directed by Evgenii Vakhtangov, in Soviet Russia (the Habima Theatre).[27] Reportedly, the most famous moment in Vakhtangov's production was the so-called Beggars' Dance; in this scene, a grotesque whirl of crippled figures which engulfs a young bride on the day of her forced marriage, becomes a simile for the woman's possession by the ghost of her dead true lover.[28] Thus, *The Dybbuk* feeds into two major areas of Haas's interest: the grotesque, which manifests itself musically through exaggeration and distortion of dance-like movement (see the discussion of the topic of 'danse excentrique' in Chapters 2 and 3), and the uncanny, which is related to themes of split subjectivity and possession by dark forces (see the discussion of *Charlatan* in Chapter 5).

The grotesque dance may also be associated, more broadly, with Jewishness. According to Esti Sheinberg, Vakhtangov's production of *The Dybbuk* was a manifestation of the 'perception of Jewish music and dance as an outlet for a grotesque *Übermarionette* [which] function[ed] as a cultural unit in twentieth-century Russian literature and theatre.'[29] It seems reasonable to assume that Haas could have been aware of these connotations. However, none of the grotesque dances in Haas's music incorporates recognisably 'Jewish' musical elements. With reference to one of the pieces in question, the 'Postludium' from Haas's Suite for Piano, Jascha Nemtsov has suggested a link between the perceived character of 'despairing cheerfulness' ('verzweifelte Lustigkeit') and the notion of 'Jewish humour' (see Chapter 3 for further discussion).[30] Again, this point may refer to an actual part of Haas's cultural heritage, but it would be difficult to construct a compelling argument to support this thesis in the absence of archival material of a personal nature.

I have chosen not to explore the problem of Jewishness in Haas's music in further detail for several reasons: the lack of relevant sources; the relatively small proportion of pieces which contain 'Jewish elements' in terms of subject matter and/or musical language; my general focus on analytical and hermeneutical reading of specific works, rather than on the personality of the composer himself; and perhaps most importantly, my belief that criteria related to style, genre, compositional technique, and recurring themes (such as the grotesque and the uncanny) bring more insight into Haas's work than the complicated and elusive notion of 'Jewishness'. Thus, Haas's Jewish heritage will be considered, where relevant, but it will not be a subject of my inquiry in and of itself.

The existing historiographical and archival sources provide limited insight into the social networks in which Haas was embedded. However, it is significant that his brother Hugo was very well connected (particularly in the 1930s) among artists, intellectuals, and other prominent figures in Prague's high society. According to Peduzzi, it was he who introduced Pavel Haas to his future wife Dr Soňa Jakobsonová, previously married to the acclaimed linguist Roman Jakobson (associated with the so-called Prague Linguistic Circle). Jakobsonová divorced her husband and married Haas in 1935.[31] Two years later (on 1 November 1937), she gave birth to their daughter Olga. Olga Haasová-Smrčková (formerly married to the writer Milan Kundera) has had a successful career as an opera singer and still lives in Brno. According to Mrs Haasová-Smrčková, Pavel Haas became acquainted, through his brother, with prominent Czech writers, including Karel Čapek, Vítězslav Nezval, and Olga Scheinpflugová.[32]

Musical culture in Brno and Haas's professional affiliations

In order to outline Haas's professional affiliations, it is useful to introduce the institutional structures of Czech musical culture in Brno, which was relatively independent of the city's German musical culture in the pre-war years and expanded rapidly in the new political circumstances of independent Czechoslovakia. One of the most important centres was the National Theatre (later called 'Zemské' Theatre) in Brno, which gained much needed new material and personal resources after 1918. The conductor František Neumann played a crucial role as the leader of the theatre's operatic ensemble from 1919 until his death in 1929.[33] He was also in charge of the concert series of the theatre's symphony orchestra (the first full-sized and fully professional symphony orchestra in the history of Brno). Neumann's progressive dramaturgy focused on the recent international repertoire as well as new works by local composers.[34] The establishment of Masaryk University in Brno in 1919 facilitated the formation of the first musicological department in Moravia. The musicologists Vladimír Helfert, Gracián Černušák, and Jan Racek all supported local musical culture through concert reviews and organisational activities.

Haas was one of the first students to enrol at the Brno Conservatoire, established in 1919 through the merger of Janáček's Organ School (established 1881) and the music school of Beseda brněnská, where Haas started his musical education in 1913. He studied music theory and composition with Jan Kunc and Vilém Petrželka (both former students of Leoš Janáček) and piano with Anna Holubová.[35] When the institution was put under state control in 1920, Janáček was appointed a professor of composition at the Prague Conservatoire, teaching in Brno. Pavel Haas attended Janáček's composition masterclass between 1920 and 1922.[36]

The most important institution for Haas's professional development was the Club of Moravian Composers (Klub moravských skladatelů); this was formally established in 1922, but its origins date back to the foundation in 1919 of the so-called Club of Young Moravian Composers (Klub mladých skladatelů moravských).[37] The initiative behind the establishment of the CYMC came from the composers Vilém Petrželka, Václav Kaprál, and the musicologist Vladimír Helfert.[38] At the inaugural meeting of the CMC, Janáček was unanimously elected president of the society, while the conductor František Neumann became vice-president.[39] The function of the CMC was to facilitate performances of new works by its members, to organise concerts of contemporary music (both Czech and foreign), to provide material support for composers and performers, to publish new works, to organise lectures, and thus stimulate musical culture in Brno. The Club's membership included not only composers, but also performers, musicologists, and enthusiasts. As a result, the CMC was strongly linked to the activities of all other musical organisations in Brno.

The activities of the CMC were mostly limited to Brno, with occasional collaboration with Prague-based institutions.[40] The CMC also had modest international affiliations. The Czechoslovak section of the International Society for Contemporary Music (ISCM) initially included the representatives of the two Prague-based musical societies: Spolek pro moderní hudbu (Society for Modern Music) and the Verein für musikalische Privataufführungen; a third delegate representing the CMC joined the board in 1923.[41] On the whole, however, the impact of the CMC on the international level was rather limited, since the Czechoslovak section as a whole had only one vote in the international forum of the ISCM.[42]

The CMC was also more or less directly involved in the visits of several internationally important figures to Brno. Following a personal invitation by Janáček, Béla Bartók came to Brno to perform works by himself and Zoltán Kodály on 2 March 1925.[43] On the very next day, the CMC organised a concert of works by Arnold Schoenberg with an introductory lecture by Helfert in anticipation of the Czechoslovak premiere of *Gurrelieder*, which took place five days later at the National Theatre in Brno in the composer's presence.[44] In 1926, Henry Cowell visited Brno during his European tour; he gave a lecture on 8 April 1926 and a concert of his works followed the next day.[45] Later that year, the CMC organised a lecture on quarter-tone music (2 December 1926) by the Czech composer Miroslav Ponc (a student of Alois Hába), followed the next day by a solo recital by Erwin Schulhoff, including both quarter-tone and half-tone works.[46]

Arguably the most important aspect of the CMC's engagement with the international musical scene was the regular inclusion of works by contemporary foreign composers in its concert series. Between 1922 and 1938, the CMC performed works by Maurice Ravel, Claude Debussy, Igor Stravinsky, Francis Poulenc, Arthur Honegger, Darius Milhaud, Bohuslav Martinů, Arnold Schoenberg, Ernst Křenek, Paul Hindemith, Egon Wellesz, Erwin Schulhoff, Fidelio Finke, Felix Petyrek, Béla Bartók, Zoltán Kodály, Alexander Scriabin, Sergei Prokofiev, Nikolai Myaskovsky, Alfredo Casella, and others.[47]

Haas maintained close contact with the CYMC and CMC throughout his life. He had one of his early works performed at the very first concert of the CYMC, he was present at the inaugural meeting of the CMC, and he remained a member of the committee until 1939, when he was excluded due to the racial laws imposed by the Nazi occupiers. Between 1926 and 1929, Haas held the position of the CMC's secretary (*jednatel*).[48] This role would have primarily entailed concert organisation, but its details are not clear from the available archival material.[49]

Most performances of Haas's chamber and solo works in his lifetime were facilitated by the CMC in collaboration with a fairly stable circle of performers. The possibility of collaboration with some of these performers and ensembles arguably provided a direct incentive for Haas's composition of specific pieces. His string quartet *From the Monkey Mountains* (1925) followed the foundation of the Moravian Quartet (Moravské kvarteto) in 1924, which premiered the piece in 1926.[50] Similarly, Haas's Wind Quintet (1929) is dedicated to the Moravian Wind Quintet (Moravské dechové kvinteto, established in 1927), which premiered the piece in 1930.[51] Haas's Suite for Piano (1935) is dedicated to Bernard Kaff, who became a member of the CMC in 1936 and premiered the work the same year.[52]

Haas also made use of other music forces available to him. His early orchestral piece *Saddened Scherzo* (*Zesmutnělé scherzo*, 1921) was premiered by the Orchestral Society (Orchestrální sdružení), directed by Vladimír Helfert.[53] His *Carnival* (*Karneval*, Op. 9, 1928–29) for male choir was dedicated to, and repeatedly performed by, the acclaimed Choral Society of Moravian Teachers (Pěvecké sdružení moravských učitelů), directed by Ferdinand Vach.[54]

Since 1927, the CMC also collaborated with the broadcasting company Radiojournal, which had run a radio station in Brno since 1924 and which became an important source of financial support for the Club's projects. The very first CMC concert to be broadcast by Radiojournal (25 April 1927) was conceived as a showcase of new Moravian music and included the premiere performance of Haas's song cycle *The Chosen One* (*Vyvolená*, 1927).[55] Haas's music appeared on the radio several times in the 1930s and one piece was composed specifically with the new medium in mind. The piece in question, the *Overture for Radio* (*Předehra pro rozhlas*, 1930–31, premiered and broadcast on 2 June 1931), is scored for small orchestra and four male voices (alternating between singing and declamation); it is based on an apotheosis of radio, written by the composer's brother Hugo.[56]

Haas also wrote several pieces of incidental music for theatre in the 1920s, mostly for productions that involved his brother Hugo.[57] Similarly, in the 1930s

Haas wrote film scores for three films featuring his brother: *Život je pes* (*Dog's Life*, 1933), *Mazlíček* (*The Little Pet*, 1934), and *Kvočna* (*Mother Hen*, 1937).[58]

The contacts between CMC and the Society for Modern Music in Prague facilitated a performance of Haas's string quartet *From the Monkey Mountains* in Prague on 26 April 1927. Several concerts which included Haas's works took place in Prague and other Czechoslovak cities in the 1930s. On at least two occasions during the composer's lifetime, Haas's music was played abroad. On 7 January 1935, Haas's Wind Quintet was performed in Vienna (Kammersaal des Musikvereins) in the first of two exchange concerts between the CMC and the Austrian Union of Composers (Österreichischer Komponistenbund).[59] On 10 February 1936, Haas's Suite for Piano was premiered in Vienna (Großer Ehrbarsaal) as part of a concert of Moravian music, organised by the Austrian society Musik der Gegenwart.[60]

On both occasions, according to reviews published in Viennese newspapers, Haas's works were considered among the best on the programme.[61] The Wind Quintet was praised as a 'work which excels in the originality of thematic [invention] as well as in the effective command of compositional technique'.[62] Reportedly, the work was received with 'stormy approval' and the third movement ('Ballo eccentrico') 'earned a separate applause'.[63] Haas's music was also singled out on account of its unusual character; with reference to the Wind Quintet, some reviewers wrote about 'a mixture of melancholy and parody' and music of 'bizarre' and 'grotesque' qualities, from which 'fantastic pictures emerge'.[64] Haas himself was characterised as a 'young, wild, and talented composer, whom one could describe as a kind of Moravian Stravinsky'.[65] The Suite for Piano was considered 'thoroughly original [and] innovative in the word's best sense', a 'highly valuable piece of pronounced, yet natural modernity'.[66] Again, reference was made to Stravinsky with respect to Haas's use of rhythm:

> In its fast movements, this interesting work develops rhythmic impulses that are reminiscent of Stravinsky's elementary power, venturing harmonically as far as the realm of polytonality. The pastoral middle movement contains echoes of Slavic folklore, which coalesce imaginatively with the [piece's] thoroughly modern constitution.[67]

The Viennese reviews constitute a fairly representative sample of the contemporary reception of Haas's music as a whole, inasmuch as they bring up many of the recurrent themes, such as grotesque/parodic/bizarre/fantastic (and yet also melancholic/mystical) character, mischievous youth coupled with compositional mastery, folk inspiration cast in thoroughly modern guise, Stravinskian rhythms, unconventional harmonies, and so on.[68]

The most substantial performance project of Haas's work was the premiere of his opera *Charlatan* by 'Zemské' (previously 'Národní'/'National') Theatre in Brno on 2 April 1938.[69] This was one of the last performances of Haas's music before the start of the German occupation of Czechoslovakia (15 March 1939), which meant the end of performance opportunities for the composer. Major works such as his String Quartet No. 3 (1937–38), Suite for Oboe and

Piano (1939), and the unfinished Symphony (1940–41) remained unperformed in the composer's lifetime.[70]

Although Haas was able to compose at a steady rate and have most of his works performed thanks to the above described professional structures, he relied on working in his father's shoe shop as his main source of income throughout most of his life. Haas also never held a teaching job at any of the musical schools in Brno; he only gave private lessons in music theory in the 1930s (Peduzzi was one of his students).[71]

The problem of a Janáček compositional school

Since the most prominent Brno-based composers of the inter-war era all studied with Leoš Janáček, the term 'Janáček's compositional school' ('Janáčkova skladatelská škola') has sometimes been used with reference to Václav Kaprál (1889–1947), Vilém Petrželka (1889–1967), Jaroslav Kvapil (1892–1958), Osvald Chlubna (1893–1971), and Pavel Haas (1899–1944).[72] Arguably, the association of these composers is based primarily on the fact that they all lived in Brno for most of their lives and based their careers as composers on virtually identical institutional structures. It is open to question whether they formed a coherent group in terms of their individual styles and aesthetic tendencies and whether they achieved some kind of organic continuation of Janáček's style, as the notion of a compositional school implies.

Paradoxically, many of these composers were strongly influenced (at least in their early works) by the Prague-based composer Vítězslav Novák (1870–1949), who, being a student of Antonín Dvořák, established himself in the pre-war years as the leading figure of Czech musical tradition. In 1940, Czech musicologist Jan Racek argued that 'virtually all members of Janáček's school in Brno were in their stylistic development more affected by the influence of Novák's oeuvre than that of Janáček's compositional idiom' and concluded that progressive Moravian music was based on a 'stylistic synthesis between Janáček and Novák'.[73] Racek's conclusion, neat as it seems, is not without problems. First, it completely disregards Haas (probably because Racek's book was published at the time of the Nazi occupation of Czechoslovakia). Second, the influence of Novák, whose work was outdated by the early 1920s with respect to Janáček's innovations and the advances of the inter-war avant-garde, is arguably a sign of conservative rather than progressive tendencies.[74]

Czech musicologist Vladimír Helfert offered a more nuanced picture in his 1936 synthetic overview of *Modern Czech Music*.[75] Helfert identified two distinct 'generational layers' of contemporary Czech composers, divided by the First World War. Whereas the artistic profile of the first layer (composers born *c.* 1890) took shape in the first two decades of the twentieth century, the composers of the second layer (born *c.* 1900) were not directly affected by late Romantic tendencies in their formative period, as they did not reach their maturity until after the war. Helfert aligned Kaprál and Petrželka (both of whom continued their studies in Prague with Novák after leaving Janáček's Organ School in Brno) with the pre-war generation, while arguing that Kvapil, Chlubna, and Haas tended towards the post-war generation.[76] Helfert, who also wrote concert reviews on a regular basis, had the advantage of first-hand knowledge of a wide range of the contemporary repertoire of Czech music, much of which is not readily available today. A comparative analysis of string quartets by these composers from the 1920s shows that works by Kaprál and Petrželka drew primarily on Novák (as well as other influences) but formed an original stylistic idiom; works by Kvapil and Chlubna gave the impression of juvenilia and relied heavily on conventions of the time; Haas's quartet 'From the Monkey Mountains' stood out on account of its unconventional, Janáčekian idiom and its avant-garde aesthetic underpinnings (which will be discussed in detail in Chapters 2 and 4 of the present study).[77] Significantly, Helfert only used the term 'avant-garde' (rather than 'modern') with reference to Haas.[78] Helfert's portrayal of Haas is worth quoting at length:

> Pavel Haas [. . .] built in his early works upon the legacy of his mentor [Janáček] in terms of expression [style] and tectonics [form]. This is clearly apparent in his orchestral piece [titled] *Saddened Scherzo* (1921). However, already in this work, elements of Janáček's influence are combined with hints of then-new West-European stimuli, particularly those of Stravinsky and Honegger, et al. These elements subsequently become dominant in Haas's style and lead the composer to remarkable individuation of compositional method in the direction of bold constructivism and uncompromising sonic invention. Haas thus becomes a courageous avant-gardist in Janáček's school, who follows the paths of new stylistic sentiments. Of course, it is not surprising that many of his works appeared as [mere] experiments (*Fata Morgana*, 1923; string quartet 'From the Monkey Mountains', 1925; Introduction and Psalm 29, 1931). However, let us not underestimate the significance of such experiments! In his Wind Quintet (1929) and especially his most recent Suite for Piano (1935) Haas appears as a full-grown artistic individuality, standing at the forefront of those who search for and create new stylistic paths [in Czech music].[79]

Nazi occupation and imprisonment in Terezín

In the early years of the war (prior to his imprisonment in Terezín), Haas composed (among others) two major works that effectively express the patriotic spirit of defiance: the Suite for Oboe and Piano (1939) and the unfinished Symphony (1940–41). Both contain full-length quotations of the Hymn to Saint Wenceslas (the patron saint of the Czech nation) and references to the Hussite chorale ('You Who Are the Warriors of God'). Peduzzi has given convincing evidence suggesting that the Oboe Suite is in fact a vocal piece in disguise.[80] However, the presumed patriotic literary text has never been found. The first movement of the Symphony makes topical allusions to religious chant and the military to portray the twofold legendary status of St Wenceslas as both a saint and a warrior. The Symphony's second movement offers a grotesquely satirical portrayal of Nazism with topical elements of 'danse macabre'.[81] The movement concludes with the superimposition of the infamous Nazi song 'Die Fahne Hoch!' (Raise the Flag!), also known as 'Horst Wessel Lied',[82] with the major-mode middle section of Chopin's 'Funeral March', both mockingly cast in the saccharine guise of a sentimental dance tune of somewhat 'mechanical' character, as if played by a barrel organ.

During the composition of the Suite and the Symphony, Haas was subjected to the tightening grip of Nazi oppression. Since Haas's wife was no longer allowed to work in the medical profession as the spouse of a Jewish person,[83] serious financial difficulties befell the family, which included not only Haas's daughter Olga and his elderly father Zikmund, but also his nephew Ivan.[84] Trying to protect his family from racial persecution, Haas got formally divorced from his wife on 13 April 1940. Dr Jakobsonová was indeed allowed to continue her medical practice, but Haas was gradually separated from the family. In April 1941, Haas and his father were forced to move to Sadová Street in a part of the city where Jewish people were concentrated and progressively isolated from the rest of society.[85] The requirement for Jews to wear the yellow Star of David was issued on 19 November 1941. By the end of the year, Haas was forced to leave Brno altogether, leaving behind his family and an unfinished score of the Symphony.

Since 2 December 1941, Haas was imprisoned in the transitional concentration camp of Terezín, better known under its German name Theresienstadt.[86] Between 1941 and 1945, this eighteenth-century fortress, comprising what was originally a garrison town, became a place in which Jewish people from the Protectorate of Bohemia and Moravia (and other Nazi-occupied territories) were imprisoned, before being transported to extermination camps, such as Auschwitz.[87] In the first months of his imprisonment, Haas had to undergo a hundred days of hard labour (the so-called 'Hundertschaft').[88] Physical exhaustion, malnutrition, and inadequate accommodation (in a room shared by 70 men on the first floor of the Sudeten Barracks) exacerbated Haas's long-term stomach problems.[89] The composer could not feasibly resume composition until he managed to find less demanding work in the so-called 'ambulatorium'.[90] According to the testimony of František Domažlický, Haas later shared a room with the medical staff, where he also gave lessons in music theory.[91] Paul Kling testified that he used to pay Haas with bread ('1/4 of a loaf per hour') for his lessons.[92]

During his incarceration in Terezín, Haas composed at least seven finished pieces, only three of which have survived: the male chorus *Al S'fod* (1942), text by David Shimoni, performance undocumented; *Study for Strings* (1943), dedicated to Karel Ančerl, performed by the Ančerl String Orchestra on 1 September and 13 September 1944; and Four Songs on Chinese Poetry for bass and piano (1944), dedicated to the singer Karel Berman, performed by Berman and Rafael Schächter on 22 June 1944.[93] Among the lost works, Peduzzi lists the following: Fantasia on a Jewish Song for string quartet (1943), performed by the Ledeč Quartet (date unknown); *Advent* (1944), three pieces for mezzosoprano, tenor, flute, clarinet and string quartet, poetry by František Halas, performance not documented; Partita in Old Style for piano (1944), dedicated to and performed by

Bernard Kaff (28 June 1944); Variations for piano and string orchestra (1944), performance not documented. Requiem for solos, chorus, and orchestra (1944), unfinished, lost.[94]

The circumstances under which these works were composed were extraordinary and deeply troubling. Terezín is well known for the remarkable concentration of elite musicians, artists, and intellectuals among the inmates, and for the vibrant cultural life which developed there, despite atrocious living conditions and constant threat of deportation. Cultural activities began as clandestine in the early days of the camp's existence. However, after the Nazis established the Council of Elders as a form of Jewish self-government within the ghetto in July 1942, cultural events were legitimately organised through the institution set up to manage 'leisure activities' ('Freizeitgestaltung').[95] The apparent benevolence of the Nazis was, in fact, part of cynical propaganda campaign. Claiming that Jews were being merely resettled (not imprisoned and systematically killed), the Nazis sought to showcase Terezín as a 'model settlement' ('Mustersiedlung') and prove that the Jews were treated well by the Nazi regime.[96]

This charade culminated during the inspection of Terezín by the International Committee of the Red Cross in June 1944. Extensive 'beautification' works had been ordered in specific parts of the ghetto (those to be visited by the committee) prior to the visit and several musical events were scheduled to take place on the day, including the performance of Verdi's *Requiem*, Krása's children's opera *Brundibár*, and an outdoor concert of popular orchestral music.[97] The Nazis also used this carefully constructed Potemkin Village to shoot the infamous propaganda film titled, significantly, *Der Führer schenkt den Juden eine Stadt* (*The Führer Gives a City to the Jews*), which actually shows Pavel Haas listening to a staged performance of his *Study for Strings* and taking a bow at the end.[98] After this, the Nazis had no more use for the artists, most of whom were transported to Auschwitz and killed between September and October 1944.[99] Haas began his last journey on 16 October 1944 and was killed in Auschwitz on the following day.[100]

The context of the Holocaust poses challenging ethical and methodological problems to scholarly interpretation of works from Terezín.[101] To begin with, the fact that Pavel Haas, Viktor Ullmann, Hans Krása, and Gideon Klein have been firmly established in the wider consciousness as 'Terezín composers' tends to obscure the individual profiles of the artists, who were rooted (prior to their incarceration) in very different backgrounds in terms of age, nationality, aesthetic affiliations, professional networks, and so on.[102] Pieces of music from Terezín are rarely analysed with respect to the particular composer's earlier works or to the broader tradition of Western art music. Critical discourse thus runs the risk of unconsciously perpetuating the 'forced fellowship' ('Zwangsgemeinschaft', to reference the subtitle of Adler's above-cited seminal study) inflicted on the artists by their Nazi oppressors. This is partly an issue of finding a suitable genre of academic writing. 'Life and work' monographs typically lack sufficient focus to bring in-depth readings of specific works,[103] while publications attempting to cover the music in Terezín in its relative entirety cannot pay enough attention to the individual artists' different pre-war affiliations.[104] Some journal articles approach a balance between the extremes, but none of these deals specifically with Haas.[105]

The age-old problem concerning the relationship between a work of art and the biography of its author gains special urgency in the context of the Holocaust. One is compelled by ethics, compassion, and piety to understand music from Terezín as a kind of a testimony of the composers' suffering. At the same time, however, one wants to avoid drawing superficial parallels between life and work, between the historiographical context and the musical text. This dilemma is encapsulated in the question put forward by Michael Beckerman in the title of his article on Gideon Klein's Trio: 'What kind of historical document is a musical score?'[106]

Beckerman's approach to music from Terezín is based largely on the premise of a 'censoring environment' in the camp, which forced the composers to maintain a certain 'façade' while incorporating secret subversive 'codes' into their works.[107] This approach is associated with focus on motivic and thematic references, typically associated with themes of death and despair.[108] While many such observations are valid, it is important to bear in mind that strategies of signification involving allusions, quotations, and other intertextual references are by no means unique to music from Terezín and that the significance of such references depends heavily on conventions of particular genres, styles, topoi, and so on.[109] Furthermore, the above constitute only one means of musical signification; a wide range of methodologies from the (broadly defined) field of musical semiotics can be used to analyse the repertoire in a more nuanced way.

Finally, the hidden 'truth', which is expected to be revealed once the code is broken, is likely to be rooted in the expectations and pre-conceived ideas held by the reader, who is prone to fall victim of confirmation bias. Particularly relevant to this point is Shirli Gilbert's critique of the notion of 'spiritual resistance', which has dominated much of the discourse on music in the Holocaust and which is directly referenced in the title of Milan Kuna's above-cited monograph on Music in Terezín: *Hudba vzdoru a naděje* (*Music of Resistance and Hope*).[110] Of course, spiritual resistance is not an entirely invalid concept, but it should be used with caution. It has strong ethical and ideological connotations and it comes with the assumption that the population of the camps was homogeneous, unified in a heroic struggle against the oppressors. Artists and works that do not fit the narrative are at risk of being marginalised or even dismissed as somehow ethically deficient.

This type of rhetoric has been used in a polemic concerning questions of leadership and influence among the composers in Terezín, which directly concerned Haas.[111] In his article titled 'Terezínské legendy a skutečnosti' ('Legends and Facts about Terezín'), Lubomír Peduzzi took issue with the way Haas was portrayed by Joža Karas in his seminal book *Music in Terezín*.[112] He referred specifically to the following passage:

As a moving spirit behind the musical activities in Terezín, Klein has to his credit the emergence of another prominent composer, Pavel Haas. A man in his forties, Haas came to Terezín with undermined health. The miserable conditions there further affected his severe depressions, resulting in total indifference to the very busy musical life of Terezín. According to his [Gideon Klein's] sister, Eliška (Lisa), Gideon Klein could not reconcile himself to seeing an artist of Haas's calibre not participating in the musical activities. So, one day, to wake him from his lethargy, Klein put in front of him several sheets of manuscript paper, on which he himself drew the musical staff, and urged Haas to stop wasting time. And indeed, Haas composed several pieces during his stay in Terezín, although only three of them have been preserved.[113]

This anecdote is seemingly innocuous and there are few obvious reasons to doubt its validity. As Peduzzi himself pointed out, Haas had long-term health problems, he was forced to leave his family with two small children (his daughter and his nephew), and he later saw his father die in the camp.[114] Nevertheless, this testimony may create the impression that Haas did not engage with the musical structures in Terezín at all, which is not true. According to Peduzzi, most of the works Haas composed in Terezín were dedicated to and/or performed by performers and ensembles active in the camp, including the pianist Bernard Kaff (Partita in Old Style, 1944), the singer Karel Berman (Four Songs on Chinese Poetry, 1944), the Ledeč Quartet (Fantasia on a Jewish Song, 1943), and the Ančerl String Orchestra (Study for Strings, 1943). Apparently, Haas composed music for the performance forces available to him, like he had done throughout his previous career in Brno. Haas's initial inactivity can be explained, at least partly, by the fact that, until the establishment of Freizeitgestaltung, all cultural activities in the ghetto were strongly limited by material conditions and official restrictions.

Peduzzi's criticism was concerned primarily with the way the story of Haas's depression was used in academic and critical discourse to raise the profile of Gideon Klein. An eloquent example of this can be found in otherwise very insightful articles on Klein by Robin Freeman.[115] Referring directly to the anecdote related by Karas, Freeman takes every opportunity to contrast Klein's 'active and supportive' approach to others with Haas's 'yearning to go home' (Freeman refers to the text of Four Songs on Chinese Poetry).[116] Ultimately, he goes further, from insisting that Klein encouraged Haas to compose, to claiming that Klein influenced what Haas composed:

> The Study for string orchestra by Pavel Haas, such exceptional stuff from him, is inconceivable in style without the Allegro vivace [recte: Molto vivace] of the Klein Trio. Even the tripping lightness of the counterpoint seems to follow on from the younger man, who gave him back his taste for writing music when he had all but given up.[117]

Unsurprisingly, Peduzzi criticized the 'myth about a "broken composer"' – and he used the rhetoric of spiritual resistance to do so.[118] To demonstrate that Haas (too) tried to raise the spirits among the community of inmates, Peduzzi invoked the text of Haas's male choral work *Al S'fod*, which he contrasted (with a degree of sarcasm) with Klein's madrigals on Hölderlin's text:

> I wonder how much consolation and strength G. Klein gave his fellow prisoners with his madrigals, particularly the one which sets the following text by Hölderlin: 'Ich bin nichts mehr, ich lebe nicht mehr gerne' (1943)? Such subjective, morbid moods may have [. . .] been experienced by many Terezín prisoners, but I question if the inmates needed to hear this kind of thing or whether they were waiting for a word of encouragement, provided for example by Haas's choir *Al S'fod*: 'Do not lament and do not cry when times are bad! Do not despair, but work, work! Thrust a path to freedom and pave it for a bright day!' (1942) Such was Haas in Terezín: determined, not reconciled with the reality but unbroken, [retaining] the fighting spirit he showed in Suite for Oboe [and Piano] and Symphony, in which he reacted through his art (as soon as 1939–41) against the [Nazis'] occupation of our country, their war against Poland and France, and their attack on the Soviet Union.[119]

Peduzzi's argument is based entirely on the positive value attached to the notion of spiritual resistance through art. Klein, whose work does not conform to the idea (at least not on the surface), is criticised on ethical and ideological grounds.

Peduzzi's choice of Haas's works is telling. Significantly, there is no mention of Haas's Four Songs on Chinese Poetry, which possess neither the defiant spirit of the earlier works (composed before the composer's deportation to Terezín), nor the beneficial social function of *Al S'fod*. Rather, they convey feelings of grief, melancholy, and alienation. Perhaps fearing that the Four Songs might be seen as containing too much of those 'subjective and morbid moods' which supposedly betray deficiency of character, Peduzzi elsewhere directed attention to the work's 'optimistic' ending and to the references to the St Wenceslas chorale (points which will be problematised in Chapter 6), through which he wished to link this work to the patriotic and defiant spirit of the Suite for Oboe and Piano (1939) and the Symphony (1940–41).[120]

It is also noteworthy that Peduzzi did not mention Haas's Study for Strings (1943) in his argument. Haas was perfectly capable, as his war-time Symphony demonstrates, of writing instrumental music that conveys the sense of patriotism, quasi-religious hope, and subversive satire. In the case of the Study, however, he wrote a piece of 'objective', 'absolute' music. As will be demonstrated in Chapter 4, Study for Strings is the most representative surviving example of Haas's engagement with Neoclassical aesthetics, which favours objective construction over subjective expression. In what way, if at all, does this work reflect the circumstances of those imprisoned in the ghetto? Is the *Study* an encrypted historical document, concealing subversive codes under its Neoclassical façade, or is it 'merely' a brilliant piece of compositional craft and musicianship – 'pure music'? Is it ethically justifiable to focus one's attention on the musical work and its aesthetic qualities, rather than on the composer and his personal ordeal? Is it possible to escape this binary perspective and find a more nuanced approach?

My analyses of Haas's works from Terezín are based on the premise that art created in the midst of the Holocaust is still primarily art – a medium which is governed by its own laws of signification and which requires specific strategies of interpretation. It may reflect specific historically and autobiographically significant events, but it cannot be reduced to a chronicle-like record of these events. Unless this art is examined on its own terms, it is hardly possible to understand and appreciate its intrinsic aesthetic value and the true nature of its relationship to the circumstances in which it was composed. This, I believe, is the only way to mediate between the two extremes which are equally unacceptable: to disregard the historical context, which would be disrespectful to the composers as victims of Nazism, or to take a reductive approach, which would be disrespectful to the composers as artists.

Notes

1 The occupation of Czechoslovakia started on 15 March 1939; Haas was transported to Terezín on 2 December 1941; he was killed in Auschwitz on 17 October 1944. See Lubomír Peduzzi, *Pavel Haas: Život a dílo skladatele* (Brno: Muzejní a vlastivědná společnost, 1993), pp. 86, 95, and 109.

2 This is partly because the Communist ideology discouraged any interest in Jewish arts and culture, fearing the rise of 'Zionism', which was readily associated with 'cosmopolitanism' and American 'imperialism'. See J.A. Labendz, 'Lectures, Murder, and a Phony Terrorist: Managing "Jewish Power and Danger" in 1960s Communist Czechoslovakia', *East European Jewish Affairs*, 44/1 (2014), 84–108 (p. 86).

3 Lubomír Peduzzi, *Pavel Haas: Život a dílo skladatele* (Brno: Muzejní a vlastivědná společnost, 1993); *Pavel Haas: Leben und Werk des Komponisten*, trans. Thomas Mandl (Hamburg: Bockel, 1996). All references to Peduzzi's monograph relate to the Czech edition.

4 Tempo Praha no longer exists; Bote & Bock has been acquired by Boosey & Hawkes.

5 See Peduzzi, *Pavel Haas*, pp. 48–9. Peduzzi described Haas's search for artistic individuality in terms of a 'journey from Janáček to Stravinsky'. Peduzzi did not elaborate on this argument much further; he suggested, though, that Haas was attracted to '[Stravinsky's] sense of the grotesque, to which [Haas] was himself inclined'. All translations from Czech sources are mine, unless stated otherwise.

6 Michael Beckerman, 'Haas's *Charlatan* and the Play of Premonitions', *The Opera Quarterly*, 29/1 (2013), 31–40.

7 The most detailed discussion to date of Haas's *Chinese Songs*, Op. 4 can be found in Vladimír Karbusický, 'Neukončená historie', *Hudební věda*, 35/4 (1998), 396–405.

8 To some extent, these issues have been explored by Peduzzi. See Lubomír Peduzzi, *Pavel Haas: Život a dílo skladatele* (Brno: Muzejní a vlastivědná společnost, 1993), pp. 26–37. See also Lubomír Peduzzi, 'Janáček, Haas a Divoška', *Opus musicum*, 10/8 (1978), Příloha (Supplement), 1–4; Lubomír Peduzzi, 'Jak učil Janáček skládat operu', *Opus musicum*, 12/7 (1980), Příloha (Supplement), 1–8. Haas's notebook containing notes from Janáček's classes is in the property of Olga Haasová–Smrčková.

9 For a recent study see Ondřej Pivoda, 'Rozhlasová hudba a Pavel Haas', *Musicologica Brunensia*, 50/2 (2015), 53–67.

10 See Lubomír Peduzzi, 'Haasova "hobojová" suita' ('Haas's "Oboe" Suite'), *Hudební rozhledy*, 12 (1959), 793–8. See also Lubomír Peduzzi, 'Vlastenecká symbolika posledních děl Pavla Haase', *Sborník Janáčkovy akademie múzických umění*, 3 (1961; Prague: Státní pedagogické nakladatelství, 1963), pp. 75–97.

11 Esti Sheinberg, *Irony, Satire, Parody, and the Grotesque in the Music of Shostakovich: A Theory of Musical Incongruities* (Aldershot: Ashgate, 2000). I will also make reference to Julie Brown, *Bartók and the Grotesque: Studies in Modernity, the Body and Contradiction in Music* (Aldershot: Ashgate, 2007). Raymond Monelle, *The Musical Topic: Hunt, Military and Pastoral* (Bloomington: Indiana University Press, 2006). Robert S. Hatten, *Musical Meaning in Beethoven: Markedness, Correlation, and Interpretation* (Bloomington: Indiana University Press, 1994). Naomi Cumming, 'The Subjectivities of "Erbarme Dich"', *Music Analysis*, 16/1 (1997), 5–44.

12 Most of Haas's estate is deposited in the Department of Music History of the Moravian Museum in Brno. Some materials are owned by the composer's daughter Olga Haasová-Smrčková, who lives in Brno. Documents relevant to Haas's time in Terezín can be found in the collections of Terezín Memorial. Some documents relevant to Haas's opera *Charlatan* and several pieces of incidental music are also kept in the archives of the National Theatre in Brno.

13 See also Lubomír Peduzzi, 'Haas, Pavel', *Grove Music Online* www.oxfordmusiconline.com [accessed 18 November 2015]. See also Michael Beckerman, 'Pavel Haas', websites of The Orel Foundation http://orelfoundation.org/index.php/composers/article/pavel_haas/ [accessed 18 November 2015].

14 Several monographs have been written about Hugo Haas (1901–1968) and his work, mostly in Czech: Valeria Sochorovská, *Hugo Haas* (Brno: Blok, 1971); Jolana Matějková, *Hugo Haas: Život Je Pes* (Prague: Nakladatelství XYZ, 2005). Hugo Haas's films – particularly those from the Hollywood era – have been recently studied by the Czech film and theatre specialist Milan Hain. See Milan Hain, *Hugo Haas a jeho (americké) filmy* (Prague: Casablanca, 2015).

15 Peduzzi, *Pavel Haas*, p. 14.

16 According to a census carried out in 1921, there were 156,000 Czechs (72.4%), 56,000 Germans (25.9%), and 3,000 (1.3%) Jews in Brno. See Jaroslav Dřímal and Václav Peša, eds., *Dějiny Města Brna*, 2 vols. (Brno: Blok, 1969–73), ii (1973), p. 91.

17 Peduzzi, *Pavel Haas*, p. 15.

18 Ibid., p. 16.

19 Ibid., pp. 16, 128–30.

20 Ibid., p. 16.

21 Ibid.

22 Ibid., p. 122.

23 This album survives as the property of Olga Haasová-Smrčková, the composer's daughter, to whom I am grateful for allowing me access to this source. The reviews quoted in this chapter are cited according to Haas's album, in which each clipping is accompanied by the title of the newspaper and the date of issue. Note that most of the reviews are signed by initials or cyphers such as '–l–' or 'St–', rather than full names. All translations from this source are mine.

24 –k, 'Z brněnských koncertů: Večer komorních novinek (Brno, 25. března)', *Lidové noviny*, 26 March 1930: 'Haas's quintet [Wind Quintet, Op. 10] successfully utilises a witty modernist diction and folk-like melodic and rhythmic invention with a certain tasteful measure of racial folklore [. . .]'; –šf–, '[untitled review of the 4th regular concert of the Brno Symphony Orchestra (13 March 1933), featuring the premiere of Haas's Psalm 29, Op. 12]', *Národní noviny*, 15 March 1933: 'Blended into [Haas's] musical idiom are Jewish elements, which invest his music with a distinctive character.'; Hrč., 'Klub moravských skladatelů v Brně', *Brněnská svoboda*, 22 April 1936: 'Haas's Suite for Piano, Op. 13, a composition [which is] temperamental to the core and musically – as we say – absolute, [. . . draws its effect from] the author's colourful sonic invention ['zvukovost'], [which is] as much racially inherited as it is artistically cultivated and sophisticated'; Hrč., 'Pavel Haas: *Šarlatán*', *Brněnská svoboda*, 5 April 1938: 'The composer Pavel Haas, the brother of the well-known and popular actor Hugo Haas, [. . .] emerged from the [compositional] school of Leoš Janáček and

combines in himself cultivated Jewish blood with pure Slavic-ness (his mother was a devoted Russian), while being, with each breath he takes, above all Czech.'

25   Haas's incidental music, which is deposited in the Archive of the National Theatre in Brno: Department of Musical Documentation (Archiv Národního divadla Brno: Oddělení hudební dokumentace), sign. 489, includes three pieces: 'Kol Nidre', 'Song about the Distant Mother' ('Píseň o matce v dáli'), and 'Short Revue Music with Foxtrot behind the Scene' ('Krátká revuální hudba s foxtrotem za scénou').

26   Gabriella Safran, 'Dancing with Death and Salvaging Jewish Culture in *Austeria* and *The Dybbuk*', *Slavic Review* 59/4 (Winter 2000), 761–81 (p. 768).

27   Ibid., p. 771.

28   Ibid.

29   Esti Sheinberg, *Irony, Satire, Parody, and the Grotesque in the Music of Shostakovich: A Theory of Musical Incongruities* (Aldershot: Ashgate, 2000), p. 307.

30   Jascha Nemtsov, 'Zur Klaviersuite op. 13 von Pavel Haas', *Musica Reanimata Mitteilungen*, 17 (December 1995), 20–3 (p. 22).

31   Peduzzi, *Pavel Haas*, pp. 65–6.

32   I visited Mrs Haasová-Smrčková in summer 2013. These names were mentioned in a telephone conversation, which took place on 20 December 2013.

33   Suzanne Vohnoutová El Roumhainová, 'Počátky Klubu moravských skladatelů: 1919–1928' ('The Origins of the Club of Moravian Composers: 1919–1928') (master's thesis, Masaryk University, 2013), see pp. 23–4 [accessed via http://is.muni.cz/th/64669/ff_m/Diplomova_prace.pdf, 15 November 2015].

34   According to Vohnoutová El Roumhainová (ibid., pp. 25–7), Neumann performed between 1919 and his death in 1929 a number of crucial pieces of international operatic repertoire including works by Debussy (*Pelléas et Mélisande*, 1921), Ernst Křenek (*Jonny spielt auf*, 1927), Ravel and Stravinsky, as well as 17 premiere performances of contemporary Czech operas. In Neumann's series of orchestral concerts, audiences in Brno had the chance to hear works by Debussy (*L'après-midi d'un faune*, 1919; *Nocturnes*, 1924), Mussorgsky (*A Night on the Bare Mountain*, 1925) Stravinsky (*Firebird Suite*, 1925; *Fireworks*, 1926, *Pulcinella*, 1927), Honegger (*Pacific 231*, 1923; *Le roi David*, 1925; *Horace victorieux*, 1926), Berg (excerpts from *Wozzeck*, 1927) and Schoenberg (*Gurrelieder*, 1925). Thirty out of 78 concerts given by Neumann in this period featured works by contemporary Czech composers, of which Osvald Chlubna, Vilém Petrželka, and Jaroslav Kvapil were the most frequently played.

35   Peduzzi, *Pavel Haas*, p. 24.

36   Haas's studies with Janáček are discussed in Peduzzi, *Pavel Haas*, pp. 26–37. See also Lubomír Peduzzi, 'Janáček, Haas a Divoška', *Opus musicum*, 10/8 (1978), Příloha (Supplement), 1–4; Lubomír Peduzzi, 'Jak učil Janáček skládat operu', *Opus musicum*, 12/7 (1980), Příloha (Supplement), 1–8.

37   Until recently, the activities of the Club of Moravian Composers remained unreflected in musicological research. So far, the most comprehensive account of the CMC in the first decade of its existence can be found in the above cited master's dissertation by Vohnoutová El Roumhainová.

38   Vohnoutová El Roumhainová, 'Počátky Klubu moravských skladatelů', p. 31.

39   Ibid., pp. 52–3.

40   I am referring particularly to Spolek pro moderní hudbu (Society for Modern Music), Přítomnost: sdružení pro soudobou hudbu (The Present: Society for Contemporary Music), and Klub českých skladatelů (Club of Czech Composers). See ibid., pp. 69–76.

41   The CMC was initially represented by František Neumann, later by Vilém Petrželka and Václav Kaprál. See ibid., p. 71.

42   Ibid.

43   Ironically, Bartók was only invited to give a recital of his piano works in Brno as a 'substitute' for the relatively little known German pianist and composer Eduard Erdmann,

who had asked for a fee too high for the Club to pay (4,000 Czechoslovak crowns). When Erdmann's conditions were refused, Janáček himself wrote a letter of invitation to Bartók, who agreed to give a concert for just 1,000 crowns. Ibid., p. 82.

44 The concert included extracts from the *Gurrelieder*, the Three Pieces for Piano, Op. 11, and the String Quartet No. 2, Op. 10. See ibid., pp. 82–3. See also Jiří Vysloužil, 'Arnold Schönberg v Brně', *Hudební rozhledy*, 37/11 (1984), 517–19.

45 Vohnoutová El Roumhainová, 'Počátky Klubu moravských skladatelů', p. 84. See also Jiří Zahrádka, 'Henry Cowell a Brno: Příspěvek k brněnským meziválečným kontaktům s představiteli světové avantgardy', in *Musicologica Brunensia. Jiřímu Vysloužilovi k 85. narozeninám* (Brno: Masarykova univerzita v Brně, 2009), 217–23.

46 Vohnoutová El Roumhainová, 'Počátky Klubu moravských skladatelů', pp. 68, 122–3.

47 For a comprehensive list of concerts organised by the CMC (and its predecessor CYMC) between 1919 and 1948, including information on repertoire, performers, dates, venues, and details concerning organisation, see ibid. pp. 105–91.

48 Ibid., p. 208.

49 Ibid., p. 54. Vohnoutová El Roumhainová also discovered the existence of several letters sent by Haas (mostly on behalf of the CMC) to the composer Emil Axman (member of the CMC, who was also a representative of the Prague-based Society for Contemporary Music). Haas's letters are deposited in the Museum of Czech music (Muzeum české hudby) in Prague, sign. G 1273, G 1735, G 1736, G 2230, G 2204, G 2207. See ibid., pp. 94–5.

50 Ibid., p. 121.

51 Ibid., p. 132.

52 Ibid., pp. 151, 196.

53 This specific concert (21 November 1926) was conducted by the conductor Břetislav Bakala. See Peduzzi, *Pavel Haas*, p. 130.

54 See ibid., p. 131.

55 There were two more premiere performances at this concert: Janáček's *Nursery Rhymes* (*Říkadla*, 1926), and Kvapil's *Con duolo* for piano (1926). See Vohnoutová El Roumhainová, 'Počátky Klubu moravských skladatelů', pp. 84–8, 125.

56 See Peduzzi, *Pavel Haas*, p. 132. See also the following: Ondřej Pivoda, 'Rozhlasová hudba a Pavel Haas', *Musicologica Brunensia*, 50/2 (2015), 53–67; A. J. Patzaková, *Prvních Deset Let Československého Rozhlasu* (Prague: Nakl. Radiojournalu, 1935), pp. 412–13, 488.

57 Reference is made here to the following plays: *R. U. R.* (1921) by Karel Čapek (premiered 9 April 1924, Brno: Divadlo na Hradbách); *Konec Petrovských* (1923) by Quido Maria Vyskočil (premiered 31 January 1923, Brno: Divadlo na Veveří); *Wozzeck* (*Vojcek*, 1923) by Georg Büchner (premiered 5 March 1923, Brno: Reduta); *Merry Death* (*Veselá smrt*, 1925) by Nicholas Evreinov (premiered 6 November 1925, Brno: Zemské divadlo); *Primus Tropicus* (1925) by Zdeněk Němeček (premiered 29 November 1925, Prague: Divadlo na Vinohradech); *Pulcinella's Victory* (*Pulcinellovo vítězství*, 1925) by Bedřich Zavadil (premiered 21 January 1926, Brno: Divadlo na Veveří); *Černý troubadour* (literally *Black Troubadour*, originally *The Jazz Singer*, 1928) by Samson Raphaelson (premiered 18 August 1928, Brno: Zemské divadlo). See Vojen Drlík, 'Tvorba Pavla Haase pro činoherní divadlo', *Opus musicum*, 35/4 (2003), 2–6. See also Peduzzi, *Pavel Haas*, pp. 130–1.

58 Peduzzi, *Pavel Haas*, pp. 64–5, 132.

59 Vohnoutová El Roumhainová, 'Počátky Klubu moravských skladatelů', p. 146.

60 Ibid., p. 151.

61 Mg., 'Komponisten aus Mähren', *Der Tag*, 9 January 1935: 'Of the young composers presented [in the concert], two seem to be particularly noteworthy. One of the two is Vilém Petrželka, whose song cycle [*Štafeta / Relay*] for voice and string quartet was performed [. . .]. The other is Pavel Haas, represented by his Wind Quintet [. . .]. The

rest [of the programme] was weaker [. . .].' See also R–i., 'Mährische Musik in Wien', *Echo*, 12 February 1936: 'Among works for piano, there was a sonata by Schäfer [. . .], pieces by Blatný, and, best of all, a suite by Paul Haas'. All Viennese newspapers are cited according to the clippings included in Haas's above mentioned album. All translations of German reviews are mine.

62 Anonymous author, 'Mährische Komponisten', *Neues Wiener Tagblatt*, 15 January 1935.

63 P. Stf., 'Im Austausch: Mährische Komponisten', *Die Stunde*, 9 January 1935.

64 P. Stf., 'Im Austausch: Mährische Komponisten', *Die Stunde*, 9 January 1935; Mg., 'Komponisten aus Mähren', *Der Tag*, 9 January 1935.

65 Réti, 'Zeitgenössische Musik aus Mähren': *Telegraf*, 9 January 1935.

66 R–i., 'Mährische Musik in Wien', *Echo*, 12 February 1936; P. Stf., 'Mährisches Austauschkonzert', *Stunde*, 12 February 1936.

67 a. r., 'Mährische Komponisten', *Tag*, 13 February 1936.

68 A critical analysis of the reception of Haas's music (based on Haas's album) has been undertaken in the following study: Michael Losen, 'Pavel Haas. Die Rezeption seiner Werke bis zum Aufführungsverbot 1939' ('Pavel Haas: Reception of his Work up till the Ban of Performance in 1939') (unpublished master's thesis, Universität Wien, 2006).

69 Peduzzi, *Pavel Haas*, p. 132.

70 Ibid., p. 133.

71 Ibid., pp. 66, 124.

72 The work of these composers (with the exception of Haas) has received very little attention in both performance and scholarship in recent decades. See Leoš Firkušný, *Vilém Petrželka: život a dílo* (Prague: Hudební matice Umělecké besedy, 1946), Ludvík Kundera, *Jaroslav Kvapil: život a dílo* (Prague: Hudební matice Umělecké besedy, 1944), Ludvík Kundera, *Václav Kaprál: kapitola z historie české meziválečné hudby* (Brno: Blok, 1968).

73 Jan Racek, *Leoš Janáček a současní moravští skladatelé: nástin k slohovému vývoji soudobé moravské hudby* [Leoš Janáček and contemporary Moravian Composers: A Sketch of the Stylistic Development of Contemporary Moravian Music] (Brno: Unie československých hudebníků z povolání, 1940), p. 16.

74 See also Jiří Vysloužil, 'Česká meziválečná hudební avantgarda' [Czech Inter-War Musical Avant-Garde], *Opus musicum*, 7/1 (1975), 1–11 (p. 6).

75 Vladimír Helfert, *Česká moderní hudba: studie o české hudební tvořivosti* [*Modern Czech Music: A Study of Czech Musical Creativity*] (Olomouc: Index, 1936), reprinted in Vladimír Helfert, *Vybrané studie: O hudební tvořivosti* (Prague: Ed. Supraphon, 1970), 163–312. Page references here and below are to the 1970 reprint.

76 Ibid., pp. 289–94. See also Jiří Fukač, 'Moravská skladatelská škola po Janáčkovi', *Hudební věda*, 4/2 (1967), 243–59.

77 See Martin Čurda, 'Smyčcové kvartety Janáčkových žáků z 20. let' [String Quartets of Janáček's Students from the 1920s] (unpublished master's dissertation, Masaryk University, 2011) [accessed via http://is.muni.cz/th/264072/ff_m/Smyccove_kvartety_Janackovych_zaku.pdf, 16 November 2015], English summary on pp. 165–6. See also Miloš Zapletal, 'Petrželkova "Štafeta" a Janáčkova "Sinfonietta" mezi sportem a ideologií: rekonstrukce dobových čtení' [Petrželka's 'Štafeta' and Janáček's 'Sinfonietta' between Sport and Ideology: the Reconstruction of Historical Readings] (unpublished master's dissertation, Masaryk University, 2013) [accessed via http://is.muni.cz/th/207024/ff_m/Zapletal-magisterska_diplomova_prace.docx, 17 November 2015].

78 Helfert, *Česká moderní hudba*, p. 294.

79 Ibid.

80 Lubomír Peduzzi, 'Haasova "hobojová" suita', *Hudební rozhledy*, 12 (1959), 793–8.

81 For a detailed analysis of the Symphony see Martin Čurda, 'Religious Patriotism and Grotesque Ridicule: Responses to Nazi Oppression in Pavel Haas's Unfinished

Wartime Symphony', in *The Routledge Handbook to Music under German Occupation, 1938–1945*, ed. David Fanning and Erik Levi (Abingdon, New York: Routledge, 2020), 377–98.

82 This quotation was first identified by Peduzzi (Peduzzi, *Pavel Haas*, p. 97). For details on the origin and political significance of the Horst Wessel Lied, see David Culbert, 'Horst Wessel Lied (1929)', in Nicholas J. Cull, David H. Culbert, and David Welch (eds.), *Propaganda and Mass Persuasion: A Historical Encyclopedia: 1500 to the Present*, (Santa Barbara, CA: ABC-CLIO, 2012), 169–70.

83 Peduzzi, *Pavel Haas*, p. 88. According to Peduzzi, Soňa Jakobsonová had Jewish ancestors, too, although she was baptised in the Russian Orthodox Church. Importantly, her Jewish roots were not apparent from her birth certificate and further documents abouth her ancestry could not be obtained, as confirmed by a letter from the Russian consulate in Prague, dated 11 September 1939. See Peduzzi, *Pavel Haas*, p. 93.

84 Hugo Haas and his wife managed to escape through France to the USA in the early months of the war, but they were unable to take the baby with them. Ivan Haas was reunited with his parents after the war. Pavel Haas sought the possibility of emigration, too, but without success. According to Peduzzi, he applied for the position of a composition professor in Tehran early in 1939, and submitted visa applications to the Coordinating Committee for Refugees in London (5 April 1939) and the American consulate in Prague (19 May 1939). See Peduzzi, *Pavel Haas*, pp. 86, 124.

85 Ibid., p. 94.

86 Ibid., p. 95.

87 See Hans Günther Adler, *Theresienstadt, 1941–1945: Das Antlitz einer Zwangsgemeinschafts* (Tübingen: JCB Mohr, 1955). For a recent English translation see *Theresienstadt, 1941–1945: The Face of a Coerced Community*, trans. Belinda Cooper (Cambridge: Cambridge University Press, 2016). For Czech translation see Hans Günther Adler, *Terezín 1941–1945: Tvář nuceného společenství* (Brno: Barrister & Principal, 2006).

88 Lubomír Peduzzi, 'Terezínské legendy a skutečnosti' [Legends and Facts about Terezín], in *O hudbě v terezínském ghettu: Soubor kritických statí* (Brno: Barrister & Principal, 1999), 38–48 (p. 46).

89 Peduzzi, *Pavel Haas*, pp. 98–9, 125.

90 Peduzzi, *Pavel Haas*, p. 98.

91 See Ludmila Vrkočová, *Rekviem sami sobě* (Prague: Arkýř, 1993), s. 115.

92 Viktor Ullmann and Ingo Schultz, *26 Kritiken über musikalische Veranstaltungen in Theresienstadt* (Hamburg: Bockel Verlag, 1993), p. 68. Kling further notes: 'Pavel Haas was a good teacher. As far as I can remember, we used Schoenberg's *Harmonielehre* and the Louis-Thuille [*Harmonielehre*]. [. . .] The book by Schoenberg was in Haas's possession; he would let us make notes and copy the excercises. [Since] these lessons already started in Brno, their resumption Terezín seemed to me almost like a continuation of "normal" life. Haas was always very kind and approachable, quite the opposite of Bernard Kaff, who – always Herr Professor – mostly kept his distance.' (pp. 68–9).

93 For a recent discussion of Haas's works from Terezín see Lubomír Spurný, 'Tvorba Pavla Haase v terezínském ghettu (1941–1944)', *Musicologica Brunensia*, 54/2 (2019), 17–28.

94 Peduzzi, *Pavel Haas*, p. 133–4. Viktor Ullmann's reviews of some of these performances can be found in Ullmann and Schultz, *26 Kritiken über musikalische Veranstaltungen in Theresienstadt*, pp. 52 (Partita in Old Style), 65 (Study for Strings), and 67 (Four Songs on Chinese Poetry).

95 Milan Kuna, *Hudba vzdoru a naděje: Terezín 1941–45* (Prague: Editio Bärenreiter, 2000), p. 15. See also Jascha Nemtsov and Beate Schröder-Nauenburg, 'Musik im Inferno des Nazi-Terrors: Jüdische Komponisten im "Dritten Reich"', *Acta Musicologica*, 70/1 (1998), 22–44 (p. 25).

96 Kuna, *Hudba vzdoru a naděje*, p. 16.

97 Ibid., pp. 17–19.
98 The film excerpt of this performance is on https://www.youtube.com/watch?v=E9g
    Szo0x4ak [accessed 22 May 2018]. For Karel Ančerl's account of the filming see
    Karel Ančerl, 'Music in Terezín', in *Terezín*, ed. František Ehrmann, Otta Hietlinger
    and Rudolf Iltis (Prague: Council of Jewish Communities in the Czech lands, 1965),
    238–41 (p. 240). See also Brad Prager, 'Interpreting the Visible Traces of Theresien-
    stadt', *Journal of Modern Jewish Studies*, 7/2 (2008), 175–94.
99 Kuna, *Hudba vzdoru a naděje*, pp. 19–20.
100 Peduzzi, *Pavel Haas*, p. 109. Peduzzi includes a different date ('probably 18 Oct
    1944') in his above cited entry in *Grove Music Online*.
101 The following discussion is based on my following book chapter: Martin Čurda,
    'Reading Meaning In and Out of Music from Theresienstadt: the Case of Pavel Haas',
    in *The Routledge Handbook of Music Signification*, ed. Esti Sheinberg and William
    Dougherty (Abingdon, New York: Routledge, 2020), 231–242.
102 This point is made in the above-cited article by Nemtsov and Schröder-Nauenburg
    ('Musik im Inferno des Nazi-Terrors', p. 35), which is also a good introduction to the
    music of 'Terezín composers'.
103 Peduzzi, *Pavel Haas*; Blanka Červinková, *Hans Krása: Život a dílo skladatele*
    (Prague: Tempo, 2003); Milan Slavický, *Gideon Klein: A Fragment of Life and Work*,
    translated by Dagmar Steinová (Prague: Helvetica-Tempora, 1996); Ingo Schultz,
    Viktor Ullmann: Leben und Werk (Kassel: Bärenreiter, 2008).
104 Joža Karas, *Music in Terezín: 1941–1945* (New York: Beaufort Books, 1985); Milan
    Kuna, *Hudba vzdoru a naděje: Terezín 1941–45* (Prague: Editio Bärenreiter, 2000).
105 See for example Robin Freeman, 'Gideon Klein, a Moravian Composer', *Tempo: A
    Quarterly Review of Modern Music*, 59/234 (October 2005), 2–18. Note that Free-
    man's remarks concerning Haas have somewhat dismissive tone, which is probably
    part of the larger Klein–Haas polemic discussed below.
106 See Michael Beckerman, 'What Kind of Historical Document Is a Musical Score?
    A Meditation in Ten Parts on Klein's Trio' [accessed via http://orelfoundation.
    org/index.php/journal/journalArticle/what_kind_of_historical_document_is_a_
    musical_score/, 26 January 2015]. Beckerman discusses the chronology of Gideon
    Klein's String Trio (1944) with respect to the dates of transports 'to the East' in 1944.
    I am not convinced that Beckerman made a sufficiently strong case for the relevance
    of the question of chronology to the reading of the work.
107 Michael Beckerman, 'Haas's *Charlatan* and the Play of Premonitions', *The Opera
    Quarterly*, 29/1 (2013), 31–40 (pp. 35–6).
108 In the above cited article, Beckerman claims that Klein made an allusion to Mahl-
    er's *Kindertotenlieder*. In my opinion, this particular comparison is less persuasive
    than other thematic parallels pointed out in the article. Perhaps more importantly,
    I find Beckerman's interpretation of this allusion as 'a statement by Klein to the effect
    that "this place is not what it seems: there are dead children here"' rather blunt. See
    Beckerman, 'What Kind of Historical Document Is a Musical Score?', no page numbers.
109 See Michael L. Klein: *Intertextuality in Western Art Music* (Bloomington: Indiana
    University Press, 2005), pp. 1–4.
110 Shirli Gilbert, *Music in the Holocaust: Confronting Life in the Nazi Ghettos and
    Camps* (Oxford: Clarendon Press, 2005), see particularly the 'Introduction: Redeem-
    ing Music – "Spiritual Resistance" and Beyond' (pp. 1–20).
111 See Lubomír Peduzzi, 'O Gideonu Kleinovi a jeho monografii' [On Gideon Klein
    and His Monograph], in *O hudbě v terezínském ghettu: Soubor kritických statí* (Brno:
    Barrister & Principal, 1999), 103–13. For a German version see 'Gideon Klein und
    seine Monographie', in *Musik im Ghetto Theresienstadt: Kritische Studien*, trans.
    Lenka Šedová (Brno: Barrister & Principal, 2005), 115–25.
112 Lubomír Peduzzi, 'Terezínské legendy a skutečnosti' [Legends and Facts about
    Terezín], in *O hudbě v terezínském ghettu: Soubor kritických statí* (Brno: Barrister &
    Principal, 1999), 38–48 (p. 46).

113 Joža Karas, *Music in Terezín: 1941–1945* (New York: Beaufort Books, 1985), p. 76.
114 Haas's father came to Terezín in March 1942 and died in the camp on 13 May 1944 (See Peduzzi, *Pavel Haas*, pp. 99, 108). Elsewhere, Peduzzi quoted the following testimony of Richard Kozderka (Haas's friend from Brno): 'In the final years of his life, Pavel Haas was very sad, pale in the expectation of horrors [to come]'. Peduzzi, *Pavel Haas*, p. 12.
115 Robin Freeman, 'Gideon Klein, a Moravian Composer', *Tempo: A Quarterly Review of Modern Music*, 59/234 (October 2005), 2–18; Robin Freeman, 'Excursus: "Nedej Zahynouti Nám Ni Budoucím, Svatý Václave": Klein, Ullmann, and Others in Terezin', *Tempo*, 60/236 (April 2006), 34–46.
116 Freeman, 'Excursus', p. 39.
117 Freeman, 'Gideon Klein', p. 18. According to Beckerman's above-cited article, the three movements of Klein's trio are dated 5 September, 21 September and 7 October 1944, respectively. Haas's *Study for Strings*, on the other hand, was performed in Terezín on 1 and 13 September 1944, and it was composed as early as 1943 (Peduzzi, *Pavel Haas*, 109 and 133). It is therefore highly unlikely that Klein's String Trio could have had any influence on Haas's *Study for Strings*.
118 Peduzzi, 'Terezínské legendy a skutečnosti', pp. 46–7. Peduzzi supports his criticism by compelling evidence about chronological inconsistencies in the testimony of Truda Solarová, on which the above cited passage from Karas's book (itself flawed with numerous factual errors) is based. See also Truda Solarová, 'Gideon Klein', in *Terezín*, ed. František Ehrmann, Otta Hietlinger and Rudolf Iltis (Prague: Council of Jewish Communities in the Czech lands, 1965), 242–5 (p. 245).
119 Ibid. See also Pavel Haas, *Al S'fod* on a Hebrew text by David Shimoni (Prague: Tempo; Berlin: Bote & Bock, 1994).
120 Lubomír Peduzzi, 'Vlastenecká symbolika posledních děl Pavla Haase', *Sborník Janáčkovy akademie múzických umění*, 3 (1961; Prague: Státní pedagogické nakladatelství, 1963), 75–97 (pp. 85–8). See also Lubomír Peduzzi, 'Haasova "hobojová" suita' ('Haas's "Oboe" Suite'), *Hudební rozhledy*, 12/18 (1959), 793–6.

Bibliography

General bibliography

Adler, Hans Günther, *Terezín 1941–1945: tvář nuceného společenství*, trans. Lenka Šedová, 3 vols. (Brno: Barrister & Principal, 2006–07), i: Dějiny (2006), ii: Sociologie (2006), iii: Psychologie (2007). For German original see *Theresienstadt 1941–1945: Das Antlitz Einer Zwangsgemeinschaft. Geschichte, Soziologie, Psychologie* (Tübingen: Mohr, 1955). For a recent English translation see *Theresienstadt, 1941–1945: the Face of a Coerced Community*, trans. Belinda Cooper (Cambridge: Cambridge University Press, 2016).
Beckerman, Michael, 'Haas's Charlatan and the Play of Premonitions', *The Opera Quarterly*, 29/1 (2013), 31–40.
'Beckerman, Michael, 'Pavel Haas', http://orelfoundation.org/index.php/composers/article/pavel_haas/ [accessed 18 November 2015].
Beckerman, Michael, 'What Kind of Historical Document Is a Musical Score? A Meditation in Ten Parts on Klein's Trio', http://orelfoundation.org/index.php/journal/journalArticle/what_kind_of_historical_document_is_a_musical_score/ [accessed 26 January 2015].
Červinková, Blanka, *Hans Krása: Život a dílo skladatele* (Prague: Tempo, 2003).
Čurda, Martin, 'Reading Meaning In and Out of Music from Theresienstadt: the Case of Pavel Haas', in *The Routledge Handbook of Music Signification*, ed. Esti Sheinberg and William Dougherty (Abingdon, New York: Routledge, 2020), 231–242.

Čurda, Martin, 'Religious Patriotism and Grotesque Ridicule: Responses to Nazi Oppression in Pavel Haas's Unfinished Wartime Symphony', in *The Routledge Handbook to Music under German Occupation, 1938–1945*, ed. David Fanning and Erik Levi (Abingdon, New York: Routledge, 2020), 377–98.

Čurda, Martin, 'Smyčcové kvartety Janáčkových žáků z 20. let' (unpublished master's thesis, Masaryk University, 2012).

Debenham, Jory, 'Existential Variations in Terezín', http://orelfoundation.org/index.php/journalArticle/existential_variations_in_terez237n/ [accessed 26 January 2015].

Debenham, Jory, 'Terezín Variations: Codes, Messages, and the Summer of 1944' (unpublished Ph.D. thesis, Lancaster University, 2016).

Doležil, Hubert, 'Svatý Václav v české hudbě', *Listy hudební matice*, 9/2 (1929–30), 43–7.

Drlík, Vojen, 'Tvorba Pavla Haase pro činoherní divadlo', *Opus musicum*, 35/4 (2003), 2–6.

Dřímal, Jaroslav, and Václav Peša, eds., *Dějiny města Brna*, 2 vols. (Brno: Blok, 1969–73).

Ehrlich-Fantlová, Zdenka, 'The Czech Theater in Terezín', in *Theatrical Performance During the Holocaust: Texts, Documents, Memoirs*, ed. Rebecca Rovit and Alvin Goldfarb (Baltimore MD: Johns Hopkins University Press, 1999), 231–49.

Ehrmann, František, Otta Hietlinger and Rudolf Iltis, eds., *Terezín* (Prague: Council of Jewish Communities in the Czech lands, 1965).

Firkušný, Leoš, *Vilém Petrželka: život a dílo* (Prague: Hudební matice Umělecké besedy, 1946).

Freeman, Robin, 'Excursus: "Nedej Zahynouti Nám Ni Budoucím, Svatý Václave": Klein, Ullmann, and Others in Terezin', *Tempo*, 60/236 (2006), 34–46.

Freeman, Robin, 'Gideon Klein, a Moravian Composer', *Tempo: A Quarterly Review of Modern Music*, 59/234 (October, 2005), 2–18.

Helfert, Vladimír, *Česká moderní hudba: studie o české hudební tvořivosti* (Olomouc: Index, 1936), reprinted in *Vybrané studie: O hudební tvořivosti* (Prague: Ed. Supraphon, 1970), 163–312.

Jeřábek, Dušan, *Brněnská romance* (Brno: Kulturní a informační centrum, 1997).

Karas, Joža, *Music in Terezín 1941–1945* (New York: Beaufort Books, 1985).

Kuna, Milan, *Hudba na hranici života* (Prague: Naše vojsko, 1990).

Kuna, Milan, *Hudba vzdoru a naděje: Terezín 1941–45: O činnosti a tvorbě hudebníků v koncentračním táboře Terezín* (Prague: Editio Bärenreiter, 2000).

Kundera, Ludvík, *Jaroslav Kvapil: život a dílo,* (Prague: Hudební matice Umělecké besedy, 1944).

Kundera, Ludvík, *Václav Kaprál: kapitola z historie české meziválečné hudby* (Brno: Blok, 1968).

Losen, Michael, 'Pavel Haas: Die Rezeption seiner Werke bis zum Aufführungsverbot 1939' (unpublished master's thesis, Universität Wien, 2006).

Migdal, Ulrike, *Und Die Musik Spielt Dazu: Chansons Und Satiren Aus Dem Kz Theresienstadt* (Munich: Piper, 1986).

Nemtsov, Jascha and Beate Schröder-Nauenburg, 'Musik im Inferno des Nazi-Terrors: Jüdische Komponisten im "Dritten Reich"', *Acta Musicologica*, 70/1 (Jan.–Jun. 1998), 22–44.

Peduzzi, Lubomír, 'Haas, Pavel', *Grove Music Online*, www.oxfordmusiconline.com [accessed 18 November 2015].

Peduzzi, Lubomír, 'Haasova "hobojová" suita', *Hudební rozhledy*, 12 (1959), 793–98.

Peduzzi, Lubomír, 'Janáček, Haas a Divoška', *Opus musicum*, 10/8 (1978), Příloha (Supplement), 1–4.

Peduzzi, Lubomír, 'Jak učil Janáček skládat operu', *Opus musicum*, 12/7 (1980), Příloha (Supplement), 1–8.

Peduzzi, Lubomír, *O hudbě v terezínském ghettu: Soubor kritických statí* (Brno: Barrister & Principal, 2nd edition, 1999); for German translation see *Musik im Ghetto Theresienstadt: Kritische Studien*, trans. Lenka Šedová (Brno: Barrister & Principal, 2005). 'Terezínské legendy a skutečnosti', 38–48. 'O Gideonu Kleinovi a jeho monografii', 103–13. 'Falešné problémy Haasových Čtyř písní', 79–84.

Peduzzi, Lubomír, *Pavel Haas: Život a dílo skladatele* (Brno: Muzejní a vlastivědná společnost, 1993); for German translation see *Pavel Haas: Leben und Werk des Komponisten*, trans. Thomas Mandl (Hamburk: Bockel, 1996).

Peduzzi, Lubomír, 'Představitel Janáčkovy školy', *Hudební rozhledy*, 17 (1964), 785–6.

Peduzzi, Lubomír, 'Vlastenecká symbolika posledních děl Pavla Haase', *Sborník Janáčkovy akademie múzických umění*, 3 (1961; Prague: Státní pedagogické nakladatelství, 1963), 75–97.

Petrželka, Vilém, and Ivan Petrželka, *Vilém Petrželka: z jeho životních osudů neznámých a zapomínaných* (Brno: Šimon Ryšavý, 2005).

Pivoda, Ondřej, *Pavel Haas: Janáčkův nejnadanější žák* (Brno: Moravské zemské muzeum, 2014).

Pivoda, Ondřej, 'Rozhlasová hudba a Pavel Haas', *Musicologica Brunensia*, 50/2 (2015), 53–67.

Racek, Jan, *Leoš Janáček a současní moravští skladatelé: nástin k slohovému vývoji soudobé moravské hudby* (Brno: Unie československých hudebníků z povolání, 1940).

Rovit, Rebecca and Alvin Goldfarb, eds., *Theatrical Performance During the Holocaust: Texts, Documents, Memoirs* (Baltimore MD: Johns Hopkins University Press, 1999).

Sen, Suddhaseel, 'The Art Song and Tagore: Settings by Western Composers', *University of Toronto Quarterly*, 77/4 (2008), 1110–32.

Schneider, Franz Markus, 'Terezínský smích', in *Terezínské studie a dokumenty* (Prague: Academia, 1999), 242–50.

Schultz, Ingo, *Viktor Ullmann: Leben und Werk* (Kassel: Bärenreiter, 2008).

Slavický, Milan, *Gideon Klein: A Fragment of Life and Work*, trans. Dagmar Steinová (Prague: Helvetica-Tempora, 1996).

Solarová, Truda, 'Gideon Klein', in *Terezín*, ed. František Ehrmann, Otta Hietlinger and Rudolf Iltis (Prague: Council of Jewish Communities in the Czech lands, 1965), 242–5.

Štědroň, Bohumír, 'Česká hudba za nesvobody', *Musikologie*, 2 (1949), 106–46.

Ullmann, Viktor, and Ingo Schultz, *26 Kritiken über musikalische Veranstaltungen in Theresienstadt* (Hamburg: Bockel Verlag, 1993).

Vohnoutová El Roumhainová, Suzanne, 'Počátky Klubu moravských skladatelů: 1919–1928' (unpublished master's thesis, Masaryk University, 2013) [accessed via http://is.muni.cz/th/64669/ff_m/Diplomova_prace.pdf, 15 November 2015].

Archival documents

Archival documents deposited in the Department of Music History of the Moravian Museum (Oddělení dějin hudby Moravského zemského muzea)

Vojcek (incidental music to play by Georg Büchner), sign. A 29.804.
Referáty z novin (Newspaper reviews), sign. J 8.

*Archival documents deposited in the Archive of the National Theatre
in Brno: Department of Musical Documentation (Archiv Národního
divadla Brno: Oddělení hudební dokumentace)*

R. U. R. (1921): incidental music to a play by Karel Čapek, sign. 168.
Konec Petrovských (1923): incidental music to a play by Quido Maria Vyskočil, sign. 274.
Veselá smrt (1925): incidental music to a play by Nicholas Evreinov, sign. 376.
Černý troubadour (1928): incidental music to a play by Samson Raphaelson, sign. 489.

Archival documents in private property of Olga Haasová-Smrčková

'Moje úspěchy a ne-úspěchy' ('My Successes and Non-successes'): a notebook containing newspaper clippings of newspaper articles on and concert reviews of Haas's works.

Musical editions

Haas, Pavel, *Al S'fod*: Male Chorus set to Hebrew words by David Shimoni, 1942 (Prague:
Tempo; Berlin: Bote & Bock, 1994).
Haas, Pavel, *Sinfonie für großes Orchester (1940–41)*, instr. Zdeněk Zouhar (Prague:
Tempo; Berlin: Bote & Bock/Boosey & Hawkes, 1994).
Haas, Pavel, Suite for Oboe and Piano, Op. 17, 1939 (Prague: Tempo; Berlin: Bote & Bock,
1993, revised by František Suchý).
Haas, Pavel, Wind Quintet, Op. 10, 1929 (Prague: Tempo; Bote & Bock/Boosey & Hawkes,
2nd rev. edn, 1998).
Haas, Pavel, Žalm 29 (Psalm 29), Op. 12 (Berlin: Boosey & Hawkes/Bote & Bock, n.d.).

1 Music and avant-garde discourse in inter-war Czechoslovakia

Introduction

In order to help situate Haas's work in the context of avant-garde movements in Czechoslovakia and beyond, this chapter contains a review of the discourse on avant-garde art and music conducted on Czech literary platforms (journals, pamphlets, books) in the inter-war period. The aesthetic landscape of the time is best described as a complex network of numerous interrelated and partially overlapping concepts (such as Poetism, Surrealism, Neoclassicism, Constructivism, and Purism), most of which are usually considered applicable to some art forms, but not to others. However, it will become apparent that the disciplinary boundaries are often elusive: music cannot be discussed separately from other art forms, aesthetics cannot be disentangled from politics and ideology, and trends in the Czech avant-garde discourse are intimately linked with concurrent developments in other countries.

Much of the discussion in this chapter revolves around the notions of Poetism and Neoclassicism. Poetism was the dominant tendency in Czech avant-garde art of the 1920s; although it is rarely associated with music (the term is most readily applicable to literature and visual arts), it will prove highly relevant to Haas's works from this decade. Neoclassicism, on the other hand, is commonly regarded as one of the two dominant stylistic tendencies (the other being the Serialism of the Second Viennese School) in the development of European art music between the two world wars. While there are a number of Neoclassical features in Haas's music (as will be demonstrated in Chapters 3 and 4), it may be problematic to speak of a clearly defined Neoclassical style.

Importantly, Poetism and Neoclassicism (like the other –isms mentioned above) are complex and problematic concepts, encompassing a number of constituent ideas (such as physiological art, everyday art, rational order, and free play of imagination), which often constitute points of overlap and create paradoxical alliances between seemingly distinct aesthetic tendencies. Therefore, the various –isms must be first 'taken apart', in order to specify which aspects are relevant to Haas's work.

In search of the Czech musical avant-garde

This chapter is concerned selectively with a particular segment of inter-war Czechoslovak music, arts, and culture. Any attempt to sketch out the variety of the musical scene alone would result in a lengthy catalogue of names, groups, and institutions. The focus here, therefore, is specifically on the Czech musical avant-garde, which started to emerge in the mid-1920s around the left-wing avant-garde group known as Devětsil (established in 1920 in Prague).[1]

The members of Devětsil were mostly artists from the fields of literature, visual art, and theatre; music was somewhat marginal. Nonetheless, there were several composers among the early members of the group, namely Emil František Burian (1904–1959), Iša Krejčí (1904–1968), and Jaroslav Ježek (1906–1942). Burian stood at the forefront of the short-lived group called Tam-tam (1925–26), the foundation of which may be regarded as an attempt to form a musical branch of Devětsil. The group, which published its own journal (*Tam-tam: Gazette musicale*) between 1925 and 1926, also included the composers Jaroslav Ježek, Erwin Schulhoff (1894–1942), Jiří Svoboda (1900–1970), and the writer Ctibor Blattný (1897–1978). Several significant avant-garde projects in the genre of musical theatre also emerged from these circles, particularly Burian's Divadlo Dada (Theatre Dada, 1927) and the so-called Osvobozené divadlo (Liberated Theatre, 1927), represented by the popular trio of Jiří Voskovec, Jan Werich, and Jaroslav Ježek.[2]

Some of the above-mentioned individuals later came together in the so-called Music Group of Mánes (Hudební skupina Mánesa, established in Prague in 1932), which included the composers Iša Krejčí, Pavel Bořkovec (1894–1972), Jaroslav Ježek, and František Bartoš (1905–1973), as well as the pianist and publicist Václav Holzknecht (1904–1988).[3] This group pledged allegiance to the aesthetic tenets proclaimed by Jean Cocteau, Erik Satie, and the composers of Les Six.

A special position was occupied by Bohuslav Martinů (1890–1959), who left Czechoslovakia to study in Paris in 1923 and took permanent residence there in 1924. Martinů published articles in Czech journals, some of which will be cited below. Although he maintained professional contacts with some of the above-mentioned groups and responded in his music to many of the tendencies that will be discussed here, he did not approve of the subversive and iconoclastic elements of the avant-garde agenda.

Haas himself, living in Brno, was necessarily somewhat removed from the epicentre of avant-garde activities, located in Prague. He was not officially a member of any of the relevant groups and did not contribute to any of the avant-garde journals such as *Pásmo*, *Tam-tam*, and *ReD* (*Revue of Devětsil*). However, Devětsil expanded from Prague to Brno in 1923. Further evidence will be provided in Chapter 2 of Haas's awareness of the activities of Devětsil in Brno, which included editing the journal *Pásmo* (1924–26)[4] and the organisation of art exhibitions, lectures, and social events.[5]

Poetism

The notion of Poetism was articulated by the avant-garde theorist Karel Teige (1900–51) and the poet Vítězslav Nezval (1900–58), the leading figures of

Devětsil. In the opening of his 1924 manifesto of Poetism, Teige announced (as avant-garde movements typically did) a breakup with the preceding artistic tradition and an assertion of 'new' art. He argued that art must no longer be the dominion of professionals, tradesmen, intellectuals and academics. The new art, he believed, would be cultivated by 'minds that are less well-read but all the more lively and cheerful'; it was intended to be 'as natural, charming and accessible as sports, love, wine and all delicacies', so that everyone could take part in it.[6] Teige's critique of artistic 'professionalism' was essentially that of the gap between 'art' and 'life', which Poetism sought to bridge, to achieve an interpenetration of the two. Teige was eager to make clear that Poetism was not intended to be just another artistic '–ism', but a life perspective, a 'modus vivendi', 'the art of living, modern Epicureanism'.[7] Its artistic manifestations were supposed to offer noble amusement and sensual stimulation, 'invigoration of life' and 'spiritual and moral hygiene'.[8] Teige implied that art could help transform human life into the state of 'poiesis' ('supreme creation').[9] Thus, all people would eventually become artists in the way they would 'live [their] "human poem[s]"': 'Happiness resides in creation. The philosophy of Poetism does not regard life and a work [of art] as two distinct things. The meaning of life is a happy creation: let us make our lives a work [of art, a creation], a poem well organised and lived through, which satisfies amply our need for happiness and poetry.'[10]

Teige's views on art were underpinned by Marxist materialism, which, however, is not entirely consistent with the emphasis on sensual pleasures, entertainment, and happiness. Teige tried to reconcile this opposition by proposing a dialectical relationship between 'Poetism', representing imagination, irrationality, and playfulness, and 'Constructivism', representing logic, rationality, and discipline.[11] Teige's pair of Constructivism and Poetism is analogous to Marx's pair of 'base' and 'superstructure'. Nonetheless, this theoretical model is not without problems; as Peter Zusi explained:

> Teige's image compulsively reproduces the fate of Marx's: it slips from an expression of dialectical unity to one of static dualism [. . .] of structure and ornament. Through such slippage, the second element (Poetism, or for Marx, the superstructure) appears not as the dialectical counterpart and completion of the first but rather as something supplemental, unnecessary, or parasitic.[12]

In any case, Teige reacted against what he saw as the anaemic, spirit-dominated art and culture of the past, as is apparent from the following statement: 'Poetism liquidates the discord between body and spirit, it knows no difference between bodily and spiritual art, between higher and lower senses. Here the Christian and ascetic dictatorship of spirit comes to an end.'[13] The 'new' art was not to be metaphysical, transcendent, elitist, complicated, speculative, and intellectual. On the contrary, it should be earth-bound, empirical, sensual, popular, accessible, and entertaining. Therefore, Poetism drew inspiration (in terms of both form and content) not only from 'low' art forms of popular urban culture, but also from phenomena of everyday life, which would commonly be excluded from art (in the conventional sense of the word). As Esther Levinger has noted, Teige's notion of art comprised 'all human activities, whether writing love letters, doing acrobatics, gardening, or cooking', and even work that would 'resemble artistic activity by being free and gamelike'.[14] Quoting Teige's article 'Pozor na malbu' ('Beware of Painting'), Levinger further explains that Poetism's shift of emphasis towards everyday experience was paralleled by recourse to corporeality and sensuality.

> [T]he Devětsil artists endeavored to arouse an awareness of everyday experience that represented the merger of art and life. They imagined that they could reawaken and reeducate the senses so that people could fully enjoy all sensory data – all sights, sounds, smells, tastes, and touches – but especially sight, for art was all around them, in 'colorful flowerbeds, posters, flags, road signs, sports clothes, the colored animation of dancing halls, popular festivities, and fairgrounds [. . .] ballet, film, games of reflections, fire-works, parades, and carnivals.'[15]

Teige's concept of 'poetry for the five senses' (among which the visual element was the most prominent) found manifestation in the so-called 'picture poem', combining the elements of poetry, typography, collage, and photomontage.[16] Teige also demanded that art should make use of all the modern media and technologies. He was particularly fascinated by the artistic potential of film. Unfortunately, financial constrictions prevented Teige and Nezval from realising some of their 'film poems' (surviving in the form of written scenarios) in which they sought to transfer the principles of 'picture poems' into a new medium.[17]

Jazz was for music what cinema was for visual art. Both brought new technological possibilities and encapsulated a modern, twentieth-century sensibility. These points were made in E. F. Burian's 1928 book *Jazz*:

> [T]here is no more jazz-like form [of art] than film and no more film-like music than jazz. [. . . The two have in common] above all their narrative and formal concision. Jazz, like film, cannot tolerate any impediments to temporal, emotional, and rhythmic shortcut [. . . which] resonate[s] with the nervous haste and rich beauty of rhythmical moments in twentieth-century life. [. . .] Jazz and film [. . .] are not without influence on other art forms. Their brevity, entertainment, and topicality [. . . finds] counterparts in theatre [. . .] and in social life (dance, clubs, and sports).[18]

Burian suggested that the genre best suited for the Zeitgeist of the twentieth century was revue, in which he saw not only a kind of modern-day 'Gesamtkunstwerk', combining music, dance and theatre, but also a parable of the modern world:

> Revue with its girls is not the product of hyper-philosophical and emotionally over-exposed [pre-war] years. Its origin goes hand in hand with jazz and film. Machines, skyscrapers, modern sports, revue, jazz, girls, stock exchange and

the class struggle. The noise of highways and the humming of millions of talking people. The orchestras of automobiles and factory sirens. The duets of aeroplanes and reflectors. A 24-hour, 365-day revue with hundreds and thousands of numbers.[19]

In Teige's thought, the characteristic features of the modern industrial age (such as speed, dynamism, functionality, precision, and so on) were correlated with physical culture and sports. All this came together under the category of 'poetry for corporeal and spatial senses (a sense of orientation, speed, spatial-temporal movement)', which comprised 'sport and its various kinds: automobility, aviation, tourism, gymnastics, acrobatics'.[20] Teige continues:

> The hunger for records, inherent to our mentality, is satisfied by athletics, the passion of victory bursts out in football matches together with the joy of teamwork, with the feeling of tensive harmony, precision and coordination. The poetry of sport [. . .] develops all senses; it yields a pure sensation of muscular activity, the pleasure of bare skin in the wind, the beauty of physical exaltation and intoxication of the body.[21]

'Physiological' music: sports, dance, and theatre

Because of the correlation of musical rhythm with bodily motion, music is very well suited for appealing to the body, which is one reason why Devětsil artists were fascinated by jazz. E. F. Burian described jazz as an art born of 'the joy drawn from movement and lively rhythm'.[22] This common view of jazz was underpinned by equally widespread stereotypical assumptions about its 'Negro' progenitors: 'Dance and dance again is the basis of the spiritual life of these primitives. One could say they live through movement.'[23]

Another manifestation of the preoccupation with physical movement can be seen in musical works inspired by sports.[24] Martinů's commentary on his orchestral *Half-time* (1924) exemplifies the contemporary rhetoric associated with sports. Martinů presented the work as a 'continuation of the new musical expression, as indicated by Stravinsky' and a 'reaction against Impressionism, sentimentality and [. . .] the metaphysical explanations of music'.[25] While warning that the piece should not be understood as a literal, mimetic representation of a game of sports, Martinů claimed *Half-time* was supposed to express 'the joy of a moment', 'the fascination with power, health, [and] movement' 'the joy of discovering and fighting', and 'the stormy life of boulevards'.[26] Nonetheless, he insisted that the piece is to be 'conceived of in purely musical terms', as an essay on the 'problems of rhythm and construction'.[27] Arguably, *Half-time* is conceptually related to Honegger's symphonic movements *Pacific 231* (1923) and *Rugby* (1928). Another example of similar tendencies in Czech music is the 'symphonic allegro' *Start* (1929) by Pavel Bořkovec.

From the perspective set by Teige, music is of less interest as an autonomous art form than as a combination of music and dance. A characteristic example of an experimental multi-media art project incorporating the element of 'poetry for corporeal and spatial senses' is the so-called *Alphabet* (*Abeceda*), which involved short poems by Nezval (each inspired by a particular letter), music by Martinů, choreography by Milada (Milča) Mayerová (reminiscent of Rudolf Laban's dance 'alphabet'), and typography by Teige (incorporating photographs of Mayerová's choreography).[28]

Comments on the 'physiological' effect of art in general and music in particular appear time and time again in Czech avant-garde discourse; the term 'physiological music' ('fyziologická hudba') is sometimes encountered, especially when music is considered in association with dance and theatre. Czech composer Iša Krejčí elaborated on this idea in an article entitled 'Proč je balet tak aktuelní?' ('Why Is Ballet So Appealing?').[29] He argued that conventional forms of theatre, based on dramatic content and 'factual logic', were obsolete:

> Nezval, Cocteau and Ribemont-Dessaignes [have created] an essentially new genre of stage art: a stage poem, illogical in its factual meaning, logical only in its form. Such a poem is not one of verse but that of stage movement, sound and decorations. [. . .] It sufficed to realise the idea of pure ballet [. . .] a physiological and purely formal music [and] musical stage [. . .]. Ballet [. . .] offers an escape from the factual logic of drama to the purely artistic logic of form, which, however, is not to be dead and devoid of effect; on the contrary, it derives its collective scenic effect from its physiological appeal: that is, from the appeal of the body and motion.[30]

Whereas Krejčí refers to French artists, other commentators associated the notion of physiological music with the developments in Russian theatre. E. F. Burian suggested that the visions of Russian theorists of theatre Aleksandr Tairov and Vsevolod Meyerhold paradoxically came to fulfilment in the dances of 'girls' in American revues, in which Burian saw the synthesis of the 'primitive' roots of dance (he drew a parallel with African row dances) and the discipline, machine-like precision, and coordination of modern sports, gymnastics, and industrial production.[31]

Czech theatre director Jindřich Honzl (1894–1953), one of the founding members of Devětsil, wrote about physiological music in his enthusiastic article about the 'Moscow State Jewish Theatre'.[32] Like Krejčí, Honzl emphasised the dominance of music and movement over text and dramatic meaning.[33] Celebrating the intimate link between music and bodily movement, Honzl marvelled at the raw, even grotesque physicality of Alexander Granovsky's productions:

> Granovsky is a director of rhythmically deformed gesture, which [. . .] falls into shunts, jerky movements, [and] spasmodic halts that are unrelated to each other, except through their rhythmic succession [. . .] determined by musical accompaniment. [. . .] The rhythmicising aspect, irrespective of

[natural] rhythms of the bodily organism, [. . . imposes] the rhythm of instrumental music upon physiological processes [. . .].[34]

The notions of physiological music and 'poetry for corporeal and spatial senses' are highly relevant to the striking emphasis on rhythm in Haas's compositional technique. Haas often uses rhythm as a means of conjuring up (even in the absence of a stage with actual dancers or actors) the image of the body in motion, which is very often subjected to grotesque exaggeration and distortion. These issues will be discussed in Chapter 2 with reference to the recurrent topic of 'eccentric dance', which appears throughout Haas's oeuvre. Haas also uses rhythm in a more abstract, or perhaps Constructivist manner. Chapter 4 will explain ways in which rhythmic and metric procedures shape the formal structure of entire movements of Haas's instrumental works.

Everyday art: Teige, Cocteau, and Les Six

Teige himself seldom referred specifically to music. However, as early as 1922 he co-authored, along with Jiří Svoboda, an article entitled 'Musica and Muzika', which effectively brought into Czech discourse the essential ideas articulated in Jean Cocteau's 1918 manifesto *Cock and Harlequin*.[35] Like Cocteau, Teige and Svoboda employed iconoclastic, anti-academic rhetoric. The Latin term 'musica' in the title refers to the music supposedly marked by the academicism, snobbism, and elitism of pre-war arts and culture. Its vernacular counterpart 'muzika' denotes the music of 'the people'.[36] 'Muzika' can be heard 'in the café, in the restaurant, in the cinema, on the street, in the park, in the Sunday dance hall, at the Salvation Army parade' or at sports events;[37] it is 'passionate, [. . .] richly colourful, strongly moving, [. . .] emotional, and immediately appealing';[38] its genres include 'rag-time, jazz-band, [. . .] fox-trot, shimmy, exotic music, couplet [popular song], cake-walk, music in cinema, [and] operetta'.[39] Music of the future, the authors believe, should engage with these rejuvenating resources. Drawing on his own area of expertise, Teige asks: 'Why should music resist new, academically unsanctioned instruments – jazz-band, accordion, the barbarian barrel organ, etc. – when architecture happily makes use of the advantages of modern materials?'[40]

Teige and Svoboda invoke French avant-garde composers as the pioneers of this new direction. Erik Satie is introduced as an influential 'comedian, humourist, and primitivist'.[41] Igor Stravinsky is celebrated for his 'love for the vulgar and the profane' that made him 'lead modern music [. . .] towards exoticism in its modern, cosmopolitan sense'.[42] Georges Auric is described as a lover of 'musical caricature' who seeks all that is 'grotesque and merry' and the author of the 'modernist foxtrot *Adieu, New York!* as well as other pieces that could be played on a barrel organ'.[43] Arthur Honegger and Darius Milhaud are also briefly mentioned. In the article's conclusion, the authors lament the 'conservatism, foolishness and narrow-mindedness' of Czech critics, who 'a priori reject such music [. . .] fearing its bold innovations'.[44]

The most comprehensive summary of the aesthetic programme surrounding Les Six can be found in the pamphlet entitled *Mladá Francie a česká hudba* (*Young France and Czech Music*), published in 1938 by the pianist and publicist Václav Holzknecht as a (somewhat belated) manifesto of the Music Group of Mánes.[45] Holzknecht's characterisation of the music of 'Young France', by which he refers to Satie and Les Six, draws heavily on Cocteau's *Cock and Harlequin*. This is immediately apparent in Holzknecht's comments on Satie, echoing Cocteau's portrayal of this composer as the father-figure who delivers French music from the grip of Wagnerism and Impressionism through a paradoxical mixture of (neo)classicism and everyday art:

> In the time of Impressionist indulgence in chromaticism, misty colours, obscured lines, and vagueness of form, [Satie] required diatonicism, and solid contours, and perfect form. Contrary to aristocratic subjectivism, [he] wanted pure and objective music. [. . .] Besides, he had a sense of the humour of everyday life. [. . .] He was one of the first to compose utility music for cafés in the style of American songs. In his ballet *Parade* [. . .] he introduced the atmosphere of circus, music-hall, machines, and exotic primitivism.[46]

Holzknecht's description of Les Six is essentially a catalogue of topoi, most of which are familiar from the context of Poetism:

> One of the characteristic features of their art is sensuality. They have infinite love for life. [. . .] Contrary to the exclusive world of the Impressionists, they want music which is popular, rhythmical and lively. They assimilate Spanish and American dances. They search for the country, the idyll, pastoral simplicity and charm; they compose [. . .] concerts with harpsichord to pay homage to Couperin. [. . .] They do not hide from the present time in the past or the future. On the contrary, they find it supremely beautiful. They have found new miracles in Chaplin's grotesques [slapsticks], they go to see clowns in the circus, and they love the elusive adventures of music halls. [. . .] Jazz opened up for them the adventures of distant places. They like its noisy sound, raw rhythms, and nostalgic melodies. [. . .] They dream about the black Haarlem, New York, and transatlantic travels. [. . .] Picasso taught them the beauty of [. . .] harlequins [. . .]. The world of *commedia dell'arte* is revived with new colours [. . .]. They are excited by modern machinery [. . . and] sports.[47]

Neoclassicism, Constructivism, Purism

In Czechoslovakia, unlike in France, the term Neoclassicism was not elevated to an over-arching stylistic category. Throughout the inter-war era, it remained one of many partially overlapping categories, such as everyday art, Constructivism, and physiological music. Holzknecht's generic designation 'Young France' in the title of his pamphlet indicates that he refers to a set of diverse, albeit interconnected tendencies, rather than a unified style. He only used the term Neoclassicism with reference to Iša Krejčí, who wrote a number of compositions in classicising small instrumental forms and the opera *Antigona* on Sophocles.[48] From the perspective of the Devětsil avant-garde, the question of a relationship with the past – classical or not – was less important than the search for resonance with contemporary reality and the Marxist revolutionary project. Indeed, many would have dismissed the notion of a return to the past as reactionary academicism.

The problematic position of Neoclassicism in Czechoslovak discourse is understandable, considering that the notion is originally rooted in a French cultural and political context. However, even in the French discourse, the concept is highly problematic. The term's literal meaning is much narrower than the variety of tendencies it has come to represent. Scott Messing has traced the origins of the generic characteristics which gradually became submerged in the rhetoric of Neoclassicism ('simple, straightforward, objective, pure, concise') to the language used during and immediately after the First World War to describe the works of 'artists associated with cubism – Picasso, Braque, and Delaunay – and the poetry of Apollinaire and Cendrars'.[49] Since such avant-garde art, as Messing himself observed, 'bore no relationship to the past', it is open to question to what extent the engagement with the 'classical' tradition is a salient feature of Neoclassicism. It appears that there was a mutually convenient alliance in the inter-war era between the tendency to return to pre-nineteenth-century 'classical' roots (which, in France, had strong nationalist overtones) and the avant-garde hunger for 'new' art, the common enemy being the (German) 'decadent' art and culture of the fin-de-siècle.

Another problem is that the current understanding of Neoclassicism as a musical style based on play with the conflicting elements of tonal and post-tonal syntax is extrapolated almost exclusively from the music of Stravinsky. The music of Satie and Les Six is frequently associated with Neoclassicism, but the term nonetheless seems too 'tight' to include the variety of tendencies these composers represent. This problem is apparent already in Cocteau's paradoxical association of Neoclassicism with everyday art and Dada (encapsulated in the work of Satie).

It is therefore not viable to assume that Neoclassicism was 'transferred' from France to Czechoslovakia as a monolithic style specific to music, because there was no such thing to begin with (the 'classicising' tendencies in the music of Stravinsky, Satie, Ravel, and others were qualitatively too different from each other to constitute a coherent musical style). However, as will be demonstrated, Czech composers and musicians were familiar with the cluster of associated ideas that floated around as a subset of a broader international and interdisciplinary avant-garde discourse.

Arguably, the writings of Karel Teige played an important mediating role. In Teige's thought, 'classical' qualities such as rational order and economy of means were encapsulated in the notion of Constructivism – the dialectical counterpart of Poetism. Thus, these tendencies were not necessarily associated with the virtues of past styles but rather with the values and merits of the modern, industrial age. Besides, the aesthetic preferences of Neoclassicism and Constructivism also overlap partially with those of Purism, which was well known among Czech architects and visual artists.[50] The notion of Purism was introduced in the journal *L'Esprit Nouveau*, edited between 1920 and 1925 by the poet Paul Dermée, the painter Amédée Ozenfant, and the architect Charles-Éduard Jeanneret (better known under the pseudonym Le Corbusier).[51]

In their 1920 manifesto of Purism, Ozenfant and Jeanneret claimed: 'One of the highest delights of the human mind is to perceive the order of nature and to measure its own participation in the scheme of things; the work of art seems to us to be a labour of putting into order, a masterpiece of human order [. . .].'[52] The authors further argued that the 'order' they invoked was the same as that underpinning Classical architecture. As David Batchelor observed, Purist works were supposed to represent 'a modern development of the Classical tradition of ancient Greece'.[53] Interestingly, the Purists also believed that the same aesthetic ideal manifested itself in 'Negro' sculpture and even modern industrial production, claiming that, for example, the development of automobile design, like that of Greek architecture, has historically evolved towards ever more 'purified' form, stripped of inessential ornamentation.[54]

The discourse of 'structure' and 'ornament', which harks back to Adolf Loos's 1908 essay 'Ornament and Crime', can also be found in Cocteau's criticism of Impressionism in *Cock and Harlequin*:[55]

> Enough of clouds, waves, aquariums, water-sprites, and nocturnal scents; what we need is music of the earth, every-day music. Enough of hammocks, garlands, and gondolas; I want someone to build me music I can live in, like a house. [. . .] Machinery and American buildings resemble Greek art in so far as their utility endows them with an aridity and grandeur devoid of any superfluity. But they are not art. The function of art consists in seizing the spirit of the age and extracting from the contemplation of this practical aridity an antidote to the beauty of the Useless, which encourages superfluity.[56]

Referring specifically to music, Cocteau emphasised the importance of rhythmic and melodic clarity and simplicity. This passage is also indicative of the anti-academic stance common to Cocteau and Teige, the preference of sensual and physical experience over intellectual contemplation.

> In music, line is melody. The return to design will necessarily involve a return to melody. [. . .] Satie teaches what, in our age, is the greatest audacity, [that is] simplicity. [. . .] he clears, simplifies and strips rhythm naked. Is this once more the music on which, as Nietzsche said, 'the spirit dances', as compared with the music 'in which the spirit swims'? Not music one swims in, nor music one dances on; MUSIC ON WHICH ONE WALKS.[57]

The binary vocabulary of Neoclassicism

As is apparent from Table 1.1, which summarises the vocabulary used in the sources cited in this chapter, the discourse of Neoclassicism was predicated on a string of correlated binary oppositions, including aesthetic, philosophical, and

Table 1.1 Vocabulary of Neoclassicism: a list of binary oppositions based on the sources
cited in this chapter

New	Old	
Clarity	Confusion	
Concision	Excess	
Simplicity	Refinement	Opposed to
Sobriety	Deliriousness	*fin-de-siècle*
Order	Chaos	
Solidness	Vagueness	
(Neo-)Classicism	Romanticism, Decadence	
'Human scale'	Titanism	
Reality	Metaphysics	
Objectivity	Subjectivity	
Form	Content	
Absolute	Programmatic	
Construction	Expression	
Concrete ('to walk on')	Fluid ('to swim in')	Aesthetic
Physiological effect	Emotional effect	
Diatonicism	Chromaticism	
Linearity	Verticality	
Rhythm		
Melody	Harmony / Colour	
Counterpoint		
Structure	Ornament	
Line	Colour	
Materialism	Idealism	
Body	Spirit	Philosophical
Rationality	Emotionality	
True	Deceptive	Ideologically
Healthy	Degenerate	connoted
French	German	Right-wing
Latin, southern	Teutonic, northern	(nationalist)
Marxist	Bourgeois	
Revolutionary	Reactionary	Left-wing
Collective	Individual	(Marxist)
Accessible	Elitist	

ideological categories, metaphorical language referring to the body and health, and examples from across artistic disciplines.

As Scott Messing has demonstrated, the aesthetic values and qualities associated with Neoclassicism were defined largely by negation of what were seen as the characteristic features of *fin-de-siècle* music, arts, and culture. Clarity, concision, simplicity, sobriety, purity, and order of objective construction were seen as preferable to confusion, excess, over-refinement, delirium, obscenity, and chaos of subjective expression.[58] Messing also showed that these binaries were strongly correlated with a rhetoric of nation and race. Neoclassicism was an attempt to recover the true and healthy spirit of French art and eliminate the influence of deceptive and degenerate German art, represented primarily by the work of Richard Wagner.[59]

It is intriguing that Teige and Cocteau used opposing ideological agendas to justify a focus on everyday art. For Cocteau, 'low' art represented the uncorrupted roots of French national culture. Teige, due to his Marxist world-view, saw 'low' art as the basis of proletarian culture. In Cocteau's case, the preference for earthly, everyday art 'built to fit man' was directed against the supposed metaphysical academicism and Teutonic titanism of Wagner (and German art in general); Teige put forward a similar aesthetic programme in his call for materialist, collectivist, and accessible Marxist art of the present day, as opposed to the idealist, individualist, and elitist bourgeois art of the past.

The pair of structure and ornament can be used to describe the aesthetic ideals of Neoclassical music. Chromaticism is denounced as superfluous ornamentation of diatonic structure. The linear dimension (contrapuntal lines, melodic contours) is preferable to vertical harmonic colouring. Cocteau demanded clearly defined shapes (music 'to walk on'), as opposed to fluid masses of sound (music to 'swim in'). Any programmatic and expressive content could be regarded as a special kind of ornament.

Neoclassicism in the writings of Czech composers

One of the earliest appearances of the rhetoric of Neoclassicism in Czech discourse was in the articles that Bohuslav Martinů published after he took residence in Paris in 1923. In one of these, he explains the basics of Stravinsky's recent stylistic orientation, which he describes as the 'revolution of return' ('revoluce návratu'). Martinů is not referring strictly to Stravinsky's most recent 'Neoclassical' works; rather, he traces the origins of the composer's 'new direction' to *The Rite of Spring* and *Petrushka*.

By renouncing all ornaments, veils of Romanticism, effeminate sensitivity of Impressionism, and subjectivism, [Stravinsky] returns through a thoroughly natural and logical process to absolute music, to purely musical values. [. . .] Against atonality, he posits clear articulation of key. Against rhythmic vagueness and chaos, he posits rational rhythmics. Although he enriches both [tonal and rhythmic organisation] with new combinations and possibilities, he does so with a sense of order, thus attaining stability and formal coherence, which had been lost in Impressionism. These are marks of a modern man who values clarity, order and economy. His revolution is actually a revolution of return.[60]

Despite the apparent overlap of ideas, Martinů did not subscribe (at least not without significant reservations) to the programmatic proclamations of Devětsil (in Czechoslovakia) and Cocteau (in France). Believing, perhaps somewhat uncritically, in the values of natural musicality and conscientious craftsmanship, Martinů criticised Les Six, whose music he found fashionably superficial and artistically irresponsible (with the exception of Honegger).[61]

E. F. Burian was attracted precisely to those 'irresponsible' experiments, which Martinů condemned, emphasising the importance of Satie and Milhaud, rather than Stravinsky and Honegger.[62] Nonetheless, even Burian occasionally added the rhetoric of the 'classic' into his eclectic mix of ideas. Burian suggested that modern jazz, represented by the orchestra of Paul Whiteman for example, possessed 'Mozart's and Haydn's lightness of invention' and was capable of 'creating a form of supreme absolute clarity and pure Mozartian texture'.[63] Burian further drew a parallel between the use of the minuet in eighteenth-century classical music and the use of modern dances in contemporary compositions. In this context, he even invoked Bedřich Smetana, the 'classical' father-figure of Czech music: 'No composer would have more passion for foxtrot than Smetana, who understood the dance rhythm of his time [. . .].'[64]

Arguably, such references to elements of dance music in the classical repertoire served mostly to legitimise the use of modern popular dances, the significance of which was primarily cultural-critical and ideological. In Burian's view, the awkward movements of the Charleston subverted the neat elegance of old-fashioned social dances, thus making an ideological statement against the hypocritical manners of decadent bourgeois society. An element of social equality was seen in the (supposed) popularity and accessibility of modern dances across all social classes. Modern dances connoted joy, optimism, physical and mental health; they were supposed to be an instrument towards the creation of a Marxist utopia.[65]

In his 1936 article entitled 'Hudba lehká a vážná' ('Light Music and Serious [Art] Music'),[66] which appeared as a contribution to a broader debate in the journal *Tempo* about popular music and its supposed negative effects on the taste of the masses, Haas, too, tried to justify the engagement with jazz and other 'light' musical genres in contemporary art music by pointing out the precedents of similar practices in the classical tradition, although he was not concerned directly with the problem of Neoclassicism and did not bring any ideological agenda into his discussion:

> Light music is not an invention of our century. It existed in pre-classical, as well as the classical era and it has its own pedigree. Like serious music, it has its good and bad authors. [. . .] [S]urely, I am not saying anything new when I point out that there are a number of beautiful, artistically valuable

and remarkable hits. Jazz music [. . .] has also influenced the development of serious [art] music, especially in terms of polyrhythmics. Jazz influences penetrate into the motoric movements of modern suites, partitas, and symphonies. [Haas's own 1935 Suite for Piano (discussed in Chapter 3) is a pertinent example.] This phenomenon, however, does not only appear in contemporary music. In the classical and pre-classical period, too, idealised social dance had its place in serious [art] music. Indeed, popular (not folk!) tunes often became the themes for variation movements.[67]

A noteworthy attempt to outline the reform of art music in terms of Teige's ideas and 'graft' the notion of Neoclassicism on this conceptual basis was made by Iša Krejčí in his 1928 article entitled 'Ponětí modernosti v dnešní hudbě' ('The Notion of Modernity in Today's Music').[68] Echoing Teige's claims, Krejčí rejected the old (Romantic) 'content'-dominated 'tendentious' art and proposed instead art which was to be 'pure' and 'functional' (devoid of 'extra-musical content', based on 'solid craftsmanship'), 'physiological' (appealing to the body), 'collective' (in the sense of Marxist ideology), and 'modern' (anti-academic, 'stemming from and designed for today's reality').[69] Finally, Krejčí forged a link between the above outlined tendencies and classical music:

Thinking of these requirements, their proximity to the tenets of classical music becomes apparent. It [music of the classical period] also wanted above all to be a good craft, pure music; it also drew on contemporary popular music, its ideals being functionality and clarity.[70]

Significantly, the term Neoclassicism comes with a caveat highlighting the necessity of relevance to contemporary cultural reality:

We strive for neoclassicism, which, however, has *nothing* to do with any kind of academicism. On the contrary: the present day has found its own tempo of life, its meaning, its style. Modern art should fully absorb the [present] time [in order to] give rise to works that are endowed with contemporary appeal or even popularity as much as they are invested with valuable content.[71]

Krejčí did not discuss the compositional-technical details of this non-academic musical Neoclassicism, apart from stating that it should be 'essentially diatonic and rhythmic' (to ensure its 'physiological' appeal), and it should draw on the 'lively themes and forms of modern dances' (as opposed to the 'dead' material of 'academic' music).[72] A more detailed characterisation of musical features associated with Neoclassicism can be found in Holzknecht's *Young France and Czech Music* (which mostly reiterates Cocteau's claims). According to Holzknecht, the composers of Les Six 'put extraordinary emphasis on rhythm, which is partly influenced by jazz';[73] they fight the 'Impressionist looseness' with the 'sharp', 'terse', and 'attacking' rhythm, drawing inspiration from machines (*Pacific 231*) and sports (*Rugby*).[74] Essentially, Holzknecht explains, their music is not intended for metaphysical contemplation but for bodily perception: 'It was necessary to turn away from music which is listened to with one's head held in one's hands. It was necessary to create music that induces movement and energy. It was necessary to return health to music.'[75] Holzknecht further claims that the French (unlike the Germans) opt for economy of means and expression: rejecting formal excess, they prefer the 'simplicity and clarity' of classical forms; turning away from the excess of total chromaticism, they 'return to diatonicism' (which is nonetheless 'understood in modern terms'); at the same time, they avoid 'monotony' by casting conventional material into 'polytonal' and 'poly-rhythmic' combinations.[76]

Holzknecht also saw traces of an 'essentially identical [aesthetic] programme' in the music of Hindemith, Bartók, and other non-French composers with some variation resulting from differences of 'cultural climate'. Thus, according to Holzknecht, Hindemith's 'roughly carved forms' are rooted in the 'Bach-Reger German tradition', whereas Bartók's music is marked by 'Asiatic temperament flavoured by Slavic tunefulness'.[77]

Haas on 'return' and 'music of the future'

Haas commented on what he saw as anachronistic tendencies in music in his 1926 article entitled 'O návratu' ('On Return').[78] He does not employ the term 'Neo-classicism' and his use of the term 'return' probably does not refer (at least not directly) to the above-cited article by Martinů, since no reference is made either to Martinů or to Stravinsky and the term has none of the positive value which Martinů attached to it. Instead, 'return' is regarded as a reactionary, escapist tendency which divorces art from contemporary reality in the name of a misinter-preted idea of 'absolute music':

> The main battle chant of these revolutionaries is: 'Down with Romanticism!' Meanwhile, they abandon their own lives, with which they are inseparably connected; they abandon the present day [. . .] and return several genera-tions back to live on the brains and blood of the old masters. [They think] the influence of the life around us and all factual perceptions and ideas [that come with it] contaminates the 'absoluteness' of music [. . .] [T]hus, they dis-regard the old truth that, inside an artist, all such things are transformed into art [. . .]. Thus, inspiration is eliminated and all that remains is a pure [and arbitrary] musical idea, not motivated or provoked by anything [. . .] [S]uch ideas are then cast into parched, conventionalised forms and thus a piece of 'absolute music' comes into being.[79]

The basis of Haas's hostility towards the notion of 'return' is clarified in his article entitled 'O hudbě budoucnosti' ('On the Music of the Future'), published around the same time.[80] Taking a Hegelian perspective, the composer argues that the evolution of art is essentially linked with the dialectical development of what might be called Zeitgeist, the agency of which manifests itself through the creative will of artists. The composer goes on to sketch a dialectical model of music history:

> After the blossom of classical form comes the time of programme music, in which loose form is dictated fully and solely by the [programmatic] subject matter. [The music of] this era goes as far as [tone-]painting and imitation of natural sounds and thus leads to chaotic formal disarray. It is therefore natural that such total freedom and looseness should be followed once again by [the re-establishment of] law and its bonds. [. . .] After the stormy, thundery, big orchestra [. . .] begins the reign of a small chamber orchestra, limited to the essential instruments [. . .]. After broad and extensive symphonic compositions, aspiring to deal with all kinds of problems (even philosophical), [resulting in] conceptual overload, heaviness of expressive means, and tiresome length [. . .] appear small, minute, carefree, parodic, and humorous pieces, which, however, only have a short life, as a result of the lack of the right measure and discipline [on part of the composers].[81]

This extract makes clear that Haas understood and recognised the historical origins of Neoclassical tendencies in music, although the anachronistic idea of 'return' was irreconcilable with his dialectical model, rooted in the present and oriented towards the future. Although Haas's music hardly ever 'returns' to the conventions of musical styles of the past, my analyses in Chapters 3 and 4 will demonstrate that much of Haas's instrumental music nonetheless displays generic characteristics associated with Neoclassicism, such as balance, concision, and clarity of form, modernist treatment of essentially diatonic musical material, and emphasis on rhythm, which becomes an important form-constitutive element.

Haas's article implies that the historical development heads towards the ideal of an 'immortal' work of musical art, which would be '*balanced* in all respects'.[82] What is described here seems to be the ultimate synthesis to which the infinite series of mutually negating theses and anti-theses points. Haas laments that, since the end of the war, art has not come anywhere near such ideal balance; instead, it finds itself in a state of disarray, struggling desperately to find a new direction. However, he points out that this is after all an appropriate reflection of the time: '[S]ince the living conditions in our time are so disorderly, [a piece of] balanced art would be a mere untruthful comedy, deprived of all connection with [the actuality of] life, which it is supposed to reflect'.[83] 'And so', the composer concludes,

> the world turns on and on, boiling and fermenting with infinite desire for [. . .] vertiginous, heavenly heights, without ever attaining its ultimate goal – and *music* awaits with anxious impatience another *master*, who will create a perfect and balanced *musical work* of the future.[84]

Of particular interest is Haas's claim that it may be a legitimate task for art to reflect the disarray of the contemporary world; indeed, some of the composer's works do precisely that. Haas's comment on the open-ended process of 'boiling and fermenting' resonates with Mikhail Bakhtin's notion of the 'carnivalesque-grotesque', which will be central to my reading of the last movement ('The Wild Night') of his 1925 string quartet 'From the Monkey Mountains' (discussed in Chapter 2). As will be argued, 'The Wild Night' and the 1935 Suite for Piano (discussed in Chapter 3), use the principle of collage to comment on the heterogeneity and disjunction of the modern world. As the following sections explain, the principle of collage is highly relevant to Poetism on the one hand and Neoclassicism on the other.

From Poetism to Surrealism: collage and other forms of play with meaning

The numerous references in Poetist works to clowns, acrobats, harlequins, magicians, and so on can be understood as references to this idea of free play or 'juggling' with words and images. This ludic creation, in which everyone could participate (or so the Poetists believed), was a way towards 'lyrical transformation' of mundane life.[85] This is illustrated by Teige's following claim: 'Poetism wants to turn life into a spectacular entertaining affair, an eccentric carnival, a harlequinade of sensations and fantasies, a delirious film sequence, a miraculous kaleidoscope.'[86] As Levinger explains, the techniques of collage and montage became an essential means of achieving this effect:

> Devětsil considered the allegorical mode of fragmentation and montage a positive value and regarded it as a privileged expression of modernity. [. . .] The whirlwind of visual metaphors became a favourite device of Devětsil's poetic language, especially in the genre they called 'film poems' [. . .]. The poems consisted of a montage of fragmented sequences strung together by a surreal logic; as such, they clearly presented an expanded version of the slightly earlier picture poems. Both genres, pictures and films, used the Russian Formalist device of defamiliarization, of which the Prague artists learned first-hand from Roman Jakobson.[87]

Poetism declined towards the end of the 1920s and Surrealism became the dominant tendency in Czechoslovak avant-garde art in the 1930s.[88] Teige and Nezval insisted that Surrealism was a natural continuation of Poetism.[89] The continuity can be seen in free play with meaning and the suspension of rational logic, motivated by a more or less overtly subversive ideological agenda. Levinger observes that Czech Surrealist photomontages of the 1930s and 1940s (such as those created by Teige or Jindřich Štýrský) continued earlier 'Poetist' practices of the 1920s in that they, too, 'produced meaning by the association of apparently unrelated signs'.[90]

Malynne M. Sternstein has argued that Poetism, like Surrealism and Dada, embarked on a 'revolution in poetic language', which in itself was part of a broader ideological mission to subvert 'symbolic constructions of power' (conventions of signification) and thus challenge the dominant social, cultural, and political establishment.[91] Part of this 'semantic revolution', Sternstein explains, was the attempt to 'liberate the word' from the bonds of linguistic signification. The liberated 'word as thing' is not merely a sign for an external object in the 'real' world; it has autonomous existence of its own.[92] Correspondingly, 'chance encounters' of words in a poem (such as Lautréamont's 'chance meeting on a dissection table of a sewing machine and an umbrella.') and 'random' juxtapositions of images in a collage or film sequence are no less real because of their unusual or magical quality.[93]

Collage in music: Stravinsky and Les Six

The notion of Surrealism has rarely been applied to music.[94] Nonetheless, as Anne LeBaron has argued, Satie's stage works *Parade* and *Relâche*, characterised by collage-like juxtapositions of styles, genres and technologies, are arguably 'representative of the transference of surrealist practices into music'.[95] The notion of collage has also been associated with Stravinsky; in his case, however, it has rarely been regarded as a Surrealist device. Jonathan Cross has argued that Stravinsky in his music devised means of 'challenging the dominant aesthetic of wholeness, connectedness, unity, continuity and directedness' and 'offered the possibility of an alternative, modernist aesthetic of fragmentation, discontinuity and opposition'.[96] Glenn Watkins has observed that '[Stravinsky's] personal style was [. . .] coined not so much through the appropriation of ingredients from a particular historical or cultural model as through their fracture and purposeful reassemblage: criticism of received materials becomes the modus operandi for the creative act'.[97]

Watkins's use of the notion of collage sheds light on a particular aspect of Stravinsky's Neoclassicism: first, the 'received materials' subjected to 'fracture' and 'reassamblage' (note the choice of 'Cubist' vocabulary) may be drawn from the realm of historical music, as well as folk music or popular music; and, second, the play with the material is in itself more important than the concern for the 'classical' aesthetic values and/or the relationship with the past. This is why Martha M. Hyde described Stravinsky's version of Neoclassicism as 'eclectic' in her seminal article on Neoclassicism.[98] Framing the discussion about Stravinsky's music in terms of collage rather than Neoclassicism makes it clear that the distance between past and present is only one of many divides that can be 'crossed' and thus made 'meaningful'.[99] For example, references to jazz can be examined not only in terms of old/new but also in terms of high/low, European/African-American, and so on.

Such juxtaposition of culturally significant elements holds substantial cultural-critical potential. Cross suggests – with reference to T. W. Adorno – that fragmentation, discontinuity, and eclecticism in Stravinsky's music reflect the disintegration of cultural value systems in the modern era.[100] Indeed, Adorno himself perceived a critical edge in Stravinsky's play with styles. Adorno and Ernst Bloch both regarded Stravinsky's (pre-Neoclassical) *Soldier's Tale*, along with Kurt Weill's

Threepenny Opera, as an example of musical 'Surrealism', by which they meant the 'refunctioning' of popular music on the principle of 'montage' for the purposes of social critique.[101] However, Adorno argued that, with the beginning of his 'Neoclassical' period, Stravinsky's music lost its critical dimension (which for Adorno was the sole justification for the use of 'dead music').[102]

Jane Fulcher has expressed a similar view, claiming that term Neoclassicism, when first applied to Stravinsky's music in the 1920s, was 'specifically associated with a restrained modernity, a socially conservative but aesthetically liberal stance'.[103] She argues that a separate kind of Neoclassicism was cultivated by the composers of Les Six, who built on Erik Satie's practice of '"play" with established "serious" meanings and styles, or his modernist "critical" classicism that evaded controls and authority':[104]

> Their neoclassicism [that of Les Six] would thus be 'cultural' and critical, unlike Stravinsky's, which they admired, but the motivation of which was more a formal and conservative exploration of styles. They rather sought a true 'modernism,' of 'critical dismantling of inherited cultural languages' as ideological constructions, in the spirit of Satie and Dada. As a result, they drew from several 'oppositional' traditions – the popular (including the folk), the commercial, and the aristocratic – which they used to define themselves against the official or academic norm. All of these they would throw into new, experimental relations, creating both new meaning and awareness not only of the reality of experience itself, but how meaning construction occurred in the past within specific conventions.[105]

Thus, Fulcher implies that Les Six used collage in a different way to Stravinsky. Whereas Stravinsky, in Watkins's words, was interested primarily in 'criticism of received materials', Satie and Les Six sought criticism of culture through manipulation of culturally significant musical elements. Arguably, the collage-like juxtapositions of contrasting musical idioms in Haas's works (namely those discussed in Chapters 2 and 3) have a similar cultural-critical significance.

The difference pointed out by Fulcher is related to that between modernism and the avant-garde. Fulcher's notion of challenging normative 'meaning construction' through 'critical dismantling of inherited cultural languages' resonates with Sternstein's claim that the Czech avant-garde artists subverted 'symbolic constructions of power' through their 'revolution in poetic language'. According to Sternstein, the avant-garde is distinguished from modernism by the presence of a political agenda, underpinning such aesthetic 'revolution':[106]

> The avant-garde is singled out as an historical movement because of its specifically political impulse: the will to attack the *institution* of art. [. . .] Literary and artistic modernism can be seen as a break with established methods and styles; as such, modernism is seen as an essentially *aesthetic* rebellion. The avant-garde likewise makes use of innovative methods [. . .] but these techniques are all intended to be somehow socially relevant.[107]

According to this definition, Haas's quartet 'From the Monkey Mountains' (discussed in Chapter 2) is the composer's only work which unambiguously qualifies as avant-garde (as opposed to 'merely' modernist). In any case, the aesthetic principles discussed here provide a useful conceptual framework for the interpretation of a significant portion of Haas's oeuvre.

Notes

1 See František Šmejkal and Rostislav Švácha, eds. *Devětsil: Czech Avant-garde Art, Architecture and Design of the 1920s and 30s* (Oxford: Museum of Modern Art, 1990). On the origins of the Czech musical avant-garde see Jiří Vysloužil, 'Česká meziválečná hudební avantgarda' [Czech Inter-war Musical Avant-garde], *Opus musicum*, 7/1 (1975), 1–11.

2 'Tam-tam' in *Slovník české hudební kultury* [Dictionary of Czech Musical Culture], ed. Jiří Fukač, Jiří Vysloužil, and Petr Macek (Prague: Editio Supraphon, 1997), p. 915.

3 See Václav Holzknecht, *Hudební Skupina Mánesa* (Prague: Panton, 1968).

4 *Pásmo* was the first regularly published literary platform of Devětsil. It published articles from the group's members resident in both Brno and Prague, as well as from European artists including (among others) László Moholy-Nagy, Theo van Doesburg, Walter Gropius, Kurt Schwitters and Le Corbusier. See Marcela Macharáčková, 'Z dějin Brněnského Devětsilu' [From the History of Brno's Devětsil], in *Forum Brunense 2009: Sborník prací Muzea města Brna*, ed. Pavel Ciprian (Brno: Společnost přátel Muzea města Brna, 2009), 79–99 (pp. 82–4).

5 Particularly noteworthy is the 1924 'Exhibition of Modern Art' [*Výstava moderního umění*]. The group organised about 30 lectures between 1924 and 1926, including (besides many others) the following: 'The Influence of Russian Theatre on Art Scene' (Jindřich Honzl, 1924), 'Russian Constructivism' (Karel Teige, 1924), 'Modern Architecture' (Theo van Doesburg, 1924), and 'Painting, Photography, Film' (László Moholy-Nagy, 1925). See ibid., pp. 96–9.

6 Karel Teige, 'Poetismus', *Host*, 3 (July 1924), 197–204, reprinted in *Avantgarda známá a neznámá* [The Known and Unknown Avant-Garde], ed. Štěpán Vlašín, 3 vols. (Prague: Svoboda, 1970–72), i: *Od proletářského umění k poetismu: 1919–1924* [From Proletarian Art to Poetism: 1919–1924] (1971), 554–61 (pp. 554–5). Page references here and below are to the 1971 reprint. All translations from Czech sources are mine, unless stated otherwise.

7 Ibid., 558.

8 Ibid., 560.

9 Karel Teige, 'Manifest poetismu', *ReD*, 1/9 (June 1928), reprinted in *Avantgarda známá a neznámá*, ed. Vlašín, ii: *Vrchol a krize Poetismu: 1925–1928* [The Peak and the Crisis of Poetism: 1925–1928] (1972), 557–93 (p. 591). Page references here and below are to the 1972 reprint.

10 Ibid., 592.

11 Teige, 'Poetismus', 560–1.

12 Peter A. Zusi, 'The Style of the Present: Karel Teige on Constructivism and Poetism', *Representations*, 88/1 (2004), 102–24 (p. 116).

13 Teige, 'Manifest poetismu', p. 592.

14 Esther Levinger, 'Czech Avant-Garde Art: Poetry for the Five Senses', *The Art Bulletin*, 81/3 (1999), 513–32 (p. 513).

15 Ibid., p. 528. Levinger quotes Teige's article 'Pozor na malbu' [Beware of Painting] published in Karel Teige, *Stavba a báseň: umění dnes a zítra 1919–1927* [Construction and Poem: Art Today and Tomorrow 1919–1927] (Prague: Vaněk a Votava, 1927), 107, translation Levinger's.

16 Ibid., p. 513.
17 Esther Levinger, 'Karel Teige on Cinema and Utopia', *The Slavic and East European Journal*, 48/2 (Summer 2004), 247–74 (p. 258).
18 Emil František Burian, *Jazz* (Prague: Aventinum, 1928), pp. 64–5.
19 Ibid., p. 57.
20 Teige, 'Manifest poetismu', p. 589.
21 Ibid., pp. 589–90.
22 Burian, *Jazz*, 18.
23 Ibid., 32.
24 For a comprehensive discussion of this matter see Miloš Zapletal, 'Sport a česká meziválečná hudba: úvod do problematiky', *Opus musicum*, 48/2 (2016), 6–40; 'Playful but Animalistically Serious: Czech Interwar Music and Sport', *Czech Music Quarterly*, 18/1 (2018), 15–25. Zapletal distinguishes three key areas of interaction between sports and music in inter-war Czechoslovakia: art music reflecting the avant-garde ideology of *Devětsil*, art music reflecting the official ideology of the Czechoslovak state, and 'functional' music associated with physical education and the Sokol movement in particular. See also 'Civilist Tendencies in the Inter-war Czech Music: at the Beginning of a Research', *Musicologica Brunensia* 54/1 (2019), 237–251.
25 Bohuslav Martinů, 'Half-time', *Anbruch*, 7/5 (1925), 292–3 (p. 292). All translations from Martinů's German article are mine.
26 Ibid.
27 Ibid.
28 See Matthew S. Witkovsky, 'Staging Language: Milča Mayerová and the Czech Book "Alphabet"', *The Art Bulletin*, 86/1 (2004), 114–35. See also Malynne M. Sternstein, *The Will to Chance: Necessity and Arbitrariness in the Czech Avant-Garde from Poetism to Surrealism* (Bloomington IN: Slavica Publishers, 2007), p. 98.
29 Iša Krejčí, 'Proč je balet tak aktuelní?', *Rozpravy Aventina*, 3 (1927–28), 159, quoted in Josef Bek, *Avantgarda: ke genezi socialistického realismu v české hudbě* [Avant-garde: Towards the Genesis of Socialist Realism in Czech Music] (Prague: Panton, 1984), p. 181.
30 Ibid.
31 Burian, *Jazz*, p. 57.
32 Jindřich Honzl, 'Státní židovské komorní divadlo v Moskvě' [Moscow State Jewish Theatre, also known as Moscow Yiddish Theatre and under the acronym GOSET], *ReD*, 1/2 (1927–28), 73–6. See also Judith Zivanovic, 'GOSET: Little-known Theatre of Widely Known Influence', *Educational Theatre Journal*, 27/2 (1975), 236–44.
33 Honzl, 'Státní židovské komorní divadlo v Moskvě', p. 75.
34 Ibid., pp. 75–6.
35 See Jiří Svoboda and Karel Teige, 'Musica a muzika', *Život*, 2 (1922), 86–9, reprinted in *Avantgarda známá a neznámá*, i, 405–12. Page references here and below are to the 1971 reprint.
36 Given his Marxist conviction, Teige used 'the people' [*lid*] interchangeably with 'proletariat'. This ideological agenda differentiates Teige from Cocteau, who – despite his opposition to cultural conservatism – employed nationalist (and thus more right-wing) rhetoric.
37 Svoboda and Teige, 'Musica a muzika', 407; the reference to sports is made on p. 409.
38 Ibid., p. 406.
39 Ibid., p. 408.
40 Ibid.
41 Ibid., p. 410.
42 Ibid.
43 Ibid., p. 411.
44 Ibid.
45 Václav Holzknecht, *Mladá Francie a česká hudba* [Young France and Czech Music] (Prague: Melantrich, Brno: Pazdírek, 1938).

46 Ibid., pp. 3–4. Italics mine.
47 Ibid., pp. 4–5. Italics mine.
48 Ibid., pp. 12–13.
49 Scott Messing, *Neoclassicism in Music: From the Genesis of the Concept through the Schoenberg/Stravinsky Polemic* (Rochester NY: University of Rochester Press, 1996), p. 108.
50 See Karel Honzík, *Ze života avantgardy: zážitky architektovy* [From the Life of the Avant-Garde: An Architect's Experience] (Prague: Československý spisovatel, 1963), pp. 26–32.
51 David Batchelor, '"This Liberty and This Order": Art in France after the First World War', in *Realism, Rationalism, Surrealism: Art between the Wars*, ed. Briony Fer, David Batchelor, and Paul Wood (New Haven CT: Yale University Press, in association with the Open University, 1993), 2–85 (p. 19).
52 Amédée Ozenfant and Charles-Éduard Jeanneret, 'Purism', *L'Esprit Nouveau*, 1 (1920), quoted in David Batchelor, '"This Liberty and This Order": Art in France after the First World War', p. 19.
53 David Batchelor, '"This Liberty and This Order": Art in France after the First World War', pp. 24–5.
54 Ibid., pp. 25–7.
55 See Adolf Loos, 'Ornament and Crime', in *Programs and Manifestoes on 20th-Century Architecture*, ed. Ulrich Conrads (Cambridge MA: MIT Press, 1970), 19–24.
56 Jean Cocteau, 'Cock and Harlequin', in *A Call to Order: Written between the Years 1918 and 1926 and Including Cock and Harlequin, Professional Secrets, and Other Critical Essays*, trans. Rollo H. Myers (New York: Haskell House Publishers, 1974), 8–82 (pp. 19, 21–2).
57 Ibid., pp. 17–18, emphasis in the original.
58 Messing, *Neoclassicism in Music*, pp. 1–2.
59 Ibid., pp. 117–27.
60 Bohuslav Martinů, 'Igor Stravinskij', *Listy hudební matice*, 4/3 (1924), reprinted in *Domov, hudba a svět: deníky, zápisky, úvahy a články*, ed. Miloš Šafránek (Prague: Státní hudební vydavatelství, 1966), 31–3 (p. 32).
61 See also Bohuslav Martinů, 'Současná hudba ve Francii' [Contemporary Music in France], *Listy hudební matice*, 4/9–10 (1925), reprinted in *Domov, hudba a svět*, 46–49. See also Bek, *Avantgarda*, p. 173.
62 Bek, *Avantgarda*, p. 175.
63 Burian, *Jazz*, pp. 26–7.
64 Ibid., p. 26.
65 Ibid., pp. 40–4.
66 Pavel Haas, 'Hudba lehká a vážná' [Light Music and Serious (Art) Music], *Tempo*, 15/8 (1936), 90. The term 'vážná hudba' (literally 'serious music') is the Czech equivalent of the German term 'ernste Musik'.
67 Ibid.
68 Iša Krejčí, 'Ponětí modernosti v dnešní hudbě', *Rozpravy Aventina*, 3/8 (1927–28), p. 97.
69 Ibid. Although Krejčí's term 'účelný' translates literally as 'purposeful', the adjective 'functional' seems to be more suitable, especially since this whole idea is clearly derived from Teige's notion of 'constructivism', which found its ultimate manifestation in 'Functionalist' architecture.
70 Ibid.
71 Ibid. Emphasis in the original.
72 Ibid.
73 Holzknecht, *Mladá Francie a česká hudba*, p. 6.
74 Ibid., p. 5.
75 Ibid., p. 8.

76 Ibid., p. 6.
77 Ibid., p. 9.
78 Pavel Haas, 'O návratu' ('On Return'), *Listy Hudební Matice / Tempo*, 5/9–10 (1926), 325–7.
79 Ibid., p. 326.
80 Pavel Haas, 'O hudbě budoucnosti', *Hudební rozhledy*, 3/3 (1926–27), 58–9.
81 Ibid. Emphasis in the original.
82 Ibid., p. 58. Emphasis in the original.
83 Ibid.
84 Ibid.
85 Sternstein, *The Will to Chance*, p. 113.
86 Teige, 'Poetismus', 557.
87 Esther Levinger, 'Karel Teige on Cinema and Utopia', p. 258.
88 Following the demise of the group Devětsil in 1931, the Czech Surrealist Group was established in Prague in 1934. An exhibition of Surrealist painting showing works by Czech as well as French painters took place in Prague in 1932. Breton's *Second Manifesto of Surrealism* was published in Czech translation in 1930 and Breton himself gave a lecture in Prague in 1935. See František Šmejkal, 'After Devětsil: Surrealism in Czechoslovakia', in *The Czech Avant-Garde of the 1920s and 30s*, ed. František Šmejkal and Rostislav Švácha (Oxford: Museum of Modern Art, 1990), 88–93 (pp. 88–9). The translation of Breton's manifesto was published in Vítězslav Nezval, *Zvěrokruh*, 2 (Prague: Ústřední Studentské knihkupectví a nakladateství, 1930), 60–74.
89 Karel Teige, 'Od artificielismu k surrealismu', in *Zápasy O Smysl Moderní Tvorby: Studie Z Třicátých Let* (Prague: Československý spisovatel, 1969), 442–68 (p. 457).
90 Esther Levinger, 'A Life in Nature: Karel Teige's Journey from Poetism to Surrealism', *Zeitschrift für Kunstgeschichte*, 67/3 (2004), 401–20.
91 Sternstein, *The Will to Chance*, p. 17.
92 Ibid., p. 54.
93 Ibid., pp. 51–2.
94 Anne LeBaron, 'Reflections of Surrealism in Postmodern Musics' in *Postmodern Music/Postmodern Thought*, ed. Judith Irene Lochhead and Joseph Henry Auner (New York: Routledge, 2002), 27–73 (pp. 30–1).
95 Ibid., p. 30.
96 Cross, 'The Stravinsky Legacy', p. 85.
97 Glenn Watkins, *Pyramids at the Louvre: Music, Culture, and Collage from Stravinsky to the Postmodernists* (Cambridge MA: Harvard University Press, 1994), pp. 2–3.
98 Martha M. Hyde, 'Neoclassic and Anachronistic Impulses in Twentieth-Century Music', *Music Theory Spectrum*, 18 (1996), 200–35. Hyde distinguishes four strategies of 'mak[ing] the distance [between past and present] meaningful', using pieces by Ravel ('reverential imitation'), Stravinsky ('eclectic imitation'), Bartók ('heuristic imitation'), and Schoenberg ('dialectical imitation') as case studies. Hyde thus draws attention to the broader preoccupation with the musical past in twentieth-century music, pointing out different ways of engagement with previous styles. Hyde draws on Harold Greene's theory of anachronism. See Harold Greene, 'History and Anachronism,' in *The Vulnerable Text: Essays on Renaissance Literature* (New York: Columbia University Press, 1986), 218–35.
99 Hyde, 'Neoclassic and Anachronistic Impulses', p. 205.
100 Cross, *The Stravinsky Legacy*, pp. 7–8.
101 Stephen Hinton: 'Weill: "Neue Sachlichkeit", Surrealism, and "Gebrauchsmusik"', in *A New Orpheus: Essays on Kurt Weill*, ed. Kim H. Kowalke (New Haven CT and London: Yale University Press, 1986), 61–82 (p. 68).
102 Theodor W. Adorno, review of Weill's *Die Dreigroschenoper* in *Die Music* 21 (December 1928), pp. 221–2, quoted in Hinton, 'Weill: "Neue Sachlichkeit", Surrealism, and "Gebrauchsmusik"', p. 66.

103 Jane F. Fulcher, *The Composer as Intellectual: Music and Ideology in France 1914–1940* (New York: Oxford University Press, 2005), p. 170. See also Jane F. Fulcher, 'The Composer as Intellectual: Ideological Inscriptions in French Interwar Neoclassicism', *The Journal of Musicology*, 17/2 (1999), 197–230.
104 Fulcher, *The Composer as Intellectual*, p. 155.
105 Ibid.
106 See Jochen Schulte-Sasse, 'Foreword: Theory of Modernism versus Theory of Avant-Garde', in Peter Bürger, *Theory of the Avant-Garde* (Minneapolis: University of Minnesota Press, 1984), vii–xlvii (p. xv), quoted in Sternstein, *The Will to Chance*, p. 11: 'Modernism may be understandable as an attack on traditional writing techniques, but the avant-garde can only be understood as an attack meant to alter the institutionalized commerce with art.'
107 Sternstein, *The Will to Chance*, p. 11. Emphasis in the original.

Bibliography

Bek, Josef, *Avantgarda: ke genezi socialistického realismu v české hudbě* (Prague: Panton, 1984).

Bek, Josef, *Erwin Schulhoff: Leben und Werk* (Hamburg: von Bockel Verlag, 1994).

Bek, Josef, *Hudební neoklasicismus* (Prague: Academia, 1982).

Bek, Josef, 'Mezinárodní styky české hudby 1924–1932', *Hudební věda*, 5/1 (1968), 628–48.

Breton, André, *Manifestoes of Surrealism* (Ann Arbor: University of Michigan Press, 1969).

Burian, Emil František, *Jazz* (Prague: Aventinum, 1928).

Chalupa, Dalibor, 'Karneval', *Host*, 4 (1924–25), 166–7.

Cocteau, Jean, 'Cock and Harlequin', in *A Call to Order: Written between the Years 1918 and 1926 and Including Cock and Harlequin, Professional Secrets, and Other Critical Essays*, trans. Rollo H. Myers (New York: Haskell House Publishers, 1974), 8–82.

Cross, Jonathan, *The Stravinsky Legacy* (Cambridge: Cambridge University Press, 1998).

Dřímal, Jaroslav and Václav Peša, eds., *Dějiny města Brna*, 2 vols. (Brno: Blok, 1969–73).

Dulavová, Marie, ed., *Dějiny české hudební kultury*, 2 vols. (Prague: Academia, 1972–81), i: 1890–1918 (1972), ii: 1918–1945 (1981).

Fer, Briony, David Batchelor, and Paul Wood, eds., *Realism, Rationalism, Surrealism: Art between the Wars* (New Haven CT: Yale University Press, in association with the Open University, 1993).

Fukač, Jiří, Jiří Vysloužil, and Petr Macek, eds., *Slovník české hudební kultury* (Prague: Editio Supraphon, 1997).

Fulcher, Jane F., 'The Composer as Intellectual: Ideological Inscriptions in French Interwar Neoclassicism', *The Journal of Musicology*, 17/2 (1999), 197–230.

Fulcher, Jane F., *The Composer as Intellectual: Music and Ideology in France 1914–1940* (New York: Oxford University Press, 2005).

Gabrielová, Bronislava, and Bohumil Marčák, *Kapitoly z dějin brněnských časopisů* (Brno: Masarykova univerzita, 1999).

Götz, František, 'Devětsil v Brně', *Socialistická budoucnost*, 28 May 1921, reprinted in Vlašín, Štěpán, ed., *Avantgarda známá a neznámá*, 3 vols. (Prague: Svoboda, 1970–72), i, 130–3.

Green, Martin, and John C. Swan, *The Triumph of Pierrot: The Commedia Dell'arte and the Modern Imagination* (Philadelphia: Pennsylvania State University Press, 1993, revised edition).

Haas, Pavel, 'Haasův kvartet "Z opičích hor": Poprvé proveden v Brně 16. března 1926', *Hudební rozhledy*, 7 (1925–26), 106.

Haas, Pavel, 'O návratu', *Listy Hudební Matice/Tempo*, 5/9–10 (1926), 325–7.

Haas, Pavel, 'O hudbě budoucnosti', *Hudební rozhledy*, 3/3 (1926–27), 58–9.

Haas, Pavel, 'Hudba lehká a vážná', *Tempo*, 15/8 (1936), 90.

Haas, Petr, 'Česká meziválečná hudební avantgarda: pojem "avantgarda" v české hudbě' (unpublished bachelor's thesis, Masaryk University, 2009).

Helfert, Vladimír, *Česká moderní hudba: studie o české hudební tvořivosti* (Olomouc: Index, 1936), reprinted in *Vybrané studie: O hudební tvořivosti* (Prague: Ed. Supraphon, 1970), 163–312.

Hinton, Stephen, *The Idea of Gebrauchsmusik: A Study of Musical Aesthetics in the Weimar Republic (1919–1933) with Particular Reference to the Works of Paul Hindemith* (New York: Garland, 1989).

Hinton, Stephen, 'Weill: "Neue Sachlichkeit", Surrealism, and "Gebrauchsmusik"', in *A New Orpheus: Essays on Kurt Weill*, ed. Kim H. Kowalke (New Haven CT and London: Yale University Press, 1986), 61–82.

Hodeir, Andre, *Jazz: Its Evolution and Essence* (New York: Grove Press, 1956).

Hoffmeister, Adolf, 'Nesmrtelnost smíchu', *Volné směry*, 26/7–8 (November 1928), reprinted in Vlašín, Štěpán, ed., *Avantgarda známá a neznámá*, 3 vols. (Prague: Svoboda, 1970–72), ii, 628–31.

Holzknecht, Václav, *Hudební skupina Mánesa* (Prague: Panton, 1968).

Holzknecht, Václav, *Mladá Francie a česká hudba* (Prague: Melantrich; Brno: Pazdírek, 1938).

Honzík, Karel, *Ze života avantgardy: zážitky architektovy* (Prague: Československý spisovatel, 1963).

Honzl, Jindřich, 'Státní židovské komorní divadlo v Moskvě', *ReD*, 1/2 (1927–28), 73–6.

Hyde, Martha M., 'Neoclassic and Anachronistic Impulses in Twentieth-Century Music', *Music Theory Spectrum*, 18 (1996), 200–35.

Jeřábek, Dušan, *Brněnská romance* (Brno: Kulturní a informační centrum, 1997).

Kelly, Barbara L., *Music and Ultra-Modernism in France: A Fragile Consensus, 1913–1939* (Woodbridge, Suffolk: Boydell Press, 2013).

Kotek, Josef, *Dějiny české populární hudby a zpěvu*, 2 vols (Prague: Academia, 1994–98), ii: *1918–1968* (1998).

Kotek, Josef, ed., *Kronika české synkopy: půlstoletí českého jazzu a moderní populární hudby v obrazech a svědectví současníků* (Prague: Supraphon, 1975).

Krejčí, Iša, 'Ponětí modernosti v dnešní hudbě', *Rozpravy Aventina*, 3 (1927–28), 97.

LeBaron, Anne, 'Reflections of Surrealism in Postmodern Musics', in *Postmodern Music/ Postmodern Thought*, ed. Judith Irene Lochhead and Joseph Henry Auner (New York: Routledge, 2002), 27–73.

Levinger, Esther, 'Czech Avant-Garde Art: Poetry for the Five Senses', *The Art Bulletin*, 81/3 (1999), 513–32.

Levinger, Esther, 'A Life in Nature: Karel Teige's Journey from Poetism to Surrealism', *Zeitschrift für Kunstgeschichte*, 67/3 (2004), 401–20.

Levinger, Esther, 'Karel Teige on Cinema and Utopia', *The Slavic and East European Journal*, 48/2 (Summer 2004), 247–74.

Locke, Brian S., *Opera and Ideology in Prague* (Rochester NY: University of Rochester Press, 2006).

Macharáčková, Marcela, 'Z dějin Brněnského Devětsilu', in *Forum Brunense 2009: Sborník prací Muzea města Brna*, ed. Pavel Ciprian (Brno: Společnost přátel Muzea města Brna, 2009), 79–99.

Martinů, Bohuslav, *Domov, hudba a svět: deníky, zápisky, úvahy a články*, ed. Miloš Šafránek (Prague: Státní hudební vydavatelství, 1966).

Martinů, Bohuslav, 'Igor Stravinskij' (1924), 31–33, originally in *Listy hudební matice*, 4/3 (1924).

Martinů, Bohuslav, 'Současná hudba ve Francii' (1925), 46–9, originally in *Listy hudební matice*, 4/9–10 (1925).

Martinů, Bohuslav, 'Half-time', *Anbruch*, 7/5 (1925), 292–3.

Messing, Scott, *Neoclassicism in Music: From the Genesis of the Concept through the Schoenberg/Stravinsky Polemic* (Rochester NY: University of Rochester Press, 1996).

Papoušek, Vladimír, *Gravitace avantgard: imaginace a řeč avantgard v českých literárních textech první poloviny dvacátého století* (Prague: Akropolis, 2007).

Peduzzi, Lubomír, *Pavel Haas: Život a dílo skladatele* (Brno: Muzejní a vlastivědná společnost, 1993); for German translation see *Pavel Haas: Leben und Werk des Komponisten*, trans. Thomas Mandl (Hamburg: Bockel, 1996).

Racek, Jan, *Leoš Janáček a současní moravští skladatelé: nástin k slohovému vývoji soudobé moravské hudby* (Brno: Unie československých hudebníků z povolání, 1940).

Schulz, Karel, 'Groteska', *Český filmový svět*, 4/2 (March 1926), reprinted in Vlašín, Štěpán, ed., *Avantgarda známá a neznámá*, 3 vols. (Prague: Svoboda, 1970–72), ii, 278–80.

Seifert, Jaroslav, and Karel Teige, eds., *Revoluční sborník Devětsil* (Prague: Večernice V. Vortel, 1922; reprinted by Prague: Akropolis ve spolupráci s Centrem výzkumu české umělecké avantgardy, 2010).

Shattuck, Roger, *The Banquet Years* (New York: Vintage Books, 1968).

Slavíček, Lubomír, and Jana Vránová, eds., *100 let Domu umění města Brna* (Brno: Dům umění města Brna, 2010).

Šmejkal, František, and Rostislav Švácha, eds., *Devětsil: Czech Avant-garde Art, Architecture and Design of the 1920s and 30s* (Oxford: Museum of Modern Art, 1990).

Štědroň, Miloš, *Leoš Janáček a hudba 20. století. Paralely, sondy, dokumenty* (Brno: Nadace Universitas Masarykiana, 1998).

Sternstein, Malynne M., *The Will to Chance: Necessity and Arbitrariness in the Czech Avant-Garde from Poetism to Surrealism* (Bloomington IN: Slavica Publishers, 2007).

Svoboda, Jiří and Karel Teige, 'Musica a muzika', *Život*, 2 (1922), 86–9, reprinted in Vlašín, Štěpán, ed., *Avantgarda známá a neznámá*, 3 vols. (Prague: Svoboda, 1970–72), i, 405–12.

Teige, Karel, 'Manifest poetismu', *ReD*, 1/9 (June, 1928), reprinted in Vlašín, Štěpán, ed., *Avantgarda známá a neznámá*, 3 vols. (Prague: Svoboda, 1970–72) ii, 557–93.

Teige, Karel, 'O humoru, clownech a dadaistech', *Sršatec*, 4/38–40 (July–August, 1924), reprinted in Vlašín, Štěpán, ed., *Avantgarda známá a neznámá*, 3 vols. (Prague: Svoboda, 1970–72), i, 571–86.

Teige, Karel, 'Poetismus', *Host*, 3 (July 1924), 197–204, reprinted in Vlašín, Štěpán, ed., *Avantgarda známá a neznámá*, 3 vols. (Prague: Svoboda, 1970–72), i, 554–61.

Teige, Karel, *Výbor z díla*, ed. Jiří Brabec, Vratislav Effenberger, Květoslav Chvatík, and Robert Kalivoda, 3 vols. (Prague: Československý spisovatel 1966–94), ii: *Zápasy o smysl moderní tvorby, Studie z třicátých let* (1969).

Tyrrell, John, *Janáček: Years of Life*, 2 vols. (London: Faber and Faber, 2006–07), ii: *(1914–1928), Tsar of the Forests* (2007).

Vlašín, Štěpán, ed., *Avantgarda známá a neznámá*, 3 vols. (Prague: Svoboda, 1970–72), i: *Od proletářského umění k poetismu: 1919–1924* (1971); ii: *Vrchol a krize poetismu: 1925–1928* (1972); iii: *Generační diskuse: 1929–1931* (1970).

Vlček, Tomáš, 'Art between Social Crisis and Utopia: The Czech Contribution to the Development of the Avant-Garde Movement in East-Central Europe, 1910–30', *Art Journal*, 49/1 (Spring 1990), 28–35.

Vojvodík, Josef, and Jan Wiendl, eds., *Heslář české avantgardy: estetické koncepty a proměny uměleckých postupů v letech 1908–1958* (Prague: Togga, 2011).

Vysloužil, Jiří, 'Česká meziválečná hudební avantgarda', *Opus musicum*, 7/1 (1975), 1–11.

Watkins, Glenn, *Pyramids at the Louvre: Music, Culture, and Collage from Stravinsky to the Postmodernists* (Cambridge MA: Belknap Press of Harvard University Press, 1994).

Witkovsky, Matthew S., 'Staging Language: Milča Mayerová and the Czech Book "Alphabet"', *The Art Bulletin*, 86/1 (2004), 114–35.

Zusi, Peter A., 'The Style of the Present: Karel Teige on Constructivism and Poetism', *Representations*, 88/1 (2004), 102–24.

2 'From the Monkey Mountains'

The body, the grotesque, and carnival

Introduction

'From the Monkey Mountains' is the title of Haas's 1925 string quartet. This piece arguably marked a turning point in the young composer's career, and singled Haas out within the group of Janáček's students. Václav Kaprál, Vilém Petrželka, and Osvald Chlubna (to name but the most important members of this group) built in their contemporary chamber works less upon Janáček's latest works than upon the pre-war tradition of Czech high-art music, represented by Antonín Dvořák's disciples Vítězslav Novák and Josef Suk.[1] Haas, by contrast, combined salient features of Janáček's compositional idiom with avant-garde tendencies that emerged during and after the First World War.

A similar assessment of the significance of Haas's quartet appears in Lubomír Peduzzi's seminal monograph,[2] but a more detailed contextualisation or critical interpretation of the work is nowhere to be found.[3] This chapter demonstrates the work's affinity to the contemporary avant-garde movement of Poetism (discussed in Chapter 1) and the associated concepts. It will become apparent that Poetism's ideal of 'everyday' art which appeals to the body corresponds with Haas's emphasis on rhythmic energy, his fascination with jazz-band music, and his penchant for grotesque exaggeration and distortion of dance-like movement. Finally, it will be shown that the string quartet conceals a reference to the theme of carnival, one of the most characteristic topoi of Poetism, the significance of which will be discussed through cultural-critical perspectives of Mikhail Bakhtin (1895–1975).

Of the four movements of the quartet, this chapter discusses the first ('Landscape'), the second ('Carriage, Horseman and Horse'), and the fourth ('The Wild Night'). The 'slow' third movement, 'The Moon and I', which is marked by a contemplative and intimate character, will not be discussed at length, because it is least relevant to the issues outlined above. Nonetheless, it will be argued that this movement is complementary to the carnivalesque features of the quartet and that, in this respect, its role in the piece is analogous to that played by contrasting sections within the other movements.

'From the Monkey Mountains': reception and Haas's commentary

At its première, Haas's quartet was met with hostility from the conservative critics.[4] This was because of its anti-academic spirit, akin to that prophesied by

Teige and Svoboda in the article 'Musica and Muzika' (discussed in Chapter 1).[5] The elements of 'low', popular music ('muzika' rather than 'musica') in Haas's work were all the more striking since they clashed with the expectations set by the genre of the string quartet, traditionally associated with 'high' art, seriousness, and refinement. This clash was further exacerbated in the last movement, when the string ensemble was joined (as if in response to Teige's call for the use of modern instruments)[6] by a percussion set – the hallmark of contemporary 'jazz bands'.[7] Many were also dismayed by Haas's use of tone-painting, which was described in terms of 'caricature', the 'burlesque', and the 'grotesque' (note that Teige and Svoboda used the same terms in their portrayal of Auric as a pioneer of everyday music),[8] and perceived by some as the mark of the influence of contemporary 'international' or 'Western' music.[9]

It is noteworthy that, despite the chauvinistic undertone of some reviews, no hostility was directed towards Haas himself and there was no mention of his Jewish origin, a factor that was used by French conservative critics against musicians like Darius Milhaud and Jean Wiéner, and that later proved fatal to Haas during the time of Nazi occupation.[10] As a recent graduate of Janáček's compositional masterclass, Haas was seen as a young talent, promising to advance the Moravian compositional tradition. Thus, most critics recognised Haas's musical gifts, but his work was nonetheless dismissed as 'modish', 'tasteless', and 'unscrupulous'.[11]

In anticipation of the work's premiere, at which Haas's quartet featured alongside works by Václav Kaprál and Osvald Chlubna, the journal *Hudební Rozhledy* (*Musical Outlooks*) published short commentaries on each of the pieces. Haas's commentary begins as follows:

> The title of the quartet comes from the colloquial name of the Moravian locality in which this composition arose. Although the movements are given programmatic titles ['Landscape'; 'Carriage, Horseman and Horse'; 'The Moon and I'; 'The Wild Night'], this is not for the sake of some kind of painting, as the listener might easily think. I simply intended to capture several strong impressions evoked by a light-hearted summer vacation in the country. [. . .] I could have entitled the movements plainly with Roman numerals and supplemented those with Italian tempo markings. I did not do that, however, because I wanted to confess openly the actual source of my inspiration and thoughts to the listener.[12]

These claims make clear that – contrary to the expectations of the chamber-music genre – Haas was not writing a serious piece of high art intended exclusively for expert audiences. This work was to be 'light-hearted' in character, and its inspiration was very much earth-bound. It should be pointed out that leisure-time activities were a typical source of inspiration for Poetism, and that travel, trips, and postcards were among its most characteristic topics, repeatedly exploited in poems and photo collages.[13]

Yet at times the proclaimed rural inspiration is brought into question by elements suggestive of an urban context. This is particularly the case with the last movement ('The Wild Night'), which, as one reviewer described it, is marked with 'the atmosphere of a bar'.[14] Whether or not the composer had spent his summer holiday in the 'Monkey Mountains', it is arguable that he chose this term – once familiar in the patois of Brno – for the title of his quartet to give it a humorous, slightly subversive ring, conjuring up as it does the common association of monkeys with mockery, cheekiness, and pulling faces.[15] In this sense, the title encapsulates the vernacular, grotesque features of the work, which will be discussed below.

The decision to avoid 'Roman numerals and [. . .] Italian tempo markings' and use 'programmatic titles' instead advertises the piece's anti-academic character and accessibility to the audience. However, Haas seems rather apologetic about the programmatic element. It is not easy to see what he means by claiming that he did not aim at 'some kind of painting'. Considering the slightly derogatory undertone of this formulation, it is possible that Haas wanted to distance himself from the aesthetic context of Romanticism or Impressionism, with which tone-painting could be associated. Haas later made his position somewhat clearer by claiming that 'the programme helps greatly to create contrasts and escalations, thus determining the piece's formal structure [and] facilitating the creation of purely musical features'.[16] This implies that the programmatic or pictorial element is treated with a high degree of abstraction and that it is ultimately subordinate to the considerations of 'pure music'. This explanation sounds plausible as far as the first movement ('Landscape') is concerned. However, some of the other movements (especially 'Carriage, Horseman and Horse') are much more overtly pictorial. Again, the composer seems to be trying to divert attention away from the more controversial features of his work – in this case the 'caricature-like' and 'grotesque' elements within the rarefied genre of the string quartet.

Finally, Haas explained that the use of the percussion set ('jazz') in the last movement was 'neither self-serving nor unnatural' since it was 'firmly bound up with the original conception of the piece, which culminates rhythmically and dynamically in its last movement'.[17] This justification plays down the association of 'jazz' with contemporary dance music and modern urban popular entertainment as a whole. In subsequent performances (Prague, 1927; Brno, 1931), the composer had the work played without the percussion part. To my knowledge, there is no archival evidence as to the reasons behind this decision. Nonetheless, Peduzzi argued that 'the composer [. . .] refrained from the use of the percussion set not so much in response to the critics as in the interest of practicality of performance'.[18]

Rhythms of 'Landscape'

Haas's commentary also betrays a considerable emphasis on physical movement and sensuality – both of which are musically conveyed by (and correlated with) rhythmic devices. Having stated that '*movement* governs throughout this light-hearted composition', the composer went on to suggest that the sensual impressions which had inspired the piece had some kind of rhythmic identity:

Whether it is the rhythm of a broad landscape and birdsong, or the irregular movement of a rural vehicle; be it the warm song of a human heart and cold silent stream of moonlight, or the exuberance of a sleepless revelry night, the innocent smile of the morning sun . . . , it is always movement that governs everything. (Even the deepest silence has its own motion and rhythm.)[19]

Haas's mention of the 'rhythm of a broad landscape' in his commentary on the quartet arguably refers to the ostinato rhythm at the beginning of the first movement. The opening section bears resemblance to the melodic and rhythmic patterns of the blues: notice the 'off-beat' rhythmic pattern in what would be the piano left-hand part (see Example 2.1) and the chromatic inflections of the solo violin melody hovering above this accompaniment (see Example 2.2). Once F is established as the 'tonic', the chromatic variability of the third and seventh degrees (the 'blue notes', in this case A/A flat and E/E flat, respectively) becomes apparent.

One contemporary critic observed that this movement ('Landscape') 'depicts the composer's rambling through a hilly landscape', portraying with 'apt humour' the 'pleasure drawn from movement and events along the journey'.[20] Of the whole movement, the passage shown in Example 2.3 is most likely to evoke the image of a rambling tourist, not least due to the march-like 'oom-pah' accompaniment figure. One could even see signs of the 'pleasure drawn from movement' in the extremely

Example 2.1 Opening ostinato. Pavel Haas, String Quartet No. 2 'From the Monkey Mountains', Op. 7, 1925 (Prague: Tempo; Berlin: Bote & Bock, 1994), first movement, bb. 1–2, violin 2 and viola.

Source: © Copyright Boosey & Hawkes Bote & Bock GmbH, Berlin. All subsequent extracts from this work refer to this edition and are reproduced by permission of Boosey & Hawkes Music Publishers Ltd.

Example 2.2 Blues scale inflections in the opening theme. Haas, String Quartet No. 2, first movement, bb. 3–10, violin 1

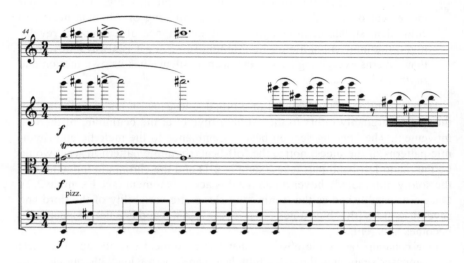

Example 2.3 Janáčekian texture. Haas, String Quartet No. 2, first movement, b. 44.

high register of the violin part and the vibrant Janáčekian texture consisting of osti-nati, trills, and melodic/rhythmic fragments scattered across the score.

Haas's reference to the 'rhythm of birdsong' in his commentary undoubtedly relates to bb. 48–52 (Example 2.4), in which a pentatonic motive (previously pre-sented in crotchets) appears in the guise of a characteristically short and sharply articulated Janáčekian melodic fragment:

Finally, the mention of a 'warm song of a human heart' corresponds with the iambic ostinato (suggestive of the slow heartbeat of a resting person) underpin-ning the movement's contrasting middle section. This is characterised by a homo-phonic texture, slow tempo (Lento ma non troppo), low dynamics, and a regular phrase structure:

Despite the presence of these programmatic or pictorial elements, there is some justification in this movement for Haas's claim that 'the programme helps greatly to create contrasts and escalations, thus determining the piece's formal structure [and] facilitating the creation of purely musical features'. Haas seems to have 'distilled' from the above described pictorial elements (articulated largely by means of rhythm) a kind of 'abstract' or 'purely musical' dynamic trajectory (also strongly dependent on rhythmic processes), which is essential for the piece's formal design. Figure 4.4 represents the occurrence of the most extensively used of the above observed ostinato patterns, which indeed give rise to such a kind of dynamic trajectory.

There are four main rhythmic patterns here, which have been arranged in descending order of rhythmic values. The schema indicates that the changes of the underlying rhythmic pattern delineate the movement's formal sections.

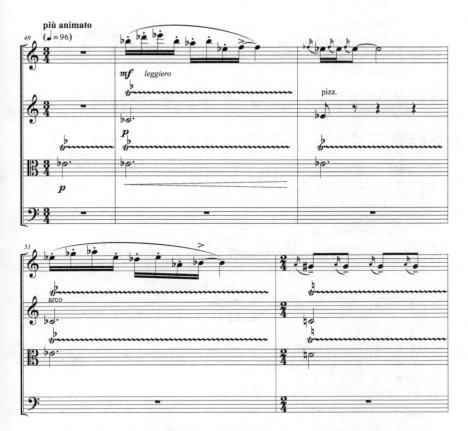

Example 2.4 'Birdsong' motive. Haas, String Quartet No. 2, first movement, bb. 48–52.

Throughout the first section (A), rhythmic values are gradually diminished. Simultaneously, the layers of ostinati are frequently superimposed to increase rhythmic activity and textural density. The momentum suddenly drops in the middle section (B) and is resumed in the final section (A'). Significantly, the resulting dynamic trajectory, which follows the pattern 'escalation–repose–finale', is also replicated on a large scale in the succession of the four movements of the piece, which thus, as the composer himself suggested, 'culminat[es] rhythmically and dynamically in its last movement'.

Arguably, Haas's emphasis on rhythmic and dynamic categories – those elements which play the most important role in the bodily perception of music – is consistent with the Poetist concept of 'poetry for the senses' (explained in Chapter 1). However, the movement's compositional-technical roots are distinctly Janáčekian. 'Landscape' will be discussed further in Chapter 4 with respect to Janáček's theory and practice of 'sčasování'.

Example 2.5 Contrasting middle section. Haas, String Quartet No. 2, first movement, bb. 90–7.

'Carriage, Horseman and Horse': a grotesque ride

The second movement is much more overtly pictorial than the first. As far as its 'programme' is concerned, the title 'Carriage, Horseman and Horse' and Haas's reference to the 'irregular movement of a rural vehicle' in his commentary are the only clues given to the listener. Nonetheless, when guided by the music, one needs no further description to imagine the creaking cart uneasily moving off, gradually picking up momentum, bouncing along an uneven track, getting out of control, and finally breaking down. Some of the contemporary critics regarded this move-ment as a parodic allusion to Honegger's *Pacific 231* (which was performed in Brno in 1924).[21] Most reviewers were put off by the frivolous humour of this movement, which provoked references to 'caricature' and the 'grotesque' in the above-cited reviews.

Musical manifestations of the grotesque have previously been discussed by Esti Sheinberg and Julie Brown.[22] The grotesque has been described as a hybrid form, a bizarre and irrational cluster of incongruities in which all kinds of boundaries are blurred – typically those between laughter and horror; merriment and frenzy; sanity and insanity; life and death; animate and inanimate; man, machine, animal, and vegetable.[23] The sense of hybridism, ambivalence, and confusion can be conveyed through the juxtaposition of musical elements that are incongruous in terms of style, character, and/or musical syntax.

The effect of the grotesque is often based on violation of an implicit bodily norm, namely through exaggeration and distortion. Sheinberg suggests that hyperbolic distortion of the bodily norm can be musically articulated by using a tempo which is too fast for human motion, a register too high for the human voice, or 'unnatural' rhythmic patterns, contrasting with the natural rhythms of human body (walk, heartbeat, and so on).[24] Musical instances of the grotesque often make use of dance gestures because of their association with bodily movement. Sheinberg proposes the following list of musical features which 'enhance a feeling of compulsive obsession that relates to the insane, bizarre side of the grotesque and to its unreal, unnatural aspects': a 'tendency to triple metre, which enhances the feeling of whirling, uncontrollable motion, sudden unexpected outbursts, loud dynamics, extreme pitches, marked rhythmical stresses, dissonances or distortions of expected harmonic progressions, and many repetitions of simple and short patterns'.[25]

The first example of grotesque exaggeration and distortion in Haas's quartet appears at the very beginning of the second movement (see Example 2.6). There the coarse opening glissandi paraphrase the opening motive of the first movement. The initial notes (E, D, E flat, D flat, C) of what was originally a fluid melody played in the upper register of the violin are now mechanically repeated, encumbered with heavy accents, played in parallel seconds in the lower register of viola and cello, and, most provocatively, disfigured by 'creaking' glissandi. As the title suggests, this musical effect may illustrate the squeaking wheels and the horse's neighing. In any case, the movement opens with a grotesque musical image of a body (possibly a hybrid body conflating the animal with the vehicle) distorted and pushed to the extreme. Another level of distortion is added when an incongruent metrical pattern (3/8 + 3/8 + 3/8) is introduced in the accompaniment, creating the sense of irregular or awkward motion (see Example 2.7). At the same time, the pitches of the initial motive are

Example 2.6 The opening glissandi. Haas, String Quartet No. 2, second movement, bb. 1–4.

Example 2.7 Metric conflict and pentatonicism. Haas, String Quartet No. 2, second movement, bb. 17–8.

adapted to yield a pentatonic collection, which, through its traditional association with exoticism, makes the section sound 'strange'.

In contrast with the rather static character of the opening, the second section (più mosso) is emphatically motoric (see Example 2.8). A new, highly repetitive theme suggestive of a horse's trot is introduced in the second violin (quavers), accompanied by semiquavers phrased in groups of three. The resulting cross-rhythms convey the impression of 'irregular' and 'bouncy' movement. The realm of pitch betrays another incongruity: like the opening theme of the first movement, the 'horse-trot' theme consists essentially of a descending blues scale, which is characterised by an inherent ambivalence between major and minor mode. As a result, the musical depiction of the ride oscillates, in Sheinberg's terms, between 'euphoric' and 'dysphoric' values, traditionally associated with 'major' and 'minor' modality, respectively.[26]

The theme, originally presented in a 'comfortable' tempo (quavers) and register, is subsequently repeated in double speed (semiquavers) and transposed to an extremely high register, with the 'bouncing' effect enhanced by dotted rhythm (see Example 2.9). Significantly, the composer annotated this section 'tečkovaný cirkus' ('dotted circus') on the margin of his autograph.[27]

Indeed, this section is marked by a musical idiom that is strikingly similar to that of the music accompanying actual circus performances. Particularly characteristic is the use of stock accompaniment patterns associating the topic of a march or a quick dance in duple metre such as a polka. In keeping with these contextual associations, the passage is marked by the typically clownish mixture of humorousness and silliness. First, the newly added components (dotted rhythm, dance/march topic) further exaggerate the already prominent emphasis on physical movement, which is thus made excessively explicit and satirised.[28] Second,

Example 2.8 'Horse trot' theme in quavers. Haas, String Quartet No. 2, second movement, bb. 24–32.

Example 2.9 'Dotted circus' theme. Haas, String Quartet No. 2, second movement, bb. 42–7.

highlighting the 'inessential' musical components introduces an element of the banal.[29] The bars that follow Example 2.9 are literally filled up by the repetitive accompaniment pattern in order to expand the four-bar 'dotted circus' theme into a neat (and in itself pronouncedly banal) eight-bar phrase.

The exaggeration of the obvious and inessential is a satirical device that invests the sense of merriment with a mocking undertone. However, the same strategy may also serve the purpose of the grotesque, which prevails once such hyperbolic distortion evokes a sense of obsession, insanity, and frenzy that overrides the initial sense of humorousness, gaiety, and merriment.[30] This is the case in the violent motoric climax that immediately follows the 'circus' section, where the 'horse-trot' theme is stated in double diminution (demi-semiquavers), played by all four instruments in unison (see Example 2.10). This 'liquidation'

Example 2.10 'Liquidation' of the theme and motoric collapse. Haas, String Quartet No. 2,
second movement, bb. 51–8.

of the theme leads to a collapse and all movement comes to a stop within a few
bars of *Tempo I*, before the whole process of gradual accumulation of momentum starts again from the opening glissandi, with minor variations to texture
and figuration.

This is likely to be the very passage that reminded the critics of Honegger's
Pacific 231. Indeed, it is arguable that Haas picked up and trivialised the idea of
acceleration and deceleration of the supposed locomotive (reduced here to a 'rural
vehicle') and thus added a parodic dimension to his piece.

What the two pieces also have in common is the technique of gradual diminution of rhythmic values, the application of which is also self-consciously trivial
(certainly in comparison with *Pacific 231*). In this case, this becomes the principal
means of grotesque distortion: the musical material associated with bodily movement is rendered 'too fast' and often simultaneously transposed to registers that

are 'too high'. This process also implicitly suggests the 'mechanisation' of the animate: what was initially a comfortable horse's trot has been accelerated into motor-like motion. The theme's gradual rhythmic diminution is reminiscent of the shifting gears of a motor vehicle. This yields a typically grotesque image of a hybrid body conflating an animal with a machine.

Cinematic aspects of the second movement

There are several reasons to draw a parallel between the second movement of Haas's quartet and the medium of film. First, the illustrative character of the music invites visual representation. The movement's title – 'Carriage, Horseman and Horse' – immediately suggests a picture, which the music sets in motion or, one might say, 'animates'. One might even wonder whether Haas was aware of René Clair's 1924 film *Entr'acte* with music by Erik Satie, in which the image of a funeral vehicle drawn by a camel gains much prominence. Starting in slow motion, the funeral procession gradually turns into a chase after the runaway hearse, racing wildly through the streets of Paris to the accompaniment of Satie's music. This film's absurd humour and satirical undertone is highly characteristic of the subversive spirit of Dada, which was closely related to the sentiments preached by Poetism.

Second, the term 'grotesque', which was repeatedly used in reviews of the piece, has also been used as a noun in Czech to refer to cartoons and short film comedies known as 'slapsticks' in English.[31] It is thus highly probable that when the Czech critics referred to Haas's music as 'grotesque', their understanding of the term was at least partly informed by its connotation with slapstick comedies of the day. Finally, American slapsticks (especially those made by Charlie Chaplin), which gained immense popularity throughout Europe in the 1920s, were celebrated by Poetism as the ultimate form of popular entertainment, outmatching circuses, cabarets, and variety shows.[32]

There are several 'technological' parallels between the second movement of the quartet and early films and cartoons. Haas inherited from Janáček elements of his 'montage' technique (to be discussed in Chapter 4), which is essentially cinematic in its juxtaposition of stretches of music divided by 'cuts' rather than transitions. The mechanistic metaphor of shifting gears, used above to describe Haas's technique of progressive rhythmic diminution, is also applicable to the speed with which a reel of film unrolls. The technological limitations of early film projectors often rendered movement unnaturally fast and therefore jerky and mechanistic, which enhanced the comical effect of slapsticks. Besides, in the above-mentioned film by Clair, slow, fast-forward, and reverse motion was purposely used (besides other visual effects) to convey the sense of the ever faster and 'wilder' ride of the runaway hearse. The repetitive nature of much of Haas's music is suggestive of the 'loop' technique widely used in early 1920s cartoons. The movement's trivial narrative is repeated several times with minor variations before the cart joyfully drives off (a moment inviting the obligatory fadeout). The whole movement is roughly five minutes in duration, which just about matches the length of contemporary 'shorties'.

There are also similarities between the types of distortion described above and the repertoire of visual gags used in 1920s cartoons, such as those made by Walt Disney, in which grotesque imagery is virtually omnipresent. Much of the comical effect of Disney's cartoons was based on the images of distorted, dismembered, and hybrid bodies mingling animate and inanimate elements. Unlike the bodies of live actors in film comedies, those of cartoon characters have no limits. They can take on hybrid forms, they can move in awkward ways that defy the laws of physics, they can be distorted or even dismembered and still, unlike static pictures to which earlier manifestations of the grotesque were confined, keep moving.[33] This is not to suggest that Haas was directly influenced by a particular Disney cartoon, but his musical illustration relies for its effects, as Disney cartoons do, on the distorted image of the body in motion. It is also worth mentioning that forms of popular entertainment such as sports events, circuses, and fairs are commonplace in Disney cartoons, and also influenced the choice of soundtracks. Thus, many of his cartoons were accompanied by circus-like music similar to that invoked by Haas in the 'dotted circus' section.[34]

The most profound affinity, however, resides in the emphasis on humour. Poetism celebrated slapstick as the art of laughter, which is universal, non-elitist, unhindered by conceptual intricacies and language barriers. 'Carriage, Horseman and Horse' was likely conceived as a musical analogue of slapsticks, a humorous mischief to be enjoyed and laughed at, one which is self-consciously simple in order to be as comprehensible as the visual gags of slapsticks. As such, it could even be regarded as a satirical commentary on the metaphysical baggage of Romantic 'programmatic' compositions, as an avant-garde statement of rejection of the preceding artistic tradition.

The grotesque, carnival, and Poetism: a Bakhtinian perspective

So far, the grotesque has been treated merely as an artistic device. However, the meaning conveyed by the device depends on its particular aesthetic and cultural context. For example, Brown's interpretation of the grotesque in Bartók's music is underpinned by the framework of Expressionism. Haas's use of the device, informed by the programme of Poetism, necessarily produces different meanings.

For the purpose of her study, Brown regards 'the grotesque body with its emphasis on distortion and abnormality, and conflations of the comic and the terrifying' as 'a perfect figurative manifestation' of 'early twentieth-century crises of subjectivity'.[35] Interestingly, the modern urban industrial world, which had been regarded as the source of alienation, fear, and anxiety by the Expressionists, was considered enchanting rather than threatening from the perspective of Poetism. As a world-view, Teige argued, Poetism was 'nothing but [. . .] excitement before the spectacle of the modern world. Nothing but loving inclination to life and all its manifestations, the passion of modernity [. . .]. Nothing but joy, enchantment and an amplified optimistic trust in the beauty of life.'[36]

Bakhtin offered an alternative notion of the grotesque that is much more compatible with the agenda of Poetism. He showed that the 'dark' side of the grotesque, while always lurking in the background, need not always dominate, and that the irrationality and hybridism need not always be threatening. As David K. Danow has explained, Bakhtin differentiated between two concepts of the grotesque according to the presence or absence of the moment of renewal or rebirth: whereas the 'medieval and Renaissance' grotesque was endowed with regenerative power stemming from the principle of laughter, the 'Romantic' grotesque lost the power of regeneration and became the expression of insecurity and fear of the world.[37] The latter type of the grotesque is static (the state of aberration, defect, and death is final and therefore threatening), whereas the former is essentially dynamic: 'The grotesque image reflects a phenomenon in transformation, an as yet unfinished metamorphosis, of death and birth, growing and becoming.'[38] As Sheinberg explains, this conception of the grotesque is based on the principle of acceptance of all ambiguities and contradictions; the resulting 'excess of meanings' is not perceived as destructive and nihilistic, but rather 'as a victorious assertion of all life's infinite "buds and sprouts"'.[39]

Bakhtin's emphasis on rebirth rather than death is matched by a focus on the (immortal) humankind rather than on the (mortal) human; as Danow points out, the transcendent laughter belongs to collectives, not to individuals.[40] Bakhtin's views on the grotesque are intrinsically linked with his interpretation of the social and cultural significance of carnival (hence his term 'carnivalesque-grotesque').[41] As Renate Lachmann explains, Bakhtin regarded carnival in his study of Rabelais in terms of the juxtaposition of 'culture and counter-culture', that is, the strictly hierarchical model of medieval society with the 'folk culture of laughter'.[42] Typically, carnival stages the world turned 'upside down', relativising and ridiculing the norms and values of the dominant culture. Importantly, the effect of this travesty is not destructive, but regenerative:

> The temporary immersion of official culture in folk culture leads to a process of regeneration that sets in motion and dynamically energizes the notions of value and hierarchy inverted by the parodistic counter-norms of the carnival. In this way the culture of laughter revives and regenerates the petrified remains of official institutions and, as it were, hands them back to official culture.[43]

Carnival thus facilitates a mythological death and rebirth through the principle of laughter, its recourse being to all that is material, corporeal, sensual or sexual, and to the 'unofficial, uncanonized relations among human beings'.[44] Bakhtin, in his study of folk culture in the work of Rabelais, construed carnival as a force which makes it possible 'to consecrate inventive freedom, [. . .] to liberate from the prevailing point of view of the world' and which 'offers the chance to have a new outlook of the world, to realize the relative nature of all that exists, and to enter a completely new order of things'.[45]

The dialectical pair of culture and counter-culture matches Teige's conceptual duality between 'Poetism', representing imagination, creativity, and playfulness, and 'Constructivism', representing logic, rationality, and discipline.[46] The industrialised modern society based on inexorable logic, rationality, and functionality represents the dominant culture which 'has succumbed to cosmic terror', since its structure and approach to work and production is goal-orientated, 'finalistic', and 'directed toward the "end"'.[47] Poetism, on the other hand, can be construed as the revitalising counter-culture of laughter. Teige's characterisation of Poetism takes on a distinctly Bakhtinian tone as he describes it as 'the culture of miraculous astonishment': 'Poetism wants to turn life into a spectacular entertaining affair, an eccentric carnival, a harlequinade of sensations and fantasies, a delirious film sequence, a miraculous kaleidoscope.'[48] Teige further claims that Poetism 'was born in the climate of cheerful conviviality, in a world which laughs; what does it matter if there are tears in its eyes?'[49] This quotation implies that Poetism as a life perspective is not turning a blind eye to the difficulties of life. Nonetheless, to put it in a Bakhtinian manner, the irreconcilable contradictions of modern existence are to be accepted through the principle of laughter.

The art of Poetism invited its recipients to participate in a carnivalesque feast, to overcome the 'cosmic terror', the frustration and alienation elicited in human subjects by the 'finalistic' modern society, to embrace Poetism as a modus vivendi and to be reborn in the state of poiesis.[50]

Haas and the 'Eccentric Carnival of Artists' in Brno

As noted in Chapter 1, the avant-garde group Devětsil expanded from Prague to Brno in 1923, where it pursued a varied range of activities, including the organisation of social events. Figure 2.1 shows the advertisement for one of the 'Eccentric Eight O'Clocks of Artists' organised as a run-up to the 'Eccentric Carnival of Artists'. Both of these events took place in 1925, just months before Haas started the composition of his quartet.

It is noteworthy that the advertisement promises an 'original American jazz band'. In fact, this is not the only time a jazz band is mentioned in connection with the 'eccentric' events of Devětsil. An article reflecting upon the Eccentric Carnival of Artists, published in the journal *Salon* (the article's first page is shown in Figure 2.2), reports that invitations to the event included the following lines from Nezval's poem *Podivuhodný kouzelník* (*Miraculous Magician*):

A básníci už neprosí	And poets no longer beg
za chudou prebendu,	for a modest stipend,
ti baví se jak černoši	they have a good time like black men do
při řvoucím JAZZ-BANDU.	with a roaring JAZZ BAND.[51]

Figure 2.1 Advertisement for the '2nd Eccentric Eight O'Clock of Artists'

Source: Pásmo, 1/7–8 (1924–5), p. 9.

It is doubtful that either of these events would host an 'original American jazz band'. An intriguing terminological issue was revealed by the Czech popular music scholar Josef Kotek, who observed that in the early 1920s, 'jazz'

> was not used as a general term denoting the new dance music, but at first just as a name for the massive, hitherto unseen percussion set. [. . .] One can easily imagine the sensation which this rackety instrument [the drum kit] elicited in the limited sonic spectrum of the day. [. . .] In the first years [of the 1920s] the typological and stylistic characterisation of new music seems to have been limited to the percussion set.[52]

Indeed, Haas himself referred to the percussion set as 'jazz' in his commentary. His decision to use 'jazz' in his string quartet gains special significance, considering the emphasis laid on this iconic feature of modern popular music in the advertisements for Devětsil's 'eccentric' events.

I. excentrický karneval umělců v Brně.

Letošní zimní období v Brně se vyznačovalo neobyčejným ruchem uměleckého života, jehož jsme dříve nepozorovali. Byla nám vždy nápadná disonance mezi uměleckým životem velikých měst Západu (Paříž, Nizza) Severu (Berlín, Stockholm) a uměleckým životem tohoto miniaturního velkoměsta — Brna. Veselí, humor, excentričnost, projevy moderních tendencí uměleckých, jež v městech s tradicí časem dosahují až varietní závratnosti a teatrální monumentálnosti, blikaly tu dosud nepatrnými světélky, o nichž se veřejnost nedověděla. Letos náhle uprostřed cyklu přednášek o moderní architektuře, jež s přednáškami Brněnského Devětsilu jsou osvěžujícím proudem ve vleklém a jaksi zdánlivě znaveném kulturním vlnobití moravské metropole, octly se v rukou zájemců prvé pozvánky na 3 excentrické eight o'clocky umělců a jejich I. excentrický karneval. Hýřily-li tyto pozvánky vtipem v úpravě, našli jsme týž vtip v jejich textu, jenž oznamoval česko-francouzsko-německy program buď takto: fox-blues, de bons vins, poèmes d'amour et d'esprit, humor, družnost — nebo touto devisou Nezvalovy Pantominy:

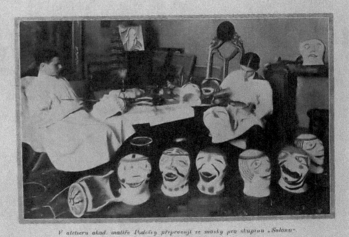

V atelieru akad. malíře Pelčáka připravují se masky pro skupinu „Salonu".
Foto Láhki Brno

Figure 2.2 '1st Eccentric Carnival of Artists in Brno'. The upper photograph shows members of Devětsil, supposedly dressed up as robots; the lower photo shows the manufacturing of masks. Reportedly, the event involved 'shooting in the manner of the people of the Wild West', 'dancing modern dances', and 'reciting of Dadaist poems'.

Source: Salon, 3/10 (1925), no page numbers.

The Eccentric Carnival of Artists was introduced by a speech, delivered by the Brno-based poet Dalibor Chalupa (1900–83),[53] who later published a poem entitled *Karneval* (*Carnival*), undoubtedly inspired by the event.[54] Significantly, this poem was set to music by Haas as the male chorus *Karneval* (*Carnival*), Op. 9 (1928–29):[55]

Karneval	*Carnival*
(Sbor huláká, jazzband lomozí)	(The choir bellows, the jazz band makes a racket)
Masky	Masks
vypouklá zrcadla	Bulging mirrors
světelné signály na moři	Light signals on the sea
Smutní umírají	Sad people die
lilie povadla	The lily has wilted
maskovaní lupiči v ulicích táboří	Masked bandits camp in the streets
lampiony zrají.	Chinese lanterns ripen.
(Sbor huláká, jazzband lomozí.)	(The choir bellows, the jazz band makes a racket.)
Čtyři levé nohy	Four left legs
spirála červenozelená	A red-green spiral
a klauni ztratili klíče	And clowns lost their keys
v ulici beze jména	In a nameless street
S bohem, Beatrice.	Goodbye, Beatrice.
(Bubny, činely, výstřel.)	(Drums, cymbals, gunshot.)
Harfou proskočil Indián	An Indian jumped through the harp
Zvony zvou vyzvánějí zvonivě	Bells bellow blasting blows
modrých zvuků lán	A field of bluebells
a vítr zvedl vlasy Godivě	And the wind blew up the hair of Godiva
činely letí k zenitu	Cymbals fly up to the zenith
ztratil se prsten	A ring got lost
není tu – není tu.	It's not here – it's not here.
(Housle.)	(Violin.)
Polibky s pomoranči	Kisses with oranges
dekolté	décolleté
malé Javanky tančí	little Javanese girls dance
v náruči Kristinu najdete	Kristina is to be found in [someone's] arms
Ó ohně ó planety	Oh fires oh planets
den začíná	The day begins
Růžová ňadra	Pink breasts
brokáty	Brocades
žije Mona Lisa	Mona Lisa lives
žije Kristina.	Kristina lives.
(Passo double.)	(Paso doble.)
Motýli	Butterflies
bělostné kotníky	White ankles
Opiovým snem pluje gondola	A gondola sails through an opium dream

Země odletěla	The Earth has flown away
a vesmírem tančí	And dances through the space
dans excentric	Danse excentrique
na jazzband hraje kolibřík.	A hummingbird plays the jazz band.
[po prstech šlape kostlivý tanečník.]	[A skeletal dancer treads on tiptoes.]
[. . .]	[. . .]
(Sbor huláká, jazzband lomozí.)	(The choir bellows, the jazz band makes a racket.)
Duhové blesky tančí	Rainbow-coloured thunderbolts dance
kolotoč na parníku	A carousel on a steamboat
Hle, radostí pláčí	Look, crying of joy are
vrcholky obelisků	The tops of obelisks
Zeppelin letí k pestré obloze	A Zeppelin flies to the multi-coloured sky
prérie v plamenech	A prairie on fire
Překrásná explose	A beautiful explosion
Jeden vzdech.	One sigh.
(Výstřel.)	(Gunshot.)[56]

Chalupa's poem contains a number of the topoi of Poetism. First of all, there is carnival itself, complete with imagery of 'gondolas', 'Chinese lanterns', 'masks', and 'clowns'. Typical also is the mild eroticism, which manifests itself in fleeting references to various female figures ('Beatrice', 'Godiva', 'Kristina', 'Mona Lisa'), all of which seem to coalesce into a single archetype of feminine beauty. Besides the obligatory element of exoticism ('an Indian', 'little Javanese girls'), there are also references to iconic features of modern civilisation ('jazz band', 'steamboat', 'Zeppelin').

Perhaps more important than this catalogue of topoi is the dream-like juxtaposition of individual elements. The imaginative use of word-play and the free association of images are reminiscent of Apollinaire's poetry, which was highly influential among the Poetists. Thus, the 'fires' of Chinese lanterns associate 'planets' and the 'pink breasts' of Mona Lisa/Kristina; the 'multi-coloured sky', illuminated by the 'rainbow-coloured thunderbolts' (perhaps of fireworks), is likened to a 'prairie on fire' and a 'beautiful explosion' of the Zeppelin; the ringing of bells conjures up the sight of a field of bluebells; a harp becomes a circus hoop through which an 'Indian' jumps; cymbals are suddenly animated and 'fly up to the zenith'; the hummingbird becomes a jazz band player, etc. This nonsensical, fantastic sequence of images, resembling a Dadaist or Surrealist film scenario, conveys the sense of bewilderment associated with carnival.

True to the dictum of 'poetry for the senses', Chalupa's poem attempts to convey not only visual but also aural sensations – particularly through bracketed illustrative remarks placed between the strophes, such as 'the choir bellows, the jazz band makes a racket' and 'drums, cymbals, gunshot'. In his musical setting, Haas drew on these indications. However, unlike in the string quartet, where he employed an actual jazz band percussion set, in *Karneval* the composer relied purely on the means offered by the chosen medium – the male-voice choir. Thus he used onomatopoeic words ('bum – džin'; 'boom – jin') in conjunction with repetitive march-like accompaniment patterns to imitate the sound of drums and cymbals; similarly, the lyrics 'ra-tada-da-ta' mimic a snare drum.[57] Since the piece is mostly in 2/4, marked 'tempo di marcia', these effects are suggestive of a military band rather than a jazz band. The concluding 'gunshot' effect is achieved by tutti declamation of the syllable 'pa'.

The poem places much emphasis on dance and erratic or spinning movement in general, thus conveying the sense of disorientation and vertigo (the physiological correlative of bewilderment). Of particular interest are the lines 'A gondola sails through an opium dream/The Earth has flown away/And dances through space/ Danse excentrique'. Significantly, Haas replaced the following line ('A humming-bird plays the jazz band') with a new line of his own: 'A skeletal dancer treads on tiptoes.'[58] By associating 'danse excentrique' with 'danse macabre', Haas underscored the 'cosmic' significance of this carnivalesque whirl, emphasising the confrontation and intermingling of life and death.

'Danse excentrique' (with or without the element of 'danse macabre') is an important topic that appears throughout Haas's oeuvre from the mid-1920s to the early 1940s. The earliest example is what Peduzzi called the 'rumba' theme from the last movement of the quartet 'From the Monkey Mountains', 'The Wild Night' (see Example 2.11).[59] This theme betrays some significant similarities (namely the 'angular' melody with pentatonic basis, and the 'hopping' gesture of staccato quavers) to the central theme of the male chorus *Karneval* (see Example 2.12). Here, the lyrics 'four left legs, a red-green spiral' suggest a kind of 'eccentric dance' (the 'red-green spiral' may be associated with the colourful outfits of the clowns mentioned in the next line of the poem). This theme, in turn, later became the basis of the third movement of Haas's Wind Quintet, Op. 10 (1929), significantly entitled 'Ballo eccentrico' (see Example 2.13).

Manifestations of this topic can also be found in Haas's later works. However, a detailed discussion of these works would require adjustments to the interpretative framework used in this chapter, which is designed to fit specifically the context

Example 2.11 'Rumba' theme (viola), Haas, String Quartet No. 2, fourth movement, bb. 19–22.

Čty - ři le - vé no - hy,   spi - rá - la   čer-ve-no ze - le - ná__

Example 2.12 Pavel Haas, male chorus *Karneval* [Carnival], Op. 9, bb. 19–21. Two manuscript scores deposited in the Moravian Museum, Brno, Department of
Music History, sign. A 22.730b, A 54.252.

Source: © Copyright Boosey & Hawkes Bote & Bock GmbH, Berlin. Reproduced by permission of
Boosey & Hawkes Music Publishers Ltd.

Example 2.13 Pavel Haas, Wind Quintet, Op. 10, 1929 (Tempo Praha; Bote & Bock/
Boosey & Hawkes, 2nd rev. edn, 1998), third movement, bb. 7–10, flute,
clarinet and bassoon.

Source: © Copyright Boosey & Hawkes Bote & Bock GmbH, Berlin. Reproduced by permission of
Boosey & Hawkes Music Publishers Ltd.

of 1920s, underpinned by Poetism. Although the third movement – 'Danza' – of
Haas's 1935 Suite for Piano can still be understood more or less in terms of the
life-affirming (Bakhtinian) carnivalesque imagery of Poetism, the second movement of his wartime Symphony (1940–41), which revisits the topic of the 'danse
macabre', inescapably veers closer to the life-threatening pole of the grotesque.

'The Wild Night'

In this historical and intertextual context, it becomes apparent that the last movement of Haas's quartet – 'The Wild Night' – features the topic of carnival. The movement's title and Haas's reference to 'the exuberance of a sleepless night of revelry' in his commentary are both consistent with this theme. However, one wonders whether the 'revelry' should be imagined as taking place in a village barn (as Haas's commentary implies) or in a city bar (as the contextual evidence suggests). The composer alludes to a variety of incongruous musical idioms linked solely by the topic of dance. There is no trace of 'jazz' in the movement's opening. Rather, 'The Wild Night' begins with a distinctly Janáčekian introduction (see Example 2.14).

Rapid trills, agitated *sul ponticello* bowing, surges of short motives, all these are devices typically used by Janáček to evoke dramatic tension. Comparison with the following passage from the second movement of Janáček's 1923 String Quartet No. 1 is illustrative (see Example 2.15). The introduction culminates in a Janáčekian folk dance of frantic, violent character, articulated by heavy

Example 2.14 Janáčekian introduction. Haas, String Quartet No. 2, fourth movement, bb. 1–5.

accentuation, played *sul ponticello* and featuring double stops, restless trills and 'savage' augmented seconds (see Example 2.16).

This Janáčekian introduction, however, suddenly gives way to the 'rumba' theme, characterised by a 3 + 3 + 2 rhythmic pattern (see Example 2.11). This theme displays properties suggestive of grotesque distortion. It is marked by an ambiguity between major and minor mode resulting, as in the previous movements, from the 'blues-scale' inflection of particular scale degrees. Although the major third (G–B)

Example 2.15 Comparison with Janáček. Leoš Janáček, String Quartet No. 1 'Inspired by Leo Tolstoy's "Kreutzer Sonata"', 1923 (Bärenreiter Praha, 2007; ed. Leoš Faltus and Miloš Štědroň), second movement, bb. 132–9.

Source: Reprinted with permission from Bärenreiter Praha (TP 520).

Example 2.16 Folk dance allusion. Haas, String Quartet No. 2, fourth movement, bb. 10–2.

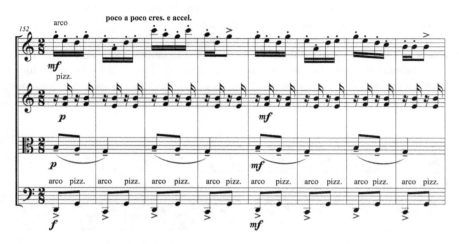

Example 2.17 The satirical polka. Haas, String Quartet No. 2, fourth movement, bb. 152–9.

dominates at first, the theme concludes with three violent G minor blows. In its subsequent reiterations, the theme is frequently distorted by ending on a 'wrong' note, particularly one a semitone away from the expected 'tonic'. The awkwardness of motion, characteristic of the grotesque, is conveyed by the 'angular' melodic design of the theme, which is marked by wide leaps, and by the irregular 3 + 3 + 2 rhythmic pattern encapsulating the incongruity between duple and triple metre.

The third distinct dance topic, polka, appears in what might be called the 'trio' section (see Example 2.17). By Haas's time, the polka was a rather old-fashioned social dance, which nonetheless was still very popular in the realm of semi-folk dance music associated with brass bands.[60] Haas's allusion to the dance is made to sound banal by the excess of 'redundant' musical material such as repetitions, fillings, and stock accompaniment patterns (the alternation of arco and pizzicato in the cello is analogous to the onomatopoeic use of 'bum – džin' in *Karneval*). In this respect, it is similar to the 'circus' section of the second movement.

Furthermore, Haas may be alluding to a particular scene from Bedřich Smetana's famous opera *The Bartered Bride* (which retained canonical status in Czech music throughout the inter-war period). Following the so-called 'March of Comedians', which marks the arrival of a circus troupe in the village, a preview performance takes place, accompanied by 'Skočná' (see Example 2.18).[61] The three-note accompaniment pattern in the viola part in Haas's quartet (Example 2.17), which is highlighted by obstinate repetition, can be seen as a trivial paraphrase of the similarly repetitive motive in the middle section of Smetana's 'Skočná' (see Example 2.18b).

Haas's treatment of the 'rumba' theme is highly characteristic. As in the second movement, the theme keeps returning in ever shorter rhythmic values. Particularly interesting is the moment when the theme is projected simultaneously in three superimposed rhythmic strata: quavers in the second violin, semiquavers in the cello, and demi-semiquavers in the first violin (see Example 2.19).

Example 2.18 Bedřich Smetana, *Prodaná nevěsta* (*The Bartered Bride*) (Prague: Editio
        Supraphon, 1982, piano reduction), 'Skočná': (a) 138–43 (opening) and (b)
        223–30 (middle section).

Source: Reprinted with permission from Bärenreiter Praha (BA 9534–90).

Through its repetitiveness, this section suggests mechanical revolving, which,
in turn, evokes a spinning carousel or barrel organ, both of which are typical attributes of the fairground. The multi-layered presentation of the theme resembles an
image of wheels within wheels or a view through a kaleidoscope. The semblance

of multiple vision suggests disorientation and vertigo, typically induced by an excessive spinning motion (such as dancing or riding on a carousel).

The last stage of the 'development' of the 'rumba' theme is its liquidation. Example 2.17 shows the theme subjugated into the metrical context of a polka,

Example 2.19 'Rumba' theme in superimposed in different rhythmic layers. Haas, String Quartet No. 2, fourth movement, bb. 71–4.

devoid of its original $3 + 3 + 2$ accentuation. Shortly afterwards, the theme reappears in demi-semiquavers, the rapid succession of which is reminiscent of the opening of Smetana's above-mentioned 'Skočná' (see Example 2.18a). The process of the theme's liquidation is finalised by its reduction to the germinal rhythmic motive, which is repeated obsessively (see Example 2.20). Thus, after the theme's metric identity has been washed off, the melodic element is likewise

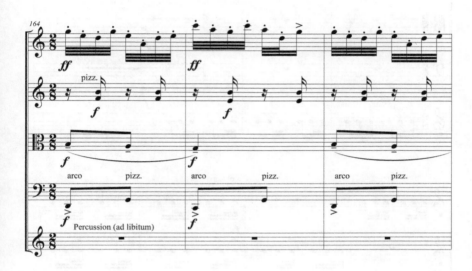

Example 2.20 'Liquidation' of the 'rumba' theme. Haas, String Quartet No. 2, fourth movement, bb. 164–78.

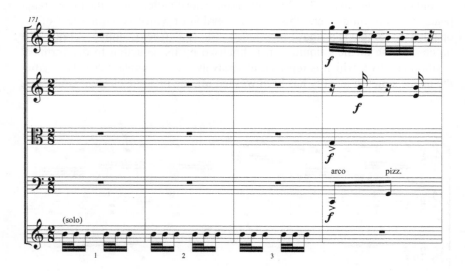

Example 2.20 (Continued)

eradicated. Even the element of pitch is partly suppressed: the instruments are instructed to play *col legno*, alternating with the percussion.

The following 'furioso' brings back the 'polka' recast into 3/8 metre, which underscores the effect of a dizzying whirl. The motive is progressively shortened until it is ultimately 'liquidated' like the rumba theme, whereupon all movement comes to a stop. Having pushed the delirious frenzy to the point of collapse, Haas inserts a four-part arrangement of his own song dedicated to a beloved girl.[62] There could hardly be a greater contrast in terms of the 'andante' tempo marking, the soft colour of the strings playing *con sordino*, the homophonic texture and the tonal clarity (see Example 2.21). However, at the end of the song's second iteration, the ethereal vision dissolves with the onset of the concluding 'furioso' section, which brings the previously interrupted dynamic escalation to a climax. Once again, all the motivic content is gradually eliminated until there is nothing left but the demi-semiquaver rhythmic pulse.

The carnivalesque mood of 'The Wild Night' results largely from the use of highly fragmentary and repetitive material, often superimposed in stratified textures. Not only does the repetition and accumulation of material, which becomes redundant and banal, connote simple-mindedness,[63] it tends to become ever more obsessive and violent. The exaggeration of stereotypical dance-like accompaniment figures and repetitive rhythmic patterns functions as a means of hyperbolic distortion of the topic of dance and bodily movement in general, conveying the sense of a delirious rapture. This accumulation of momentum is conjoined with

Example 2.21 Quotation of Haas's early song. Haas, String Quartet No. 2, fourth movement, bb. 205–12.

distortion and degeneration of the musical 'bodies': note the 'development' of the rumba theme, which is first stripped of its essential traits and ultimately destroyed. The initial merriment draws ever closer to frenzy and the whirl of dance is exaggerated to the point of collapse, eliciting a hallucination.

Conclusion: the play of polarities and incongruities

The positioning of the contrasting section in the last movement refers to the 'escalation–repose–finale' pattern of the first movement, which, moreover, applies to the quartet as a whole. The third movement ('The Moon and I'), which includes a quotation of the 'slow' section of 'Landscape', thus appears as a larger-scale 'repose' section inserted between two emphatically dynamic movements. The essence of the schema observed here is the juxtaposition of polar opposites. The 'fast–slow–fast' model is but one manifestation of this generic principle; other binaries include light and darkness, joy and sadness, sincerity and irony, seriousness and farce, and so on.

The work as a whole is deliberately heterogeneous in character. The first movement, despite its 'programmatic' inspiration, is rather 'serious' and 'abstract' in its focus on the development of the form-constitutive dynamic trajectory. The second movement, on the other hand, uses similar techniques based on rhythmic diminution to create a farcical musical caricature. The juxtaposition of the two encapsulates Teige's duality of Constructivism and Poetism. Similarly, the contrast between 'The Moon and I' and its surrounding movements brings into focus a number of characteristically modernist incongruities. This can be explained by analogy with the contrasting episode within 'The Wild Night'.

The dominant carnivalesque character of 'The Wild Night' is contrasted (yet, in a way, enhanced) by the insertion of Haas's amorous song. This section, metaphorically speaking, throws a spotlight on an individual, singling him out from the crowd, suspending the surrounding rave, and revealing his inner subjective experience. This is a moment of authenticity and sincerity; it is devoid of all the irony, masquerade, and role-playing inherent in carnival. The section thus offers a statement about the challenge posed by modern cultural reality to the human subject and the viability of subjective expression (here confined to the realm of 'hallucination' functioning as quotation marks). However, the resulting effect is not one of Expressionist despair; the carnivalesque celebration of modernity is subtly qualified but not subverted. After all, to paraphrase Teige, Haas's piece was 'born [. . .] in a world which laughs; what does it matter if there are tears in its eyes?'

Juxtaposition of incongruities (binary or not) is a salient feature of carnivalesque imagery. It is therefore significant that, in 'The Wild Night', Haas juxtaposes musical idioms that are incongruous in terms of style and that are associated with different socio-cultural contexts. Thus, the rumba theme with its 'oriental' pentatonicism, 'South American' rhythmic pattern, and 'African-American' blues-scale inflection, appears next to the 'East European' folk modality of the Janáčekian introduction. Janáček's folk primitives, Smetana's rather old-fashioned comedians, and modern cosmopolitan 'jazz band' lovers all take part in the dizzying whirlpool of dance. 'The Wild Night' thus appears as a carnivalesque allegory of the perplexing heterogeneity of the modern world, disorienting and potentially threatening, replete with contradictions that cannot be reconciled but that can be rendered harmless through the principle of laughter.

As 'The Wild Night' constitutes the climax of the piece, carnival assumes prominence as a point of view, from which all the characteristic and culturally connoted features, contrasts and contradictions of the work are regarded. Thus, carnival functions in Haas's work not only as a prominent topos of Poetism but also as a world-view, a pertinent metaphorical characterisation of the particular culture from which Haas's quartet emerged and of which it remains a testimony.

Notes

1 See Martin Čurda, 'Smyčcové kvartety Janáčkových žáků z 20. let' [String Quartets of Janáček's Students from the 1920s] (unpublished master's thesis, Masaryk University, 2011), English summary on pp. 165–6 [accessed via http://is.muni.cz/th/264072/ff_m/Smyccove_kvartety_Janackovych_zaku.pdf; 16 November 2015].

2 Lubomír Peduzzi, *Pavel Haas: Život a dílo skladatele* (Brno: Muzejní a vlastivědná společnost, 1993). The work in question is discussed on pp. 42–9. All translations from Czech sources are my own, unless stated otherwise.

3 This chapter is based on my previous article published as follows: Martin Čurda, *'From the Monkey Mountains*: The Body, the Grotesque and Carnival in the Music of Pavel Haas', *Journal of the Royal Musical Association*, 141/1 (2016), 61–112. Copyright ©The Royal Musical Association, reprinted by permission of Taylor & Francis Ltd, www.tandfonline.com on behalf of The Royal Musical Association.

4 The première took place in Brno on 16 March 1926 under the auspices of the Club of Moravian Composers (Klub moravských skladatelů). In my discussion of the work's reception, I cite the original newspaper articles, unless stated otherwise. Where originals could not be accessed, reviews are cited according to Haas's album of newspaper clippings entitled 'Moje úspěchy a ne-úspěchy' ('My Successes and Non-successes'), which survives as the property of Olga Haasová-Smrčková. Since the reviews are mostly signed by initials or cyphers such as '–l–' or 'St–', the names of the authors cannot always be established.

5 Jiří Svoboda and Karel Teige, 'Musica a muzika', originally published in *Život*, 2 (1922), 86–9, reprinted in *Avantgarda známá a neznámá* [The Known and Unknown Avant-Garde], ed. Štěpán Vlašín, 3 vols. (Prague: Svoboda, 1970–72), i: *Od proletářského umění k poetismu: 1919–1924* [From Proletarian Art to Poetism: 1919–1924] (1971), 405–12. Page references here and below are to the 1971 reprint.

6 Ibid., p. 408: 'Why should music resist new, academically unsanctioned instruments – jazz-band, accordion, the barbarian barrel organ, etc. – when architecture happily makes use of the advantages of modern materials?'

7 The review in *Moravské noviny* blames the composer for seeking to be 'fashionable at all costs'. See lk., 'Nová kvarteta', *Moravské noviny*, 19 March 1926.

8 Svoboda and Teige, 'Musica a muzika', p. 411.

9 See –l–, 'Kulturní obzor: V koncertu Klubu moravských skladatelů', *Stráž socialismu*, 18 March 1926; –k–, 'Z brněnských koncertů: Večer kvartetních novinek', *Lidové noviny*, 18 March 1926; [unknown], 'Koncerty v Brně', *Tribuna*, 19 March 1926 (cited from Haas's album); L.K. [Ludvík Kundera], 'Koncert Klubu moravských skladatelů', *Národní osvobození*, 19 March 1926.

10 See Barbara L. Kelly, *Music and Ultra-Modernism in France: A Fragile Consensus, 1913–1939* (Woodbridge, Suffolk: The Boydell Press, 2013), p. 5.

11 See St–, 'Klub moravských skladatelů', *Rovnost*, 18 March 1926; lk., 'Nová kvarteta', *Moravské noviny*, 19 March 1926; L. K., 'Koncert Klubu moravských skladatelů', *Národní osvobození*, 19 March 1926; V. H. [Vladimír Helfert], 'Koncerty v Brně: Klub mor. skladatelů', *Ruch*, 20 March 1926.

12 Pavel Haas, 'Haasův kvartet "Z opičích hor": Poprvé proveden v Brně 16. března 1926' [Haas's Quartet "From the Monkey Mountains": Premièred in Brno on 16 March 1926], *Hudební rozhledy*, 7 (1925–6), 106.

13 See Esther Levinger, 'Czech Avant-Garde Art: Poetry for the Five Senses', *The Art Bulletin*, 81/3 (1999), 513–32 (p. 523).

14 *Stráž socialismu*, 18 March 1926.

15 The reviewer in *Stráž socialismu* who questioned the 'rural' inspiration of the work also pointed out that the term 'Monkey Mountains' (as a name for the particular locality) was 'derisory rather than [just] vernacular' and thus 'rather dangerous for Haas's work'.

16 Haas, 'Haasův kvartet "Z opičích hor"'.

17 Ibid.

18 Peduzzi, *Pavel Haas*, p. 42.

19 Haas, 'Haasův kvartet "Z opičích hor"'. Emphasis in the original.

20 *Tribuna*, 19 March 1926.

21 The date of the performance of *Pacific 231* in Brno (5 October 1924) is mentioned in Peduzzi, *Pavel Haas*, p. 49. The reference to Honegger's *Pacific 231* is made in the following reviews: V. H. [Vladimír Helfert], 'Koncerty v Brně: Klub mor. skladatelů', *Ruch*, 20 March 1926; L. K. [Ludvík Kundera], 'Koncert Klubu moravských skladatelů', *Národní osvobození*, 19 March 1926.

22 Esti Sheinberg, *Irony, Satire, Parody, and the Grotesque in the Music of Shostakovich: A Theory of Musical Incongruities* (Aldershot: Ashgate, 2000); Julie Brown, *Bartók and the Grotesque: Studies in Modernity, the Body and Contradiction in Music* (Aldershot: Ashgate, 2007).

23 See Brown, *Bartók and the Grotesque*, p. 54. See also Sheinberg, *Irony, Satire, Parody, and the Grotesque*, pp. 221–5.

24 See Sheinberg, *Irony, Satire, Parody and the Grotesque*, p. 211.

25 Ibid., p. 221.

26 Ibid., pp. 302 and 305–6.

27 Haas's autograph is deposited in the Moravian Museum, Department of Music History, sign. A 29.801a, p. 15.

28 In Sheinberg's theory, the principal strategies of satirical distortion of an object include such 'insertion of a new component' which serves to 'satirize an implicit quality of the object by enhancing it, thus making it explicit'. See Sheinberg, *Irony, Satire, Parody, and the Grotesque*, p. 98.

29 Among other strategies of satirical distortion, Sheinberg mentions the 'removal of the essential' and the 'manifest presence of the inessential'. The latter typically involves 'the emphatic use of musical banalities, musical clichés and/or musical background material'. See ibid., pp. 88–9.

30 See ibid., 221.

31 This use of the word 'grotesque' was probably inspired by the German terms 'Film-Grotesken' or 'Grotesk-Filme'. See Peter Jelavich, review of Thomas J. Saunders, *Hollywood in Berlin: American Cinema and Weimar Germany* (Berkeley: University of California Press, 1994), in *Central European History*, 28 (1995), 105–7.

32 See Karel Schulz, 'Groteska', *Český filmový svět*, 4/2 (March 1926), repr. in *Avantgarda známá a neznámá*, ed. Vlašín, ii: *Vrchol a krize Poetismu* [The Peak and the Crisis of Poetism] (1972), 278–80 (pp. 279–80).

33 Such images could be appalling had the overall purport not been predominantly humorous. Nonetheless, in certain instances the comic element does not unequivocally dominate. For instance, Disney exploited the quintessentially grotesque topic of the Dance

of Death in the 'Skeleton Dance' episode of his Silly Symphonies and in the 'Haunted House' episode of the Mickey Mouse series (both 1929).

34 For an example of a 'bouncy' horse ride and a grotesque dance (performed by a 'baddie' with a wooden leg) accompanied by a circus-like soundtrack, see the Disney cartoon 'The Cactus Kid' [accessed via https://www.youtube.com/watch?v=1UoD6bDoKY0, 28 December 2014].

35 Brown, *Bartók and the Grotesque*, p. 46.

36 Karel Teige, 'Poetismus', *Host*, 3 (July 1924), 197–204, repr. in *Avantgarda známá a neznámá*, ed. Vlašín, i, 554–61 (p. 557). Page references here and below are to the 1971 reprint.

37 David K. Danow, *The Spirit of Carnival: Magical Realism and the Grotesque* (Lexington: University Press of Kentucky, 2004), p. 36.

38 Mikhail Bakhtin, *Rabelais and His World*, trans. Helene Iswolsky (Cambridge MA: MIT Press, 1968), p. 24, quoted in Danow, *The Spirit of Carnival*, p. 35.

39 Sheinberg, *Irony, Satire, Parody, and the Grotesque*, pp. 208–9.

40 Danow, *The Spirit of Carnival*, p. 37.

41 See Danow, *The Spirit of Carnival*, p. 31: 'Bakhtin rightly combines (in recognition of their potential convergence) the two concepts in a single expression, the carnivalesque-grotesque.'

42 Renate Lachmann, 'Bakhtin and Carnival: Culture and Counter-Culture', in *Mikhail Bakhtin*, ed. Michael E. Gardiner, 4 vols. (London: Sage, 2002), ii, 60–90 (p. 75).

43 Ibid., p. 72.

44 Danow, *The Spirit of Carnival*, p. 3.

45 Bakhtin, *Rabelais and His World*, p. 34, quoted in Danow, *The Spirit of Carnival*, p. 142.

46 Teige, 'Poetismus', pp. 560–1.

47 Lachmann, 'Bakhtin and Carnival', p. 73.

48 Teige, 'Poetismus', p. 557.

49 Ibid., pp. 556–7. Translation as in Matthew S. Witkovsky, 'Staging Language: Milča Mayerová and the Czech Book "Alphabet"', *The Art Bulletin*, 86/1 (March 2004), 114–35 (p. 114). Witkovsky himself uses a modified translation from a reprint of Teige's article in *Between Worlds: A Sourcebook of Central European Avant-Gardes, 1910–1930*, ed. Timothy O. Benson and Eva Forgacs (Los Angeles: Los Angeles County Museum of Art; Cambridge MA: MIT Press, 2002), 579–82 (p. 580).

50 Teige, 'Poetismus', p. 557.

51 These lines from the poem are quoted in -ak-, 'I. Excentrický karneval umelců v Brně' ('1st Eccentric Carnival of Artists in Brno'), *Salon*, 3/10 (1925), no page numbers. *Podivuhodný kouzelník* was first published in *Revoluční sborník Devětsil* (*Devětsil Revolutionary Almanac*), ed. Jaroslav Seifert and Karel Teige (Prague: Večernice J. Vortel, 1922).

52 Josef Kotek, *Dějiny české populární hudby a zpěvu*, 2 vols. (Prague: Academia, 1994–98), ii: *1918–1968* (1998), pp. 67–8.

53 Macharáčková, 'Z dějin Brněnského Devětsilu', pp. 85–6.

54 Dalibor Chalupa, 'Karneval', *Host*, 4 (1924–5), 166–7.

55 Two manuscript scores of this piece are deposited in the Moravian Museum, Department of Music History, sign. A 22.730b and A 54.252. A printed edition was published by Boosey & Hawkes/Bote & Bock in 2006.

56 Chalupa, 'Karneval', pp. 166–7. In the interest of accuracy, I did not attempt to replicate rhyming patterns in the translation. The only exemption is the verse 'zvony zvou vyzvánějí zvonivě'/'bells bellow blasting blows', where the onomatopoeic effect (the repetition of 'zv'/'bl') is arguably more important than literal meaning.

57 Haas, 'Karneval' (sign. A 22.730b), pp. 5, 14.

58 Ibid., p. 10.

59 Peduzzi, *Pavel Haas*, p. 46.

60 The polka originated in Bohemia in the first half of the nineteenth century and enjoyed widespread popularity in the patriotic circles of the higher society of the time. In the latter part of the century, it entered the standard repertoire of brass bands and assumed the status of folk music. See Gracian Černušák, Andrew Lamb and John Tyrrell, 'Polka', *Grove Music Online*, www.oxfordmusiconline.com [accessed 2 December 2015].

61 This piece was later used in several of Disney's *Road Runner* cartoons.

62 See Peduzzi, *Pavel Haas*, p. 48.

63 See Sheinberg, *Irony, Satire, Parody, and the Grotesque*, pp. 88–9.

Bibliography

General bibliography

Anonymous author (-ak-), 'I. Excentrický karneval umelců v Brně', *Salon*, 3/10 (1925), n. p.

Bakhtin, Mikhail, *Rabelais and His World*, trans. Helene Iswolsky (Cambridge MA: MIT Press, 1968).

Brown, Julie, *Bartók and the Grotesque: Studies in Modernity, the Body and Contradiction in Music* (Aldershot: Ashgate, 2007).

Burian, Emil František, *Jazz* (Prague: Aventinum, 1928).

Chalupa, Dalibor, 'Karneval', *Host*, 4 (1924–25), 166–7.

Cocteau, Jean, 'Cock and Harlequin', in *A Call to Order: Written between the Years 1918 and 1926 and Including Cock and Harlequin, Professional Secrets, and Other Critical Essays*, trans. Rollo H. Myers (New York: Haskell House Publishers, 1974), 8–82.

Černušák, Gracian, Andrew Lamb and John Tyrrell, 'Polka', *Grove Music Online* www.oxfordmusiconline.com [accessed 2 December 2015].

Čurda, Martin, 'Druhý smyčcový kvartet Pavla Haase: mezi Janáčkem a Ravelem', *Opus musicum*, 42/4 (2010), 29–46.

Čurda, Martin, '*From the Monkey Mountains*: The Body, the Grotesque and Carnival in the Music of Pavel Haas', *Journal of the Royal Musical Association*, 141/1 (2016), 61–112.

Čurda, Martin, 'Smyčcové kvartety Janáčkových žáků z 20. let' (unpublished master's thesis, Masaryk University, 2012).

Čurda, Martin, 'Smyčcové kvartety Pavla Haase z 20. let' (unpublished bachelor's thesis, Masaryk University, 2010).

Danow, David K., *The Spirit of Carnival: Magical Realism and the Grotesque* (Lexington: University Press of Kentucky, 2004).

Götz, František, 'Devětsil v Brně', *Socialistická budoucnost*, 28 May 1921, reprinted in Vlašín, Štěpán, ed., *Avantgarda známá a neznámá*, 3 vols. (Prague: Svoboda, 1970–72), i, 130–3.

Haas, Pavel, 'Haasův kvartet "Z opičích hor": Poprvé proveden v Brně 16. března 1926', *Hudební rozhledy*, 7 (1925–26), 106.

Hoffmeister, Adolf, 'Nesmrtelnost smíchu', *Volné směry*, 26/7–8 (November 1928), reprinted in Vlašín, Štěpán, ed., *Avantgarda známá a neznámá*, 3 vols. (Prague: Svoboda, 1970–72), ii, 628–31.

Kotek, Josef, *Dějiny české populární hudby a zpěvu*, 2 vols. (Prague: Academia, 1994–98), ii: *1918–1968* (1998).

Kotek, Josef, ed., *Kronika české synkopy: půlstoletí českého jazzu a moderní populární hudby v obrazech a svědectví současníků* (Prague: Supraphon, 1975).

Lachmann, Renate, 'Bakhtin and Carnival: Culture and Counter-Culture', in *Mikhail Bakhtin*, ed. Michael E. Gardiner, 4 vols. (London: Sage, 2003), ii, 60–90.

Levinger, Esther, 'Czech Avant-Garde Art: Poetry for the Five Senses', *The Art Bulletin*, 81/3 (1999), 513–32.

Levinger, Esther, 'A Life in Nature: Karel Teige's Journey from Poetism to Surrealism', *Zeitschrift für Kunstgeschichte*, 67/3 (2004), 401–20.

Levinger, Esther, 'Karel Teige on Cinema and Utopia', *The Slavic and East European Journal*, 48/2 (2004), 247–74.

Macharáčková, Marcela, 'Z dějin Brněnského Devětsilu', in *Forum Brunense 2009: Sborník prací Muzea města Brna*, ed. Pavel Ciprian (Brno: Společnost přátel Muzea města Brna, 2009), 79–99.

Peduzzi, Lubomír, *Pavel Haas: Život a dílo skladatele* (Brno: Muzejní a vlastivědná společnost, 1993).

Schulz, Karel, 'Groteska', *Český filmový svět* 4/2 (March 1926), reprinted in Vlašín, Štěpán, ed., *Avantgarda známá a neznámá*, 3 vols. (Prague: Svoboda, 1970–72), ii, 278–80.

Schwandt, Erich, 'Trio', *Grove Music Online*, www.oxfordmusiconline.com [accessed 2 December 2015].

Sheinberg, Esti, *Irony, Satire, Parody, and the Grotesque in the Music of Shostakovich: A Theory of Musical Incongruities* (Aldershot: Ashgate, 2000).

Slavíček, Lubomír, and Jana Vránová, eds., *100 let Domu umění města Brna* (Brno: Dům umění města Brna, 2010).

Svoboda, Jiří and Karel Teige, 'Musica a muzika', *Život*, 2 (1922), 86–89, reprinted in Vlašín, Štěpán, ed., *Avantgarda známá a neznámá*, 3 vols. (Prague: Svoboda, 1970–72), i, 405–12.

Teige, Karel, 'Manifest poetismu', *ReD*, 1/9 (June 1928), reprinted in Vlašín, Štěpán, ed., *Avantgarda známá a neznámá*, 3 vols. (Prague: Svoboda, 1970–72), ii, 557–93.

Teige, Karel, 'O humoru, clownech a dadaistech', *Sršatec*, 4/38–40 (July–August 1924), reprinted in Vlašín, Štěpán, ed., *Avantgarda známá a neznámá*, 3 vols. (Prague: Svoboda, 1970–72), i, 571–86.

Teige, Karel, 'Poetismus', *Host*, 3 (July 1924), 197–204, reprinted in Vlašín, Štěpán, ed., *Avantgarda známá a neznámá*, 3 vols. (Prague: Svoboda, 1970–72), i, 554–61.

Teige, Karel, *Výbor z díla*, ed. Jiří Brabec, Vratislav Effenberger, Květoslav Chvatík and Robert Kalivoda, 3 vols. (Prague: Československý spisovatel 1966–94), ii: *Zápasy o smysl moderní tvorby, Studie z třicátých let* (1969).

Vlašín, Štěpán, ed., *Avantgarda známá a neznámá*, 3 vols. (Prague: Svoboda, 1970–72), i: *Od proletářského umění k poetismu: 1919–1924* (1971), ii: *Vrchol a krize poetismu: 1925–1928* (1972), iii: *Generační diskuse: 1929–1931* (1970).

Newspaper reviews

–l–, 'Kulturní obzor: V koncertu Klubu moravských skladatelů', *Stráž socialismu*, 18 March 1926.

lk., 'Nová kvarteta', *Moravské noviny*, 19 March 1926.

L. K. [Ludvík Kundera], 'Koncert Klubu moravských skladatelů', *Národní osvobození*, 19 March 1926.

–k–, 'Z brněnských koncertů: Večer kvartetních novinek', *Lidové noviny*, 18 March 1926.

St–, 'Klub moravských skladatelů', *Rovnost*, 18 March 1926.

[unknown], 'Koncerty v Brně', *Tribuna*, 19 March 1926 (cited from Haas's album).

V. H. [Vladimír Helfert], 'Koncerty v Brně: Klub mor. skladatelů', *Ruch*, 20 March 1926.

Archival documents

Archival documents deposited in the Department of Music History of the Moravian Museum (Oddělení dějin hudby Moravského zemského muzea)

Karneval, sign. A 22.730 b and A 54.252.
Z opičích hor, sign. A 29.801 a.

Archival documents in private property of Olga Haasová-Smrčková

'Moje úspěchy a ne-úspěchy' [My Successes and Non-successes]: a notebook containing newspaper clippings of newspaper articles on and concert reviews of Haas's works

Musical editions

Haas, Pavel, String Quartet No. 2 'From the Monkey Mountains', Op. 7, 1925 (Prague: Tempo; Berlin: Bote & Bock, 1994).

Haas, Pavel, Wind Quintet, Op. 10, 1929 (Tempo Praha; Bote & Bock/Boosey & Hawkes, 2nd rev. edn, 1998).

Janáček, Leoš, String Quartet No. 1 'Inspired by Leo Tolstoy's "Kreutzer Sonata"', 1923 (Prague: Bärenreiter Praha, 2007; ed. Leoš Faltus and Miloš Štědroň).

Smetana, Bedřich, The Bartered Bride (Prague: Bärenreiter Praha, 2011, the composer's piano arrangement).

3   Suite for Piano, Op. 13 (1935)
Neoclassical tendencies

Introduction

In the introduction to his short article on Haas's Suite for Piano (1935), Jascha
Nemtsov has associated Haas's music (and this piece in particular) with the
'anti-Romantic' stylistic orientation of Stravinsky, Bartók, and the composers
of Les Six, as opposed to the 'post-Romantic' style of the Second Viennese
School.[1] The 'anti-Romantic' aesthetic camp is often referred to through the
broadly conceived term Neoclassicism,[2] which Nemtsov, surprisingly perhaps,
does not invoke. Although Haas's Suite for Piano may not be representative of
a fully-fledged Neoclassical style, it arguably displays a number of Neoclassical
features. As the following analysis will demonstrate, the work reflects several of
the key concepts trending in the aesthetic discourse of the inter-war era, namely
the notions of Neoclassicism, everyday art, and collage (see Chapter 1). At the
same time, the piece displays a continuation and further development of Haas's
use of grotesque distortion and the topic of 'danse excentrique' (discussed in
Chapter 2). The difference in style between the 1935 Suite for Piano and the
1925 string quartet 'From the Monkey Mountains' resides largely in the emergence of Neoclassical tendencies.

   In the inter-war era, a number of composers who participated in the generational reaction against the intellectual baggage and overblown proportions of late
Romantic music turned to the 'light' genre of the suite, traditionally based on a
succession of short contrasting dance movements.[3] The new compositions could
emulate historical dance types in a Neoclassical manner or update the genre by
the inclusion of modern contemporary dances, not to mention other possibilities
(a suite did not necessarily have to consist exclusively of dance movements).
Besides, given its inherent principle of contrast, the genre of the suite provided
a suitable medium for Haas's preoccupation with the juxtaposition of contrasting, oppositional, or even incongruous musical elements (previously observed in
'From the Monkey Mountains'). Haas's Suite for Piano comprises five carefully
crafted musical miniatures: two pieces of more or less 'abstract' music ('Praeludium' and 'Con molta espressione'), two 'jazzy' dance movements ('Danza' and
'Postludium'), and a 'Pastorale', marked by an atmosphere of antiquity (besides
other connotations of the pastoral).

The structure of this chapter follows the succession of individual movements in the suite, each of which raises different questions: the two initial movements provide insight into Haas's compositional technique and its Neoclassical features; the two dance movements are significant in terms of grotesque exaggeration and distortion; and the 'Pastorale' features an intriguing play with musical topics. The significance of collage-like juxtaposition of culturally significant musical fragments throughout the suite will be discussed in the conclusion.

The Neoclassical 'Praeludium'

Nemtsov's articulate summary of Haas's compositional technique offers a useful starting point for the exploration of the suite:

> [The Suite displays] striking thematic compactness. Each movement is based for the most part on a short melodic unit, an elementary germinal cell. [. . .] Because the cell on its own is very short, generic, and essentially neutral, a musical idea only arises as a sum and result of many repetitions and variations.[4]

Haas's use of repetitive motivic cells is apparent from the very beginning of 'Praeludium'. The essence of the movement's motivic content is encapsulated in the initial four bars (see Example 3.1). The texture consists of two interlocking parts, associated with two corresponding repetitive patterns. Note the prevalence of fifths and fourths in the example: D – A and E – B in the right hand; C sharp – G sharp and F sharp – C sharp in the left hand. These pitches constitute seven adjacent points along the cycle of fifths; when put into an ascending (scalar) order within the space of a single octave, the same pitches produce a diatonic scale. Thus, fourths and fifths, rather than triads, are the building blocks of Haas's diatonicism.

Highly relevant to Haas's use of diatonicism is an observation made by Václav Holzknecht in his 1938 pamphlet *Mladá Francie a česká hudba* (discussed in Chapter 1).[5] Holzknecht argued that music which follows what might broadly be called Neoclassical tendencies is characterised by 'diatonicism understood in

Example 3.1 Interlocking ostinato patterns in 'Praeludium'. Pavel Haas, Suita pro klavír (Suite for Piano) (Praha Hudební matice, 1937), first movement, bb. 1–4.

modern terms', that is, diatonicism in which complexity is achieved by 'multiplication', resulting in 'polytonal' and 'polyrhythmic' combinations.[6] The notion of multiplication is readily apparent in Haas's (vertical) superimposition and (horizontal) reiteration of the two diatonic fragments. The resulting texture, which is rather 'pandiatonic' than 'polytonal', can also be described as 'polyrhythmic' or 'polymetric': the right-hand pattern (which employs mostly white keys) is repeated twice in each bar and thus implies 6/8 metre; the complementary left-hand pattern (which is confined to black keys) has a different rate of reiteration, suggestive of 3/4 metre.

This repetitive motivic material is elaborated mostly by sequential transposition, intervallic transformation (expansion/contraction/inversion), metro-rhythmic transformation, and change of modal colour (diatonicism occasionally yields to whole-tone modality). The transpositional sequences of the reiterating fragments give rise to ascending or descending 'melodic' gestures. The changes of such vertical direction typically occur at key points of the form, which is also often punctuated by changes of metro-rhythmic configuration, textural arrangement, and intervallic structure of the motives.

For example, in the a – b – a' outline of the movement's first part, the middle section (shown in Example 3.2) is distinguished by the disruption of the established metric-rhythmic pattern (note the conflict between 3/2 and 12/8 metre), by exchange of parts coupled with intervallic inversion of the initial motive (now

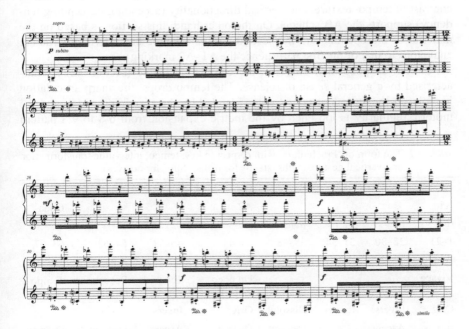

Example 3.2 Small-scale middle section (b) of 'Praeludium'. Haas, Suite for Piano, first movement, bb. 22–32.

rising rather than falling), and by the corresponding ascending tendency of the bass, leaping by a perfect fifth at the beginning of each bar (D – A – E – B – [F sharp] – C sharp – G sharp – E flat – B flat). Once this succession reaches its highest point (the B flat in b. 29), having traversed the space of several octaves, a re-transition begins (marked by intervallic and textural re-inversion), leading to the beginning of a recapitulation at the original transpositional level (in the penultimate bar of the example).

The small-scale recapitulation is suddenly brought to an end when the interlocking pattern disintegrates and 'vanishes' in an ascending arpeggio. Here ends the first part of the overall binary form. What follows is a contrasting theme (see Example 3.3), which is nonetheless derived from the original motivic cell (the two superimposed diatonic fragments) through the principle of variation. Nemtsov uses the term 'montage' (discussed in detail in Chapter 4) to refer to such rapid juxtapositions of contrasting musical elements:[7]

> Besides analogy [variation], montage – the immediate succession of oppositional materials – plays an important role in the formal design. Haas uses both methods in dialectic unity: different fragments, which clash with each other, mostly have a common origin.[8]

The overall form displays a certain degree of ambiguity between an AB and an AA' (A1–A2) layout (see Table 3.1). The fact that the slow section brings contrast in tempo, texture, and vertical directionality (ascending/descending tendency) supports the AB schema. On the other hand, this section is based on the material of the opening and the second part as a whole has a ternary structure analogous to that of the first part (hence the A1–A2 marking).

Marked 'un poco meno mosso', the contrasting theme (section a2) is characterised by a general sense of release. The tempo drops, the sharp articulation is replaced by slurred sustained notes blended by the sustaining pedal, and the motoric regularity is loosened by the metric expansion from 6/8 to 9/8 pattern

Table 3.1 The form of 'Praeludium' with respect to key, tempo, intervallic transformation and vertical gesture ('5ths' stands for fifths; '8ths' for octaves).

A				B			
A1				A2			Coda
(a1	b1	a1')	trans.	(a2	b2	a2')	
1–21	22–30	31–34	35–38	39–44	45–53	54–62	63–67
A natur.		A natur.		A flat		A natur.	
Vivace				Un poco meno mosso	Tempo I.	Poco meno mosso	Tempo I.
Orig.	Invers.	Re-inv.	Dissolut.	Orig.	Invers.	Re-inv.	
	Ascent (5ths)		Descent (chrom.)	Descent (5ths)	Ascent (chrom.)	Descent (5ths)	Descent (8ths)

Example 3.3 Contrasting section of 'Praeludium' (A'/B). Haas, Suite for Piano, first movement, bb. 39–41.

(as in the second and third bar of Example 3.3), which allows the music to linger on the dotted minim, embellished by chromatically encircling quavers (marked 'poco espressivo'). Furthermore, the section is underpinned by a sequence of descending fifths, which counter-weights the succession of ascending fifths in section b1. The contrasting middle section b2 starts with no transition when the initial tempo and textural pattern is resumed in b. 45. Like the analogous section b1, it is marked by an exchange of parts and intervallic inversion of the two diatonic fragments. The general ascending tendency (which contrasts with the descending tendency of a2) also manifests itself in the transpositional sequence of the three-note left-hand pattern, each iteration of which appears a semitone higher than the previous one.

The structural weight of the movement's formal design is concentrated in the recapitulation of a2 (a2'), which is adequately expanded. As before, the section consists of two iterations of a three-bar unit. This time, the second iteration appears in rhythmic augmentation, thus occupying the space of six bars. This horizontal expansion is accompanied by vertical expansion in terms of register, as well as rhythmic and textural enrichment. Thus, the conclusion of 'Praeludium', marked by augmentation of the theme, prominent pedal points, rich figurative embellishment and broad spans of register, resembles the closing sections of historical organ preludes. It is also noteworthy that the theme is underpinned by a clearly discernible tonal progression, concluded by a perfect authentic tonal cadence (b. 61), and followed by a coda, which consists of three successive home-key iterations of the opening motive, each transposed an octave lower than the previous one.

'Praeludium' possesses a number of features that can be described as Neoclassical. The very title of the opening piece suggests an 'old' practice. The expectations thus raised are met by the piece's almost exclusively diatonic pitch structure, its toccata-like character, and the semblance of improvisation. The brevity, simplicity, and clarity of formal design (despite the ambiguity between AA' and AB) is perhaps not exceptional in this genre (binary structures were common in Baroque suites). However, the piece also displays economy of means in that it derives maximal effect from minimal motivic material, using simple but highly efficient methods of transformation. There is also an element of expressive restraint. This is apparent in Haas's treatment of the climactic final cadence, which – despite its lyrical and perhaps even slightly sentimental character – is not dwelled upon longer than necessary, being strictly confined to the pre-established model. Moreover, any excess of sentiment is prevented by the motoric movement, which permeates the majority of the 'Praeludium'; for example, the lyrical character of the slow theme's final iteration is 'neutralised' by the return of the semiquaver 'perpetuum mobile' in the coda.

Finally, the music's gestural properties, gauged in terms of metre (regular/irregular), tempo (slow/fast), register (high/low), and melodic tendency (ascending/descending) are an essential means of articulating the piece's formal structure. Such comprehension of musical form relies largely on kinaesthetic analogy with elementary categories of physical movement. This may be understood as one of the possible realisations of the notion of physiological music, a response to Cocteau's call for music 'to walk on' rather than 'to swim in' (see Chapter 1).

'Con molta espressione': the negative image of 'Praeludium'

In contrast to the prevailing diatonicism of the 'Praeludium', the second movement, entitled 'Con molta espressione', is marked by radical chromaticism. However, there are a number of analogies between the two. In both cases, the opening theme, from which the rest of the movement is derived, consists of two superimposed elementary units (diatonic in the first movement and chromatic in the second), each occupying a different metric layer (compare Examples 3.1 and 3.4). Both themes also seem to be underpinned by the same diatonic skeleton, consisting of the perfect fifths A – E in the right-hand part and F sharp – C sharp in the left-hand part.

Furthermore, there are considerable similarities between the slow section (a2) of 'Praeludium' (see Example 3.3) and the beginning of the second piece. First, the two have in common the tendency towards descending motion – diatonic in the former (the succession of falling fifths) and chromatic in the latter (stepwise semitone descent).[9] Second, the second bar of the slow section of 'Praeludium' seems to contain the germ of the opening right-hand motive of the second movement; there are similarities in texture, contour (chromatic 'encircling'), articulation (slurs, 'tenuto' marking), and performance directions ('poco espressivo'/'con molta espressione').

Example 3.4 Opening bars of 'Con molta espressione'. Haas, Suite for Piano, second movement, bb. 1–9.

On the large scale, both movements are similar in formal layout, consisting of two iterations (AA') of a ternary small-scale design (a1 – b1 – a1'; a2 – b2 – a2'). In both cases, a2 appears in a tonally contrasting transpositional level with reference to a1 (the two sections stand in a neighbour-note relationship in the first movement and a tonic-dominant relationship in the second), and a2' re-establishes the tonic level. The form of the second movement is slightly more ambiguous (see Table 3.2). First, a2 is not a contrasting variation of a1; it merely presents the theme on the 'dominant' transpositional level (a^D). Second, the transitional sections (tr./retr.), which facilitate the modulation to the dominant region and back, are the main source of contrast in the movement. Therefore, the transition gives the impression of an independent contrasting section (B).

Table 3.2 The form of 'Con molta espressione' with respect to tonality, tempo, intervallic transformation and a vertical (ascending/descending) tendency ('4ths' stands for fourths).

A			(B?)	A'			
a1	b1	a1'	trans.	a2	retrans.	b2	a2'
a^T	a^{INV}	$a^{T'}$		a^D		a^{INV}	$a^{T'}$
1–18	19–28	29–37	38–45	46–63	64–71	72–84	85–91
Tonic		Tonic		Dominant			Tonic
Orig.	Invers.	Re-inv.		Orig.		Invers.	Re-inv.
Desc. (chrom.)	Asc/Desc. (chrom)	Desc. (chrom.)	Asc. (4ths)	Desc. (chrom.)	Asc. (4ths)	Asc/Desc. (chrom)	Desc. (chrom.)

As in 'Praeludium', changes of texture, tempo, and melodic direction mark significant form-constitutive events. Both of the contrasting sections in the second movement (b1 and tr/B) are distinguished by techniques familiar from the 'b' sections of 'Praeludium'. Exchange of parts (hand swapping) and intervallic inversion are apparent in b1 (hence the alternative designation a^{INV}); here the left-hand descending chromatic tetrachord from the opening bars appears in the right-hand part in an ascending form. The transition (quasi B) is marked by an altered textural and metro-rhythmic pattern, faster tempo ('poco piu mosso'), intervallic inversion (in the inner voices), an ascending tendency (a sequence of rising transpositions), and an overall sense of accumulation of momentum (see Example 3.5).

On the whole, the second movement can be regarded as a negative image of the first one, setting up binary oppositions such as diatonic/chromatic and fast/slow. Moreover, 'Con molta espressione' appears as an expressive counterpart of the affectively neutral 'Praeludium', although both movements have equally rigorous (or 'objective') formal structures. Another oppositional pair emerges from the juxtaposition of the second movement's lament-like descending chromaticism and the comic character of the following 'Danza'.

Example 3.5 Transition (quasi B). Haas, Suite for Piano, second movement, bb. 38–48.

'Danza': the eccentric dance

The third movement of Haas's suite, the 'Danza', alludes to one of the most famous early twentieth-century popular dances – ragtime. Although the era of ragtime had long been over by the mid-1930s, it should be taken into consideration that, by this time, there had been a long history of employing ragtime elements in art music. The best-known examples include Debussy's *Golliwog's Cakewalk* from his 1908 piano suite *Children's Corner*, Stravinsky's *l'Histoire du Soldat* (1918), Ragtime pour onze instruments (1919), and *Piano Rag Music* (1919), Hindemith's *Suite 1922*, and various works by Erwin Schulhoff (Fünf Vortragsstücke, Op. 3, Fünf Pittoresken, Suite for Chamber Orchestra, Op. 37).[10]

'Danza' is another instance of the topic of 'danse excentrique', previously observed in Haas's works from the 1920s, namely in the last movement ('The Wild Night') from Haas's 1925 string quartet 'From the Monkey Mountains', in the male choir *Karneval* (1928), and in the third movement ('Ballo eccentrico') of the 1929 Wind Quintet (see Chapter 2). There are qualities and connotations inherent to ragtime and its predecessor, the cakewalk, which are consistent with the comic or even grotesque character of Haas's 'eccentric' dances. The cakewalk is believed to have originated as black slaves' parody of the social customs (modes of dressing, posture, highly stylised social dances) of their white masters.[11] Ironically, the dance was popularised by white performers' imitations in blackface minstrel shows.[12] The most characteristic element of ragtime is its syncopated rhythm, 'grafted onto an existing stock of conventions associated with the duple-metre march and two-step [as well as polka and schottische]'.[13]

The typical rhythmic patterns of ragtime are similar to those employed by Haas in his earlier 'eccentric' dances, where rhythmic irregularities were used to create the comical effect of awkward motion. Moreover, the typical left-hand accompaniment pattern characterised by the alternation of single tones and chords invests the music with a clownish, mechanical, puppet-like character. The image also involves the stereotypical notion of 'black primitivism', which is associated with ragtime.

The opening ragtime theme of 'Danza' (see Example 3.6) displays all of the above-mentioned characteristic features: the left-hand accompaniment pattern, the right-hand syncopation working against this obstinate rhythm, and the clearly outlined 16-bar structure divided into four four-bar phrases, marked by a distinct tonal identity and rhythmic patterning:

Table 3.3 Formal outline of the ragtime theme (numbers refer to groups of semiquavers in each bar).

basic idea	(A major)	2/4:	| 4 4 | 3 3 2 | 4 4 | 3 3 2 |
basic idea	(C sharp minor)		| 4 4 | 3 3 2 | 4 4 | 3 3 2 |
continuation	(F sharp minor)		| 3 3 2 | 4 4 | 3 3 2 | 3 3 2 |
cadential phrase	(F sharp minor)		| 4 4 | 3 3 2 | 3 3 2 | . . . |

In his above cited article, Nemtsov comments on the ragtime theme: 'The clownish accentuation and parallel minor seconds in the melody make this dance [appear] grotesque rather than cheerful. I imagine a crowd of hideously dancing puppets – as if they came out of the pictures by James Ensor.'[14] I fully agree with Nemtsov, with the slight reservation that the overall character of 'Danza', like that of the earlier 'eccentric' dances, is closer to the humorous rather than the terrifying pole of the grotesque.

The theme is marked by modal ambivalence between major and minor, which, by means of correlation, creates the characteristically grotesque conflation of euphoric and dysphoric elements. The modal shifts result on the one hand from the transpositions of the basic idea from A major to third-related minor keys and, on the other hand, from blues-scale alterations of particular scale degrees within the phrases. The latter is particularly obvious at the end of the second four-bar phrase, cast in C sharp minor, where the major-mode third degree (E sharp) unexpectedly appears on the downbeat of the cadential bar (see Example 3.6). The humorous effect is underscored by articulation: the staccato semiquavers scattered between the two parts might well be heard as the onomatopoeic representation of a giggle, further implying a clownish persona. The semitone clashes, dissonant clusters of fourths, and chromatic voice leading also contribute to the overall sense of comic awkwardness.

With its binary AA' outline, the large-scale form of 'Danza' resembles that of the previous movements.[15] However, 'Danza' does not possess virtues of economy and concision; on the contrary, it is deliberately 'excessive'. Like 'The Wild Night' from the 1925 string quartet, 'Danza' is characterised by purposeful abundance of redundant musical material, designed to evoke the sense of mind-less and obsessive repetition, all of which contributes to the disorientating purport of the grotesque. Much of the movement is occupied by static musical material, animated solely by means of rhythm: syncopations, dotted rhythms, and cross-rhythms. Such motivic material, which is already quite elementary, is subject to further fragmentation and distortion.

These tendencies escalate towards the end of the movement. The gradual inten-sification of momentum (indicated by the markings *presto – poco a poco acceler-ando – prestissimo*) pushes the dance to the point of collapse. All melody, indeed, all motivic content is gradually eliminated and all that remains are violent bursts of a dissonant cluster of fourths, which is eventually suspended by the sustaining pedal and deprived of resolution (see Example 3.7).

The movement actually concludes with a 'thickened' suspended dominant chord in A major (the root E emerges as a pedal in the last two bars). Note that in

Example 3.6 The 'Ragtime' theme. Haas, Suite for Piano, third movement, bb. 1–8.

Example 3.7 Motoric ending of 'Danza'. Haas, Suite for Piano, third movement, bb. 94–104.

the first three bars of the example, the only melodic element (found in the lowest voice of the right-hand part) highlights the pitches E – F sharp – G sharp, which are heard as scale degrees ^5 – ^6 – ^7 in A major. Even this rudimentary melody is eliminated in the fourth bar as the G sharp (^7) is suspended in a fourth-based cluster which, significantly, contains the entire A major scale. Given the use of static, repetitive motivic fragments and the emphasis on rhythm as an indispensable means of driving the movement to its end, this is arguably one of the most Stravinskian passages in the whole of Haas's oeuvre.

'Pastorale': the pastoral dream

At the beginning of the fourth piece of Haas's suite, pastoral imagery is invoked by a flute-like motive, embellished by trills, which subsequently gives rise to a modal melodic line, floating weightlessly in the right-hand part (see Example 3.8).[16] The left-hand part provides simple contrapuntal accompaniment. Although the austere texture is reduced to two parts throughout this introduction, it nevertheless gives the impression of a more complex imitative texture with recognisable quasi-fugal entries (bb. 4, 7, 12).

Following the last of these entries, a 'chorale' theme emerges from the contrapuntal flow (see Example 3.9). This theme derives its religious connotations not only from generic features of phrasing, texture, and modality, but also from motivic similarity with the ancient Czech Hymn to Saint Wenceslas. Since St Wenceslas is the patron of the Czech people, the appearances of the 'Wenceslas' motive are particularly significant in Haas's wartime pieces. However, the significance of the motive in earlier works is less straightforward.[17] In the case of 'Pastorale', the allusion to the Wenceslas Hymn may be motivated by the religious connotations of the pastoral, which is concerned with a nostalgic longing for a place of primordial harmony, innocence, and safety.[18] As a saint and a national patron, St Wenceslas represents two places consistent with this description: heaven and homeland.

The chorale theme dissolves after no more than four bars in a chromatic descent and reappears immediately in the guise of a dance-like folk tune (see the second part of Example 3.9). The right-hand melody has some affinity to the compound metre of a siciliana (traditionally 12/8, here 12/16), although

Example 3.8 The 'flute' tune. Haas, Suite for Piano, fourth movement, bb. 1–3.

Example 3.9 The (St Wenceslas) chorale theme and the folk-like theme. Haas, Suite for Piano, fourth movement, bb. 12–9.

this is obscured by the 3/4 notation of the right-hand part and the left-hand ostinato pattern suggestive of 9/16 metre.[19] The characteristic parallel thirds do not appear here, but there is a readily apparent C sharp drone in the left-hand part. On the other hand, details of modality and rhythm invest the folk tune with an East European flavour.

Thus, within the space of no more than 20 initial bars, a shift has taken place from a shepherd's flute tune through an old-style contrapuntal prelude to a religious chant, transformed into a folk tune. The piece thus displays the merger of sacred and profane elements which is characteristic of the pastoral.[20] The generic qualities of antiquity, simplicity, and purity associated with the pastoral are signified musically by the use of 'simple' texture and melodies, 'pure' diatonicism, and 'ancient' modality.[21]

One more connotation of the pastoral remains to be commented upon: the notion of an idyll or a dream, something that only exists as an unattainable ideal outside the human world. Thirteen bars before the end, having gone through several more transformations between its sacred and profane guises, the chorale theme dissolves in a 'misty' chromatic passage marked by a slow rocking rhythm. As the music 'vanishes' with the concluding arpeggio (an ascending series of fourths), the idyllic pastoral vision disappears like a dream.[22] This ending is significant for the interpretation of the relationship between 'Pastorale' and the surrounding movements; this issue will be further discussed in the concluding section of this chapter.

'Postludium': the dysphoric dance

The last movement, 'Postludium', summarises much of what has occurred in the preceding parts.[23] It appears as a chromatic and 'jazzy' counterpart of 'Praeludium', with which it shares toccata-like texture and articulation (at least initially). In its radical chromaticism, especially in the slow central section, 'Postludium' harks back to the second movement. However, most parallels can be seen between 'Postludium' and 'Danza'. The two have in common their dance-like character, syncopated rhythmic pattern, metronome marking (the 'Postludium' is notated 'alla breve'), as well as the element of grotesque exaggeration and distortion. 'Postludium' seems to pick up on the dynamic momentum which had accelerated towards the end of 'Danza', before getting temporarily lost in 'Pastorale'. 'Postludium' thus appears as a (remarkably dissonant) dynamic climax of the whole suite.

Above all, 'Postludium' is characterised by its vigorous, percussive, motoric rhythm, stubborn repetition of fragmentary motives, clashing dissonances, and pervasive chromaticism. It has even been suggested that, in this movement, rhythm dominates over melody. Peduzzi has described the thematic material of 'Postludium' (which is largely based on a single motive) as 'ditty-like', if not utterly 'melodically indifferent'.[24] Indeed, the introductory phrase consists of little more than an irregularly accentuated chromatic descent (see Example 3.10).

However, despite the absence of a conventional diatonic melody, the movement has distinct phrase structure and voice-leading contours. As was the case in 'Praeludium', the repetitive motivic material draws attention to patterns of transposition (ascending/descending motion) and intervallic transformation of the reiterating fragments; such events, in turn, are crucial for the demarcation of formal units. For example, the overall shape of the introduction shown in Example 3.10 is essentially that of an archetypal eight-bar sentence: 2 + 2 + (1 + 1) + 2. The contour of the phrase is defined by its linear directionality: the 'basic idea' (bb. 1–2) is marked by a chromatic descent, which is continued throughout its restatement (bb. 3–4). With the onset of the 'continuation', however, the direction changes, as the fragmented material is sequentially transposed upwards. The 'cadential' section is a kind of leading-note prolongation, preparing the onset of the main theme.

Example 3.10 The introductory phrase of 'Postludium'. Haas, Suite for Piano, fifth movement, bb. 1–8.

The main theme (see Example 3.11) also has a recognisable phrase structure (that of a parallel period), which, however, is not underpinned by a conventional harmonic progression but rather by the symmetry of melodic lines: the four-bar-long chromatic descent from C to F in the top voice underpinning the antecedent is counterweighted by a corresponding chromatic ascent in the bass, rising from B flat to F throughout the consequent. Thus concludes the first section of the movement, which is subsequently repeated with some variation.[25] Despite the semblance of improvisation and loose formal organisation, the following section continues to adhere to conventional models of phrase structure. In its second presentation, the theme is expanded into a compound sentence (bb. 28–44).

As in the 'Praeludium', there is a contrasting slow section, based on augmentation of the elementary rhythmic motive (see Example 3.12). In its descending melodic tendency and its radically chromatic pitch structure, this section bears a strong resemblance to the theme of the second movement. The 'jazzy' harmony of the slow section results from the use of fourth-based sonorities and seventh-chords, shifted around in chromatic parallels (with contrary motion in the inner voices). The most striking feature of the slow section's theme is the continuous chromatic descent, traversing the space of an entire octave, which has a strong

Example 3.11 The main theme of 'Postludium'. Haas, Suite for Piano, fifth movement, bb. 9–16.

Example 3.12 Contrasting slow section. Haas, Suite for Piano, fifth movement, bb. 58–64.

association with the topic of lament. The descent is divided into three two-bar (four-note) units, the last of which is broken up into two separate 'sighs', as if due to a lack of breath, thus enhancing the expressive gestural effect.

Besides its dysphoric character evoked by high levels of chromaticism and dissonance, the middle section is characterised by abrupt contrasts in dynamics (*pp/ff*) tempo (slow/fast), rhythm (augmentation/diminution of the elementary three-note motive), gesture (ascending/descending transpositional sequences of the motive), and articulation (legato/staccato). Such oscillation between opposing extremes is a typical feature of the grotesque, indicating a conflicted emotional state.

Once the original tempo has been restored (b. 87), the movement draws rapidly to its end, propelled by motoric figuration. In the recapitulation, the accumulation of momentum is enhanced by fragmentation and repetition of (already fragmentary and repetitive) thematic material (see Example 3.13). The main theme is reduced to its first bar and immediately repeated (bb. 99–100), so that the two iterations form a continuous chromatic descent. The introductory figure (bb. 101–103) is likewise abridged into a single bar and repeated three times in an ascending sequence with a gong-like pedal marking the downbeat of each bar. The theme of the slow section (bb. 104–105) is distorted in a similar way as the main theme (curtailed, metrically altered, and repeated in a descending succession) and subsequently re-cast in diminution and displaced in a high register (bb. 106–107).

Example 3.13 Accummulation and distortion of motivic material in the recapitulation. Haas, Suite for Piano, fifth movement, bb. 99–108.

Four bars before the end, after some more convolutions of the main-theme fragment, a cadential progression is initiated in the bass which arrives on the tonic G in the penultimate bar. However, the accumulated momentum does not seem to be fully discharged in the cadence; a succession of heavily accentuated descending chromatic parallels ensues, leading to a suspended dissonant sonority, which is left unresolved.

In his article, Nemtsov provided the following summary of 'Postludium', which is worth quoting at length:

> The form of the final movement would be chaotic, were it not for the fact that even the smallest of the fragment-splinters, which follow each other in highly hectic succession, are derived from the main theme. The middle part, which shows light hints of blues, brings repose for a short while. Then the whirlwind starts again even more intensely. This kaleidoscope gives rise with its unusual dynamic momentum to a fairground atmosphere – a favourite subject for Haas. ['Postludium' has] the peculiar character of 'despairing cheerfulness', which seems to me to be typical of Jewish humour – one dances and makes jests so as not to cry (this has also been perfectly conveyed by Shostakovich in his song cycle 'From Jewish Folk Poetry').[26]

The association of 'Jewishness' with 'despairing cheerfulness' or 'laughter through tears' has been commented upon by Esti Sheinberg with reference to the views of the Russian composer Mikhail Gnesin.[27] Sheinberg explains the perceived conflation of contradictory emotional states by the peculiarity of the 'Jewish Dorian' mode, in which 'major' and 'minor' scale degrees (associated with 'euphoric' and 'dysphoric' character, respectively) are mixed. Sheinberg also points out klezmer music's tendency to 'repetitiveness' or, as Gnesin called it, 'ecstatic automatisation', capable of evoking the image of a dancing 'grotesque Übermarionette'.[28]

Neither Nemtsov nor I have identified any specifically musical features in Haas's suite that might be considered Jewish. Correspondingly, there are no references to Jewishness in the contemporary reviews of the piece, with the exception of one oblique remark about Haas's 'racially inherited sonic invention'.[29] Nonetheless, 'Postludium' is arguably characterised by a conflation of euphoric and dysphoric elements. This effect results from an incongruity between the ragtime-influenced dance gestures, on the one hand, and the pervasive lament-like chromatic descent, on the other. The grotesque effect is enhanced by exaggeration and distortion of physical movement. The repetition, accumulation, and deformation of musical material (particularly in the final section) are fittingly described by adjectives such as obsessive, vertiginous, convulsive, and violent.

Conclusion

The study of Suite for Piano is important for the understanding of the development of Haas's compositional language in the 1930s, in which emerging Neoclassical tendencies coexist with the composer's continuing interest in jazz, collage-like juxtaposition of contrasting elements, and the grotesque. The work's Neoclassical features include formal concision and brevity, economy of means (efficient use of minimal motivic material), focus on linear contours (melodic lines, ascending/descending transpositional sequences) rather than vertical harmonic 'colouring', emphasis on rhythm and 'anti-sentimental' motoric drive, modern use of diatonicism, and overall balance between wit and discipline, simplicity and mastery.

On the other hand, Haas does not play with classical tonal syntax in the way Stravinsky does; his music does not employ anachronistic clichés. In fact, there are very few allusions to music of the past in Haas's suite, with the exception of the 'Pastorale'. Haas made a further step in this direction in his opera *Charlatan* (1934–37), which employs a historicising musical idiom to evoke the atmosphere of a seventeenth-century fairground (see Chapter 5). Elements suggestive of historical fairground music subsequently penetrated the 1943 Study for Strings (discussed in Chapter 4), which is the most characteristic surviving example of Haas's Neoclassicism. Unfortunately, the Partita in Old Style (*Partita ve starém slohu*; Terezín, 1944), which would have been highly relevant to the issues discussed here, has been lost.[30]

There appears to be a tension in Haas's suite between the classical ideal of order and restraint and the grotesque features of confusion and excess. However, both tendencies arguably serve to create a sense of distance: gestures of subjective investment are either avoided or exaggerated. On another level, this apparent conflict is part of Haas's broader preoccupation with the juxtaposition of oppositional elements. The relatively restrained character of the first two movements (which constitute a complementary pair) contrast with the excessive nature of 'Danza' and 'Postludium' (which also complement each other in many respects). Moreover, a whole cluster of binary oppositions emerges with the interpolation of 'Pastorale' between the latter two. The ancient, rural, and religious connotations of 'Pastorale' contrast with the modern, urban associations evoked by the ragtime-influenced, jazzy idiom of 'Danza' and 'Postludium'. 'Pastorale' occupies the position of an idyllic, dream-like interlude inserted between two dance movements linked by similarities of tempo, articulation, and rhythmic pattern. The view of the 'Pastorale' as a dream episode is encouraged not only by its own 'vanishing' ending, but also by the way the previous movement ('Danza') ends, or rather fails to end: instead of a genuine conclusion, the dance is intensified to the point of ecstatic obsessiveness and ultimate collapse, which creates the impression of losing one's consciousness or attaining some sort of trance through dance. It is in such a 'state of mind' that the 'Pastorale' appears.

In the previous chapter, a similar kind of musical collage in the last movement ('The Wild Night') of Haas's 1925 string quartet 'From the Monkey Mountains' was interpreted through Bakhtinian perspectives on carnival and Teige's notion of Poetism. However, since Poetism declined towards the end of the 1920s, it is open to question whether the same model can be applied to the suite, composed in 1935. The central problem concerns the mutual relationship between the incongruous elements. In 'The Wild Night', the signifiers of the old, folk, rural world were conflated with attributes of the modern, urban world in a carnivalesque whirl where contradictions seemed to coexist without being mutually exclusive. By contrast, in the suite, the two realms are carefully separated; the ancient, folk, and religious elements are confined to the 'Pastorale', the territory of nostalgic reminiscence, and they are treated without the ironic distance that facilitated the conflation of incongruities in 'The Wild Night'.

The position of 'Pastorale' between 'Danza' and 'Postludium' in the suite is analogous to that of the slow movement 'The Moon and I' between 'Carriage, Horseman, and Horse' and 'The Wild Night' in the string quartet. In both cases, the framing movements create the effect of the comic/carnivalesque/grotesque hyperbole of physical motion; they are also connected by similarity of syncopated rhythmic patterns (besides other common features), which underscores the paren- thetical nature of what comes in between. Another parallel can be drawn between 'Pastorale' and the episode which appears within 'The Wild Night': at one point in the movement, the dizzying carnivalesque rave is temporarily suspended, giv- ing way to a quotation of Haas's own song which he once dedicated to a girl he loved. In both of these cases, moments associated (more or less explicitly) with subjectivity are confined within the carefully constructed framework of a dream, hallucination, or reminiscence. Finally, 'Pastorale' is correlated with other slow/ reflective/subjective sections of the suite, most of which are subtly connected, as has been demonstrated, by similarity of motivic material, contour, and/or articu- lation: the slow second movement (located between two emphatically motoric movements) builds on the slow section of 'Praeludium' and anticipates the slow section of 'Postludium'.

The positioning of such episodes between two related movements or within a single movement is a particular example of the correlation which may occur, as Michael Puri has observed in his study of memory and decadence in Ravel's music, between 'interior' parts of a formal design and 'psychological interior- ity'.[31] Although Haas's music does not lend itself fully to interpretation through the prism of Decadence (at least not in the case of this particular piece), it is appar- ent that Haas, like Ravel, often employs an objective 'mask' (typically in the form of motoric and/or humorous music) which occasionally 'slips to reveal a longing subject'.[32] This is the case in at least two of the above-mentioned parenthetical sections in Haas's works: the reminiscence of a beloved girl (in 'The Wild Night') and the dream-like vision of pastoral antiquity (in 'Pastorale'). Thus, 'Pastorale' is not (at least not primarily) the product of a Neoclassical tendency to honour, emulate, build upon, or deconstruct (as Stravinsky does) the past; the emphasis here is on the remembering/dreaming subject.

Of particular interest is what Puri calls the question of 'transformation': 'How has the past been altered in its reappearance in the present?'[33] Since in Haas's case the past interjects in the present, the more appropriate question is: 'How does the appearance of the past alter the present?' Unlike in Haas's string quartet, where the section following the inserted love song retains the humorous, life-affirming character of what came before, in the suite, the comic character of 'Danza' con- trasts with the more ambiguous and, at times, explicitly dysphoric atmosphere of the 'Postludium'. In other words, the episode ('Pastorale') seems to effect a change of perspective, whereby the following part ('Postludium') appears as a critical commentary on or even a negative image of the previous part ('Danza'). The euphoric eccentric dance becomes a dysphoric grotesque dance. To conclude, the use of collage in the suite, unlike in the earlier string quartet, appears not as a celebration of the invigorating stimuli the world has in stock for twentieth-century people, but rather as a critical statement about the ambivalent subjective experience of the modern world and the (subconscious?) longing for the irretrievably lost pastoral utopia.

Notes

1 Jascha Nemtsov, 'Zur Klaviersuite op. 13 von Pavel Haas', *Musica Reanimata Mitteilungen*, 17 (December 1995), 20–3 (p. 20).
2 The opposition between Stravinsky's Neoclassicism and Schoenberg's Serialism was coined in the 1920s. See Scott Messing, *Neoclassicism in Music: From the Genesis of the Concept through the Schoenberg/Stravinsky Polemic* (Rochester NY: University of Rochester Press, 1996), pp. 139–49.
3 Jan Trojan, 'Suita' in *Slovník české hudební kultury* [Dictionary of Czech Musical Culture], ed. by Jiří Fukač, Jiří Vysloužil and Petr Macek (Prague: Editio Supraphon, 1997), pp. 885–7 (886): 'The suite type is [in the early 20th century] modernised by being conceived as a succession of new and non-traditional dances, taken over from modern dance music or musical folklore (Bartók's suites; Hindemith's *Suite 1922*; E. Křenek's *Kleine Suite*). [. . .] The suite conveys new stylistic surges in the case of Janáček's wind sextet *Youth* (1924), in the works of B. Martinů (*Small Dance Suite*, 1919; *Jazz Suite*, 1928) and – in a very particular way – in the music of Alois Hába.' Italics and translation mine. All translations from Czech sources are my own, unless stated otherwise.
4 Nemtsov, 'Zur Klaviersuite op. 13 von Pavel Haas', p. 22. All translations from Nemtsov's article are my own.
5 Václav Holzknecht, *Mladá Francie a česká hudba* [Young France and Czech Music] (Prague: Melantrich; Brno: Pazdírek, 1938). See also Holzknecht's 16-page essay *Klavír v moderní hudbě* [Piano in Modern Music] (Prague: Melantrich; Brno: Pazdírek, 1938).
6 Ibid., p. 6.
7 The notions of collage and montage are closely related, but not interchangeable. I use the term 'collage' with reference to issues of semantics to describe the juxtaposition of elements invested with contrasting or incongruous meanings; the term 'montage', as I use it, applies to issues of compositional technique and designates the succession of distinct and discontinuous musical materials. For further discussion of montage see Chapter 4.
8 Nemtsov, 'Zur Klaviersuite op. 13 von Pavel Haas', p. 22.
9 The theme of the slow section of 'Praeludium' is derived from the sequential transposition of the movement's initial ostinato motive by a major second in bars 3–4; this may also be the model for the sequential major-second drop in the opening theme of the second movement, especially considering the correspondence of absolute pitch (E–D) in the right-hand part.
10 See Andre Hodeir, *Jazz: Its Evolution and Essence* (New York: Grove Press, 1956).
11 H. Wiley Hitchcock and Pauline Norton, 'Cakewalk', *Grove Music Online*, www.oxfordmusiconline.com [accessed 4 November 2013].
12 Ibid.
13 Edward A. Berlin, 'Ragtime', *Grove Music Online*, www.oxfordmusiconline.com [accessed 4 November 2013].

14 Nemtsov, 'Zur Klaviersuite op. 13 von Pavel Haas', p. 21. James Ensor (1860–1949) was a Belgian painter; his work, which typically features grotesque figures, carnival masks, and various kinds of fantastic and macabre imagery, has been associated with Symbolism, Expressionism, and Surrealism. See Ian Chilvers, 'James Ensor', in *The Oxford Dictionary of Art and Artists*, 4th ed. (Oxford: Oxford University Press, 2009) [accessed via www.oxfordreference.com, 23 May 2016].

15 There is a parallel between 'Danza' and 'Praeludium' in tonal layout. The beginnings of both are marked by an ambivalence between A major and F sharp minor. In both cases, the opening material is transposed a semitone lower (A flat/F) on its return (at the beginning of A˙) and return to A major towards the end of the A˙ (although the cadence is conspicuously frustrated in 'Danza').

16 The reference to flute is also made in Nemtsov, 'Zur Klaviersuite op. 13 von Pavel Haas', p. 21.

17 Peduzzi expressed the opinion that the apparent allusions to the Wenceslas chorale in Haas's earlier pieces are to be considered cases of an 'unwitting, only later consciously exploited resemblance' of melodic shapes [between Christian and Jewish religious chant], originally borrowed by the composer from the melodies of synagogue chants in order to personalise his musical idiom'. See Peduzzi, *Pavel Haas*, p. 52. This explanation, however, raises the even more difficult question of Haas's familiarity with Jewish synagogue music, which has been briefly discussed in the Introduction.

18 I am drawing on the discussion of the pastoral in Raymond Monelle, *The Musical Topic: Hunt, Military and Pastoral* (Bloomington: Indiana University Press, 2006). See particularly pp. 185, 195–8.

19 Ibid., p. 215 and onwards.

20 Monelle provides an early example of this association, observing that Virgil's description of 'the "Golden Age", a period in history in which justice reigned [. . .] and men were like children, innocent and happy' was considered by the medieval critics as 'a Christian prophecy, and it earned for Virgil a place on the facades of cathedrals'. See ibid., p. 186.

21 See ibid.

22 See also Nemtsov, 'Zur Klaviersuite op. 13 von Pavel Haas', p. 21: 'the beautiful images vanish as a reflection in the water, smudged by light wind'.

23 A similar point has been made by Nemtsov (ibid.).

24 Peduzzi, *Pavel Haas*, p. 69: 'Two musical thoughts alternate [in this movement]: the introductory, based on the irregular alteration of accentuation in melodically indifferent music, and the main one – of ditty-like character'.

25 See also ibid.: '[The main theme] is the main material for the following music, which is based on loose variations interspersed by interludes derived from the introduction'.

26 Nemtsov, 'Zur Klaviersuite op. 13 von Pavel Haas', p. 22.

27 Esti Sheinberg, *Irony, Satire, Parody, and the Grotesque in the Music of Shostakovich: A Theory of Musical Incongruities* (Aldershot: Ashgate, 2000), pp. 302, 305–7.

28 Ibid., p. 307. Sheinberg refers to Mikhail Gnesin, 'O yumore v muzyke', in *Stat'i, Vospominaniy, Materiali*, ed. R. V. Gl'ezer (Moscow: Sovetskii Kompozitor, 1961), p. 201.

29 Hrč., 'Klub moravských skladatelů v Brně', *Brněnská svoboda*, 22 April 1936: 'Haas's Suite for Piano, Op. 13, a composition [which is] temperamental to the core and musically – as we say – absolute, [. . . draws its effect from] the author's colourful sonic invention ['zvukovost'], [which is] as much racially inherited as it is artistically cultivated and sophisticated'. Quoted from a newspaper clipping included in Haas's album 'Moje úspěchy a ne-úspěchy' ('My Successes and Non-successes'), which survives as the property of Olga Haasová-Smrčková. Translation mine.

30 According to Peduzzi, this was a six-movement piece; the incipit of the sixth movement (Gigue) was preserved on a keepsake sheet dedicated by the composer to K. Herrmann. Peduzzi refers to the so-called Heřman's collection (Heřmanova sbírka)

deposited in the Terezín Memorial (Památník Terezín), inv. no. 3914/G 731. See Peduzzi, *Pavel Haas*, p. 133. Viktor Ullmann's review of the piece is available in Viktor Ullmann and Ingo Schultz, *26 Kritiken über musikalische Veranstaltungen in Theresienstadt* (Hamburg: Bockel Verlag, 1993), p. 52. 'Bernard Kaff played boldly a modern programme. Modern music is dreaded because of its harmonic [language] [. . .]. The abandonment of the tonal system and the natural overtones corresponds with the abolition of true imitation of nature in painting. Pavel Haas does not carry this process further, on the contrary, he introduces new sounds within tonality; one could speak of a tonal twelve-tone music. The "Partita in Old Style" maintains the forms, or at least the primal features ['Urphänomene'] of the suite form. Here, too, Haas's music is thoroughly praiseworthy; it is playfully powerful, naturally polyphonic, transparent in the piano texture, interesting, and graceful. I give the prize to the small Air, without diminishing the merit of the other movements. Whether the term "Partita" should be used for tonally volatile pieces with individual movements set in different keys, is a separate question. In a partita, all movements were originally connected by an identical key. Therefore, I would have preferred the title 2nd Suite. Kaff played the Partita with verve and mastery.' Translation mine.

31 Michael J. Puri, *Ravel the Decadent: Memory, Sublimation, and Desire* (New York: Oxford University Press, 2011), p. 26. Puri's point concerns the appearance of musical material which is associated with memory of the past through its 'historical content' (references to styles, genres, techniques, or other features which recognisably belong to the past) or 'contextual content' (successive appearances of musical material in a cyclic formal design). See also p. 22.

32 Ibid., pp. 39–40.

33 Ibid., p. 22.

Bibliography

Berlin, Edward A., 'Ragtime', *Grove Music Online*, www.oxfordmusiconline.com [accessed 4 November 2013].

Hasse, John Edward, ed., *Ragtime, Its History, Composers and Music* (New York: Schirmer Books, 1985).

Hitchcock, H. Wiley and Pauline Norton, 'Cakewalk', *Grove Music Online*, www.oxford musiconline.com [accessed 4 November 2013].

Hodeir, Andre, *Jazz: Its Evolution and Essence* (New York: Grove Press, 1956).

Holzknecht, Václav, *Hudební skupina Mánesa* (Prague: Panton, 1968).

Holzknecht, Václav, *Klavír v modern hudbě* (Prague: Melantrich; Brno: Pazdírek, 1938).

Holzknecht, Václav, *Mladá Francie a česká hudba* (Prague: Melantrich; Brno: Pazdírek, 1938).

Monelle, Raymond, *The Musical Topic: Hunt, Military and Pastoral* (Bloomington: Indiana University Press, 2006).

Nemtsov, Jascha, 'Zur Klaviersuite op. 13 von Pavel Haas', *Musica Reanimata Mitteilungen*, 17 (December, 1995), 20–3.

Peduzzi, Lubomír, *Pavel Haas: Život a dílo skladatele* (Brno: Muzejní a vlastivědná společnost, 1993); for German translation see *Pavel Haas: Leben und Werk des Komponisten*, trans. Thomas Mandl (Hamburg: Bockel, 1996).

Puri, Michael J., *Ravel the Decadent: Memory, Sublimation, and Desire* (New York: Oxford University Press, 2011).

Trojan, Jan, 'Suita' in *Slovník české hudební kultury* [Dictionary of Czech Musical Culture], ed. Jiří Fukač, Jiří Vysloužil and Petr Macek (Prague: Editio Supraphon, 1997).

Archival documents (Pavel Haas)

Archival documents in private property of Olga Haasová-Smrčková

'Moje úspěchy a ne-úspěchy' ('My Successes and Non-successes'): a notebook containing newspaper clippings of newspaper articles on and concert reviews of Haas's works.

Musical editions

Haas, Pavel, Suita pro klavír (Suite for Piano) (Prague: Hudební matice, 1937).

4 Rhythmic layers and musical form

Janáček̇ian elements in Haas's compositional practice

Introduction

The rhythmic vigour of Haas's music has often been highlighted as one of its characteristic features, attributed to the influence of Janáček and/or Stravinsky. Some contemporary reviewers perceived Janáček's influence in Haas's use of 'terse, short, sharply rhythmicised motives', which tend to be either 'repeated' or dropped and 'succeeded by another [motive]' but never developed into 'broad-breathed melodic lines'; others argued that the 'motoric' quality of Haas's music 'has its roots in the West, in Stravinsky'.[1] According to *Grove Music Online*, Haas 'productively assimilated Janáček's compositional technique' in that he 'explored a method of modal composition and the rhythmic layering of structures'.[2] Peduzzi has claimed that the development of Haas's compositional style followed a trajectory leading naturally from Janáček to Stravinsky, arguing that the two shared 'a similar [technique of] work with a motive and a common tendency towards polyrhythmics'.[3]

The most articulate assessment of the importance of rhythm in Haas's music comes from Jasha Nemtsov, who identified two basic principles underpinning Haas's compositional language: 'analogy' – repetition and variation of a very short, elementary melodic 'cell', which gives rise to larger musical ideas and even whole movements; and 'montage' – rapid juxtaposition of contrasting musical materials (which may nonetheless be derived from the same germinal 'cell' through the principle of 'analogy').[4] Nemtsov further argues that

> the principles of analogy and montage, which cut the form into cells, rule out the constitution of large-scale tonal relations. Rhythm thus gains particular importance, [since it] provides the static music with a dynamic aspect [through] polyrhythmic and polymetric combinations, as well as rhythmic transformations [of musical material].[5]

Nemtsov's observations introduce a number of key problems which will be discussed below. The following chapter will demonstrate that some of the most characteristic features of Haas's music are rooted in Janáček's compositional practice, namely the use of ostinati, fragmentary thematic materials, stratified textures, vertical superimposition of rhythmic and melodic patterns, and horizontal, montage-like juxtaposition of contrasting materials. Janáček's theory of *sčasování* and his notion of 'metro-rhythmic layers' will be instrumental to explain the roles played by rhythm and metre in Haas's formal designs. Finally, Haas's compositional practices will be related to broader issues concerning early twentieth-century musical syntax that have been discussed in connection with the music of Stravinsky: the crisis of tonality and goal-directed linear progression, the fragmentation of conventional phrase structure, the use of repetitive motivic 'cells', and the resulting problems of stasis, (non)development, and (dis)continuity.

Introduction: Janáček's compositional idiom in the context of early twentieth-century musical syntax

Fragmentation, repetition, stasis, discontinuity, blocks, mosaics, and montage

As Christopher Hasty has demonstrated, the early twentieth-century crisis of tonality raised substantial problems of succession and continuity in music.[6] The tension-resolution propelling principle inherent to tonality was an essential means of ensuring directionality in music, the causal relationship between 'before' and 'after' enabling the listener to 'predict the future course of events'.[7] From a Schenkerian perspective, a continuous, linear progression towards a tonal centre is the essence of tonal music. This principle of goal-directed motion is the most important source of tonal music's teleological drive, capable of producing a sense of formal closure. Tonality also plays an essential role in the articulation of musical form, from the small-scale level of individual phrases (underpinned by certain patterns of harmonic progression) to large-scale structures of entire compositions (determined largely by relations between key areas).

In terms of pitch structure, stasis typically results from the use of non-diatonic collections (whole-tone, octatonic, twelve-tone) in which there is no hierarchical system of distinct scale degrees with a tonic or finalis functioning as its base (and the goal of melodic progression). However, diatonic material can also be treated in a static, non-developmental manner when subjected to fragmentation and repetition. This approach is particularly strongly associated with Stravinsky, whose melodies, as Gretchen Horlacher has demonstrated, often have 'identifiable intervallic shapes' and therefore raise the expectation of goal-directed linear progression, but this expectation is nonetheless frustrated by their fragmentary, repetitive nature.[8] Thus, Stravinsky's music typically features, in Jonathan Cross's words, 'immobile' ostinati and 'static' melodies 'built from limited motifs or cells which are then repeated/varied in various guises rather than developing thematically'.[9] The problems of fragmentation, discontinuity, stasis, and non-development also affect large-scale formal structures of Stravinsky's works; this is apparent, as Cross pointed out, in the composer's exploration of '"block" construction', 'mosaic structure', and cinematic juxtapositions akin to the 'montage techniques of Eisenstein'.[10]

Particularly pertinent is Cross's following point, concerning the importance of rhythm as a means of compensating for such static musical features:

> It should hardly surprise us that, in the face of the collapse of tonality with its guarantee of directedness, early twentieth-century composers should look to the rhythmic parameter in order to find new means of investing their apparently harmonically static and non-developmental music with a renewed dynamism.[11]

Cross refers to the strategy of using stratified textures, consisting of vertically superimposed rhythmically differentiated layers, which is characteristic not only of Stravinsky, but also of Debussy:

> [Stravinsky's] modernist concerns [with fragmentation, opposition, disruption, and so on] overlap with Debussy's [in whose music] repetition also has a non-developmental function and results, as Arthur Wenk has explored, in a static, circular music, or as Derrick Puffett has argued [. . . in] 'static, non-developmental textures [based on] ostinato [. . . which can be regarded] as an anti-developmental device substituting mechanical (!) repetition for German motivic development.' Aspects of the anti-Teutonic characteristics of *both* composers' music certainly have their roots in Russia, especially in the shared models offered by Mussorgsky – this is clearly a significant issue in any understanding of the pre-history of the parallel modernisms of Debussy and Stravinsky.[12]

Another composer who arguably stood outside the German tradition (at least in his late works), had keen interest in all things Russian, and shared similar composition-technical concerns, is Janáček. All of the issues discussed so far – fragmentation, repetition, stasis, discontinuity, montage, stratification of texture and preoccupation with rhythm – are highly characteristic of Janáček's music. Of particular interest are the observations made by Czech composer and musicologist Josef Berg in his brief essay entitled *On Janáček's Compositional Idiom* (*K Janáčkovu skladebnému projevu*).[13] Berg characterised the type of texture which typically appears in Janáček's late music as 'polymelodic', arguing that it consists of 'autonomous, equally important melodic lines' and therefore 'lacks accompaniment or figuration in the traditional sense'.[14]

Berg distinguished two types of melodic elements in Janáček's music: *nápěv* ('melody'; pl. *nápěvy*), longer melodic fragments resembling traditional motives or themes, and *sčasovka* (pl. *sčasovky*), shorter melodic fragments, typically reiterating and thus forming ostinato 'accompaniment' layers.[15] A parallel with Horlacher's 'reiterating fragments' (understood as 'a larger group to which ostinati belong as a special subset') is immediately apparent.[16] Berg emphasised that the two types differ in 'function' but not in essence, because they typically stem from a common motivic basis and because each *nápěv* can be easily transformed into *sčasovka* and vice versa.[17] Such exchange of roles through rhythmic augmentation

Example 4.1 Rhythmic strata in Janáček's music. Leoš Janáček, String Quartet
No. 1 'Inspired by Leo Tolstoy's "Kreutzer Sonata"', 1923 (Bärenreiter
Praha, 2007; ed. Leoš Faltus and Miloš Štědroň), second movement,
bb. 179–87.

Source: Reprinted with permission from Bärenreiter Praha (TP 520). All subsequent examples from
this piece refer to this edition.

and diminution is illustrated by the extract from Janáček's String Quartet No. 1
(1923) shown in Example 4.1.

This example also illustrates Janáček's use of layered textures, consisting of
superimposed melodic and rhythmic strata. The term 'montage' has often been
used with reference to Janáček's techniques of 'vertical' superimposition of
reiterating fragments (potentially involving overlap, phase shift, and so on) or
'horizontal' juxtaposition of consecutive contrasting sections without mitigating
transitions.[18] In this case, the change of the ostinato pattern and textural configuration as a whole is an important source of contrast.

Janáček's treatment of melodic fragments defies the syntactic principles of
conventional phrase structure most of the time. However, fragmentation is also
apparent on the level of large-scale form. Berg compared the formal designs he
observed in Janáček's late works to a 'mosaic', arguing that 'simple reiteration,
the juxtaposition of successive statements of a theme (as well as juxtaposition
of different themes without a transition) is more common than development'.[19]
Berg refers particularly to the first movement of Janáček's late String Quartet
No. 2 'Intimate Letters', in which '*nápěvy* and *sčasovky* [. . .] are juxtaposed so
conspicuously (often without any transition and with sudden contrast) that they
seem to be mechanically put together'.[20] Nonetheless, a sense of unity results
from the 'monothematic' structure of the movement,[21] which, according to Berg,
derives most of its motivic content from a common germ through 'traditional
means of motivic transformation (i.e. variation, expansion, division, [and] trun-
cation)'.[22] It follows that these processes engender a sense of development.
However, Berg argues that development in Janáček's music is non-linear and
discontinuous and his formal designs are essentially additive, that is, consisting
of a succession of distinct variants of one or several recurring motivic fragments
(see Figure 4.1).

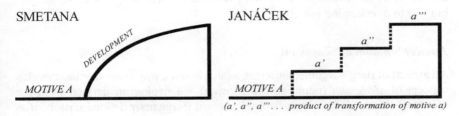

(a', a'', a'''. . . product of transformation of motive a)

Figure 4.1 Berg's schema comparing developmental strategies used by Smetana and Janáček.

Source: Berg, *K Janáčkovu skladebnému projevu*, p. 20. Translation mine.

Successive formal sections may be distinguished not only by variation of the thematic melodic fragments (*nápěvy*), but also by the transformation of the context in which they appear – a particular metro-rhythmic, modal, and textural configuration. Changes of such configurations amount to significant form-constitutive events. Of particular importance in this respect are the underlying ostinati (*sčasovky*), which often persist throughout whole formal sections, investing them with a distinctive identity.

A parallel emerges here with Edward T. Cone's notion of 'stratification'. Cone's seminal essay on discontinuous blocks in Stravinsky's music (which post-dates Berg's study on Janáček), begins with the observation that 'Stravinsky's textures [are marked by] sudden breaks affecting almost every musical dimension: instrumental and registral, rhythmic and dynamic, harmonic and modal, linear and motivic'.[23] 'Stratification' is defined as 'the separation in musical space of ideas – or better, of musical areas juxtaposed in time'. Cone's preference for the term 'musical areas' over 'ideas' indicates that the contrast between successive sections is not only motivic or thematic. In traditional tonal repertoire, themes and keys would be the primary form-constitutive elements; parameters such as tempo, rhythm, metre, texture, instrumental colour, dynamics, and so on (despite being arguably part of the identity of each theme) would mostly be considered of lesser structural significance. From Cone's perspective, all of the above parameters are of equal importance in that they are all capable of differentiation and unification of individual musical areas. In other words, the successive musical areas are characterised by specific combinations of musical parameters concerning motivic/thematic units, pitch structure, tempo, rhythm, metre, texture, instrumentation, articulation, colour, dynamics, and so on. Finally, reconfiguration of these parameters offers the possibility of a 'synthesis', defined by Cone as a process of 'transformation' and mutual 'assimilation' through which 'the diverse elements are brought into closer and closer relation with one another'.[24]

Cone points out that successive formal 'blocks' in Stravinsky's music, discontinuous as they are in most musical parameters, mostly have at least one element in common.[25] Similarly, Berg observes that Janáček's *nápěvy* and *sčasovky* often do not change simultaneously. The introduction of a new *nápěv* or its variant (what Berg calls 'thematic differentiation') may be mitigated by continuity of an unchanged *sčasovka* ('textural unification') or vice versa, giving rise to overlapping patterns.[26]

Janáček's notion of Sčasování

All aspects of Berg's argumentation are related in some way or another to Janáček's concept of *sčasování* (noun; adj.: *sčasovací*) – a neologism derived from the root 'čas' ('time').[27] Czech musicologist Jarmil Burghauser defined *sčasování* as (a) 'metro-rhythmics' (a general designation for the complex of rhythmic and metric phenomena), and (b) 'rhythmicising' (the 'compositional activity' of 'forming' and 'structuring' in this area).[28] For the sake of convenience, Janáček's adjective *sčasovací* and Burghauser's adjective 'metro-rhythmic' will be used used interchangeably from now on.

In his theoretical writings, Janáček combines under the heading of *sčasování* music-theoretical observations on metro-rhythmic relations in music with psychologically oriented aesthetic reflections. The composer's well-known fascination with the so-called *nápěvky mluvy* ('speech melodies') stemmed from his belief that rhythmic patterns of speech convey the speaker's immediate psychological state. Correspondingly, he believed that a particular mood could be musically articulated by means of rhythm. This is illuminated by the following quotation from his *Complete Theory of Harmony* (*Úplná nauka o harmonii*):

> I have arrived at the significance of sčasování through the study of speech melodies ['nápěvky mluvy']. [. . .] The ultimate sčasovací truth resides in words, the syllables of which are stretched into equal beats, a pulse which springs from a certain mood. Nothing compares to the sčasovací truth of the rhythms of words in [the flow of] speech. This rhythm enables us to comprehend and feel every quiver of the soul, which, by means of this rhythm, is transmitted onto us, evoking an authentic echo in us. This rhythm is not only the expression of my inner spirit, it also betrays the impact of the environment, the situation and all the mesological influences to which I am exposed – it testifies to the consciousness of a certain age. We can feel a fixed mood clinging to the equal beats [i.e. the pulse] of sčasovka [a noun referring either generally to the 'sčasovací layer' or, as Berg uses it, to a recurring rhythmic pattern].[29]

From this perspective, each particular metro-rhythmic configuration in Janáček's textures seems to carry a specific 'mood'. The ostinati (*sčasovky*) are the principal means of sustaining the mood over longer periods of time. Drawing on Janáček's above-cited thoughts, Berg described *sčasovka* as a 'unique means of expression' and explained its operation as follows:[30]

> *Sčasovka* imposes its frozen mood [upon a musical area] by ceaseless repetition of a single melodic fragment. [. . .] When such a small fragment pounds

incessantly throughout a prolonged section of a piece, it creates for the time of its duration an atmosphere governing the section; it invests the section with its character, its pulse, its mood.[31]

Berg further argues that Janáček's 'non-functional' treatment of harmony, which results in the sense of harmonic 'stasis', is another aspect to the 'frozen mood' of *sčasovka*:[32]

> The mood-evoking effect of *sčasovka* is not based only on rhythm. Most of the time, *sčasovka* is also the sole carrier of harmony. [. . .] The considerable harmonic inertia (i.e., the [long] duration of each harmony) [in Janáček's music] is directly related to the function of *sčasovka* to communicate mood. A chord [or perhaps rather a modal colour, since *sčasovky* are mostly non-triadic] thus gains a new role. It produces a sonic effect and creates for the time of its duration a specific atmosphere, which is an irreducible part of the overall effect of *sčasovka*.[33]

In more technical terms, Janáček's notion of *sčasování* was based on a hier-archical model of metro-rhythmic organisation, in which the '*sčasovací* base' (defined by Michael Beckerman as 'fundamental temporal unit [. . .] which fills an entire measure') functions as a common denominator, from which 'higher' lay-ers are derived through subdivision (see Figure 4.2).[34] The distance between the 'highest' layer and the 'base' was referred to as the 'depth of *sčasování*' ('hloubka *sčasování*') or, more conveniently, 'metro-rhythmic depth'.[35]

Janáček also commented on how movement across such rhythmic layers con-tributes to a satisfactory conclusion of a musical phrase.

> To conclude a composition means to bring all its inner rhythmic[36] vibration to a stop; thereby its *sčasovací* life is lost and with it also the harmonic life and melodic development. [. . .] The vibration of each layer can be terminated by a longer beat, the beat of [the layer's] own *sčasovací* base, or the *sčasovací* base of a lower layer. The more *sčasovací* layers concur, the more abrupt the cut is.[37]

Janáček's *sčasovací* layer is defined as regular rhythmic pulse, a succession of even beats or time segments of equal duration. Hence, *sčasovací* layers are pri-marily rhythmic layers. However, the superimposition of layers, all of which are derived by means of subdivision from the '*sčasovací* base', necessarily results in the grouping of beats into larger metric units (groups of two, three, four, etc.). As Janáček put it, 'accentual [metric] activity [which] gives rise to accentual shapes [. . .] emerges from the coaction of two harmonic, i.e. simultaneous *sčasovky* [rhythmic layers]'.[38] Janáček distinguishes three types of *sčasovky*:[39] *sounding sčasovka* ('sčasovka znějící') – a succession of equal beats in sounding music; *counting sčasovka* ('sčasovka čítací') – an echo of 'sounding sčasovka'

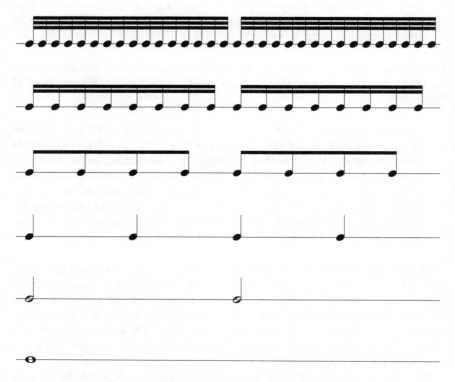

Figure 4.2 Janáček's model of '*sčasovací* layers' stemming from a semibreve '*sčasovací* base'

Source: Leoš Janáček, 'Můj názor o sčasování (rytmu)'/'My Opinion of *Sčasování* (Rhythm)', in *Teoretické dílo: Články, studie, přednášky, koncepty, zlomky, skici, svědectví, 1877–1927 (Theoretical Works: Articles, Studies, Lectures, Concepts, Fragments, Outlines, Testimonies, 1877–1927)*, ed. Leoš Faltus, Eva Drlíková, Svatava Přibáňová, and Jiří Zahrádka, 2 vols. (Brno, 2007–08), ii/1 (2007), 361–421 (p. 393). Reproduced by permission of Editio Janáček, o.p.s.

in the listener's mind, which continues to 'count the beats' during longer notes or pauses;[40] and *grouping sčasovka* ('sčasovka scelovací') – a 'lower' rhythmic layer (unfolding in longer rhythmic values), which divides the 'higher' levels into metric groups.[41] Janáček's illustration (see Figure 4.3) shows how a metrically undifferentiated pulse of equal beats (*sounding* or *counting sčasovka*) gains 'accentual shape' through the addition (in performance or in mind) of a *grouping sčasovka*:

The notion of '*sčasovací* layers' is of considerable importance to Janáček's methods of motivic transformation. Any motive can be 'transposed' to any of the layers (moving 'higher' or 'lower'). This technique can be observed, for example, in the third movement of Janáček's 'Kreutzer Sonata' string quartet, which is based on a single motive. Example 4.2 shows the opening bars, in which the

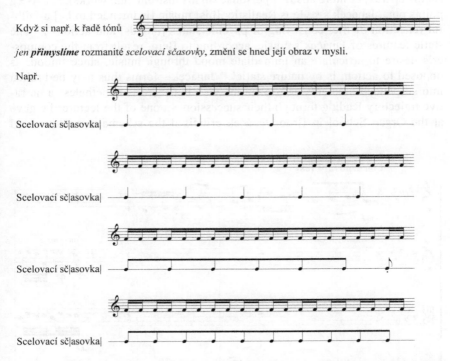

Když si např. k řadě tónů

jen **přimyslíme** rozmanité *scelovací sčasovky*, změní se hned její obraz v mysli.

Např.

Scelovací sč|asovka|

Scelovací sč|asovka|

Scelovací sč|asovka|

Scelovací sč|asovka|

Figure 4.3 Janáček's example of the emergence of metric groupings from the interaction of two rhythmic layers. Janáček, 'Základy hudebního sčasování', p. 25: 'If we add – albeit *just in our minds* – various *grouping sčasovky* to a succession of notes such as this [. . .], its shape in the mind changes instantly'.

Source: Reproduced by permission of Editio Janáček, o.p.s. Translation mine.

germinal four-note motive appears (with some variation) on three distinct rhythmic levels (quavers, semiquavers, and demi-semiquavers). This example also demonstrates Janáček's 'montage' technique: each of the two contrasting guises of the motive (the lyrical *nápěv* and the violently agitated *sčasovka*) is delivered by two superimposed voices that are 'out of phase' with each other. Moreover, the juxtaposition of the two elements, which is gradually intensified in the following bars (the fragments get progressively shorter and alternate with increasing frequency), is an example of 'horizontal' montage.

Finally, it should be pointed out that, despite the parallels with Stravinskian compositional practices, Janáček's aesthetic convictions were fundamentally different from those espoused by Stravinsky. The 'impersonal', 'detached', or 'objective' character, often ascribed to Stravinsky's manipulation of musical material, is alien to Janáček, whose ideal was to capture in music with expressive immediacy the affects moving the psyche of dramatic characters (in his operas) or more abstract personae (in his instrumental works).[42] As Berg points out, 'Janáček's style is Realistic; [his] music [is intended to be] a faithful reflection of life, consisting of psychic states [moods] and actions'.[43] The static features of Janáček's music, according to Berg, result from the composer's desire to articulate an immediate mood through music, since 'mood, as opposed to action, is by nature static'.[44] Janáček's forms thus may be broken into suspended moments or 'frozen moods', but there is nonetheless a narrative trajectory leading through their succession. In one of the lectures he gave at the Organ School in Brno, Janáček criticised the schematic, architectural

Example 4.2 Janáček, String Quartet No. 1, third movement, bb. 1–7.

conception of traditional musical forms and advocated what he called 'developmental formation' ('formace vývojová') or 'fantasia', which he understood as a (narrative) succession of moods, concluded by 'the expression of the resultant mood, the resultant emotional vibration'.[45] If Janáček's 'moods' correspond with Cone's 'strata', then the expression of the 'resultant emotional vibration' can be achieved by means similar to those described by Cone with reference to his notion of 'synthesis'.

Case Study No. 1: String Quartet No. 2 (1925), mov. 1: 'Landscape'

The first movement entitled 'Landscape' of Haas's 1925 String Quartet No. 2, 'From the Monkey Mountains', has already been discussed at some length in Chapter 2. It is useful to quote again Haas's comments concerning the significance of rhythm and movement in 'Landscape':

> I simply intended to capture several strong impressions evoked by a light-hearted summer vacation in the country. The programme helps greatly to create contrasts and escalations, thus determining the piece's formal structure [and] facilitating the creation of purely musical features. [. . .] *Movement* governs throughout this light-hearted composition. Whether it is the rhythm of a broad landscape and birdsong, or the irregular movement of a rural vehicle; be it the warm song of human heart and cold silent stream of moonlight, or the exuberance of a sleepless revelry night, the innocent smile of the morning sun . . ., it is always movement that governs everything. (Even the deepest silence has its own motion and rhythm.)[46]

Haas's emphasis on rhythm and movement has previously been related to his engagement with the tendencies of the inter-war Czechoslovak avant-garde, namely with Poetism's emphasis on corporeality and sensuality. However, now that Janáček's theory and practice of *sčasování* has been introduced, it also becomes apparent that Haas's claims regarding the expressive potential of rhythm echo Janáček's thoughts on the correlation between rhythm and 'mood'. The following analysis will also demonstrate Janáček's influence on Haas's compositional technique. Haas's use of Janáčekian rhythmic layers is apparent from Figure 4.4 (previously referred to in Chapter 2), which tracks the occurrence of the most prominent ostinato patterns in 'Landscape', demonstrating that changes of ostinato pattern correspond with the boundaries between formal sections.

Movement across Janáčekian rhythmic layers facilitates the transition between sections marked 'a' and 'b', shown in Example 4.3. The initial ostinato comes to a stop by moving down two rhythmic layers (that is, by gradual augmentation from semiquavers through quavers to crotchets). The beginning of a new section is marked by the onset of a new ostinato, which is based on the same rhythmic pattern, projected onto a higher (demi-semiquaver) rhythmic layer.

Figure 4.4 Ostinato rhythms and form in 'Landscape'

Example 4.3 Transition from 'a' to 'b' through cessation and reinvigoration of the ostinato rhythm. Pavel Haas, String Quartet No. 2, Op. 7 'From the Monkey Mountains', 1925 (Prague: Tempo; Berlin: Bote & Bock, 1994), first movement, bb. 38–40.

Source: © Copyright Boosey & Hawkes Bote & Bock GmbH, Berlin. All subsequent extracts from this work refer to this edition and are reproduced by permission of Boosey & Hawkes Music Publishers Ltd.

The beginning of the small-scale recapitulation (section 'a'') is marked by the return of the opening semiquaver ostinato (shown in the first bar of Example 4.3) on the level of demi-semiquavers. This ascent along the ladder of rhythmic layers is part of a gradual escalation of momentum, which spans the entire first section of the movement. As indicated in Figure 4.4, the increasing rhythmic activity is enhanced by the addition of an extra layer of triplets.

When the intensification reaches its climax, a rapid, montage-like cut in tempo, rhythm, and texture announces the beginning of a contrasting middle section (see motive 'c' in Figure 4.6). This is characterised by homophonic texture, slow tempo (lento ma non troppo), and a regular, albeit ambivalent metric pattern (whereas the melody is cast in 3/4 metre, the chordal accompaniment is in 6/8). The regular slow pulse of this section roughly corresponds with the rate of the human heart during rest (note the composer's mention of 'the warm song of the human heart' in the above quoted commentary). The middle section, which is permeated by this regular beat, thus physiologically associates the moment of repose following the escalation of activity in the movement's first part. At its end, however, the slow pulse is progressively disturbed by outbursts of the first section's ostinato, the assertion of which marks the beginning of the recapitulation (section 'A''). This agitated rhythmic pulse subsequently persists until the end of the movement.

The entirety of the movement is based, similarly as in Janáček's above discussed works, on a small number of germinal motivic 'cells' (see Figure 4.5). The opening theme (bb. 3–10) features two distinctive motives: 'x', which initiates the theme's characteristic blues-scale descent, and 'y', which emphasises key scale degrees (^5 and ^1) within this descent. Motive 'y' later gives rise to *sčasovka* 's''. The pentatonic motive 'a' arguably originates as an extension of

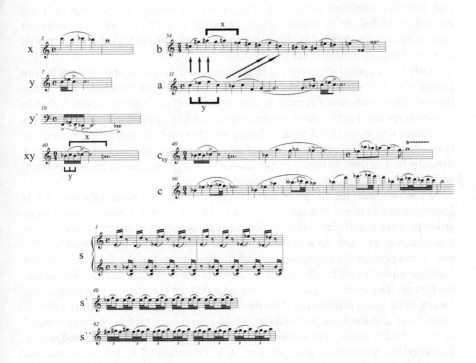

Figure 4.5 Motivic Material in 'Landscape'

the minor-third step of motive 'y' by addition of neighbouring pitches above and below. The chromatic motive 'b' in 5/4 is derived by means of horizontal and vertical expansion from the pentatonic motive 'a', combined with the 'descending sinusoid' contour of motive 'x'. Motive 'c', on which the contrasting middle section is based, is conceived relatively independently, although it is anticipated at the beginning of section 'b' by what I have labelled motive 'c_{xy}', consisting of three successive statements of motive 'xy', each of which 'reaches' higher than the previous one, while preserving the original melodic contour (+ - + -).

In common-practice tonal music, thematic and tonal contrasts would play an important role in articulating formal structure. These factors are also at work in Haas's movement, albeit to a lesser extent. Since the piece consists for the most part of relatively short thematic fragments, developed almost exclusively by means of sequential transposition, distinct key areas are not clearly established throughout much of the movement. It is significant, though, that the succession of motives 'a' and 'b' in the recapitulation follows the same transpositional pattern as in the first section. Moreover, there is large-scale tonal correspondence between the opening phrase, which is 'in F' (tinted by 'blue' notes) and the concluding V-I cadence in F major (the theme of the middle section, is introduced in E flat and subsequently repeated in D flat/C sharp).

Since the movement's tonal architecture is rather skeletal, changes of metro-rhythmic and textural configuration play an important role as a means of formal differentiation and unification. Particularly important in this respect is the Janáčekian technique of 'transposition' across rhythmic layers, which applies not only to ostinato patterns (as shown in Figure 4.4), but also to the movement's motivic/thematic material (see Figure 4.6).

Motive 'a' appears successively in crotchets, semiquavers, and quavers before giving way to its new variant (motive 'b'), unfolding in crotchets. The variation of other elements of texture is also significant: the ostinato appears first in semiquavers and later in demi-semiquavers, yielding occasionally to trills.[47] It is significant that moments of recapitulation, which round off what might become an open-ended series of variations, do not rely so much on the return of a particular thematic unit as they do on the reappearance of a rhythmic and/or textural pattern, which in itself acquires motivic significance.

In contrast with the diversity of sections A and B, the recapitulation (A') is homogeneous in terms of metro-rhythmic and textural configuration. These properties provide a unifying 'context' for the recapitulation of thematic material in a similar way as a key does in traditional tonal music. All of the motives 'a', 'b', and 'c' are presented in crotchets against the background of the demi-semiquaver ostinato, embellished by chromatic counter-melodies. The recapitulation, unlike the first section, creates a continuous melodic flow of chromatically interweaving contrapuntal lines, distinguished rhythmically by syncopation and triplet subdivisions. Note also the melodic flexibility of the *sčasovka*, which is no longer 'static' as in Janáček's music, but rather participates in the contrapuntal voice-leading. Considerable momentum emerges from this saturation of texture with melodic and rhythmic activity, which drives the movement to its conclusion.

DIFFERENTIATION (sections A + B)

MOTIVE: *a* (crotchets)   *a* (semiquavers)   *a* (quavers)   *b* (crotchets)   *c* (crotchets)

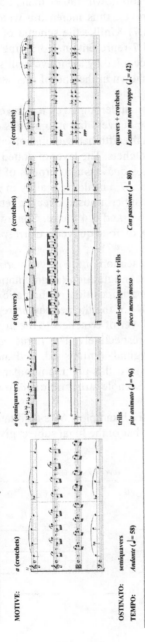

OSTINATO: semiquavers   trills   demi-semiquavers + trills   quavers + crotchets

TEMPO: *Andante* (♩ = 58)   *più animato* (♩ = 96)   *poco meno mosso* (♩ = 80)   *Con passione* (♩ = 80)   *Lento ma non troppo* (♩ = 42)

UNIFICATION (section A')

MOTIVE: *b* (crotchets)   *c* (crotchets)

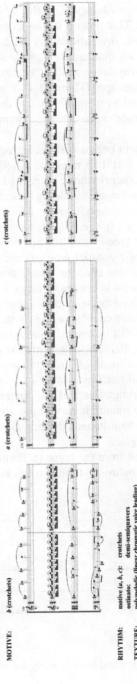

RHYTHM: motive (*a*, *b*, *c*):   crotchets
                 ostinato: demi-semiquavers
               polymelodic (linear chromatic voice leading)
               rhythmic individuation of voices (syncopation and triplets)

TEXTURE:

TEMPO: *Appassionato* (♩ = 76)

Figure 4.6 Formal Functions: Differentiation and Unification

Case Study No. 2: Study for Strings (1943)

Haas's Study for Strings (Terezín, 1943) is a suitable complement to the early string quartet. This piece's dynamic trajectory is similar to that of 'Landscape', but in this case, rhythmic levels are added 'top-down' rather than 'bottom-up', descending from quavers through to semibreves, thus increasing what Janáček called 'metro-rhythmic depth' (see Figure 4.7). Unlike the schema of rhythmic layers in 'Landscape' (Figure 4.4), Figure 4.7 represents not only the rhythmic layers employed by ostinati, but also those occupied by the movement's thematic material. Another, more detailed schema is shown at the end of this section (see Figure 4.8).

The movement begins with the Introduction, underpinned by a pulse of quavers (see Example 4.4). It is not clear whether the quavers fall into groups of two or three, until another rhythmic layer is added in the fifth bar with the introduction of a tetrachordal ostinato, unfolding in dotted crotchets. The layer of dotted crotchets functions as *grouping sčasovka*, which divides quavers into groups of three and thus coins the 6/8 metre. Theme 1 enters in b. 17, unfolding mainly in groups of three crotchets (see Example 4.5). Since it is superimposed over the tetrachordal ostinato, a subtle conflict emerges between 6/8 and 3/4 metre. Somewhat later, the ostinato pattern changes, now consisting of four quavers. Correspondingly, Theme 1 is re-cast in groups of four crotchets (b. 47).

Haas conceived the second, developmental section of the piece (starting b. 60) as a fugue, which enables metro-rhythmic reconfiguration (augmentation, diminution, metric displacement) and textural superimposition of thematic material. Diminution (b. 101) and augmentation (b. 104) of the theme may be regarded in terms of its 'transposition' from the original layer of crotchets to the higher layer of quavers, and the lower layer of minims, respectively. The fugue culminates with the superimposition of the theme's original, diminished, and augmented form in a contrapuntal texture (mm. 104–125). At this point, a number of rhythmic layers are simultaneously 'activated'; the whole structure of *sčasování* thus becomes 'energised'.

The transition from the fugue to Theme 2 (see Example 4.6) is facilitated by the descent across metro-rhythmic layers. The last bar of the fugal subject gives rise to

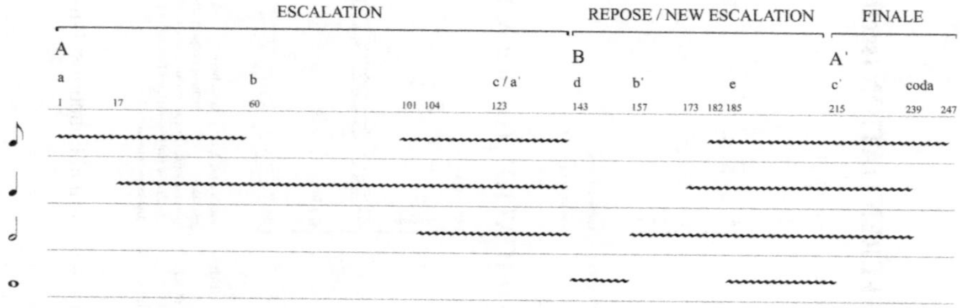

Figure 4.7 Rhythm and form in Study for Strings

Example 4.4 Opening ostinato and a 'mirroring' tetrachordal motive. Pavel Haas, Studie pro
smyčcový orchestr (Study for Strings), 1943 (Berlin: Bote & Bock; Prague:
Tempo Praha, completed and revised by Lubomír Peduzzi, 1991), bb. 1–8.

Source: © Copyright Boosey & Hawkes Bote & Bock GmbH, Berlin. All subsequent extracts from
this work refer to this edition and are reproduced by permission of Boosey & Hawkes Music Publishers Ltd.

a quaver ostinato pattern, which, in turn, is transformed into Theme 2 by the gradual extension of rhythmic values. As a result, a new metric pattern (3/2) is formed
and the 'metro-rhythmic depth' is increased with the establishment of the rhythmic
layer of minims. Brackets are used to differentiate implied minim beats (*counting
sčasovka* or *grouping sčasovka*) from 'actual' minim beats (*sounding sčasovka*); a
certain degree of rhythmic reduction mediates the distinction between the two.

By now it seems to have become a pattern that each new theme should reach
a lower metro-rhythmic level than that of the previous one: there are groups of
three quavers in the Introduction, three crotchets in Theme 1, and three minims in
Theme 2. With the thematic variants gradually moving away from the origin, the
problem of formal unification arises. Similarly as in 'Landscape', the first section
of the movement is rounded off by the return of the tetrachordal ostinato of the
Introduction (with its implied 6/8 metre), which is now superimposed over the
second iteration of Theme 2 (see Example 4.7).

Example 4.7 shows not only the superimposition of the two thematically significant metro-rhythmic patterns but also the transition to the slow middle section.
This transition and the previous one have in common the same ostinato pattern and
the technique of gradually extending rhythmic values. In this case, the extension
of the last note of the pattern gives rise to a hemiola rhythm, which establishes

the layer of semibreves, on which the Adagio is based (semibreves are notated as crotchets).[48] The middle section thus descends to the composition's lowest rhythmic level. All of the 'higher' rhythmic layers become 'extinguished' in the Adagio (except for the iambic pulse, marking the beginning of each semibreve beat).

The Adagio ends with the return of the fugal subject (m. 160). The latter part of section B is permeated by what can be described as a 'struggle' to restore the lost momentum by gradually climbing the rhythmic levels all the way up to quavers. This process begins in m. 157 with the incomplete iteration of the fugal subject: the four accentuated minims (notated as quavers) of the theme's head re-establish the layer of minims, thus lifting the music from the semibreve stillness of the Adagio. The theme subsequently undergoes gradual rhythmic diminution, which eventually gives rise to a new ostinato pattern, projected simultaneously in quavers and crotchets (see second violin and viola in Example 4.8). Although the original rhythmic level has now been re-established, the recapitulation does not follow just yet. Instead, a new theme emerges (see Example 4.8). Flowing mostly in long values (reaching the layer of semibreves), Theme 3 is suspended above an increasingly complex ostinato texture, which 'activates' all rhythmic layers from quavers to semibreves plus their triplet subdivisions. The 'metro-rhythmic depth' of this section is unequalled anywhere else in the movement. Located just before the beginning of the large-scale recapitulation (the return of Theme 2), it functions as the piece's 'structural dominant'. The momentum resulting from the superimposition of metro-rhythmic layers is discharged with the return of Theme 2, which appeared already in the first part of the movement as the peak of dynamic activity, not least thanks to its semblance of folk dance.

As before, Theme 2 is rounded off by the return of the Introduction's rhythmic pattern. This persists even after the last iteration of the theme has been completed, giving rise to a coda (see Example 4.9). Stripped of all thematic material, the coda appears as a summary of the movement's metro-rhythmic patterns. It plays out the tension between duple and triple groupings of quavers and minims. Particularly interesting is the movement's conclusion, which is essentially rhythmic. The only surviving melodic element, the basic tetrachordal motive of the Introduction, is compressed horizontally (from four dotted crotchets to four quavers) and forced into vertical superimposition. Eventually, melody is suppressed altogether in a vertical pile of perfect fourths. The movement is driven to its conclusion by the accumulated rhythmic momentum. In the last three bars, the rhythmic pulse drops down two levels from quavers through to minims. A further descent to the level of semibreves is implied by a hemiola rhythm, articulated by the three concluding blasts. The movement is thus concluded by descending once again (this time for good) to the lowest rhythmic level.

Figure 4.8 summarises graphically the results of the preceding analysis. It takes into account both themes and ostinati (treated as two separate layers) and shows the relationship between their metro-rhythmic properties and the piece's formal design. It is important to point out that the layers traced in this schema are rhythmic rather than metric. Duple and triple groupings are regarded as 'modal' variants of a single rhythmic layer. Themes are assigned to layers according to their lowest and/or most frequent notated rhythmic value, which mostly coincides with what is commonly called 'beat' or 'tactus'. This is relatively straightforward in the case of Theme 1 in its original 3/4 guise. In its subsequent 2/2 guise, the beat arguably shifts to the level of minims; however, since the theme still consists primarily of crotchets, it occupies the crotchet layer in the schema. Theme 2, cast in 3/2 metre, is also under-pinned by a minim beat; in this case, however, minims are sufficiently prominent in the theme itself to be considered a sounding rhythmic layer (this is more apparent from Example 4.6). The same principle applies to Theme 3, where a semibreve beat is implied by the underlying ostinato, as well as the theme itself, which repeat-edly reaches the layer of semibreves. In Janáček's terms, the themes are catego-rised according to their lowest traceable *sounding sčasovka* (and its corresponding *counting sčasovka* evoked in the listener's mind). The schema does not take into account *grouping sčasovky*, such as 'beat' (the special position of which has been explained), '*sčasovací* bases' of individual bars (dotted minim in 3/4, semibreve in 2/2, dotted semibreve in 3/2, etc.), and 'lower' metric or even hyper-metric units.

It is tempting to say that the layer of minims (reached in the Adagio, in Theme 3, and at the end of the Coda) is the movement's large-scale '*sčasovací* base'. However, an important distinction must be made. The level of minims may be the work's 'rhythmic base' (the lowest rhythmic level), but not its 'metric base' (a fun-damental metrical unit from which all the other units in the composition are derived by means of subdivision). Nonetheless, there are elements of triple metric grouping on the level of semibreves. The 5/1 (notated as 5/4) bar of the Adagio mostly con-sists of a group of three semibreves with two 'extra' beats filled by 'echoes' of the iambic pattern in lower voices. Semibreves also tend to form groups of three (with some irregularity) towards the end of Theme 3 (see Example 4.8). Finally, the con-clusion of the work by a hemiola in a 3/2 bar produces a group of three semibreves. This is significant because the emerging 3/1 bar can be subdivided in such ways as to produce all the other bar types in the composition: 3/2 (half), 2/2 (third), 3/4 and 6/8 (quarter). In this sense, the Adagio, Theme 3, and the Coda can indeed be considered as touching the movement's large-scale *sčasovací* base.[49]

Example 4.5 Theme 1 in 3/4. Haas, Study for Strings, bb. 17–30.

Example 4.6 Transition from Fugue to Theme 2. Haas, Study for Strings, bb. 118–9, 122–7.

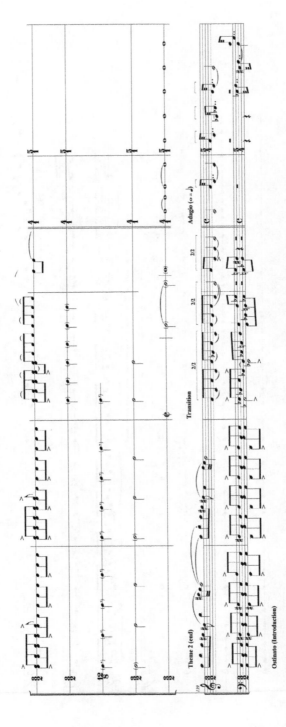

Example 4.7 Small-scale recapitulation (a') and transition to slow middle section (B). Haas, Study for Strings, bb. 139–144.

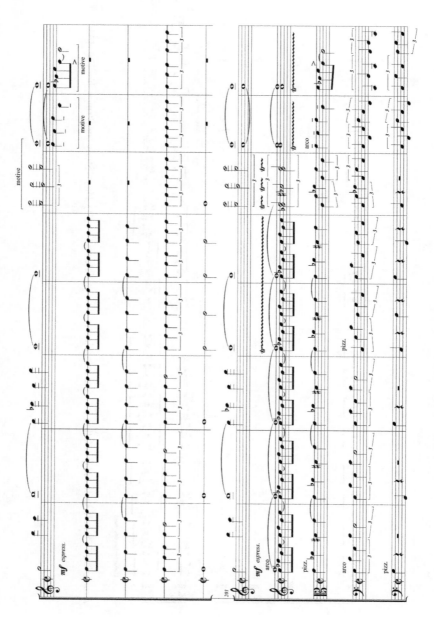

Example 4.8 Theme 3, the structural dominant. Haas, Study for Strings, bb. 201–8.

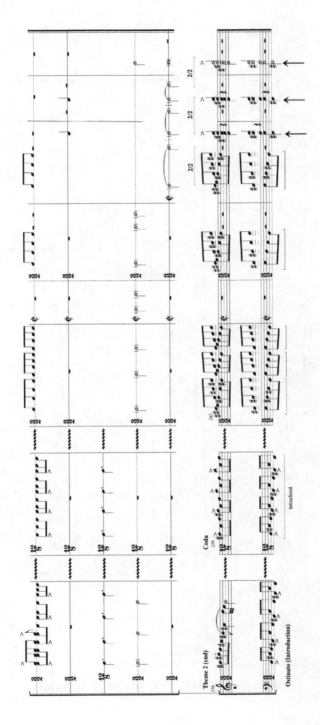

Example 4.9 Coda. Haas, Study for Strings, bb. 236, 239, 242–7.

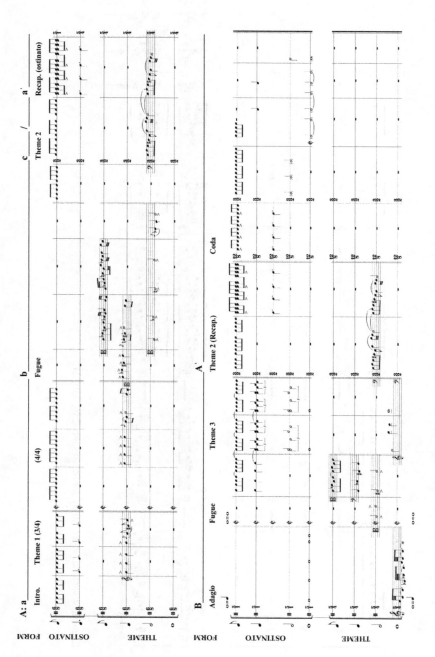

Figure 4.8 Rhythmic layers and form in Study for Strings

Figure 4.9 shows large-scale proportional relationships within the movement. The whole piece, which includes 247 bars in total, can be divided relatively effortlessly into four quarters of *c*. 60 bars. The first quarter itself breaks into two symmetrical 30-bar sections, both of which are further divided into two groups, comprising 16 and 14 bars, respectively. Thus, remarkably, the Introduction and the Transition both comprise 16 bars, despite their different internal subdivisions, and Theme 1 occupies 14 bars in both of its metric guises (3/4 and 4/4). It is also significant that the following Fugue comprises exactly 60 bars, thus balancing out the 60-bar area of Theme 1. In the second half of the movement, formal sections fall less neatly into equal-length units. Nonetheless, Theme 2, together with Adagio and Fugue (as well as a couple of short transitions), occupies the total of 62 bars. The last (approximate) quarter of the movement encompasses 66 bars, divided equally between Theme 3 (with its brief surrounding transitions) and Theme 2 with the following Coda.

	Introduction	1–16	16 bars: (8 x 2)
	Theme 1　　(3/4)	17–30	14 bars: (6+5+3)
1/8			
	Transition	31–46	16 bars: (6+4+3+3)
	Theme 1　　(4/4)	47–60	14 bars: (6+5+3)
1/4			
	Fugue	60–119	60 bars: (elision) 6 + 6 + (2) + 6 + (4) + 6 + (4) + 6 + (1) + 3 + 12 + (4)
1/2			
	Transition	120–122	3 bars
	Theme 2	123–140	18 bars: (2+3+3) + 2 (trans.) + (2+3+3)
	Transition	141–142	2 bars
	Adagio	143–156	14 bars: 1 + 1 + 1 + ...
	Fugue	157–181	25 bars: 3 + 10 + 3 + 3 +3 + 3
3/4			
	Transition (Ostinato)	182–184	3 bars
	Theme 3	185–211	27 bars: (2+3) + (2+2+2) + (2+3) + (3+2+3+3)
	Transition	212–214	3 bars
7/8			
	Theme 2	215–236	22 bars: (1+3+3) + 1 (trans.) + (2+3) + 4 (trans.) + (2+3)
	Coda	237–247	11 bars: 4 + 2 + 1 + 2 + 2

Figure 4.9 Large-scale proportions in the Study for Strings

There does not seem to be any rigorous organising principle underpinning the phrase structure of individual themes. All of the themes are based on repetition and variation of short, asymmetrical motivic units. Theme 1, for example, consists of three groups, comprising 6, 5, and 3 bars, respectively (see Example 4.5). The absence of an underlying harmonic progression (resulting from the melody's fixation on the pitch B and its static tetrachordal accompaniment) makes the theme appear as a succession of fragments derived from a common motivic basis. It is noteworthy that Haas took care to preserve the theme's original bar count and phrase structure in its second iteration in 4/4. Because simple conversion into 4/4 would shorten the theme in terms of bar count, the composer added a (truncated) repetition of the first fragment at the end to compensate; moreover, he altered the order of the other fragments in order to keep the theme's original layout (6 + 5 + 3 bars).

Given their fragmentary and repetitive nature, the themes do not form phrases in the traditional sense of the word. The length of thematic units is more or less arbitrary; it seems to be guided proportional relationships. The 16-bar Introduction (the only part of the movement which can be divided squarely into eight-, four-, and two-bar units) constitutes an elementary building block of the form (roughly one sixteenth of the overall bar count) and arguably functions as a template for the approximate length of thematic units (up till the final quarter of the movement, where themes are expanded to help create the sense of drive towards the end).

Diatonicism, folk modality, Neoclassicism

As far as pitch structures are concerned, Study for Strings is characterised by pervasive diatonicism and the use of folk modality (Dorian in Theme 1, Lydian in Theme 3). B is apparently the tonal centre of the composition, since the initial presentation of Theme 1 is in B Dorian and the final presentation of Theme 3 in the recapitulation is in B Lydian. The themes are not underpinned by harmonic progressions confirming a particular key; instead, the modal centre is affirmed by the tetrachordal ostinato pattern, confined to the fourth interval B – F sharp.

The kind of thematic material found in Study for Strings is very different from that encountered in 'Landscape'. The folk-like, diatonic modality of the Study contrasts with the use of pentatonicism, the blues scale, and richly chromatic material in 'Landscape'. Correspondingly, the two pieces also employ different kinds of contrapuntal textures. In 'Landscape', Haas embellished the thematic units by chromatic counter-melodies in the other voices, thus giving rise to dense poly-rhythmic and poly-melodic textures, which facilitated the continuity between the successive iterations of short fragments. In other words, the relatively indistinct thematic units were integrated into a continuous melodic flow of chromatically interweaving contrapuntal voices. In the Study, the themes constitute full-grown (albeit irregular) musical phrases and their contrapuntal elaboration in the fugal passages gives rise to more conventional, essentially diatonic contrapuntal textures.

Although there is a conceptual similarity in the overall shape of both movements, the means of its execution is very different in each case. The comparison made here indicates a shift of Haas's compositional idiom in the 'Neoclassical' direction – towards the values of rational construction, clarity of design, and flawless craftsmanship. The 'Constructivist' element of the composition (the title itself suggests a kind of technical exercise) resides in metro-rhythmic manipulation of motivic and thematic material. The piece's rhythmic vigour and prevailing dance-like character are also highly characteristic. It is also significant that the motivic and thematic material in the movement bears resemblance to Haas's opera *Charlatan* (discussed in Chapter 5), specifically to the music accompanying the fairground performances of the title character – a seventeenth-century itinerant quack doctor. Haas's Neoclassicism, as manifested in the Study, thus alludes thematically to historical folk/popular/fairground music (rather than the Viennese classical style), while using contrapuntal techniques that hark back to the Baroque tradition.

Interpreting Study for Strings in the context of Terezín

Although this chapter focuses on issues of compositional technique, it presents a unique opportunity to show how analytical insight may help to interpret the significance of Study for Strings with reference to Haas's imprisonment in Terezín. The work's rhythmic drive and occasional dance-like features produce an overall life-affirming character. However, the sudden cessation of rhythmic activity in the central section creates a conspicuous incongruity, which demands interpretation.

There are a number of instances in Haas's earlier music of subjective, contemplative, lyrical episodes being inserted between more exuberant, dynamic, or even humorous sections. Examples of this strategy include 'The Moon and I' in the quartet 'From the Monkey Mountains', the love song in 'The Wild Night', and 'Pastorale' in Suite for Piano (see Chapters 2 and 3). The 'escalation–repose–finale' trajectory followed by the Study can already be found in 'Landscape'. In both cases, the contrasting slow sections are marked by a nocturnal atmosphere of stillness (the contrasting theme from 'Landscape' reappears in 'The Moon and I') and underpinned by a slow-moving iambic ostinato (associated with the 'warm song of the human heart' in the case of 'Landscape'). Another slow section with very similar properties can be found in the first movement of String quartet No. 3 (discussed later in this chapter).

These examples seem to confirm Michael Beckerman's view on the significance of 'middle' sections of musical works (expressed in his discussion of Gideon Klein's music from Terezín):

I have become a great believer in middles. [. . .] [W]hat is placed in the middle is often what the thing is really about. It is the secret that [. . .] is too valuable, too delicate, too dangerous, or too dependent to touch the real world. So in middles we find [. . .] confessions, erotic tensions, funeral marches, the unaccountable, the delicate and the inscrutable; expression writ large.[50]

Elsewhere, Beckerman suggests that there is 'a chilling similarity' between the middle section of the Study and the so-called Windmill Scene from *Charlatan*.[51] This similarity is not motivic, but rather topical, and it is related to Beckerman's previous point. The nocturnal Windmill scene, which is located in the opera's second (middle) act and surrounded by daytime scenes of the charlatan's fairground performances, is another middle episode, in this case associated with intimacy, erotic desire, madness, violence, war, and death (see Chapter 5). Importantly, Haas used similar kinds of contrasting musical materials in *Charlatan* and in the Study. While the outer sections of the Study use a Neoclassical musical idiom similar to that found in the fairground scenes from *Charlatan*, its middle section is similar to the Windmill Scene in the use of slow-moving, repetitive music, characterised by densely chromatic voice-leading within a claustrophobically narrow pitch-range. This intertextual association underscores the dysphoric connotations of the Study's middle section.

Perhaps the best way to interpret the striking contrast inherent to the Study for Strings is to take the preceding analysis of the work's rhythmic structure as the starting point. When the activity of the 'higher' rhythmic layers is extinguished in the Adagio, all that is left is the iambic 'heart beat', marking the beginning of each semibreve. This reduction of the movement's 'rhythmic life' to its 'bare essence' brings to mind existential issues of life and death. There is a sense of agency, even physical labour, in the way the movement 'struggles' to resume its previous rhythmic activity one layer at a time. This is particularly apparent from the return of the fugal subject (b. 157): the four accentuated notes of the theme's 'head', marked 'molto espressivo' and moving in dissonant chromatic parallels, appear as four heavy, painful steps, through which the music is set to motion again (by re-establishing the rhythmic layer of minims). Eventually, the lost momentum is restored, producing a sense of transcendence, with Theme 3 floating weightlessly in long values (in the manner of a cantus firmus) on top of a vibrant ostinato texture. Finally, the return of the dance-like Theme 2 brings the movement to a life-affirming conclusion.

This proces of 'reviving' rhythmic activity and 're-conquering' rhythmic layers is, I believe, what the Terezín survivor Thomas Herbert Mandl referred to in the following commentary:

> I learned something about the kind of person Pavel Haas was when I played violin in Karel Ančerl's Symphonic String Orchestra at the performances of Haas's *Study for String Orchestra*. It suddenly became clear to me that not only was Haas a gifted master of melody and rhythm, that his personality was informed by a will to conquer and overcome ['sieghafte Wille'] (especially apparent in the theme of the fugue) and that it was this that helped him to triumph over the degrading conditions of his internment.[52]

Mandl's testimony taps into some of the crucial questions concerning the interpretation of music from Terezín. Is the Study a piece of 'pure music', or an encrypted testimony reflecting the compsoer's imprisonment in Terezín? It turns out that it can (and perhaps even must) be both. All humans are psychologically conditioned to interpret patterns of movement of an abstract, inanimate object (in Mandl's case the musical structure unfolding in time) as if they were intentional behavioural actions of an animate, anthropomorphic agent (whom Mandl identified with the composer) in a particular environment (Terezín, in this case). The overlap between my analytical description and Mandl's interpretation of Haas's Study for Strings thus exemplifies the capacity (if not the necessity) of purely musical structures to signify beyond themselves and carry profound meanings for those who interpret them.

Case Study No. 3: String Quartet No. 3, Op. 15 (1937–38), mov. 1 (untitled)

The first movement of Haas's String Quartet No. 3 serves as the final case study (for the sake of convenience, the untitled movement will be referred to according to its initial tempo marking as Allegro moderato). As is apparent from the schema shown in Figure 4.10, the formal layout of the Allegro moderato does not follow the 'escalation–repose–finale' pattern observed in 'Landscape' and the Study for Strings. This piece is cast in a symmetrical 'arch' structure, consisting of seven formal sections, each comprising *c*. 20 bars. There are two distinct thematic areas, alternating with sections of developmental character. Following the central developmental episode, both themes are recapitulated in reverse order.

Besides changes in ostinato rhythmic patterns and tempo, Figure 4.10 also represents the movement's 'tonal' trajectory. Despite the complexity of pitch structure, which will be discussed later, tonal centres are relatively clearly defined at key points of the movement. The first theme gravitates towards the tonic of E flat, but its attempted cadence (in b. 19) is frustrated in the theme's initial presentation. The second theme is rather conventionally in the dominant key (B flat), albeit it is in a minor mode and with a plagal character. Correspondingly, the iambic ostinato pattern, which underpins almost the entire movement, appears on two rhythmic levels, analogous to tonic and dominant tonal levels.

The return of the iambic ostinato to the tonic E flat (in the bass) and to the initial rhythmic level (in b. 94) suggests the beginning of a recapitulation, albeit a 'deceptive' one, since the pedal subsequently moves to the leading-tone level (b. 101). This semblance of recapitulation is one of the reasons why the 'exposition–development–recapitulation' pattern of sonata form is superimposed over the symmetrical 'arch form' schema in the diagram. The other reason is that, as will be shown, there is a tendency in the recapitulation toward increased continuity and the accumulation of teleological drive, which contrasts with the relatively more discontinuous presentation of material in the exposition.

Figure 4.11 summarises the motivic content of the movement. It is readily apparent that the motives of thematic units are similarly fragmentary and closely interconnected as those found in 'Landscape'. The three main motives, labelled 'scissors', 'sinusoid', and 'linear' according to their contours (indicated by +/- signs in the schema), are morphological variants of the seven-note cell, first

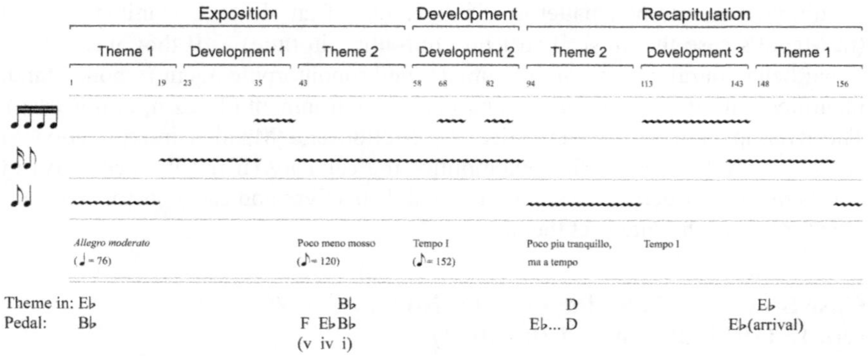

Figure 4.10 Form of Allegro moderato with reference to rhythm, tempo, and tonality

Figure 4.11 Motivic material of the movement

introduced by the opening scissors motive. As in 'Landscape', the means of developing such fragmentary material are mostly limited to repetition, transposition, and the variation of textural and metro-rhythmic context. Longer musical phrases are only created by linking successive iterations of various units or, more commonly, repeated iterations of a single unit. The resulting successions (rarely conjoining more than three units) are 'rounded off' in this movement by the cadential figure, which is derived from the last four notes of the linear motive.

The 'Lyrical' theme (Theme 2) is in many respects analogous to the theme of the middle section of 'Landscape': both are motivically more or less independent from the rest of the movement, they form relatively long musical phrases with a clear affinity to a tonal or modal centre, and they contrast with the preceding material by slow tempo, simplified, homophonic texture, and low dynamic level. Finally, both themes are underpinned by an iambic ostinato pattern, previously associated with the 'warm song of the human heart'.

Pitch structure: diatonicism v. symmetry

The Allegro moderato is characterised by a constant tension between diatonic and symmetrical pitch structures. The duality between diatonicism and pitch symmetry is correlated with other oppositional pairs, such as progression and stasis, linearity and circularity, as well as temporality and spatiality. These problems have far-reaching consequences for the movement's large-scale formal design, which itself reflects the preoccupation with symmetrical construction.

Following analytical graphs are based on a modified Schenkerian notation: 'empty' and 'filled' note heads, note stems of various lengths, slurs, and beams to indicate the hierarchical relationships between pitches that constitute diatonic structures. 'Angular' slurs are used to connect pitches belonging to an interval cycle, that is, symmetrical partitioning of the octave pitch space into equal steps: two tritones (IC6), three 'major thirds' (IC4), four 'minor thirds' (IC3), or six 'whole tones' (IC2), not to mention further possible divisions that are not relevant here. The key pitches of an interval cycle may be 'embellished' by 'neighbour-tones' (indicated by slurs) and passing tones.

The prominence of pitch symmetry is announced at the very beginning of the movement (see Example 4.10) by the appearance of the scissors motive, the shape of which is a typical product of inversional pitch symmetry. The motive first appears centred on D, sliding chromatically in opposing directions towards the tritone C flat – F. Note that this tritone is adjacent to the pedal B flat from above. Then the sinusoid motive appears, which is also based on the principle of symmetry, despite the difference in shape. This motive – as presented by violin 2 – chromatically fills the same tritone space (that between C flat and F) as the scissors motive. The sinusoid motive also appears in the cello, doubled by first violin. Here it is transposed in such a way that it outlines the tritone E flat – B double flat. This tritone neighbours the B flat pedal from below, thus 'balancing out' the tritone C flat – F. This assertion of balance concludes the first small-scale formal unit.

The passage is subsequently repeated, transposed by a perfect fourth, so that the pedal moves to E flat. However, towards the end of the passage, the cello breaks the sinusoid pattern and follows a descending major triad, in which the pedal E flat is the upper fifth. This is the first unambiguously diatonic shape in the movement.

Example 4.10 Pitch symmetry in the opening bars. Score and analytical reduction. Pavel Haas, String Quartet No. 3, Op. 15, 1937–38 (Berlin: Bote & Bock; Prague: Tempo Praha, 1991), first movement, bb. 1–15.

Example 4.11 (which immediately follows the previous extract) demonstrates the ambiguity and interaction between diatonic and symmetrical pitch structures in the first theme. The theme consists of three iterations of the linear motive, based on a diatonic 5^ to 1^ descent in the minor mode, embellished by

Example 4.11 Diatonicism v. symmetry in Theme 1. Score and analytical reduction (fore-ground and middleground). String Quartet No. 3, first movement, bb. 16–22.

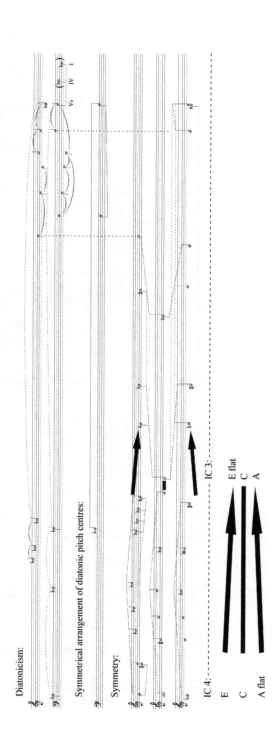

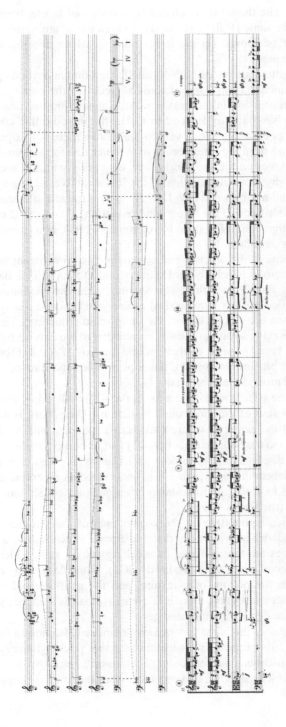

Example 4.12 Problems of continuity in Development 1. Score and analytical reduction (foreground and middleground). String Quartet No. 3, first movement, bb. 32–43.

neighbour notes. The theme is concluded by a cadential figure, based on a tri-adic descent to the tonic (E flat). However, an element of ambiguity is induced by the chromatic 'shadows' (in the lower voices), which accompany each of these diatonic shapes.

The top and bottom staves of both levels (foreground and middleground) of the analytical reductions show the diatonic skeleton of the passage. Although the IV – V – I progression in the bass is rather vaguely implied and ultimately frustrated, as the bass fails to descend to E flat, the melodic line convincingly articulates E flat as the tonic. However, on the whole, there is a large degree of ambiguity resulting from the interference of symmetrical formations (accounted for in the inner staves on the diagram). First, beginning with the second bar of the example, the rhythmic punctuation of the linear motive highlights a whole-tone series descending from A flat to D and – after a transfer of register – back to A flat (see the third line of the foreground reduction). Thus, the D can be seen either as the leading tone in E flat (in the diatonic system), or as a focal point of the symmetrical axis A flat – D.

The tension between diatonicism and symmetry is also apparent in the alter-nation in the first violin part between D natural and D flat ($7^\wedge$ in E flat), as well as F natural and F flat ($2^\wedge$ in E flat). The seemingly random oscillation between these variants is due to their symmetrical arrangement around the symmetrical axis D – A flat (see the second line of the foreground reduction). This, in turn, throws into question the seemingly diatonic character of the closing figure, which is symmetrical in terms of pitch content around the axis of A flat. From this per-spective, the outer pitches D flat and E flat appear to be subordinated to a whole-tone scale formed around the axis A flat – D.

Meanwhile, there is another tritone axis (C flat – F) outlined by the viola (see the second lowest staff of the foreground reduction). The pattern is only broken in the third bar of the example, where viola runs in parallel with the first violin and thus conforms to the other axis (A flat – D) and its corresponding whole-tone scale. The violin displays affinity to both axes (hence its division to two staves in the schema), depending on whether it is understood as a continuation of the chromatic descent in viola (the fifth stave) or an independent stratum of pitches centred around D (the fourth stave).

The higher (middleground) level shows that each of the symmetrically con-ceived strata, sandwiched within the diatonic frame, is centred on a particular pitch. These pitches are those of two interlocking tritone axes, which combine to produce an interval cycle of minor thirds (IC3). Thus, despite the rich voice-leading activity in the polymelodic texture, and the goal-oriented descending tendency of the diatonic stratum, there is an element of stasis induced by this sym-metrical complex underpinning the passage.

Example 4.12 shows the latter part of Development 1, leading to the onset of the second theme. Its purpose is to demonstrate that pitch symmetry does not strictly rule out voice-leading continuity. The passage begins with the familiar scissors motive, which gives rise to a sequential ascent in the first violin to E flat, paralleled from below by the second violin and viola (see the top stave of the foreground reduction). This is followed by a descent from E flat to A flat ($5^\wedge$ to $1^\wedge$ in A flat minor).

Again, however, there is an alternative reading in terms of symmetrical structures (see the three staves below). The initial three bars in first violin can be seen as an IC 3 ascent from E to F flat (an octave above), followed by a whole-tone descent back to E. The second violin and viola follow a similar arch-shaped trajectory, centred on C and A flat, respectively. The three parts thus prolong an interval cycle of major thirds: E – C – A flat.

The next three bars bring a new ostinato, based on the scissors motive, as well as a new iteration of the sinusoid motive. Importantly, the pitches outlined by the two combine to produce a complete interval cycle of minor thirds: C – D sharp – F sharp – A. The following two bars are essentially a transposition of the same material within the interval cycle.

The symmetrical pattern is broken with the assertion of the diatonic cadential figure in the outer voices, descending from A to D ($5^\wedge$ to $1^\wedge$ in D minor). Meanwhile, however, F asserts itself as a modal centre in the inner voices. The assertion of F as the bass pedal marks the beginning of a plagal v – iv – i cadential progression in the bass, which establishes B flat as a tonal centre and thus leads to the onset of the secondary theme (itself marked by plagal character).

Moving to the middle ground (shown in the upper part of Example 4.12), this section begins with the prolongation of an IC4, followed by a prolongation of an IC3. It is significant that there is an apparent voice-leading continuity between the two. The diatonic stratum is quite sparse in this case. There is a prolongation of A flat towards the beginning, followed by a prolongation of D towards the end. On a higher level, A flat and D could be seen as subordinated to F, which initiates the plagal cadence leading to the second theme. It is characteristic of an omnipresent ambiguity that the key pitches in the diatonic stratum are symmetrically arranged.

Problems of continuity, differentiation, and unification

A detailed discussion of the movement's pitch structure on the scale of the whole movement is beyond the scope of this study. Suffice it to say that a continuity of voice leading (in which the standard principle of diatonic linear progression is constantly interfered with by symmetrical structures) can be traced throughout the movement. The following discussion focuses on the 'surface' discontinuities resulting from the juxtaposition of different kinds of thematic material, tempo, texture, and metro-rhythmic configuration. It will become apparent that some sections of the movement are more continuous than others. Arguably, the varying degree of continuity is a significant factor in the movement's formal design.

The montage-like juxtaposition of sharply contrasting formal sections is most apparent in the exposition. Particularly illustrative is the discontinuity of tempo, metro-rhythmics, texture and pitch material, which separates Theme 2 from the surrounding sections (see Example 4.13). There is a degree of formal ambivalence added by the fact that the theme is framed by the reappearance of material referring to the beginning of the movement: the iambic ostinato, the scissors motive, the opening tempo and texture. The use of these 'signposts' to punctuate the form creates the expectation of a recapitulation, which proves to be deceptive time and time again. The movement appears to 'rewind' to its beginning a number of times, only to then go in a different, unexpected direction. This enhances the semblance of discontinuous and non-linear developmental trajectory in the movement.

The recapitulation, on the other hand, is characterised by an increased sense of continuity. This is apparent in Example 4.14, which shows the transition from the second theme to the last developmental section. In this case, there is no 'scissor cut' marking the seam, there is no change of tempo, and all of the motives are presented on the common rhythmic level of crotchets. Rather unusually, the linear and sinusoid motives are cast in a common textural and metro-rhythmic guise. As a result, the three motives are linked into a single, continuous melodic line. As is apparent from the last part of Example 4.14, melodic activity is further enhanced by stretto-like superimposition of the sinusoid motive.

These tendencies grow in strength towards the end of the final developmental section, immediately preceding the recapitulation of the first theme (see Example 4.15). Again, a relatively long, continuous melodic line is created out of three consecutive elided iterations of the sinusoid motive. Note also the accumulation of motivic material, achieved by the superimposition of sinusoid and scissors motives. The beginning of the recapitulation is punctuated by the arrival on the 'tonic' pedal, the return of the iambic ostinato, the scissors motive, and the cadential figure, which facilitates the arrival on the tonic E flat in the upper voice. Unlike in the exposition, this punctuation does not produce a sense of discontinuity because it is 'cushioned' by the continuity of voice-leading and texture, as well as by the anticipation of the scissors motive and the iambic ostinato.

An important aspect of this 'synthesising' tendency in the recapitulation is voice-leading integration of previously distinct and discontinuous material. The upper part of Example 4.15 shows the contrapuntal skeleton underpinning the retransition: the outer voices (the first violin and cello) approach the tonic E flat by a minor-third step from above and below, respectively (by this time, the pitch symmetry of this progression comes as no surprise). Meanwhile, in the inner voices (not shown in the example), there are two more contrapuntal strata: symmetrical (based on the scissors motive) and diatonic (mostly consisting of triadic parallels). Both are contrapuntally related to the top voice (mostly by means of parallel motion) and thus participate in the rich, continuous contrapuntal flow.

Such saturation of texture facilitates a build-up of momentum, which drives the movement to the recapitulation of Theme 1 and eventually to its end. Example 4.16 shows the last bars of Theme 1 and the final cadence. The recapitulation of Theme 1 is underpinned by the tonic pedal E flat (as opposed to the dominant pedal B flat found in the exposition). Again, the theme is concluded by the cadential figure, which is repeated sequentially over the next few bars, prolonging the tonic E flat (as is indicated by the diagonal beam in the example). The example also shows that the sequential iterations of the cadential figure are interspersed with blocks of parallel triads, the roots of which outline a descending B flat major (dominant) triad. In other words, the final cadence takes the form of an interlocking superimposition of the tonic (affirmed by the pedal E flat) and the dominant (the B flat triad). It is also noteworthy that the harmonic dissonance resulting from this superimposition is accompanied by a metric dissonance, induced by the hemiola rhythm which distinguishes the triadic blocks from the surrounding material. Finally, in the last two bars, the iambic ostinato descends to its original, tonic level and eventually comes to a complete stop.

Example 4.13 Discontinuities in the exposition. String Quartet No. 3, first movement, bb. 35–7, 43, 47, 58–9.

Example 4.14 Increased continuity in the recapitulation. String Quartet No. 3, first movement, bb. 102–4, 113–6, 127–9.

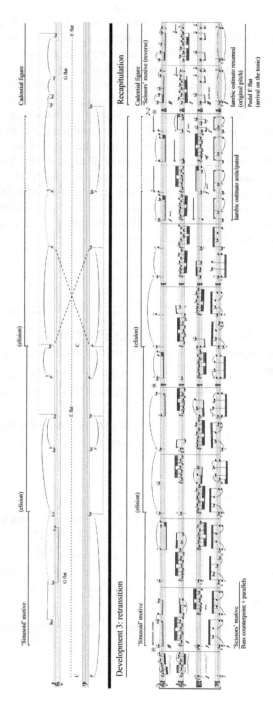

Example 4.15 The final part of Development 3 (a retransition to the recapitulation of Theme 1). Score and middle-ground reduction of the counterpoint of outer voices. String Quartet No. 3, first movement, bb. 136–46.

Example 4.16 The final cadence. String Quartet No. 3, first movement, bb. 150–7.

The movement's 'uncanny' properties

Some of the properties of Allegro moderato observed above have strong relevance to Haas's opera *Charlatan,* the completion of which immediately preceded the composition of the quartet. In fact, some of the motivic material from the opera was used in the quartet. Particularly significant is the case of the 'Lyrical' theme of Allegro moderato, which was not used in the final version of *Charlatan,* but which appeared in a draft of Haas's libretto – specifically on the first page of the so-called Windmill Scene (see Figure 4.12).

The symbolism of this scene will be discussed in Chapter 5 through Freud's notion of the uncanny, which will also be relevant to the analysis of the Four Songs on Chinese Poetry in Chapter 6. Interestingly, some elements of the imagery associated with the uncanny (mirror reflections, shadows, repetition and circular motion) are apparent in the Allegro moderato. The idea of 'mirroring' manifests itself in the preoccupation with symmetry throughout the movement (from the scissors motive to the large-scale 'arch' form). The inseparable association of diatonic motives with their chromatic 'shadows' is another manifestation of the same idea, as is the 'splitting' of syntax into two opposing, yet inseparable layers (diatonic and symmetrical). The aforementioned semblance of multiple returns or rather fleeting 'echoes' of preceding musical material, which appear throughout the movement, resonates with what Freud called 'involuntary repetition' (the 'déjà vu' effect), which is one of the most typical of 'uncanny' phenomena. All these considerations contribute to the anxious atmosphere which characterises the movement.

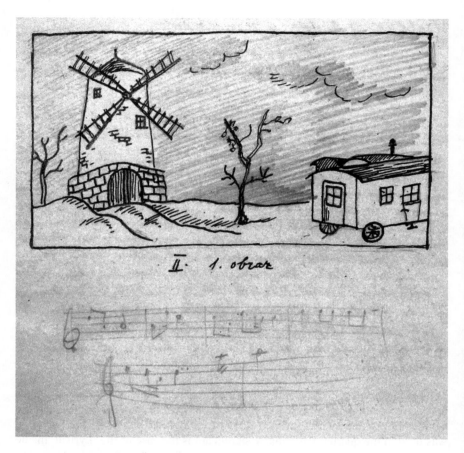

Figure 4.12 Pavel Haas, *Šarlatán: Návrhy libreta* [Charlatan: Sketches of the Libretto],
Department of Music History of the Moravian Museum, sign. B 832. Notebook entitled 'Doktor Bledovous' ('Bledovous' crossed out and replaced with
'Pustrpalk') and marked 'II. verse' ('2nd version'), act 2, scene 1, first page
(no page number).

Source: Reproduced by permission of the Department of Music History of the Moravian Museum.

Conclusion

The previous analyses demonstrate that, in Haas's music, properties of metro-
rhythmics, or *sčasování*, to use Janáček's term, perform many of the formal functions traditionally secured by tonal organisation. Each particular metro-rhythmic
and textural configuration provides context for the appearance of thematic material in a similar way that a key does in tonal music. It can differentiate successive iterations of a single theme as well as unify appearances of distinct themes,
previously associated with different configurations. Furthermore, specific configurations have a strong referential function, which means that their changes and

reappearances help articulate formal structure. Although the use of textures with varying levels of rhythmic activity to distinguish formal sections and to emphasise formal functions is not strictly unique to Haas and Janáček, these strategies gain increased significance in the music of these composers due to the negative effects of fragmentation and repetition on phrase structure and tonality.

A more or less clear tonal plan is discernible in all of the pieces; the effect of recapitulation and cadence relies partly on the restoration and confirmation of a tonal/modal centre established in the first section. Nonetheless, the form-constitutive role of tonality is weakened by Haas's frequent use of fragmentary thematic material (the sequential treatment of which prevents the establishment of extended tonal areas), as well as by his use of symmetrical pitch structures, which interfere with tonal syntax. Features of rhythm, metre, and texture acquire particular importance in these circumstances.

With some modifications, Edward T. Cone's notions of 'stratification', 'interlock' and 'synthesis' are useful to describe characteristic features of Haas's formal designs. Relatively clear examples of stratification can be found in the contrasting, 'lyrical' themes of Haas's string quartets, each of which constitutes a wholly separate stratum, differentiated from the rest of the movement in terms of rhythm, metre, texture, tempo, modality, and type of thematic material. What distinguishes them from 'mere' contrasting themes in the conventional sense is that they are discontinuous (at least on their original presentation) with the surrounding material, from which they are separated by montage-like 'cuts' at both ends. The closest Haas's works get to the interplay between strata described by Cone is in the 'arch' form of the Allegro moderato, where the contrasting theme returns (on a lower rhythmic level) in the second half of the movement.

Haas's use of Janáčekian rhythmic layers in his Study for Strings may function as a means of stratification in Cone's sense; the form can to some extent be regarded in terms of initiation, suspension, and resumption of activity in various rhythmic strata. However, there are some significant reservations. First, the Study for Strings is perhaps the least discontinuous of the pieces studied here, especially since transitions between layers are facilitated by rhythmic 'modulations' based on the augmentation and diminution of motives, as well as hemiola rhythms. Second, the strata are occupied in this particular composition by relatively fully formed themes (the level of fragmentation and repetition is quite low, compared to the material of Stravinsky's blocks). Finally, the movement across rhythmic strata is gradual and cumulative; layers are 'conquered' one by one and the ultimate aim seems to be the simultaneous 'resonance' of all layers. Study for Strings, like 'Landscape', follows a relatively conventional A B A' template, conceived as a linear (or, more precisely, gradual) accumulation of momentum, interrupted in the middle section. This model is conceptually very different from Cone's non-linear, and perhaps even non-narrative, interlocking design, encapsulating some of the most emblematic features of Stravinsky's modernism.

Cone's notion of 'synthesis' is useful to describe Haas's strategies for achieving formal closure. In the recapitulation sections of 'Landscape' and Allegro moderato, previously heterogeneous elements are brought into 'close relation with one another' by finding a common denominator primarily in terms of rhythm, meter, tempo, and/or texture, as well as by horizontal conjunction, vertical superimposition, and contrapuntal integration of motivic fragments. These processes produce an increased sense of continuity, as well as escalation of motivic, rhythmic, melodic, contrapuntal, and textural activity (these elements are, in fact, inseparable).

To some extent, the compositional strategies described here seem to supplement the dynamics of tension and release found in traditional tonal music. In the latter two case studies, the onset of the final section (an abridged recapitulation consisting of the return of one of the themes) is preceded by an accumulation of 'tension' by means of metro-rhythmic, textural, and/or contrapuntal complication. In Theme 3 of the Study for Strings, this is achieved by the superimposition of numerous ostinato patters, which increases the 'metro-rhythmic depth' of the section. In the final section of Development 3 of Allegro moderato (immediately preceding the recapitulation of Theme 1), momentum is accumulated by horizontal linking and vertical superimposition of melodic material, integrated into a dense, chromatic, contrapuntal texture. In both cases, however, the recapitulation of the theme is marked by notable simplification in all of these parameters, which produces a sense of 'release'. All this helps to create a kind of forward-propelling force, which is essential for the creation of formal closure, traditionally facilitated by the teleological drive of tonality.

Whether there is a hierarchical relationship between metro-rhythmic layers on the large scale, analogous to tonal hierarchy, is a separate question. In the first case study ('Landscape'), the use of metro-rhythmic layers serves to gradually increase or decrease dynamic activity in the movement, but the layers do not seem to relate in a hierarchical fashion to any kind of tonic level. In the third case study (Allegro moderato), the movement 'up' and 'down' the rhythmic layers seems to be analogous to the tonal movement in the dominant and subdominant direction, respectively. Interestingly, the tonal and rhythmic hierarchy work against each other in this movement: the second theme appears on dominant and leading-tone tonal levels, but, at the same time, it tends towards the 'subdominant' rhythmic level, since it is based on the same iambic pattern as the pervasive ostinato, 'transposed' to a lower rhythmic layer. This, of course, is a natural result of the second theme's traditional role as the slow and lyrical counterpart of the first theme. For the same reason, the recapitulation cannot occupy the tonic rhythmic level unless the dynamic schema of the movement is reversed ('slow–fast–slow'), which is not the case in any of the pieces studied here.

The sense of hierarchical rhythmic organisation is the strongest in the Study for Strings, where all of the rhythmic layers can be related to a common '*sčasovací* base'. This makes theoretically possible a parallel between metro-rhythmic and tonal space (based on a succession of fifths rooted in the tonal base). The purpose of sonata-form development is to take motivic material through a variety of remote key areas, to traverse multiple levels of the tonal space before settling on its base in the recapitulation. By analogy, the developmental sections in the Study for Strings (the fugues and Theme 3), serve to 'energise', by means of metro-rhythmic transformation of thematic material, numerous levels of the hierarchical metro-rhythmic architecture. Finally, the eventual descent to the basic rhythmic level of semibreves is analogous to the descent to the tonic. Thus, in this piece, more so than in the others, metro-rhythmic processes are capable of relatively independently articulating formal closure.

Notes

1 See extracts from reviews of Haas's works compiled in Michael Losen, 'Pavel Haas. Die Rezeption seiner Werke bis zum Aufführungsverbot 1939' (unpublished master's thesis, Universität Wien, 2006), Anhang G5, pp. 2–3. Translation mine.

2 Pukl, Oldřich, Smaczny, '*Czech Republic*'. *Grove Music Online*, www.oxfordmusiconline.com [accessed 10 May 2010].

3 Lubomír Peduzzi, *Pavel Haas: Život a dílo skladatele* (Brno: Muzejní a vlastivědná společnost, 1993), p. 117.

4 Jascha Nemtsov, 'Zur Klaviersuite op. 13 von Pavel Haas', *Musica Reanimata Mitteilungen*, 17 (December 1995), 20–3 (p. 22). All translations from Nemtsov's article are my own.

5 Ibid., pp. 22–3.

6 Christopher Hasty, 'On the Problem of Succession and Continuity in Twentieth-century Music', *Music Theory Spectrum*, 8 (1986), 58–74.

7 Ibid., p. 62.

8 Gretchen G. Horlacher, *Building Blocks: Repetition and Continuity in the Music of Stravinsky* (New York: Oxford University Press, 2011), p. 32.

9 Jonathan Cross, *The Stravinsky Legacy* (Cambridge: Cambridge University Press, 1998), pp. 10–11. Richard Taruskin has traced the origins of this technique to the Russian folk practice of singing 'popevki' – repetitive tunes that are 'inherently static, iterative, open-ended, noncadential (hence tonally suspensive, recursive, infinitely extendable)'. See Richard Taruskin, *Stravinsky and the Russian Traditions: A Biography of the Works Through Mavra*, 2 vols. (Oxford: Oxford University Press, 1996), ii, p. 1363, quoted in Horlacher, *Building Blocks*, p. 37.

10 Ibid., p. 10. Cross also invokes Richard Taruskin's notions of 'drobnost'' ('"splinteredness"; the quality of being formally disunified, a sum-of-parts') and 'nepodvizhnost'' ('immobility, stasis; as applied to form, the quality of being nonteleological, nondevelopmental'). See Taruskin, *Stravinsky and the Russian Traditions*, ii, pp. 1677–78, quoted in Cross, *The Stravinsky Legacy*, p. 10.

11 Ibid., p. 89.

12 Ibid., p. 11. Cross refers to Arthur C. Wenk, *Claude Debussy and Twentieth-Century Music* (Boston: Twayne, 1983) and Derrick Puffett, *Papers in Musicology, 4: 'Debussy's Ostinato Machine'* (Nottingham: University of Nottingham, Dept. of Music, 1996). See also Derrick Puffett, 'Debussy's Ostinato Machine', in *Derrick Puffett on Music*, ed. Kathryn Puffett (Aldershot: Ashgate, 2001), 231–85 (p. 263). Italics in Cross's original; exclamation mark in Puffett's original.

13 Josef Berg, *K Janáčkovu skladebnému projevu* [On Janáček's Compositional Idiom] (Brno: Společnost Leoše Janáčka, 1991). The essay was written as early as 1948 but remained unpublished until 1991.

14 Ibid., p. 10. All translations from Czech sources are mine, unless stated otherwise.

15 Ibid., pp. 10–1. Berg draws on Janáček's terminology: 'nápěv' (singular form of the word) translates conveniently as 'tune'; however the translation 'vocal melody' would be more appropriate since it reflects the etymological link with 'zpěv' ('singing'). There is also related to a more familiar term of Janáček's, that of 'nápěvky mluvy' ('nápěvky' is the dimminutive of 'nápěvy'; 'mluvy' is the genitive of 'mluva' – 'speech'), which is

usually translated as 'speech melodies'. The term *sčasovka* will be explained later along with Janáček's concept of *sčasování*, which is also linked to 'nápěvky mluvy'.

16 Gretchen Horlacher, 'The Rhythms of Reiteration: Formal Development in Stravinsky's Ostinati', *Music Theory Spectrum*, 14/2 (Autumn 1992), 171–87, p. 180.

17 Berg, *K Janáčkovu skladebnému projevu*, p. 11.

18 The term was coined in the 1960s and 1970s by Czech composers and theorists Miloš Štědroň, Miloslav Ištvan, Ctirad Kohoutek, and Alois Piňos, most of whom were involved in pioneering the techniques of electro-acoustic music, hence their interest in the cinematic techniques of Sergei Eisenstein. The term was also adopted by John Tyrrell. See Miloš Štědroň, *Leoš Janáček a hudba 20. století: paralely, sondy, dokumenty* [Leoš Janáček and Twentieth-Century Music: Parallels, Probes, Documents] (Brno: Nadace Universitas Masarykiana, 1998), pp. 147–56.

19 Berg, *K Janáčkovu skladebnému projevu*, p. 10.

20 Ibid., p. 25. Italics mine.

21 Ibid., p. 26.

22 Ibid., p. 19.

23 Edward T. Cone, 'Stravinsky: The Progress of a Method', in *Perspectives on Schoenberg and Stravinsky*, ed. Benjamin Boretz and Edward T. Cone (New York: W.W. Norton, 1972), 156–64 (p. 156).

24 Ibid., pp. 157–8.

25 Ibid., p. 157.

26 Berg, *K Janáčkovu skladebnému projevu*, pp. 27–29. Berg's terms are 'sjednocení/diferenciace tematiky' and 'sjednocení/diferenciace faktury'.

27 The translation 'in-time-putting' has been suggested in Jiří Fukač, 'Janáček and the Dance of "Categories"', in *Janáček and Czech Music: Proceedings of the International Conference (Saint Louis, 1988)*, Studies in Czech Music No. 1, ed. Michael Beckerman and Glen Bauer (Stuyvesant NY: Pendragon Press, 1995), 371–88 (p. 387).

28 Jarmil Burghauser, 'Hudební metrika v Janáčkově teoretickém díle' [Musical Metrics in Janáček's Theoretical Works], in *Sborník prací Filosofické Fakulty Brněnské University*, series H (Řada hudebně vědná/Musicological Studies), 33–4 (1984–85), 137–53 (p. 138). See also Michael Beckerman, *Janáček as Theorist* (Stuyvesant NY: Pendragon Press, 1994), p. 82.

29 See Leoš Janáček, *Úplná nauka o harmonii* [Complete Theory of Harmony], in *Teoretické dílo: Články, studie, přednášky, koncepty, zlomky, skici, svědectví, 1877–1927*, ed. Leoš Faltus, Eva Drlíková, Svatava Přibáňová, and Jiří Zahrádka, 2 vols. (Brno: Editio Janáček, 2007–08), ii/1 (2007), 459–661 (p. 462). Translation mine; emphasis in the original; (de)italicisation of 'sčasování/sčasovací/sčasovka' mine. For a slightly different translation see Beckerman, *Janáček as Theorist*, pp. 82–3.

30 Berg, *K Janáčkovu skladebnému projevu*, p. 15.

31 Ibid.

32 Ibid., pp. 29–30, 35.

33 Ibid., pp. 16, 35.

34 See Beckermann, *Janáček as Theorist*, p. 83.

35 Zdeněk Blažek, 'Leoš Janáček o skladbě a hudebních formách na varhanické škole v Brně' [Leoš Janáček on Composition and Musical Forms at the Organ School in Brno], *Opus musicum*, 20/4 (1988), 107–11 (p. 107).

36 Janáček uses idiosyncratically the adjective 'časový', which literally translates as 'temporal'. It seems, however, that 'časový' is used interchangeably with 'sčasovací' in this case, for which reason I prefer to translate it as 'rhythmic'.

37 Janáček, *Úplná nauka o harmonii*, p. 605.

38 Leoš Janáček, 'Základy hudebního sčasování' [Basics of Musical *Sčasování*], in *Teoretické dílo (Theoretical Works)*, ii/2 (2007–2008), 13–131 (p. 25). Janáček's thoughts on the origins of metre in the interaction of rhythmic strata resonate with the ideas put

forward by Maury Yeston, as summarised by Harald Krebs in the following quotation: 'Yeston defines musical meter as "an outgrowth of the interaction of two levels – two differently-rated strata, the faster of which provides the elements and the slower of which groups them." In other words, a sense of meter can arise only when a given stratum of regular pulses is associated with a slower stratum that organizes the pulses into equivalent groups.' See Harald Krebs, 'Some Extensions of the Concepts of Metrical Consonance and Dissonance', *Journal of Music Theory*, 31/1 (Spring 1987), 99–120 (p. 100); Krebs quotes Maury Yeston, *The Stratification of Musical Rhythm* (New Haven CT and London: Yale University Press, 1976), p. 66.

39 See Janáček, 'Základy hudebního sčasování', pp. 15–26.

40 Ibid., pp. 16–17.

41 Ibid., pp. 25–6.

42 Take for example the way Janáček described the inspiration behind his 1923 string quartet, in a letter to Kamila Stösslová (14 October 1924): 'I imagined a poor woman, tortured, beaten, beaten to death, as portrayed by the Russian writer Tolstoy in his work Kreutzer Sonata.' Quoted in Milan Škampa's preface to the following edition of Janáček's quartet: Leoš Janáček, String Quartet no. 1, 'Inspired by Tolstoy's Kreutzer Sonata', 1923 (Prague: Supraphon; 2nd edn, revised by Milan Škampa, 1982).

43 Berg, *K Janáčkovu skladebnému projevu*, p. 16.

44 Ibid. A similar point was made by Czech musicologist Jaroslav Jiránek, who argued that the tendency in Janáček's music to repetition and harmonic stasis is due to Janáček's 'desire to grasp [. . .] *the uniform mood of the life moment* [a moment in life]'. See Jaroslav Jiránek, 'The Controversy between Reality and Its Living in the Work of Leoš Janáček', in *Janáček and Czech Music: Proceedings of the International Conference (Saint Louis, 1988)*, Studies in Czech Music No. 1, ed. Michael Beckerman and Glen Bauer (Stuyvesant NY: Pendragon Press, 1995), 365–70 (p. 368), emphasis in the original.

45 Blažek, 'Leoš Janáček o skladbě a hudebních formách na varhanické škole v Brně', p. 107. The opposite of 'formace vývojová' ('developmental formation') is 'formace seřadná', which is an ambiguous, idiosyncratic term. The adjective 'seřadná' could be translated as 'ordered' or 'additive'.

46 Haas, 'Haasův kvartet "Z opičích hor"', 106. Emphasis on 'movement' ('pohyb') in the original.

47 Trills are also highly characteristic of Janáček's textures. Berg regards trill as a special case of *sčasovka* because it functions as a 'vehicle of mood': 'From Janáček's perspective it always signifies tensions, this effect stems from its association with whirling, unrest [. . .] the same holds true of tremolo'. See Berg, *K Janáčkovu skladebnému projevu*, p. 17.

48 Note the markings in the Boosey & Hawkes score: 'crotchet = semibreve' in b. 143 and 'quaver = minim' in b. 160.

49 The idea of hierarchically organised metro-rhythmic space has been explored in analyses of selected pieces by Brahms. See particularly David Lewin, 'On Harmony and Meter in Brahms's Opus 76 No. 8', *Nineteenth-Century Music*, 4/3 (1981), 261–5; Richard Cohn, 'Complex Hemiolas, Ski-Hill Graphs, and Metric Spaces', *Music Analysis*, 20/3 (2001), 295–326; and Scott Murphy, 'On Metre in the Rondo of Brahms's Op. 25', *Music Analysis*, 26/3 (2007), 323–53. My approach is different in that I focus primarily on the activity of rhythmic layers. While I take into account metric groupings on the level of individual bars, I do not believe Haas's Study for Strings (and the other works studied in this chapter) can be analysed in terms of hypermetric organisation (which is essential to the analyses referenced above) because of the fragmentary and repetitive nature of Haas's thematic material (discussed in the following paragraphs).

50 Michael Beckerman, 'Klein the Janáčkian', in *Musicologica Brunensia*, 44/1–2 (2009), 25–33 (pp. 28–9).

51 Michael Beckerman, 'Haas's *Charlatan* and the Play of Premonitions', *The Opera Quarterly*, 29/1 (2013), 31–40.
52 Thomas Herbert Mandl, liner notes to *Janáček, L.: String Quartet No. 2, 'Intimate Letters'/Haas, P.: String Quartet No. 2*, CD recording by Petersen Quartet (EDA Records, 1999). Available at www.eda-records.com/177-1-CD-Details.html?cd_id=62 [Accessed 21 May 2018]. Translation as in Jory Debenham, 'Terezín Variations: Codes, Messages, and the Summer of 1944', unpublished Ph.D. thesis (Lancaster University, 2016), p. 83.

Bibliography

General bibliography

Agawu, Kofi V., 'Stravinsky's "Mass" and Stravinsky Analysis', *Music Theory Spectrum*, 11/2 (Autumn, 1989), 139–63.
Beckerman, Michael, *Janáček as Theorist* (New York: Pendragon Press, 1994).
Beckerman, Michael and Glen Bauer, eds., *Janáček and Czech Music: Proceedings of the International Conference (Saint Louis, 1988), Studies in Czech Music No. 1* (Stuyvesant NY: Pendragon Press, 1995).
Berg, Josef, *K Janáčkovu skladebnému projevu* (Brno: Zprávy společnosti Leoše Janáčka, Vol. 6, 1991).
Blažek, Zdeněk, 'Janáček – učitel', *Opus musicum*, 18/3 (1986), 65–71.
Blažek, Zdeněk, 'Leoš Janáček o skladbě a hudebních formách na varhanické škole v Brně', *Opus musicum*, 20/4 (1988), 107–11.
Burghauser, Jarmil, 'Hudební metrika v Janáčkově teoretickém díle', in *Sborník prací Filosofické Fakulty Brněnské university*, 32–33 (1984), 137–53.
Carter, Chandler, 'Stravinsky's "Special Sense": The Rhetorical Use of Tonality in "The Rake's Progress"', *Music Theory Spectrum*, 19/1 (Spring 1997), 55–80.
Code, David J., 'The Synthesis of Rhythms: Form, Ideology, and the "Augurs of Spring"', *The Journal of Musicology*, 24/1 (Winter 2007), 112–66.
Cohn, Richard, 'Complex Hemiolas, Ski-Hill Graphs, and Metric Spaces', *Music Analysis*, 20/3 (2001), 295–326.
Cohn, Richard, 'Inversional Symmetry and Transpositional Combination in Bartók', *Music Theory Spectrum*, 10 (Spring 1988), 19–42.
Cone, Edward T., 'Stravinsky: The Progress of a Method', in *Perspectives on Schoenberg and Stravinsky*, ed. Benjamin Boretz and Edward T. Cone (Princeton NJ: Princeton University Press, 1968), 156–64.
Cross, Jonathan, *The Stravinsky Legacy* (Cambridge: Cambridge University Press, 1998).
Čurda, Martin, 'Druhý smyčcový kvartet Pavla Haase: mezi Janáčkem a Ravelem', *Opus musicum*, 42/4 (2010), 29–46.
Čurda, Martin, 'Smyčcové kvartety Pavla Haase z 20. let' (unpublished bachelor's thesis, Masaryk University, 2010).
Debenham, Jory, 'Terezín Variations: Codes, Messages, and the Summer of 1944', unpublished Ph.D. thesis (Lancaster University, 2016).
Fukač, Jiří, 'Janáček and the Dance of "Categories"', in *Janáček and Czech Music: Proceedings of the International Conference (Saint Louis, 1988)*, Studies in Czech Music No. 1, ed. Michael Beckerman and Glen Bauer (Stuyvesant NY: Pendragon Press, 1995), 371–88.

Hasty, Christopher, 'On the Problem of Succession and Continuity in Twentieth-century Music', *Music Theory Spectrum*, 8 (1986), 58–74.

Horlacher, Gretchen Grace, *Building Blocks: Repetition and Continuity in the Music of Stravinsky* (New York: Oxford University Press, 2011).

Horlacher, Gretchen Grace, 'The Rhythms of Reiteration: Formal Development in Stravinsky's Ostinati', *Music Theory Spectrum*, 14/2 (Autumn 1992), 171–87.

Janáček, Leoš, 'Úplná nauka o Harmonii', in *Teoretické dílo: Články, studie, přednášky, koncepty, zlomky, skici, svědectví, 1877–1927*, ed. Leoš Faltus, Eva Drlíková, Svatava Přibáňová, and Jiří Zahrádka, 2 vols. (Brno: Editio Janáček, 2007–08), ii/1 (2007), 459–661.

Janáček, Leoš, 'Můj názor o sčasování (rytmu)', in *Teoretické dílo: Články, studie, přednášky, koncepty, zlomky, skici, svědectví, 1877–1927*, ed. Leoš Faltus, Eva Drlíková, Svatava Přibáňová, and Jiří Zahrádka, 2 vols. (Brno: Editio Janáček, 2007–08), ii/1 (2007), 361–421.

Janáček, Leoš, 'Základy hudebního sčasování', in *Teoretické dílo: Články, studie, přednášky, koncepty, zlomky, skici, svědectví, 1877–1927*, ed. Leoš Faltus, Eva Drlíková, Svatava Přibáňová, and Jiří Zahrádka, 2 vols. (Brno: Editio Janáček, 2007–08), ii/2 (2007–08), 13–131/

Jiránek, Jaroslav, 'The Controversy between Reality and Its Living in the Work of Leoš Janáček', in *Janáček and Czech Music: Proceedings of the International Conference (Saint Louis, 1988)*, Studies in Czech Music No. 1, ed. Michael Beckerman and Glen Bauer (Stuyvesant NY: Pendragon Press, 1995), 365–70.

Kielian-Gilbert, Marianne, 'The Rhythms of Form: Correspondence and Analogy in Stravinsky's Designs', *Music Theory Spectrum*, 9 (Spring 1987), 42–66.

Kielian-Gilbert, Marianne, 'Stravinsky's Contrasts: Contradiction and Discontinuity in his Neoclassic Music', *The Journal of Musicology*, 9/4 (Autumn 1991), 448–80.

Krebs, Harald, 'Some Extensions of the Concepts of Metrical Consonance and Dissonance', *Journal of Music Theory*, 31/1 (Spring 1987), 99–120.

Lewin, David, 'On Harmony and Meter in Brahms's Opus 76 No. 8', *Nineteenth-Century Music*, 4/3 (1981), 261–5.

Limmer, Martin, 'Studien zur motivischen Arbeit im Werk von Pavel Haas' (unpublished Ph.D. dissertation, Universität Mozarteum Salzburg, 2013).

Mandl, Thomas Herbert, liner notes to *Janáček, L.: String Quartet No. 2, 'Intimate Letters'/Haas, P.: String Quartet No. 2*, CD recording by Petersen Quartet (EDA Records, 1999). Available at www.eda-records.com/177-1-CD-Details.html?cd_id=62 [Accessed 21 May 2018].

Mawer, Deborah, *Darius Milhaud: Modality and Structure in Music of the 1920s* (Aldershot: Scolar Press, Ashgate Publishing, 1997).

Murphy, Scott, 'On Metre in the Rondo of Brahms's Op. 25', *Music Analysis*, 26/3 (2007), 323–53.

Peduzzi, Lubomír, *Pavel Haas: Život a dílo skladatele* (Brno: Muzejní a vlastivědná společnost, 1993); for German translation see *Pavel Haas: Leben und Werk des Komponisten*, trans. Thomas Mandl (Hamburg: Bockel, 1996).

Perle, George, 'Symmetrical Formations in the String Quartets of Bela Bartók,' *Music Review*, 16 (1955), 300–12.

Puffett, Derrick, 'Debussy's Ostinato Machine', in *Derrick Puffett on Music*, ed. Kathryn Puffett (Aldershot: Ashgate, 2001), 231–85.

Rehding, Alexander, 'Towards A "Logic of Discontinuity" in Stravinsky's "Symphonies of Wind Instruments": Hasty, Kramer and Straus Reconsidered', *Music Analysis*, 17/1 (1998), 39–65.

Štědroň, Miloš, *Leoš Janáček a hudba 20. století. Paralely, sondy, dokumenty* (Brno: Nadace Universitas Masarykiana, 1998).

Tyrrell, John, *Janáček: Years of Life*, 2 vols. (London: Faber and Faber, 2006–07), ii: *(1914–1928), Tsar of the Forests* (2007).

Ullmann, Viktor, and Ingo Schultz, *26 Kritiken über musikalische Veranstaltungen in Theresienstadt* (Hamburg: Bockel Verlag, 1993).

Waters, Keith, *Rhythmic and Contrapuntal Structures in the Music of Arthur Honegger* (Aldershot: Ashgate, 2002).

Wingfield, Paul, 'Janáček, Musical Analysis, and Debussy's "Jeux de vagues"', in *Janáček Studies*, ed. Paul Wingfield (Cambridge: Cambridge University Press, 1999), 183–280.

Musical editions

Haas, Pavel, String Quartet No. 2 'From the Monkey Mountains', Op. 7, 1925 (Prague: Tempo; Berlin: Bote & Bock, 1994).

Haas, Pavel, String Quartet No. 3, Op. 15, 1937–38 (Berlin: Bote & Bock; Prague: Tempo Praha, 1991).

Haas, Pavel, Studie pro smyčcový orchestr, 1943 (Berlin: Bote & Bock; Prague: Tempo Praha, completed and revised by Lubomír Peduzzi, 1991).

Janáček, Leoš, String Quartet No. 1 'Inspired by Tolstoy's Kreutzer Sonata', 1923 (Prague: Supraphon; 2nd edn, revised by Milan Škampa, 1982).

Janáček, Leoš, String Quartet No. 1 'Inspired by Leo Tolstoy's "Kreutzer Sonata"', 1923 (Prague: Bärenreiter Praha, 2007; ed. Leoš Faltus and Miloš Štědroň).

5 Haas's *Charlatan*

A tragi-comedy about old comedians, modern individualists, and uncanny doubles

Introduction

Charlatan, Haas's first and only opera, was composed between May 1934 and June 1937, and premiered in Brno on 2 April 1938.[1] In a newspaper interview published a week before the premiere, the composer introduced the work as follows:

> I had been thinking about writing an opera for a long time [but] it was not until 1934 that I found a subject which appealed to me. It depicts the itinerary life of a seventeenth-century doctor-charlatan. [. . .] The variegated subject, the attractive setting in which the story takes place, the comedy and drama of adventurous stories – all this captivated me so [strongly] that I started the work with joy and enthusiasm. [*Charlatan*] is a musical tragi-comedy; it switches from grotesque [farcical] to tragic situations. The story tells about the life of the itinerant quack [. . .] Pustrpalk, who performed in fairgrounds, and depicts, to put it shortly, the fame and fall of this adventurer.[2]

Charlatan's premiere marked the climax of Haas's career. The reviews were overwhelmingly positive and expressed high hopes for the composer's further works in this genre.[3] Haas was complimented for the opera's dramatic traction and forward-propelling dynamism (enhanced by Janáčekian musical diction), effective use of contrasts and twists, and apt portrayal of individual characters.[4] Haas was also praised for the opera's effective orchestration and original musical language, combining Janáčekian features (rhythmic energy, declamation, and the use of short, repetitive motives at the expense of broad melodic units and enclosed arias) with historicising elements suggestive of a seventeenth-century fairground (diatonic modality and occasional use of strophic songs).[5]

Later that year, Haas received the prize of the Smetana Foundation for his achievement in *Charlatan*.[6] His professional success was paralleled by happy family life, as demonstrated in the above-mentioned newspaper interview by a photograph of the composer holding his infant daughter Olga (born on 1 November 1937). However, Haas's professional and personal life were soon to be drastically affected by the rapidly deteriorating political situation. The annexation of Austria by Nazi Germany in March 1938 was followed by the so-called Munich

Agreement in September 1938, which paved the way for the German occupation of Czechoslovakia in March 1939. In the newly established Protectorate of Bohemia and Moravia, Haas's music could no longer be performed due to the composer's Jewish origins. Since *Charlatan* was the last major work of Haas's to be performed prior to the occupation, it also marks the end of the composer's public career.

These historical circumstances have influenced the interpretation of the work. In a recent article entitled 'Haas's *Charlatan* and the Play of Premonitions', Michael Beckerman highlights the opera's ambivalent, tragi-comical genre, arguing that a proper reading of *Charlatan* 'refuses to take the work at face value' and seeks its true meaning under the comic 'facade'.[7] In order to 'peel away some of the layers of [this] facade', Beckerman continues, one must look to the practices of Terezín composers who 'used a range of codes, from expressive topoi such as funeral dirges to quotations from such works as Suk's *Asrael symphony*, the Verdi *Requiem* [etc.]' in order to create 'reverse Potemkin villages', that is, seemingly innocuous pieces of music with 'subversive cores' perceptible to the 'insiders'.[8] Crucially, Beckerman suggests that 'it was not only Haas's Terezín works that were written in such a manner, but [. . .] his opera as well'.[9] In his view, Haas's *Charlatan* functions as a 'premonition' of the monstrosities of Nazism:

> In *The Charlatan* a crowd robotically chants "Long Live Pustrpalk!" [the 'charlatan'] as if aping a Nazi spectacle; a miller is burned alive in his mill while crowds sing outside; Pustrpalk kills a Catholic priest, probably unintentionally; [a] vanished village [. . .] presages the Nazi liquidation of Lidice in 1942 [as retribution for the assassination of the Reich-Protector Reinhard Heydrich]. The framing of these events raises potent questions about Haas's state of mind during the opera's composition, and the figure of the Charlatan looms large as the most enigmatic aspect of the work.[10]

Beckerman's approach is not without problems. While it is plausible to suggest that Haas reflected the ominous rise of Nazism (well underway at the time of the opera's composition) and perhaps even made 'a kind of projection based on contemporary reality',[11] the retrospective mapping between fictional and historical events (intriguing as it may be) is hard to justify, as is the view of *Charlatan* through the lens of Terezín. The danger here is that the context might completely overwhelm the text, so to speak, and impose upon it a particular kind of interpretation.

On the other hand, Beckerman made some highly insightful observations, which the following analysis will elaborate upon. For example, he was right to draw attention to the theme of disturbing 'premonitions' and to the opera's 'enigmatic' nature. As will be shown, premonitions, omens, curses, mysterious malevolent forces, and other features associated with the notions of the uncanny and the fantastic, play an important role in the opera and in its literary source. In a way, Beckerman's essay is a case of transference of some characteristic literary themes and devices from the text itself to the meta-textual level of its critical reflection.

Beckerman also aptly characterised the ambiguity of Pustrpalk's character and its affinity with various literary models:

> [Pustrpalk's] character as conceived by Haas purposely incorporates some of the greatest 'actors' to walk the world stage. In the opening scene he appears as Don Giovanni, seducing the beautiful Amarantha, wife of a 'professor' [. . .]. He later becomes a kind of Napoleon, a dictator in confrontations with his troupe, and seems to channel Faust in his confrontation with the priest. [. . .] At the beginning of the opera's final scene, his men refer to him conspicuously as 'Don Quixote' [. . .]. [. . . Pustrpalk's] many aspects combine to create a classic archetype.[12]

Indeed, Pustrpalk's affinity with the literary types of Don Juan, Faust, and Don Quixote (three of Ian Watt's 'myths of modern individualism') will help to explain many aspects of the story – especially the moral issues it raises.[13] On the other hand, the archetypes and theatrical practices of the *commedia dell'arte* will prove relevant to the comic facet of Haas's tragi-comedy. The following examination of the opera's literary sources, their dramatic adaptation, and musical setting will yield a nuanced view of this enigmatic work.

Winckler's *Doctor Eisenbart*: genre and themes

The principal literary source of Haas's opera is the novel *Doctor Eisenbart* (first version published in 1929) by the German writer Josef Winckler (1881–1966), which describes the adventures of the famous itinerant physician of the Baroque era, Johann Andreas Eisenbart (1663–1727).[14] Interestingly, Haas never officially acknowledged this was the case. During his work on the libretto, he gradually removed all references to German geographical locations and even changed the name of the main character to Pustrpalk.[15] In Peduzzi's view, this was an intentional disguise necessitated by the so-called Nuremberg Laws (introduced in Germany in 1935), which, as he explains, 'ruled out the collaboration of a German writer with a Jewish composer'.[16]

Winckler's book is quite ambivalent in terms of genre. It consists largely of anecdotal stories, often based on the strophes of the once familiar German song *Ich bin der Doktor Eisenbart*.[17] This song belongs to the genre of satirical songs sung in the fairground for popular amusement, possibly illustrated by humorous pictures such as those included in Winckler's book (see Figure 5.1).

Correspondingly, Eisenbart appears partly as a folk buffoon from a popular jest-book. He states early in the book that his 'only true medicine is humour' and, indeed, most of his 'cures' are little more than pranks played on his patients, who came almost exclusively from the higher social ranks: nobility, clergy, and rich townsmen.[18]

However, contrary to his Harlequinian stage persona, Eisenbart also has the facet of an intellectual driven by desire for scientific and philosophical knowledge and a self-assured surgeon with proven skills, which he is accordingly proud of.

Figure 5.1 llustration to Chapter 23: 'How Eisenbart cured the Gluttony Count' (by drill-
ing him a second anus).

Source: Winckler, *Eisenbart*, p. 302.

There are a number of 'reflective' passages in the book in which Eisenbart con-
templates the philosophical underpinning of medicine and science. Here Eisenbart appears as a tragic figure with a strong affinity with Faust, which will be
discussed later on. Eisenbart is also portrayed as a transitional figure between the
'old' age of superstition (he is keen on horoscopes and obsessed with collecting
pickled human eyes) and the rational, scientific rigour of the Enlightenment.

Winckler's novel reflects the questionable reputation surrounding itinerant
quacks and the ambivalence that their association with fairground entertainment
tended to shed on their medical skills. As M.A. Katritzky explains:

> Quacks such as Johann Andreas Eisenbart [. . .] drew heavily on publicity
> and spectacle to create and bolster their celebrity persona. But ultimately
> their success rested on their medical track records [. . .] in routine procedures
> regarded by the medical establishment as undignified, such as tooth care or
> venereal disease management, or potentially dangerous [procedures], such as
> cataract, hernia and bladder-stone surgery.[19]

Correspondingly, Winckler's Eisenbart, having no officially recognised education, is looked down upon by university-trained doctors. He reciprocates the
disdain but, at the same time, he aspires to gain recognition for his medical skills.
Moreover, Eisenbart's 'dishonourable' itinerant fairground practice using a troupe

of comedians as a means of commercial promotion elicits contempt from the 'respectable' townsmen and the church, not to mention restrictions from political authorities. Eisenbart is thus portrayed as an anti-establishment figure, proudly defying social and political constraints.

The overarching narrative of Winckler's otherwise episodic book is based on Eisenbart's love affair with a young lady called Amarantha, who leaves her husband (a respectable professor) to travel with Eisenbart, although he is himself married to a woman called Rosina. Midway through the book, Amarantha disappears without a trace. Eisenbart is left in the dark as to the reasons for her disappearance, tormented by speculations that Amarantha may have left him for another man – perhaps one with less questionable social and professional status.[20] It is not until one of the last chapters that Eisenbart manages to find Amarantha in the home of her husband. By that time, however, Eisenbart is an old, dying man, unable to pursue the affair any further.

The other narrative line spinning throughout the book is Eisenbart's ongoing struggle against the intrigues of the monk Jochimus, who is a friend of Amarantha's husband. Jochimus embodies the narrow-minded morality of bourgeois society by which Eisenbart is castigated and to which he stands in opposition. In his vicious pursuit of Eisenbart, Jochimus resorts to bribery and all kinds of machinations in order to bring the 'charlatan' to 'justice'.[21] Even the disappearance of Amarantha turns out to be Jochimus's doing: during their final encounter, Amarantha reveals to Eisenbart that she was abducted by Jochimus and forcefully returned to her husband.

Ironically, Jochimus comes to seek Eisenbart's help towards the end of the book when he becomes mortally ill. More ironically still, he dies during an operation, casting a shadow of doubt over Eisenbart's medical skills and moral integrity. This is despite the fact that Eisenbart apparently genuinely tried to save the monk's life; he did not even know that Jochimus was responsible for the abduction of Amarantha at the time of the operation. In his last days, Eisenbart is haunted by feelings of guilt and bitter disappointment. The complex questions concerning the nature of Eisenbart's guilt and the reasons for his declining fate will be the subject of further discussion.

Eisenbart/Pustrpalk and the myths of modern individualism

In terms of character type, Eisenbart is closely affiliated to Don Juan, Faust, and Don Quixote – three of Ian Watt's 'modern individualists'. The figure of Faust is most directly relevant, because its numerous literary representations relate (more or less loosely) to the historical figure of Georgius Faustus, a wandering magician, necromancer, and astrologer, who was widely known in Germany in the first four decades of the sixteenth century.[22] Faust's itinerant existence and disputable reputation present an obvious parallel with Eisenbart. In fact, the split in Eisenbart's character between a folk buffoon and a tragic hero is prefigured by the 1587 *Faustbuch*, which, like Winckler's book, was for the most part an episodic compilation of miscellaneous stories about magic tricks and farcical feats attributed to Faust.[23]

In Goethe's *Faust* the element of farcical folk humour is suppressed in favour of the portrayal of Faust as a gloomy intellectual, a tragic embodiment of humanity's struggle for knowledge and power. The Faustian problem is articulated in an episode from Winckler's novel which Haas did not include in his opera but which is well worth mentioning: Eisenbart's encounter (framed as a nightmarish dream) with Ahasverus, the Wandering Jew, condemned to plodding the Earth eternally.[24] Having met the lamenting Ahasverus beside the road, Eisenbart decides to relieve him from his pain and punishment in a radical way – by cutting his legs off. Ahasverus rejoices: 'You have thwarted God's curse; you have wrested me from God's vengeance!'[25] Eisenbart, full of pride, puts Ahasverus 'on public display [. . .] as the greatest triumph of his brilliant art, which has circumvented heaven and hell and snatched the offering from the furious cosmos!'[26] The trick seems to have worked for several days, but one night Eisenbart's caravan starts to move, pulled by Ahasverus walking on his stubs into a horrendous nocturnal landscape.[27] When Eisenbart wakes up, the lesson he takes from this nightmare is that he must 'quickly turn away from monstrous cures before it is too late'.[28] He feels that he had become too intoxicated with his self-assurance and fame; that he has to temper his tendency to transgress the principles of nature, fate, and ethics, or else he will face eternal damnation.

On another level, the encounter with Ahasverus may reflect on Eisenbart's itinerant lifestyle.[29] In fact, as Watt points out, all of the modern individualists live solitary and itinerant lives outside social structures and moral constrictions.[30] Eisenbart also possesses the 'monomania' of modern individualists who 'are not particularly interested in other people; they are completely engaged in their own individual enterprise; they are defined by whatever they have somehow decided to do or be'.[31] Towards the beginning of Winckler's book, Eisenbart proclaims himself an heir of the medieval vagrants and a prophet of a 'new era [. . .] of freedom in the world'.[32] Both the novel and the opera contain a direct reference to Eisenbart/Pustrpalk as the 'Don Quixote of medicine'.[33] The character's individualist, monomaniacal, and transgressive features will help to explain the reasons behind Eisenbart/Pustrpalk's downfall.

Charlatan **and the legacy of fairground theatre**

To shed light on the farcical aspect of the story, it is useful to draw attention to the legacy of 'illegitimate' fairground theatre, which is strongly embedded in the narrative. Haas, who participated in a strand of early twentieth-century avant-garde work preoccupied with topoi and practices of *commedia dell'arte* and other forms of 'unofficial theatre' (including circus, carnival, pantomime, and the like), was undoubtedly aware of the presence of these elements in Winckler's novel.[34] It is also no coincidence that the composer 'rechristened' Eisenbart as Pustrpalk – a character in the anonymous fourteenth-century Czech play known as *Mastičkář* (literally a 'quack ointment seller').

Mastičkář is part of a broader literary tradition – the so-called merchant scene, which developed as a secular appendix to medieval Easter liturgical plays. The merchant scene relates to the description of *Visitatio sepulchri* in the Gospel of

Mark: 'when the Sabbath [after the crucifixion] was past, Mary Magdalene, and Mary the mother of James, and Salome, had bought sweet spices, that they might come and anoint [the body of Jesus]'.[35] According to Katritzky, the merchant scene, which is characterised by 'humour based squarely on profanities, scatology and sexual misconduct',[36] exploits the rhetoric and comic routines of 'the harangues and theatrical shows offered by marketplace quacks', which represent 'the earliest, most long-standing and most successful form of commercial promotion'.[37] Katritzky thus argues that, in the Middle Ages, quackery and popular theatre went hand in hand, coexisting in mutually beneficial symbiosis. Eisenbart's troupe, which at the peak of its activity comprised over a hundred comedians, musicians, and other assistants, was one of the most spectacular and also one of the last examples of this practice.[38]

The cast of *Mastičkář* includes the quack called Severin, his wife, and his servants Rubín and Pustrpalk. The essence of the play is satirical ridicule of the master by the servants and comic squabbling between the husband and his wife. Importantly, Katritzky argues that the merchant scene prefigures the most significant comic archetypes underpinning popular theatre:

> The quack's assistant Rubin is often identified as a forerunner of the stage fools of the itinerant professionals, such as the English troupes' Pickelhering or Jean Potage, or the Harlequin or Zanni of the Italian *commedia dell'arte* [. . .]. In fact, many centuries before the *commedia dell'arte* developed its characteristic improvised stock comic stage business, or *lazzi*, the merchant scene featured stock roles with predictable verbal, visual and physical comic routines, and the clear potential for improvisation. Taken as a whole, its three main roles, the quack couple and their servant, herald the central *commedia dell'arte* trio of master, servant and inamorata [. . .].[39]

Indeed, in Winckler's novel, Eisenbart's troupe includes the characters of Pickelhering and Jean Potage, whose specific identities are nonetheless obscured in Haas's libretto by translations of their names: Zavináč (literally 'Rollmop') and Kyška (literally 'Sour Soup'). The other characters in the troupe include Bakalář ('Bachelor', originally Bakkalaureus, a theology student and Eisenbart's closest companion), Pavučina (literally 'Cobweb', originally Spinnfresser), and Provazochodec (literally 'Ropewalker', originally Seiltänzer).

However, the archetypes identified by Katritzky also manifest themselves on the 'higher' level of Winckler's (and Haas's) narrative. Most of the characters remain 'within' their archetypal comic roles even when encountered 'off stage', that is, when they are not involved in their ('stage-within-stage') fairground production. Winckler reduced Eisenbart's wife from a 'real' historical character (Anna Rosina Albrecht, described by Katritzky as a 'woman with a successful itinerant healthcare record', who effectively functioned as Eisenbart's 'business partner') to the comic archetype of a bossy wife.[40] The reference to Socrates's wife Xanthippe ('Xantippa') is made in *Mastičkář*, as well as in Winckler's book and Haas's opera.[41] Amarantha is the Columbine of this story, whose arrival establishes another archetype of farce: the love triangle.

The character of Amarantha's husband (the Professor) is marginal in Winckler's novel and does not appear at all in Haas's opera, apart from in references made by Amarantha and Jochimus. The Professor functions as the tip of the other love triangle (Eisenbart/Pustrpalk – Amarantha – Professor) and as the oppositional counterpart of Eisenbart/Pustrpalk: an academically sanctioned scientist and virtuous member of the social establishment. Haas goes further than Winckler in stereotypical reduction of this character as he replaces Winckler's relatively neutral name 'Professor Lautenschläger' with 'Profesor Puntičkář' ('Hairsplitter'), aptly translated by Pavel Drábek as 'Professor Meticuloso'.[42]

Eisenbart/Pustrpalk alternates between a number of archetypes in rapid succession: within his troupe, he is the master, frequently satirised by his servants; in his marriage with Rosina, he plays the role of a hen-pecked husband; and his affair with Amarantha makes him look like a foolish old man, blinded by desire for a young bride. He approaches the archetypes of Dottore and/or Pantalone in his self-important demeanour and the pride he takes in his knowledge and wealth. When Eisenbart/Pustrpalk persuades Amarantha to join his troupe, he effectively steals her from her husband, thus becoming a kind of Harlequin. This facet of his character is further enhanced by his role as an arch-comedian and, in the broadest sense, an anti-establishment figure keen on ridiculing the respectable, wealthy, and powerful. However, in relation to Amarantha, Eisenbart/Pustrpalk increasingly appears less as Harlequin and more as Pierrot – a melancholic dreamer hopelessly in love with Columbine, who is typically lured away by Harlequin.

The first act

The Fairground Scene (Act 1, Scene 1)

The first act remains unambiguously within the comic genre, suggesting little about the tragic turns to come. The opening scene brings the audience to the middle of a fairground performance by Pustrpalk's troupe.[43] Haas's brief orchestral overture sets the scene effectively, evoking the opening scene of Stravinsky's *Petrushka* (performed in Brno in 1923). A dance-like ostinato is the basis for a superimposition of distinct metric and motivic layers – mostly repetitive melodic fragments of diatonic or pentatonic nature. Thus, as Haas himself claimed in the above-mentioned newspaper interview, the music 'has folk-like ['lidový'] character' and serves to 'illustrate the historical setting of the story', while 'using modern means of expression'.[44] The composer specified this point in his commentary on the orchestral suite from the opera:[45]

By using thematic material rooted in diatonicism and periodicity, I wish to draw closer to the historical, popular nature of the subject. [. . .] I should like to point out that the music's overall folk-like character ['lidovost'] is not conceived in terms of folklore but rather along the lines of a popular street song or fairground tune, tinted by classicising historicity.[46]

Example 5.1 Pentatonic ostinato and anticipation of the Peregrination Song (see Example 5.4). Haas, *Šarlatán*, piano reduction (Department of Music History of the Moravian Museum, sign. A 22.688), p. 1.

Example 5.2 The 'fairground' theme. Haas, *Šarlatán*, piano reduction (DMH MM, sign. A 22.688), p. 2.

The overture does not constitute a self-contained 'number'; it flows seamlessly into Kyška's summoning of the audience: 'Come, come! People! This world will trap you with its charms!'[47] At the same time, a (non-diegetic) trumpet call cuts through the orchestral texture and mutes the multitude of overlapping voices that illustrate the soundscape of the fairground. The performance begins with Kyška (tenor) and Pavučina (bass) exchanging humorous and characteristically satirical stories about their master's healing practices. Once a crowd of spectators has gathered, Pustrpalk (baritone) himself makes his appearance, accompanied by (diegetic) fanfares, and addresses the people in a solemn voice: 'Ladies and gentlemen! I'm the famous Pustrpalk!'

With the exception of several strophic songs illustrating the fairground setting, the whole opera is based on prosaic text, set to music in Janáčekian declamatory style. Like Janáček, Haas avoided enclosed arias in order not to interfere with the realistic pace of dramatic action. As the composer explained, 'the overall style of the opera is certainly influenced by rapid changes of situation, contrasts of character, and ceaseless movement [in the drama]'.[48] Naturally, such declamatory approach is particularly suitable for the depiction of stage-within-stage fairground performances.

Pustrpalk's performance, which follows closely (often word for word) Winckler's description of the scene, contains some of the typical routines through which

historical quacks, in Katritzky's words, 'demonstrat[ed], by natural or supernatural means, [their] personal authority over death'.[49] Correspondingly, Pustrpalk
saves the life of a snake-bitten boy and awes the audience by performing the
snake-charmer's dance with a poisonous snake (accompanied by music of an oriental flavour). He then proceeds to demonstrate the power of 'Theriak', a miraculous universal antidote. He feeds a pill of arsenic to a volunteer (doubtlessly a
disguised member of Pustrpalk's company), whom he revives with Theriak, gathering enthusiastic applause from the audience.

The return of the opening ostinato (with the associated motivic material) in
the orchestra indicates that one part of the scene has come to an end. Although
the opera is not divided into conventional 'numbers', Haas punctuates the overall form (much like in his instrumental music) by reintroducing familiar ostinato
patterns in the 'accompaniment', even when there is no sense of thematic return
in the 'melodic' voices. This may be what the composer had in mind when he
claimed: 'There are no arias [in the opera], but I tried to create certain melodic
units in the orchestra.'[50]

At this point, according to Haas's stage directions, the monk Jochimus appears
among the spectators; his presence is supposed to be conspicuous visually, but he
remains silent (for now) and his arrival is not associated with any new orchestral
music.[51] At the same time, Zavináč announces the arrival of a carriage carrying
a beautiful lady. The appearance of Amarantha on stage is accompanied by a
lyrical theme marked by sensuous chromaticism, wide melodic leaps, and slow,
graceful motion (see Example 5.3). Suggestive of cinematic romance, the theme
seems to suspend time in a way that corresponds with the transfixing beauty

Example 5.3 Amarantha's theme. Haas, *Šarlatán*, autograph score (DMH MM, sign. A
         22.687 a), p. 61.

of Amarantha. Indeed, Pustrpalk's response to Amarantha's self-introduction is 'enveloped' by her theme (continuing in the orchestra), which suggests that he is 'under her spell'.

Amarantha's theme takes on a comic character as Pustrpalk starts the preparations for his prankish cure. The lady, who has been unable to move 'since a bad fright, at a troubled childbirth', springs to her feet (to the crowd's great amusement) when she is made to sit in a large basket filled with nettles.[52] While Pustrpalk helps Amarantha take her first steps, he persuades her to join his company as a 'concubine'.

Pustrpalk is applauded enthusiastically. However, the crowd's cheering ('Praise him!'), accompanied by the fairground theme, is suddenly disrupted by the protest of the monk Jochimus (baritone): 'Silence! You scheming fraud! I'll denounce you right now!'[53] The monk's words resonate ominously in total silence. After momentary bewilderment, Pustrpalk 'composes himself and smiles contemptuously'. As Jochimus walks away, the crowd 'turns after him with a threatening hiss'.[54] Correspondingly, the music continues from where it stopped, leading seamlessly to the second scene through a brief orchestral interlude.

Peregrination Song (Act 1, Scene 2)

The second scene illustrates the wandering lifestyle of the troupe. On the stage, the scenery depicting various towns and landscapes moves behind the static caravans. An off-stage male choir sings in unison a strophic Peregrination Song, accompanied by orchestral variations.

The song (which has no textual precedent in Winckler's novel) paints a romanticising image of the itinerant life of Pustrpalk's troupe, putting an emphasis on cyclic temporality (travelling 'from dusk to dawn', 'from winter to summer', for

Example 5.4 Peregrination Song. Haas, *Šarlatán*, piano reduction (DMH MM, sign. A 22.688), pp. 46–7. Transcription mine.

'days, weeks, months, years') and the death-defying, redemptive power of laughter (an echo of Haas's earlier, Poetism-inspired works):

[. . .]

Dny, týdny, celé měsíce,
ba roky dlouhé jdou.
Zázračný doktor Pustrpalk
s divou svou spřežinou.

[. . .]

Po celý den jen vtipkuje
i se svou družinou.
Takoví lidé, věřte nám,
ti nikdy nezhynou.

Ať je doba dobrá nebo zlá,
na rtech měj stále smích.
Do pláče vždycky času dost
v hodinách posledních.

Kdo věčně mračí se jak čert,
ten ať jde do háje.
Kdo zpívá, jásá, zná i žert,
ten přijde do ráje!

[. . .]

For days on end, for weeks – whole months,
nay, for years they travel on.
The magical Doctor Pustrpalk
with his wild companions.

[. . .]

And all day long he's full of jests,
and so are all his mates.
Such people, as you may be sure,
will never die away.

In good times, and in bad times too,
have a smile upon your face.
There still is time ahead for tears,
in our final days.

Who is always sulking and all frowns,
let them vanish from our eyes;
while they who sing, rejoice and jest
will come to Paradise![55]

The Crinoline Episode (Act 1, Scene 3)

The third scene opens on the square of another city.[56] The company is apparently about to leave, waiting for the return of the ladies (Amarantha has gone to the tailor's shop and Rosina to the market). Amarantha enters in an excessively wide crinoline, which makes it impossible for her to get inside the caravan. Pustrpalk and Bakalář try to help her get in with comic clumsiness. Suddenly, Jochimus appears again and explains that he is a friend of the respectable Professor, to whom Amarantha is married. He objects to her association with what he regards as dishonourable company and is outraged at Pustrpalk's indifference to his moralising rebuke. He retreats with a threat on his lips.

When Rosina comes back, she finds Pustrpalk kneeling before Amarantha, as he is trying to squeeze the crinoline to make it pass through the caravan's narrow door. A comic fight breaks out between the two women. As a crowd of laughing onlookers starts gathering, Pustrpalk cuts the crinoline with his scalpel, pushes Amarantha inside the caravan and shouts out a command for departure. As the company leaves hurriedly, Jochimus reappears and 'climbs on the roof of one of the caravans'; sitting with 'his legs hang[ing] down', he 'makes a threatening gesture with his fists' and shouts 'Vengeance! Vengeance!' while the assembled 'audience, laughing, waves goodbye to them all.'[57] This concluding scene, although it does not take place on an actual stage, effectively becomes a farcical performance.

The Windmill Scene (Act 2, Scene 1)

The Windmill Scene is a turning point in *Charlatan*; it makes clear that the opera will not be as unambiguously comic as the first act suggested. Its nocturnal setting, which contrasts with the preceding daytime scenes, has deeper symbolic meaning as part of a string of correlated binary oppositions: light/darkness, comedy/tragedy, public/private, overt/covert, and so on. Haas's stage directions provide the first hints of the scene's haunted, mysterious atmosphere:

> Flat, bleak landscape. Towards the left [. . .] there is an abandoned windmill with a large gate. Spring night. Clouds pull across the sky. [. . .] Towards the mill, there is a bare tree. [. . .] Pustrpalk sits on the steps of a caravan, deep in thought. Amarantha leans against the tree.[58]

The dark, melancholic character of the scene is conveyed musically by a slow-moving chromatic ostinato, confined to a claustrophobic tritone ambit and accompanied by a lament-like chromatic descent in the bass. The ostinato seems to reflect Pustrpalk's 'thoughtful' state of mind in its slow, repetitive,

Figure 5.2 Haas's drawing of the scene

Source: Haas, *Šarlatán*, autograph score (DMH MM, sign. A 22.687 b), unnumbered first page. Reproduced by permission of the Department of Music History of the Moravian Museum.

cyclic motion. Pustrpalk's speech emerges seamlessly from his silent rumination (see Example 5.5):

> There, there, used to be a village . . . And the Swedes set it on fire, ravaged it all, turning it to ruin. Misery seized all the land, all the country. Just the mill, that's all that's left now. Now only the old miller's fighting his coming death. Delirious, and raving. His young beautiful niece attending to his illness. Other than that the mill is a desolate place. Except for armies of bats and mice. The old miller is on fire. An inner fire is scorching him. The poor man's raving in madness . . .[59]

Pustrpalk's mood suddenly changes with the appearance of the moon:

> The moon emerges from behind the clouds, flooding the whole landscape with silver glare. Pustrpalk becomes absorbed in his thoughts. Suddenly he gets up. He walks around for a while, thinking. Then he stops by Amarantha and takes her firmly by her hand.[60]

As if hypnotised by the moonlight, Pustrpalk confesses to Amarantha his uncontrollable passion for her: 'I can't control myself any longer! You've set my feelings all on fire! You are a castaway star! You're like a radiating fire, divine, or even infernal! Hear me now! Hear me now!'[61] Pustrpalk's excitement is musically conveyed by the marking 'Appassionato' and by a 'trembling' ostinato figure, supported by timpani beats.

From the midst of this rapture emerges a tender declaration of love: 'My dragon sweet, God's Paradise! You're a blooming fiery flash of lightning, Amarantha dear!'[62] The tone of the music correspondingly changes (see Example 5.6): marked 'poco piu largamente' and 'dolce', the passage is characterised by sensuous chromaticism, ambivalence between major and minor modes (perhaps

Example 5.5 Pustrpalk's entry. Haas, *Šarlatán*, autograph score (DMH MM, sign. A 22. 687 b), p. 186.

Example 5.6 Pustrpalk's declaration of love (the 'sweet dragon' theme). Haas, *Šarlatán*, piano reduction (DMH MM, sign. A 22.688), p. 80.

reflecting the bitter-sweet torment of love) and ascending gestures in the accompaniment (suggestive of the elevation of the spirit to the heights of 'paradise'). There are notable similarities with Amarantha's theme from the first act, namely the marking 'largamente' with slow minim beat, and the broad, chromatically embellished melodic line with a penchant for repeated notes.

Amarantha is surprised, questions the durability of his feelings for her, and urges Pustrpalk to control his feelings. This, however, only exacerbates his excitement: 'No! No! I'll be even worse still! Like a demon bad! All evil I'll have brought about shall be all your own fault! I'm like a man possessed!'[63] With these ominous words, the 'appassionato' marking returns, along with the fast tempo and the 'trembling' pattern, with an extra beat (a blast of timpani and brass) added for emphasis at the end of each bar.

When Pustrpalk embraces Amarantha passionately, she breaks from him and bids him good night. On her way, she 'gracefully drops a handkerchief', which Pustrpalk picks up and presses to his lips as a token of her inclination.[64] A comic element is added when Rosina appears on the roof of one of the caravans, equipped with a telescope. As the two lovers leave, Rosina waves the telescope in a threatening gesture.[65] As Pustrpalk-Pierrot climbs inside his caravan, the moon, too, 'disappears partly behind the clouds', leaving the scene 'dark and empty'.[66]

An unexpected chain of events starts when two of the comedians appear on stage and conspire to steal Pustrpalk's money. In accord with the stereotypical master–servant comic routine, Pustrpalk overhears their scheming and takes them by surprise with a pistol. However, Pustrpalk's witty scolding of his cunning servants gradually transforms, somewhat surprisingly, into a monologue, in which Pustrpalk extols the beauty of the troupe's companionship and the nobility of their quest: 'And yet we form a troupe and a brothers' guild, just like a pack of wolves. [. . .] We are a touring faculty, and follow with assiduity our common goal, our only precious goal, participating in one fate!'[67]

To the astonishment of the perpetrators, Pustrpalk decides to make a magnanimous gesture of camaraderie – to divide all his money between his companions. This decision is the turning point of the whole scene. The comedians start a wild revelry, during which an alcohol-fuelled fight breaks out. The mad old miller, irritated by the uproar, throws a lantern into the crowd of fighting men and kills Zavináč. In retribution, the comedians set the windmill on fire. Pustrpalk flees the scene with Amarantha, accompanied only by Bakalář, his closest servant.

This tragic turn of events gives rise to one of the most powerful instances of the grotesque in Haas's oeuvre. This, however, is not an instance of the life-affirming, Bakhtinian 'carnivalesque-grotesque' character, found in Haas's earlier works. Rather, it is designed to convey a sense of emotional disturbance, a mixture of merriment and horror: the comedians sing cheerfully while the miller burns to death (see Example 5.7). What the audience hears is the comedians' music, a simple, major-mode, march-like song, accompanied by percussion instruments. Since the song is meant to be diegetic (there are musicians on the stage among the comedians), it does not reflect the horror experienced by Pustrpalk and Amarantha. The disturbing incongruity and emotional ambiguity effectively convey the scene's violent madness to the audience.

It is noteworthy that Haas praised the dramatic effect of such juxtapositions in his newspaper review of Shostakovich's *Lady Macbeth of the Mtsensk District*, performed in Brno on 30 April 1936:

> [Shostakovich's] fierce expression masters the [dramatic] situation, using a broad and long affective scale, ranging from gut-wrenching brutality to lyrical tenderness and from the depths of hopeless sorrow to grotesque caricature. Completely oppositional affects are often not only juxtaposed, but even mutually entangled and wedged into each other. These masterful scenes are particularly effective and hugely persuasive. Take for example the scene in which a ragged and drunk muzhik discovers Izmailov's corpse. At the tragic moment of the scene (monologue) appears in a ferocious fortissimo a banal and vulgar hackneyed song. This stunning moment, in my view, is the most boisterous climax of the work.[68]

The Windmill Scene raises a number of questions: Does Pustrpalk's 'obsession' with Amarantha have anything to do with the tragic turn of events? If so, in what way? Why does Pustrpalk decide to share all his money with the comedians, who just tried to rob him? Is his own reasoning plausible? Why does the old miller get so upset that he kills one of the comedians? Is his reported madness a satisfactory explanation? What is the nature of his madness anyway? And why should there be any mention of his 'young' and 'beautiful' niece, who plays no role in the scene whatsoever? Is the image of the burnt village merely an illustration of the destruction following a recent war? Is the whole spectacle of horror to be taken at face value, or does it have some kind of symbolic significance?

Example 5.7 The comedians' song: 'Long live our glorious lord! Long live all those with him on board! [. . .] [(In the window of the mill appears the head of the miller, who screams desperately. Everyone waves at him.)] Long live our reverend lady Rosina! Hurrah! Hurrah! Hurrah! [(Everyone leaves the scene joyfully.)]'[69]. Haas, *Šarlatán*, piano reduction (DMH MM, sign. A 22.688), p. 131.

Winckler's version of the Windmill Scene

Answers to most of these questions can be found by comparing Haas's version of the scene with the relevant chapters of Winckler's book. The Windmill Scene is based mostly on the chapter entitled 'The Events in the Old Mill and What a Disturbance of Spirits Was Unleashed Here'.[70] References to omens, premonitions, and ghosts occur throughout Winckler's book, but they are particularly prominent in the 'Windmill' chapter. The burning of the windmill appears to be a fulfilment of an earlier omen. The previous chapter, entitled 'The Apocalyptic Journey: Eisenbart's First Despair', starts with the description of Eisenbart's unease resulting from an unsettling dream:[71]

> Eisenbart [. . .] could not find any sleep and gazed up into the starry sky, because he had dreamt the previous night that his whole caravan burnt. He opened the Dreambook of Apomasaris [. . .] and read in Chapter 159: '[. . .] when one dreams about a house burning down, the owner of the house or its occupier will be ruined by war or illness'.[72]

Indeed, Eisenbart's business is badly affected by the misery inflicted upon German cities (described in some detail in this chapter) by war. At the beginning of the 'Windmill' chapter, the dream comes back to Eisenbart, as he travels through the land, hoping to find refuge at some peaceful corner:

> As he crouched, his chin propped up by his fists, at the front of the rattling wagon, going further and further, he was unable to suppress an oppressive nightmare and saw in a dream all of the caravans fearfully burning and the whole troupe being burnt alive. [. . . He] huddled like a shivering ghost: 'That means Death! Death! Death!'[73]

Shortly afterwards, the troupe arrives at the windmill. The first draft of the Windmill Scene in Haas's libretto begins at this point, closely following Winckler's book. Originally, the history of the place is not narrated by Pustrpalk himself, but by Kyška/ Jean Potage: 'Does my sight fail me? Is it a dream? Was it here? There used to be a village. The Swedes burnt it down. I lay wounded in this mill.'[74] The questioning of the border between reality and illusion in these words contributes to the scene's otherworldly character, which is enhanced by Bakalář's/Bakkalaureus's warning that 'ghosts and spectres inhabit abandoned mills'.[75] The delirium of the dying miller completes the horror-like picture: 'The sick miller [. . .] in a delirium of epilepsy believed he heard ghosts and pressed himself motionlessly against the wall'.[76]

All of these details are compressed into Pustrpalk's opening speech in the final version of Haas's libretto. Pustrpalk's declaration of love to Amarantha, the dialogue of the two plotters, and Pustrpalk's ensuing monologue follow closely Winckler's original and remained essentially unchanged throughout Haas's work on the libretto. One of the noteworthy alterations made in later versions of the libretto, however, is the virtual elimination of the character of the miller's niece. Originally, it was she who overheard the dialogue of the plotters and came to warn Eisenbart.[77]

Winckler's version offers more insight into Eisenbart's private thoughts. Having been told about the plot, Eisenbart lies awake, awaiting the robbers, and gets absorbed in self-reflection, thinking that 'he has not been a good master [and] a caring father [but] only a selfish, greedy man [. . . who] healed fewer than he capitalised on'.[78] This might illuminate his motivation to share his wealth with the members of his troupe.

Winckler's account of the following revelry differs from Haas's adaptation in that Pickelhäring/Zavináč is killed in the fight that breaks out among the drunk comedians – not by the mad miller.[79] Nonetheless, the miller's throwing of a lantern among the comedians, which only happens moments later, becomes an incentive for the comedians to set the mill alight.[80] Amarantha and Eisenbart do not flee in Winckler's version; they, too, get carried away by the upsurge of collective madness.[81] The two only decide to run away from the troupe two chapters later.[82]

Winckler's description of the fire contains a sublime image of the burning mill, which Haas included in the first draft but later dropped:

> [As the windmill was gradually consumed by fire,] the wings started turning to the left [. . .] and the horrendously beautiful, fantastic spectacle unfolded

with ever-increasing speed: the mill waved around itself and reached up to the sky with fiery arms and the giant, burning cross rotated through the darkness.[83]

This image captures the fantastically horrifying and grotesque atmosphere of the scene. It also brings to mind Green and Swan's observation that the combination of spinning motion and fairground imagery (merry-go-rounds, barrel organs) constitutes an Expressionist topos, signifying 'chaos', 'a whirlpool into which the self is in danger of plunging'.[84]

The rest of Winckler's chapter is occupied by Eisenbart's contemplation over Pickelhering's dead body, concerned with the unknown secrets of life and death, the dead man's 'evil look', and the 'curse' which lies upon the unfortunate place:

> [Eisenbart] suddenly thought about Pickelhering's 'evil look', constantly discussed among the fellow travellers – and, blimey, may there be something to it? When the moon exerts influence upon the body, when the spirit ascends all the way to the eyes, why should not the powers of evil spirits flow along? Perhaps through the feet by means of the earth's magnetism, since the land is cursed . . .?[85]

Eisenbart's thoughts suggest that the 'cursed' place (retaining the evil spirit of war) inspires violence and madness in all that set foot upon it – hence the miller's madness, the comedians' fight, and the destruction of the windmill. The whole scene thus functions as a memento of the horrors of war, which Winckler graphically described in the preceding chapter.

Haas's version of the Windmill Scene: an alternative reading

Haas's version retains the vague sense of the involvement of some kind of dark power, corrupting the sanity of the characters, but this menace is associated less directly with the war. Haas's libretto does not make it entirely clear whether the war is ongoing or whether it is a matter of the past, and there are no direct references to the war in any other scene of the opera's final version.[86]

Instead, the possibility arises that the mysterious force may be rooted in Pustrpalk's love affair with Amarantha. This theme is foregrounded at key moments of Haas's dramatic adaptation of the scene, which begins with Pustrpalk's rendezvous with Amarantha and ends with the two lovers fleeing together from the scene of horror, abandoning the rest of the troupe. The love affair is also one of the main reasons behind the plot against Pustrpalk. The two robbers (Zavináč and Pavučina) reveal in their dialogue that they want to steal Pustrpalk's money because they suspect (not incorrectly) that he will soon run away with Amarantha to live a comfortable, sedentary life and leave the troupe to their own devices.[87] Finally, Pustrpalk's words 'All evil I'll have brought about shall be all your own fault! I'm like a man possessed!

I swear! Amarantha dear!' seem to function as an omen of the impending tragedy (as Eisenbart's nightmares about fire did in Winckler's original).

Many aspects of the Windmill Scene lend themselves to interpretation through the concept of the uncanny. According to Nicholas Royle's definition,

> the uncanny [. . .] is concerned with the strange, weird and mysterious, with a flickering sense (but not conviction) of something supernatural. The uncanny involves feelings of uncertainty, in particular regarding the reality of who one is and what is being experienced. Suddenly, one's sense of oneself [. . .] seems strangely questionable. It is a peculiar commingling of the familiar and unfamiliar.[88]

One of the characteristic uncanny phenomena described by Sigmund Freud in his seminal essay is 'involuntary repetition'.[89] Freud gives the example of being lost in the forest and coming again and again to 'one and the same spot, recognisable by some particular landmark'.[90] Pustrpalk's arrival at a place (distinguished by the windmill) which is evidently familiar to him on his travels across the German lands may be an example of such 'involuntary repetition'. Another case in question is the recurring motive of fire in Winckler's book: Eisenbart's repeated dream functions as an omen, which comes true with the destruction of the windmill. Moreover, the Windmill Scene, which is suspended between reality and illusion, is in itself a kind of nightmarish premonition, foreshadowing further tragedies that come later in the opera.

Another typical feature of the uncanny mentioned by Freud is the presence of 'doubles', including 'reflections in mirrors', 'shadows', 'guardian spirits', and so on. Freud points out that these images can have various meanings: duplication of the self may signify fear of death; mirror reflection may be related to 'the function of observing and criticizing the self and exercising a censorship within the mind'; the double may also represent 'unfulfilled but possible futures [. . .], all those strivings of the ego which adverse external circumstances have crushed'.[91]

The best candidates for Freudian doubles in the Windmill Scene are the characters of the mad old miller and his young, beautiful niece. Neither of these obscure figures speaks or even appears on stage in the final version of Haas's libretto, with the significant exception of the miller's intervention in the comedians' fight and his intermittent appearances in the window of the mill. It is also intriguing that Haas did not remove the reference to the miller's niece, even though he crossed out all of her lines in the second draft of the libretto. It is a striking 'coincidence' that the first reference to the 'mad old miller' and his 'young beautiful niece' is made by Pustrpalk (immersed in his 'thoughtful' or perhaps 'self-reflective' mood) during his rendezvous with Amarantha. I suggest that the miller functions as Pustrpalk's double, a critical, self-censoring projection of the self as a 'delirious and raving', moribund old man, 'scorched by an inner fire', that is, by a pathological desire for Amarantha, whose alias is the 'young beautiful niece'. Moments later, Pustrpalk uses similar terms to express his passion for Amarantha: 'I can't control myself any longer! You've set my feelings all on fire! You are a castaway star! You're like a radiating fire, divine, or even infernal!'

There is a subtle hint of this 'doubling' in Haas's musical setting. Most of Pustrpalk's monologue about the destroyed village is based on the four-note ostinato and lament-like descending chromatic lines. However, the mention of the miller and his niece is immediately preceded by an anticipation of the 'sweet dragon' theme that would later underpin Pustrpalk's above described declaration of love (see Example 5.6).

As noted above, Pustrpalk's sudden outburst of passion for Amarantha coincides with the appearance of the moon (and the reappearance of the 'sweet dragon' theme). The moon may have various meanings. In Winckler's novel, it is associated with a mysterious power, which draws 'evil spirits' out of the 'cursed land' into one's head. In the context of this amorous episode, the moonlight makes Pustrpalk appear as a moonstruck Pierrot. However, the moon may also function as a symbol of reflection (or self-reflection) and the reverse side of all things (moonshine is the 'inauthentic' reflection of sunshine). In this case, all of these meanings seem to overlap. Pustrpalk/Pierrot struggles with the uncontrollable and ultimately destructive force of his passion for Amarantha/Columbine, which is initially projected outwards in the figure of the delirious miller and subsequently reflected back (by the moon) onto himself.

If this is the case, however, then the whole scene (including details of landscape, characters, and events) potentially becomes a symbolic portrayal of Pustrpalk's disturbed subjectivity. For example, the silhouette of the windmill, which dominates the landscape, can be understood as a representation of a phallus. The fact that the miller and his young niece are confined to the phallic object seems to affirm their allegorical nature. This 'symbolic' perspective does not quite take priority over the 'realistic' perspective, but it cannot be entirely dismissed either. The effect produced by this irresolvable ambiguity is encapsulated in concept of the fantastic, described by Lucie Armitt as a 'borderline phenomenon', 'a site of hesitancy, uncertainty and disquieting ambivalence' which results from questioning the boundary between the 'real' and the 'imaginary'.[92]

The question is to what extent the Freudian perspective helps to explain the ensuing tragic events. Such interpretation would be based on the premise of Pustrpalk's above-mentioned inner conflict between two contrary tendencies: to continue his itinerant life within the troupe or to break away with Amarantha, associated with the vision of a settled life. In other words, the love affair with Amarantha is in conflict with Pustrpalk's individualistic, monomaniacal quest for an undefined ideal ('We are a touring faculty, and follow with assiduity our common goal, our only precious goal, participating in one fate!').

Pustrpalk's surprising gesture of camaraderie towards his troupe is accompanied by a shadow of anxiety, ostensibly motivated by fear of his wife: 'Let us make a pact now, a brotherhood treaty [. . .]. [But] my wife must not ever get to find out that I've divided all! [(The moon shines.)]'[93] As the appearance of the moon suggests, this may be another case of uncanny doubling: Pustrpalk's fear of Rosina (the 'Xanthippe') may be a projection of his anxiety resulting from his inner conflict between his allegiance to the 'brotherhood' on the one hand and Amarantha on the other.

Significantly, Pustrpalk's first attempt to calm the comedians down ('Silence! Silence! Don't wake up my wife!'), is accompanied by the return of the opening ostinato, associated with Pustrpalk's rendezvous with Amarantha and his narration about the burnt village and the mad miller (see Example 5.8).[94] Besides, there are prominent instances of musical 'mirroring', which may refer to Pustrpalk's conflicted subjectivity and/or to the doubling of Rozina and Amarantha. The opening ostinato (see Example 5.5) consists of a four-note chromatic ascent, mirrored by a corresponding chromatic descent (disguised by the re-ordering of pitches); on its return (see Example 5.8), the pattern is extended, giving rise to longer (six-note and eight-note) progressions.

Pustrpalk's ever-increasing anxiety is disproportional to the ostensible husband–wife conflict. In his second attempt to temper the escalating revelry, he cries 'Silence!' (his exclamation is accompanied by three loud blows of the timpani) and, 'startled by his own voice, he glances fearfully back towards the carriage in which Rosina sleeps'.[95] His following utterance ('Just be quiet, quiet, unless my wife should take us by surprise!') is, again, accompanied by symmetrical voice leading and menacing beats on the timpani.[96]

As noted above, in Haas's final version, Zavináč is killed directly by the mad miller, not by another comedian. This detail is of great significance for the reading proposed here, since it can be regarded as an instance of another class of uncanny phenomena, which Freud refers to as 'omnipotence of thought' or 'wish fulfilment'.[97] The miller's violent reaction against the comedians' rioting appears to be a continuation of Pustrpalk's previous efforts to calm them down. Moreover, when the miller is regarded as Pustrpalk's double, representing his unrestrained

Example 5.8 Return of the opening four-note motive. Haas, *Šarlatán*, piano reduction (DMH MM, sign. A 22.688), pp. 106–7: ('Silence! Silence! Don't wake up my wife! And mind you, not a word now! My wife must not know about it!').

desire, his disapproval of the celebration of 'brotherhood' appears as the manifestation of Pustrpalk's will to dissociate himself from the troupe and devote himself completely to Amarantha. Conversely, the comedians' destruction of the windmill is an attack on Pustrpalk's libido, a symbolic act of castration.

Whether the tragic outcome of the Windmill Scene is understood as a memento of the deadly fury of war, or as a Freudian allegory of Pustrpalk's pathological sexuality, it is surely more than a simple image of the rioting of a group of drunken rogues. Not only is there a strong sense of foreboding leading up to the the outbreak of violence, but this event itself seems to prefigure a series of further adverse events, which will ultimately lead to Pustrpalk's ruin. The reversal of euphoric into dysphoric mood will become a fixed pattern: Pustrpalk's success in the King's city will be spoilt by the disappearance of Amarantha. His seemingly successful operation on Jochimus will result in the monk's death and Pustrpalk's defamation. Finally, the merriment of Pustrpalk's song in the concluding scene will be immediately juxtaposed with his death.

Carnival Scene (Act 2, Scene 2)

In the second scene of the second act (the Carnival Scene), Pustrpalk, Amarantha, and Bakalář arrive in the King's city in the midst of carnival festivities.[98] Similarly as in the opening scene, there is a short instrumental prelude. The theme is based on the characteristic rhythmic patterns of the Baroque dance *bourrée* (see Example 5.9).[99] Much of the scene is based on this theme, which is embellished in a Neoclassical manner by mildly dissonant counter-melodies.

Having abandoned his troupe, Pustrpalk joins forces with Doktor Šereda. Šereda warns Pustrpalk to beware of the eccentric King who, as he claims, likes to spy on his subjects, takes sadistic delight in torture, indulges in throwing exuberant dance parties, is consumed by an ambition to conquer the whole world, and – to finish off the list of alpha-male qualities – has an insatiable appetite for women.

Inspired by Šereda's advice, Pustrpalk decides to focus his trade on the extract from his 'Spiritus Universale', which is particularly effective as a stimulant of manly power. On the arrival of the carnival procession (which is made up of courtiers in costumes and includes the King himself, disguised as a peasant) Bakalář

Example 5.9 Bourrée. Haas, *Šarlatán*, piano reduction (DMH MM, sign. A 22.688), p. 133.

sings a humorous song to attract the crowds and advertise Pustrpalk's medicine (see Example 5.10):

Starý velbloud sežral tento lék,
se slepicí spářil se jak rek,
oba zmizeli pak jako sen,
slepic velbloudích tak vznikl kmen.
Zakrněli, se slabostí pryč,
Pustrpalk vám k tajemství dá klíč,
lék na vlastní kůži zkuste už,
slovo má teď zázračný náš muž.

An old camel ate this elixir,
Topped an old hen with utmost plaisir;
They both flamed up like a meteor,
Made a breed that never was before!
If you're weak, small, shrunk or in decay,
Master Pustrpalk will make your day!
Try this potion! Everyone now can!
While I pass the word to our great man![100]

Pustrpalk's medicine is enthusiastically praised by the King himself:

King: Silence! Citizens! Long live he, the most glorious man of all our era! Long live great Pustrpalk and his renowned Spiritus Universale!
Folk: (Chanting) Long live Pustrpalk! Long live he! [. . .]
King: I declare [. . .] Spiritus Universale [. . .] the world's [greatest] wonder!
             (The King pins on Pustrpalk an especially big medal.
             The enthusiasm of the crowd keeps escalating.)[101]

Pustrpalk's triumph is duly accompanied by fanfares (previously associated with the King's arrival). However, the overall character of the music is somewhat ominous. This is due to the combination of the crowd's 'robotic' chanting (to use Beckerman's metaphor), the ever-increasing tempo of the passage, the minor modality and chromatic counterpoint of the fanfares, and dissonant clusters in the

Example 5.10 Bakalář's song. Haas, *Šarlatán*, piano reduction (DMH MM, sign. A 22. 688), p. 159.

ostinato. The sense of foreboding is fulfilled when Bakalář announces that Amarantha has disappeared:

Bakalář: Amarantha [has] disappeared!
            Left in a carriage! [. . .]
            Right next to her, there I saw a mysterious friar!
Pustrpalk: [declamation] A friar? Jochimus! Abduction! Revenge!
King: The fireworks now begin!
Folk: Hurrah! Hurrah![102]

Once again, an emphatic reversal occurs from a euphoric to a dysphoric mood and the tragedy of Pustrpalk's loss is juxtaposed with the collective merriment of the carnival celebrations (the fireworks), accompanied by cheerful, dance-like music (the bourrée theme).

Although Pustrpalk asserts that Amarantha was abducted by Jochimus, there is still a certain degree of ambiguity. In Winckler's novel, Amarantha's disappearance remains surrounded by mystery for a long time, leaving Eisenbart tormented by uncertainty and speculation amidst the rumours that she ran away with the 'kapellmeister of an Italian commedia troupe' or a handsome courtier.[103] It is noteworthy that Haas retained in his final version some clues suggesting that Amarantha is indeed susceptible to the attractions of other men and the King in particular. At the beginning of the scene, Šereda gives Pustrpalk the following warning: 'Be careful, do not ever take your eyes from your lady. In the moment you turn . . . she's gone! The King's a lover of women.'[104] When Amarantha accidentally overhears Šereda's following remark that the King 'often hosts up to eight baronesses all night',[105] she 'closes her eyes' and produces a conspicuous 'admiring' sigh,[106] which is echoed by sweeping glissandi in the string section of the otherwise silent orchestra for extra emphasis.

Another problem is that Haas's description of Amarantha's behaviour prior to her disappearance seems to be at odds with the claim that she was 'abducted'. While Pustrpalk is fully engaged in his enterprise, Jochimus appears in the crowd, 'catches Amarantha's attention', they 'give each other a sign', and once Amarantha 'understands', she 'climbs off the stage' and 'quietly leaves the scene'.[107] This discrepancy might be explained as Haas's attempt to stage Winckler's version of Amarantha's kidnapping, according to which she was deceptively lured to a meeting, where she was seized by Jochimus and his accomplices and brought back to her husband by force.[108] On the other hand, the ambiguity may be the desired effect.

Haas may have deliberately planted such seeds of uncertainty in the audience's minds to make them speculate about mysterious premonitions and their uncanny fulfilments. Has Amarantha all along been in some sort of collusion with Jochimus, unknown to Pustrpalk? Does her disappearance have something to do with her excitement at the sexual capacity of the King? Who is he, anyway – this obscure figure creeping around in disguise, surrounded by the mysterious aura of a lascivious brute – perhaps another of Pustrpalk's doubles? Is there any symbolic significance in the fact that both figures are cast as baritones? Does the King reflect Pustrpalk's own lust, reckless ambitiousness, and vanity, which the King so conspicuously feeds with his exaggerated praise of Pustrpalk's medical art?

The need to ask such questions is more important than finding definitive answers. If there were clear answers at hand, the effect of compulsive wondering would be lost. In any case, at the end of the scene, Pustrpalk appears as a power-less tragic clown, a Pierrot who has lost his Columbine (as he always does) due to her attraction to a Harlequinian figure or due to the machinations of a mysterious adversary. The context of a carnival festivity, complete with masks, fireworks (an allusion to the 'horrendously beautiful spectacle' of the burning windmill?), and other attributes of fairground imagery results in another instance of grotesque commingling of euphoric and dysphoric emotions, portraying the confusion and psychological turmoil experienced by the protagonist.

The Operation (Act 3, Scene 1)

The first scene of the opera's third act takes place 'a relatively long time later' (as indicated by an echo of the Peregrination Song) in 'the square of another city'; 'night is falling' and 'Pustrpalk sits in front of his tent broodily, holding his head in his hands'.[109] Suddenly, Jochimus is brought before Pustrpalk, seeking the lat-ter's help in his mortal illness.[110]

Jochimus: I'm Jochimus. Doctor, forget all that has happened till now. I have done you wrong. I have heard wonders about your operations! All those you've kindly performed . . . I will expiate my guilt now and show my respect and trust to you.

Pustrpalk: (Recollecting) You, sir? What sort of guilt, sir? (He waves his hand.) I must examine you, and if necessary, I'll perform an operation.[111]

It appears that no grudge remains between the two men. However, just before entering the doctor's tent, the monk makes an ominous remark:

(Jochimus steps towards the tent, . . . but stops as if facing a decision. He crosses himself. His servant leaves; so do the men who helped carry him.)

Jochimus: Et in puncto ad infernum . . . In a moment to hell! Ha ha ha.' (He laughs devilishly)

(Jochimus enters [the tent] with determination and a sideward smile, followed by Pustrpalk. Empty stage. The moon rises. The tent is illuminated from inside. The silhouettes of Pustrpalk and Jochimus appear [on the tent wall].)[112]

Jochimus's sinister utterance is underpinned by a chromatic descent (as if lead-ing to the depths of hell) and a death knell played by triangle and timpani (see Example 5.11). The music accompanying the operation is dark and mysterious, not least due to the slow tempo, dense chromatic textures, sustained dissonant

Example 5.11 Jochimus's sinister proclamation. Haas, *Šarlatán*, autograph score (DMH MM, sign. A 22.687 c), p. 448.

sonorities, whole-tone modality, and echoes of the iambic death knell. Later on, the music approaches the character of a 'danse macabre', conveyed by waltz-like tempo and metre and 'spooky' instrumental effects, such as repetitive high-pitched whole-tone figures in the woodwinds, the 'skeletal' sound of pizzicato strings, and the 'otherworldly' timbre of harp and vibraphone. Finally, at the end of the operation, the death knell returns in the guise of an ominous sustained pedal (timpani and contrabassoon).

The symbolism of death anticipates the tragic outcome of the operation. Just as Pustrpalk congratulates himself on his 'masterful operation', Kyška announces that Jochimus is dead.[113] Shaken by the outcome, Pustrpalk sorrowfully comments on the divine power's superior authority over a physician's skills: 'This hand did do its utmost best! But the Angel of Death stood by ripping the poor man away from me.'[114]

The incident immediately attracts public attention. One of the first to come to the scene is a local Apothecary (Lékárník), who immediately asserts that the monk was intentionally killed. The tent is soon surrounded by soldiers and a crowd of onlookers gathers around. The people are divided over Pustrpalk's guilt. The last to arrive is the local physician (Fyzikus/Physicus). In Winckler's version, the Physicus, having examined the corpse, testifies that Eisenbart's operation was exemplary and the crowd disperses.[115] Haas's final version paints a much grimmer picture.[116] Like the Apothecary before him, the Physicus asserts Pustrpalk's guilt and when he notices that the 'charlatan' has fled, he incites anger in the crowd:

> (A wild fight commences between the two camps of the gathered people.)
>
> *Physicus:*   [declamation] Silence! The Charlatan has vanished! Coward! Murderer! Catch him, quickly! Hang him on the gallows!
> *Folk:*   [declamation] Catch him! Hang him on the gallows!
> *Chorus:*   (behind the scene): [singing] Charlatan!
> *Folk:*   [declamation] Hang him on the gallows!
> *Chorus:*   (behind the scene): [singing] Charlatan!
> *Folk:*   [declamation] Hang him on the gallows![117]

This alternative ending apparently mirrors the emphatic celebration of Pustrpalk in the preceding scene, where, too, the crowd parroted (in unsung declamation) the words of an authoritative figure. Not only did Haas strengthen the formal coherence of the drama and highlight the declining trajectory of Pustrpalk's fate, he also produced another uncanny effect, that is, 'involuntary repetition' coupled with polar reversal from extreme acclamation to extreme condemnation (neither of which seems justified by Pustrpalk's actions). Particularly noteworthy are the non-diegetic calls 'Charlatan!' heard from behind the scene (see Example 5.12). This voice of judgement seems to be coming from some kind of 'transcendent' authority (Jochimus? Heaven? Hell?), or perhaps from Pustrpalk's conscience.

Example 5.12 Pustrpalk's denunciation. Haas, *Šarlatán*, piano reduction (DMH MM, sign. A 22.688), p. 216.

The Tavern Scene (Act 3, Scene 2)

The opera's concluding scene is set in a tavern. Bakalář, Kyška, and others talk about Pustrpalk, whom they describe as a 'fearful figure', 'decrepit, ruined with drinking', wandering through the streets 'like a silent demon', and unable to recognise any of his former companions.[118] Pustrpalk staggers in and offers to treat three wandering students to wine. When they want to know the identity of their benefactor, Pustrpalk makes them guess, boasting about his fame. When he is finally recognised, Pustrpalk climbs on top of a table and starts singing a self-satirising song:

Já Pustrpalk, já lékař jsem,	Doctor Pustrpalk, you'd know my name,
vše léčím vlastním způsobem:	My methods have secured my fame:
uzdravím slepce, chodí zas	I cure the blind, they hop and sing;
a chromým vracím zraku jas!	The lame can soon see everything!
[. . .]	[. . .]
A hrabě jeden žral jak hřích,	One Count there was, an eater staunch,
že bezmála mu puknul břich.	Who almost overstuffed his paunch!
I bez váhání hned jsem vstal,	Quick as a flash I knew my role:
mu druhou díru navrtal.	And drilled for him another hole![119]

For the most part, this is Haas's literal translation of the above-discussed German song *Ich bin der Doktor Eisenbart*, as included in Winckler's novel. Winckler cleverly adds a bitter, self-destructive flavour to the song's overtly humorous, satirical character by having it sung by Eisenbart himself. The song thus becomes

Já, Pu - str - palk, já___ lé - kař jsem, vše lé - čím vlast - ním způ - so-bem,

u - zdra-vím slep - ce, cho - dí zas a chro - mým vra - cím zra - ku jas!

Example 5.13 Pustrpalk's song. Haas, *Šarlatán*, autograph score (MZM, sign. A 22.687 c), pp. 548–9. Transcription mine.

'the outcry of [Eisenbart's] innermost dichotomy' – that between a serious physician and a prankster:

> Here he pilloried the whole art of medicine in his person and relieved in a burst of sarcasm the suffocating anxiety, [which had accumulated] as he gave innumerable superb examples of his grotesque science and revealed his whole inner abstruseness year after year. [. . .] But in this last and greatest self-expression, the meaning of his existence, which hereby became a parable and a legend, seemed to get extinguished.[120]

Haas's setting of the song (see Example 5.13) clearly alludes to Papageno's aria *Der Vogelfänger bin ich ja* from *The Magic Flute*. Pustrpalk thus appears in the guise of Papageno: boastful and clownish. The difference is that Papageno is truly a comic figure, whereas Pustrpalk merely poses as one, making an ironic commentary on his tragic fate.

While singing, Pustrpalk is gradually joined by the former members of his dispersed company, who happen to witness the scene, until all of them are dancing and singing together. The last notes of the song are interrupted by the return of the ominous chanting of 'Charlatan' (heard, again, from behind the scene). At that moment, Pustrpalk starts hallucinating that Jochimus is coming to 'choke' him.

Pustrpalk: Quiet!
Chorus: (behind the scene) Charlatan!
Pustrpalk: (Speaks.) There, look!
  (Points into the auditorium.) Coming this way!
Chorus: (behind the scene) Charlatan!
Pustrpalk: It's him! Jochimus!
  (Pulls out his sword and stands on guard as if expecting a duel.)
  Ah, he wants to choke me!
  (Charges towards the auditorium as if against an invisible enemy [. . .] and falls as if he took a hit.)
  Ah, ah! Ah, God, have mercy on me.
  Ah! People, pray for my wretched soul!
  (Dies.) (The people kneel and cross themselves.)[121]

Haas's version of Pustrpalk's death is a dramatically effective compression of Winckler's original. The idea of Eisenbart being haunted by apparitions (including not only Jochimus, but also by the comedian killed in the Windmill Scene and by mistreated former patients) is present in Winckler's novel, but not directly associated with Eisenbart's death.[122] Eisenbart dies in the following chapter (apparently of a weak heart) at the end of his lengthy disputation with his son concerning the ethical and philosophical issues underpinning medicine.[123] In all versions of Haas's libretto, Eisenbart/Pustrpalk's death is juxtaposed with the merriment of the song: the doctor 'suddenly grabs at his heart', says 'Pray for my wretched soul!' and dies.[124] However, it was not until the late stages of his work on the opera that Haas decided to associate Pustrpalk's death with the hallucination of Jochimus and the return of the chants 'Charlatan!', both of which only appear in the orchestral score. This modification was apparently made in conjunction with the revision of the events following Jochimus's death, where the 'Charlatan!' chants were introduced for the first time.

Jochimus: the uncanny punitive force

Through his revisions, Haas highlighted the conflict between Pustrpalk and Jochimus, strengthened the latter's dramatic agency, and emphasised the moralising aspect of the story. When Pustrpalk is denounced as 'coward', 'murderer', and 'charlatan', the audience (both on and off stage) is being convinced that Pustrpalk is the villain and Jochimus is the martyr. The appearance of Jochimus in the midst of Pustrpalk's revelry seems to be an allusion to the arrival of the 'stone guest' to Don Juan's dinner (although there is no allusion to Mozart's *Don Giovanni*). By means of analogy, Pustrpalk is portrayed as a shameless trickster and murderer, whereas Jochimus appears as the moral authority, the executioner of justice.

And yet the moral message of this conclusion is profoundly problematic. It is not clear of what Pustrpalk is guilty. Winckler's Eisenbart has a guilty conscience because of the many patients he tricked and mistreated with his prankish curing practices. However, very few such cases appear in Haas's opera and Jochimus is apparently not one of them. Haas's version of the story draws more attention to the suspicion that Pustrpalk may have intentionally killed Jochimus out of revenge for the monk's intervention in his love affair with Amarantha (note the parallel with Don Juan's killing of Don Pedro).

However, Pustrpalk's behaviour before and after the fatal operation suggests no murderous intentions. Jochimus, on the other hand, appears as dishonest and malevolent: initially, he asks for forgiveness and help, but then he makes a sinister remark about hell, followed by 'diabolic laughter'. Significantly, these demonic features only appear in Haas's adaptation; in Winckler's original Jochimus's utterance 'et in pucto ad infernum' is not meant as a threat, but as an expression of the monk's fear for his life in the face of a dangerous surgery.[125] Haas does not portray Jochimus as an innocent victim, but rather a malicious architect of Pustrpalk's doom. Thus, Jochimus undergoes a gradual transformation from a 'real' character to a mysterious supernatural force.

At the same time, Pustrpalk seems to be drawn inevitably to his tragic end. He starts off as a successful impresario but his encounter with Amarantha has a destabilizing effect; the two fatal blows come when Amarantha disappears and Pustrpalk's medical skills – his most secure domain – are called into question (both through the agency of Jochimus). Thus, Pustrpalk seems to be gradually diminished to a mere puppet, while Jochimus (or whatever he represents) increasingly appears as the almighty puppet-master – one who takes away Pierrot's Columbine, ruins his reputation, and finally delivers his death.[126] In this sense, the end of *Charlatan* is a reversal of Petrushka's triumph over the Magician (sometimes referred to as 'Charlatan'!), in Stravinsky's well-known ballet: Jochimus, the true 'Charlatan', makes his triumph over the dead body of his puppet.

One might even wonder if Jochimus may have engineered Pustrpalk's encounter with Amarantha in the first place. According to Haas's stage directions, Jochimus's first appearance on stage occurs at the very same moment when whip cracks are heard, announcing the arrival of Amarantha's carriage.[127] From this Hoffmannesque perspective, Jochimus appears as Coppélius/Coppola from Hoffmann's *Sandman*, who (as if with a pair of magic glasses) makes Nathanael/Pustrpalk blindly fall in love with a puppet-like female (Olympia/Amarantha), only to take her away from him later. Significantly, both Nathanael and Pustrpalk are driven to their deaths by an uncanny reappearance of the mysterious puppet-master.

Finally, Jochimus, like the old miller, may be regarded as Pustrpalk's double. He is the embodiment of all those features that Pustrpalk stands in opposition to: morality, authority, official establishment, religion, sedentary life, bourgeois values and conventions, and so on. The reading of Jochimus in these terms is supported by the fact that both figures are cast as baritones. Moreover, Jochimus's appearances in the third act are associated with musical signifiers of the uncanny.

Example 5.14 shows the music accompanying the encounter of Pustrpalk and Jochimus prior to the operation. As in the opening ostinato of the Windmill Scene, the stepwise chromatic ascent in the upper voice is mirrored by an inversional descent in the lower voice. This mirroring suggests that in this encounter, Pustrpalk may be facing his own 'mirror image'. Note also the persistent

Example 5.14 Jochimus's arrival prior to the operation (Act 3; Scene 2): 'I'm Jochimus. (Pustrpalk is startled.)' Haas, *Šarlatán*, piano reduction (DMH MM, sign. A 22.688), p. 186.

clash between adjacent pitches in the bass. Similar instances of mirroring can be found throughout the music which underpins the operation. It is also striking that, as Haas has specified in his stage directions, the moon (the symbol of self-reflection) should appear at the very moment when Jochimus enters Pustrpalk's tent to undergo the fatal operation, which the audience is supposed to view as a shadow play (with silhouettes of the two men projected onto the tent's wall).[128] This imagery suggests that the operation can be regarded (on one level) as a symbolic act of Pustrpalk's communion with his alter-ego. From this perspective, the dark forces involved should be understood as internal (psychological) rather than external (infernal).

By the same token, Jochimus's final appearance is to be seen as a modern reinterpretation of the *ombra* scene (a scene involving a ghost or another supernatural figure) in terms of the uncanny. Michael Klein explains that, since the nineteenth century, the 'object of fright, indeed of the supernatural itself is not some outside force, like a god, but an inner force that splits the ego'.[129] Klein further observes that musical signifiers of the uncanny include those of the *ombra* topic ('tremolos, diminished seventh chords, Neapolitans') with the addition of 'enharmonicism, strange uses of chromaticism, odd voice-leading, and mechanical repetitions of musical material'.[130] Of these musical features, Haas's death motive displays 'mechanical repetition' and 'strange chromaticism' (see Example 5.15): it is based on chromatic parallel motion of a highly dissonant sonority, comprising a tritone (G flat – C) and a semitone clash (G flat – F), which might symbolise the uncanny doubling of one particular tone by its polar opposite (tritone) and near equivalent (the adjacent semitone). Whichever tone is 'the one', it is followed by chromatic 'shadows' in parallel motion. The uncanny character of the motive is enhanced by the 'otherworldly' sound of woodwinds in high register.

Example 5.15 The 'death' motive ('Pustrpalk charges with his sword against the auditorium as if it was an invisible enemy . . .'). Haas, *Šarlatán*, piano reduction (DMH MM, sign. A 22.688), p. 257.

Pustrpalk: transgressor, victim, or psychopath?

The crucial question posed by the opera concerns the reasons behind Pustrpalk's fall. Compared to Winckler's novel, Haas placed much more emphasis on the psychological portrayal of Eisenbart/Pustrpalk. This is apparent from the play with uncanny doubles in the Windmill Scene and the accentuation of the demonic features of Jochimus, who flicks freely between a 'real' character, an external supernatural figure, and an internal Doppelgänger, confined to Pustrpalk's subjective, psychological world. As a result, Pustrpalk seems to be driven to his ruin, at least partly, by psychological forces rooted in his disturbed subjectivity. Pustrpalk's uncontrollable desire for Amarantha interferes in an explosive mix with his radically individualist, monomaniacal personality, destabilised by anxieties concerning his social and professional status, all of which fundamentally undermines his moral and psychological integrity.

However, the core of the opera (and the novel) resides in the negotiation of the ethical questions concerning the character's inherent ambiguity between a trickster and a serious physician. In this sense, Pustrpalk's downfall seems to be driven by ('objective' or 'external') forces of ethical and/or social order. Pustrpalk is a figure of transgression, which resides (besides the petty fraud he commits in his dubious business) in the vanity, pride, and monomania he shares with the modern individualists, all of whom, as Watt has observed, 'have an undefined kind of ideal, but do not succeed in reaching it. They are not, in any obvious sense, achievers, but rather emblematic failures. Moreover, they are [. . .] punished for their attempt to realize their aspirations [. . .]'.[131]

Relevant to Watt's thoughts on the modern individualists are Kierkegaard's reflections on the problems of modern secular society and culture through the archetypal figures of Don Juan, Faust, and the Wandering Jew. As George Pattison explains, Kierkegaard saw these figures 'as representing the three great forms of life outside religion, namely, sensuous passion, doubt and nihilistic despair', which he regarded as various stages of self-awareness in a developmental schema heading towards an increasingly pessimistic world-view.[132] Arguably, all of these stages can be identified in the declining fate of Eisenbart/Pustrpalk, whose appearance in the final scene bears a striking resemblance to the Wandering Jew – a man who is (in Pattison's words) 'inescapably aware of his own perdition as he wanders the earth, indifferent to the affairs of those around him, longing only for extinction'.[133]

Indeed, there is a redemptive element in Haas's depiction of Pustrpalk's death, which moves the audience to compassion. Once Pustrpalk dies, urging his companions to 'pray for his wretched soul', the melody of his song is heard once again, this time cast in a prayer-like guise, while 'all [people on stage] kneel silently and cross themselves'.

The transgressive features of Pustrpalk's character are clear enough. However, Pustrpalk also seems to be, at least to some extent, a victim of repression rooted in the narrow-minded morality, intolerance, and xenophobia of the social/political/

professional establishment and its leading figures. In fact, itinerant groups such as that of Johann Andreas Eisenbart faced fierce opposition from the sedentary establishment.[134] As Katritzky explains:

As a major economic threat, performing quacks suffered a relentless and increasingly coordinated three-pronged establishment attack. If the medical establishment was primarily concerned [especially in the eighteenth century] to curb the activities of unqualified healers, and sedentary musicians and actors to discourage itinerant performers, the Church recognized that its authority was undermined by both the performative and medical authorities of itinerants.[135]

Moreover, there is a strong element of social control through moral and religious doctrines embedded in the Faustian template of Eisenbart's story. As Watt observed, the 1587 *Faustbuch* is largely a didactic work of 'complacent moralism', which echoes the 'devil-haunted aspect of Lutheran Germany' and the 'curse which the Reformation laid on magic, on worldly pleasure, on aesthetic experience, on secular knowledge'.[136] Watts links these features of the *Faustbuch* directly to the ideology underpinning witch trials:

It was pressure from Lutheran Wittenberg which brought about a revision of the law of Saxony; after 1572 a witch was to be burnt merely for having made a pact with the devil, 'even if she has harmed nobody with her sorcery'. The ideology of damnation was strengthened by being internalised; and the *Faustbuch* embodies this in two ways. On the one hand, there was no need to show that Faust had done anyone any harm; and on the other hand, the punitive force was subjectivised.

Watt's points apply to Eisenbart/Pustrpalk: he is not unambiguously guilty of consciously and willingly harming anyone and the punitive force (embodied by Jochimus) is internalised to such extent that it appears as his own hallucination, as if stemming from his conscience.

From the perspective outlined above, Pustrpalk appears as social outcast and victim of prejudice. Since the middle ages, this was the position shared by travelling comedians, musicians, quacks – and Jews. Indeed, the possible view of Pustrpalk as a Jew has been suggested by Beckerman:

Accusations that Jewish doctors killed their patients, or engaged in charlatanry for either ritual or sexual purposes, have echoed over the centuries, coming to a kind of 'fruition' both in Nazi doctrine and several years later in the notorious 'doctors' plot' in the Soviet Union. This is one of the reasons that the power of Haas's *The Charlatan* crystallizes in our own time, on the heels of both the Shoah and the Gulag.[137]

Conclusion

Beckerman's reading of *Charlatan* as a premonition of the Holocaust reveals connotations which 'crystallise in our own time' from a retrospective view of the twentieth century. The question is whether Winckler's novel and Haas's opera were conceived in their own time as a reflection – or even deliberate critique – of the contemporary socio-political atmosphere, marked by the rise of totalitarianism.

The main ambition of Winckler's novel is to reinvent the man behind the legend, to portray Johann Andreas Eisenbart, remembered in popular consciousness as a shadow of his stage persona (encapsulated in the Eisenbart song), as a human being with all his joys and sorrows, virtues and vices, achievements and failures, in a life-long struggle against internal conflicts and external adversities. At the same time, the book wants to be an entertaining read, making the best out of the subject matter, populated by fairground shows, adventurous travels, and Eisenbart's marvellous feats. Although Winckler's novel deals with themes that have political implications (such as Eisenbart's opposition to the norms set by social, professional, religious, and political structures) and that may have had particular resonance in the 1930s, it would be an overstatement to claim that the book aspires to function allegorically as a critical commentary on the social and political situation of its time.

Haas's opera is a relatively faithful stage adaptation of Winckler's book. It effectively highlights the polarity between Pustrpalk's comic stage persona and his tragic private personality and amplifies (as has been noted) the psychological conflicts within his subjectivity. The commingling of popular entertainment and human tragedy in Winckler's book was apparently a major source of attraction for Haas. In his above-quoted commentary, Haas highlighted the subject's entertaining aspect ('the attractive [fairground] setting', 'the comedy and drama of adventurous stories') and hinted at its tragic undertones, but he gave no clues to suggest that the opera contained an element of social commentary. Of course, Haas may have had various reasons to be not entirely forthcoming in the press, but the comparison between the opera and its literary model yields little evidence to suggest that Haas developed the critical potential of the subject matter any further than Winckler. The scenes of Pustrpalk's unmerited celebration and unfair defamation may bring to mind images familiar from Nazi propaganda (to which the composer would have been exposed), but their primary purpose is to juxtapose Eisenbart/Pustrpalk's 'fame and fall', and their moral is best understood along the lines of 'what goes around, comes around' or 'wealth obtained by fraud will dwindle'.

Importantly, newspaper reviews reflecting on the opera's premiere contain no references to the work's social and political implications or to the state of affairs in contemporary politics; instead, the reviewers focused on the ethical questions surrounding Pustrpalk's ambiguous character as the key subject of the opera, mostly regarding the 'charlatan' in a compassionate manner:

[Pustrpalk] is a character torn between real and farcical moments in the story, a man who staggers between tragical and comical life situations, a man who [. . .], having experienced successes and failures, comes to a tragic end [. . .].[138]

[Pustrpalk] is not a fraudster and cunning trickster, exploiting people's weakness [. . .], but rather a devoted servant of his medical art, [. . .] a man with good and noble heart.[139]

[Pustrpalk] is not a mere charlatan and fraudster; he is a man who, despite his fraudulent trade, has a bit of humanity in his heart. That is why we feel close and sympathetic to him.[140]

The very title of Haas's opera – *Charlatan* – implies a judgement; Pustrpalk is put on trial and found profoundly human. Interestingly, one of the reviewers pointed out Pustrpalk's kinship with the modern individualists, arguing that *Charlatan* tells 'a profound life story of a [character] type, which has perpetual relevance, just like the types of Faust, [Don] Juan or [Don] Quixote.[141] Thus, while it is justifiable to interpret *Charlatan* with respect to the rise of Nazism in the 1930s, it is by no means necessary to do so, since the work's essential philosophical and ethical message about the human condition, embodied in a 'timeless' character type, is largely independent of a particular historical context.

Pustrpalk's position somewhere between flesh-and-blood character and archetype (in fact, a number of different archetypes) encourages the reading of the story as a kind of parable. Many can recognise elements of themselves (or someone else) in Pustrpalk, his follies, vices, and anxieties. This is the basis of the comic effect of *commedia dell'arte* and the moral appeal of stories of Don Juan and Faust. Who can be sure, having witnessed Pustrpalk's encounters with his uncanny doubles (the old miller, the King, Jochimus – each reflecting or subverting a particular aspect of his character), that Pustrpalk is not their own doppelgänger? The play about premonitions itself becomes a premonition. This is what makes *Charlatan* such a powerful statement about ambiguity and uncertainty as the fundamental conditions of human existence.

Notes

1 This chapter expands on my previous article published in Czech as follows: Martin Čurda, 'Haasův Šarlatán: tragikomedie o starých komediantech, moderních individualistech a podivných dvojnících', *Hudební věda*, 55/3–4 (2018), 391–427.

2 -vk-, 'Nová česká opera v Brně: Premiéra "Šarlatána" od brněnského skladatele Pavla Haase 2. dubna na scéně Zem. Divadla – Rozhovor se skladatelem', *Moravské slovo*, 26 March 1938, p. 3. Translation mine.

3 All of the reviews quoted below are cited according to Haas's album of newspaper clippings entitled 'Moje úspěchy a ne-úspěchy' ('My Successes and Non-successes'), which survives as the property of Olga Haasová-Smrčková. All translations from this source are mine.

4 V.P., 'Nová česká opera: *Šarlatán* od Pavla Haase', *České slovo*, 7 April 1938; –rr., 'Šarlatán', *Moravské noviny*, 5 April 1938. One of few reservations concerned the portrayal of Jochimus, Pustrpalk's main adversary, who, according to some reviewers, was characterised too skeletally (–k, 'Haasův Šarlatán: Premiéra v brněnském divadle', *Lidové noviny*, 5 April 1938; V.S., 'Z brněnské opery', *Národní politika*, 5 April 1938).

5 Emanuel Ambros, 'Haasova opera "Šarlatán"', *Národní listy*, 5 April 1938; –b–, 'Opera v Brně: Pavel Haas: Šarlatán', *Moravský přítel lidu*, 5 April 1938.

6 Lubomír Peduzzi, *Pavel Haas: Život a dílo skladatele* (Brno: Muzejní a vlastivědná společnost, 1993), p. 84.

7 Michael Beckerman, 'Haas's *Charlatan* and the Play of Premonitions', *The Opera Quarterly,* 29/1 (2013), 31–40 (p. 36).

8 Ibid., pp. 34–5.

9 Ibid., p. 36.

10 Ibid.

11 Ibid.

12 Ibid., pp. 32, 37.

13 Ian Watt, *Myths of Modern Individualism: Faust, Don Quixote, Don Juan, Robinson Crusoe* (Cambridge: Cambridge University Press, 1997).

14 Josef Winckler's book was published in several editions of various lengths: *Des verwegenen Chirurgus weltberühmbt Johann Andreas Doctor Eisenbart [. . .]* (Stuttgart: Deutsche Verlags-Anstalt, 1929, 589 pages); *Des verwegenen Chirurgus weltberühmbt Wunder-Doktor Johann Andreas Eisenbart [. . .]* (Berlin: Deutsche Buchgemeinschaft, 1933, 401 pages); *Des verwegenen Chirurgus weltberühmbt Johann Andreas Doctor Eisenbart [. . .]* (Stuttgart: Deutsche Verlags-Anstalt, 1953, 471 pages). Haas worked with the abridged 1933 Berlin edition; all references to Winckler's book made here relate to this edition and all translations from this source are mine. According to Peduzzi, Haas also owned a dramatic adaptation of Eisenbart's story drawing on Winckler's book, entitled *Doctor Eysenbarth,* and written by Ernst Fürst. See Lubomir Peduzzi, *Haasův Šarlatán: Studie o opeře: Původní nezkrácená verze* (Brno, 1994), pp. 6–7. However, Haas's opera bears very little resemblance to this text. Fürst's drama was published as follows: Ernst Fürst, *Doctor Eysenbarth* (Stuttgart and Berlin: Chronos Verlag, 1932). I am indebted to Prof. Pavel Drábek for helping me to obtain a copy of this source.

15 In the second version of the libretto, Haas replaced 'Eisenbart' ('Iron-beard') with 'Bledovous' ('Pale-beard'). The final name 'Pustrpalk' was introduced in the third version. Pavel Haas, *Návrhy libreta* [Sketches of the libretto], Department of Music History of the Moravian Museum, sign. B 832. The first version of the libretto is contained in a notebook marked (in red pencil) 'Opera: I. verse' ('Opera: 1st version'). The second version is in another notebook entitled 'Doktor Bledovous ["Bledovous" crossed out and replaced with "Pustrpalk"]: Dle románu Josefa Wincklera volně zdramatisoval a slova napsal Pavel Haas' ('Doctor Pale-Beard/Pustrpalk: According to the novel by Josef Winckler freely dramatised and written by Pavel Haas'). This notebook is marked (in red pencil) 'II. verse' ('2nd version'). The third version is written on the reverse sides of concert programmes of the Club of Moravian Composers (A4 sheets glued together). There is no title page; the first page (containing a list of characters) is marked (in red pencil) 'III. [verse]' ('3rd' [version]). The fourth version, virtually identical with the third, is typewritten on sheets of paper of unconventional format (similar to A4 but taller), bound together.

16 Peduzzi, *Pavel Haas,* p. 69. All translations from Peduzzi's book are my own.

17 Ibid., p. 124 (endnote no. 39): 'The text of this song, but not its melody, is derived from the popular eighteenth-century song *Ich bin der doctor Eisenbart,* widely known across the whole of Germany and the surrounding countries (including Switzerland and France).'

18 Winckler, *Eisenbart,* p. 25.

19 M.A. Katritzky, *Women, Medicine and Theatre, 1500–1750: Literary Mountebanks and Performing Quacks* (Aldershot: Ashgate, 2007), p. 121.

20 Winckler, *Eisenbart,* p. 195.

21 Ibid., pp. 34–5, 77–9, 107–8.

22 Watt, *Myths of Modern Individualism,* pp. 3–4.

23 Ibid., pp. 24–5.

24 Winckler, *Eisenbart*, pp. 324–30 (chapter 25: 'Gott Schütze Andreas!').

25 Ibid., p. 327.

26 Ibid.

27 Ibid., p. 329.

28 Ibid.

29 Ibid., p. 128: '[Speaking to himself] Frankly, Eisenbart [. . .] your restless blood chases you viciously like Father Ahasverus.'

30 Watt, *Myths of Modern Individualism*, pp. 123–4.

31 Ibid., p. 233.

32 See also Winckler, *Eisenbart*, p. 31.

33 Ibid., p. 356; see also Pavel Haas, *Šarlatán*, autograph score (Department of Music History of the Moravian Museum, sign. A 22.687 c), pp. 507–8.

34 See Martin Green and John Swan, *The Triumph of Pierrot: Commedia dell'Arte and the Modern Imagination* (University Park: Pennsylvania State University Press, 1993, revised edition), pp. 1–2.

35 Quoted in Katritzky, *Women, Medicine and Theatre*, p. 37.

36 Katritzky, *Women, Medicine and Theatre*, p. 33. Opinions vary about the significance of this episode in the liturgical plays. Katritzky suggests that it had a 'didactic' function: it is intended to 'heighten the intensity of religious plays' theologically motivated contrast between profane and spiritual concerns, not by glorifying worldly pleasures, but by ridiculing them' and thus to inspire the spectators to 'recognize and laugh at their human folly, and to reject it in favour of spiritual redemption' (p. 35).

37 Ibid., p. 35.

38 Ibid., pp. 168–9.

39 Ibid., p. 36.

40 Ibid., p. 167.

41 Pavel Haas, *Šarlatán*, autograph score (Department of Music History of the Moravian Museum, sign. A 22.687 a), p. 97. See also Winckler, *Eisenbart*, p. 19.

42 Winckler, *Eisenbart*, p. 28. See also Haas, *Šarlatán*, autograph score (DMH MM, sign. A 22.687 a), p. 62. I am grateful to Professor Pavel Drábek, who kindly shared with me his excellent unpublished English translation of Haas's libretto to *Charlatan*. All translations of extracts from Haas's libretto (its final version) presented below are Drábek's, unless stated otherwise.

43 This scene is based on the first chapter of Winckler's book, entitled 'The Cures Begin' ('Die Kuren beginnen'). See ibid., pp. 9–35.

44 -vk-, 'Nová česká opera v Brně: Premiéra "Šarlatána" od brněnského skladatele Pavla Haase 2. dubna na scéně Zem. Divadla – Rozhovor se skladatelem', *Moravské slovo*, 26 March 1938, p. 3.

45 The reference here is to Haas's Suite Op. 14 (1936) from the opera *Charlatan*; premiered in Brno on 14 June 1937. See Peduzzi, *Pavel Haas*, p. 132.

46 Pavel Haas, 'Suita z tragikomické opery Šarlatán', *Radiojournal*, XV/24 (1937), 10.

47 Haas, *Šarlatán*, autograph score (DMH MM, sign. A 22.687 a), pp. 5–6.

48 -vk-, 'Nová česká opera v Brně: [. . .] Rozhovor se skladatelem', *Moravské slovo*, 26 March 1938, p. 3.

49 M.A. Katritzky, *Women, Medicine and Theatre*, p. 87.

50 -vk-, 'Nová česká opera v Brně: [. . .] Rozhovor se skladatelem', p. 3.

51 Haas, *Šarlatán*, autograph score (DMH MM, sign. A 22.687 a), p. 57.

52 Ibid., p. 65.

53 Ibid., pp. 106–7.

54 Ibid., p. 107. Translation mine.

55 Ibid., pp. 117–26.

56 This scene is based on the fourth chapter of Winckler's book, entitled 'The Crinoline' ('Die Krinoline'). Winckler, *Eisenbart*, pp. 70–9.

57 Haas, *Šarlatán*, autograph score (DMH MM, sign. A 22.687 a), pp. 181–2. Translation mine.
58 Haas, *Šarlatán*, autograph score (DMH MM, sign. A 22.687 b), pp. 183–5. Translation mine.
59 Ibid., pp. 186–92.
60 Ibid., pp. 194–7. Translation mine.
61 Ibid., pp. 196–9.
62 Ibid., pp. 199–201.
63 Ibid., pp. 210–12. See also Winckler, *Eisenbart*, p. 119.
64 Haas, *Šarlatán*, autograph score (DMH MM, sign. A 22.687 b), pp. 211–15.
65 Ibid., pp. 213–15.
66 Ibid., pp. 216–17. Translation mine.
67 Ibid., pp. 246–54.
68 Pavel Haas, 'Katěrina Izmailová v Brně', *Národní noviny*, 3 May 1936.
69 Ibid., pp. 317–21. Translation by Drábek; additions mine.
70 Winckler, *Eisenbart*, pp. 109–43.
71 Ibid., pp. 94–108.
72 Ibid., p. 94.
73 Ibid., p. 110.
74 Haas, *Návrhy libreta* (DMH MM, sign. B 832), notebook marked 'Opera: 1. verse', act 2, p. 1 (pages in each act are numbered separately). Translation mine. See also Winckler, *Eisenbart*, p. 111.
75 Ibid., p. 3. Translation mine. See also Winckler, *Eisenbart*, p. 113.
76 Winckler, *Eisenbart*, p. 116.
77 Haas, *Návrhy libreta*, (DMH MM, sign. B 832), notebook marked 'Opera: 1. verse', act 2, p. 13. See also Winckler, *Eisenbart*, p. 126.
78 Winckler, *Eisenbart*, p. 127.
79 Ibid., pp. 133–4: 'the musicians conspired against the comedians [. . .] and after a short dispute, during which many drew their daggers and swords, a horrible scream rang out among two or three duels! [. . .] Pickelhering was lying in the grass with a stream of black blood coming out from a wound in his forehead'.
80 Ibid., p. 134: 'Racketing, shouting, and banging was heard from the mill; the epileptic [miller] sprang out of his bed in frenzy, grabbed a glowing lantern and threw it among the fighting men, so that blazing flickers sprang up. The men did not know where it came from, but it became a blind signal for them to set fire all around [. . .]'.
81 Ibid.: 'Amarantha seemed to be seized by madness as she was running around the mill, declaiming Molière [. . .]. Eisenbart [. . .] suddenly started shouting into the night the strophe "Morpheus in mentem trahit impellentem ventum jenem"'.
82 Ibid., pp. 152–78 (chapter 9: 'Die Badkur [. . .]').
83 Ibid., p. 135. See also Haas, *Návrhy libreta* (DMH MM, sign. B 832), notebook marked 'Opera: 1. verse', act 2, p. 22: 'The wings of the windmill start turning, slowly at first, then faster and faster – even frenziedly!' Translation mine.
84 Green and Swan, *The Triumph of Pierrot*, p. 142. Reference is made specifically to early Expressionist cinema and particularly to *The Cabinet of Dr Caligari*, where images of marry-go-rounds and barrel organs abound, accompanying the performance at one of the fairground booths of Dr Caligari (puppet-master figure, controlling his assistant Cesare, who is in a trance). The authors also note that *commedia*-inspired art in general betrays a fascination with the circle (circular motion, round shape of Pierrot's face, associated with the full moon, 'circular' narratives, etc.).
85 Winckler, *Eisenbart*, p. 142.
86 The most direct clue is Amarantha's vague reference to 'hard and frightening times' in her response to Pustrpalk's love declaration: 'I think you're rushing now, you're just

seeking a sanctuary, dearest Master! These are hard times and frightening times!' See Haas, *Šarlatán*, autograph score (DMH MM, sign. A 22.687 b), pp. 209–10.

87 Ibid., pp. 224–6: 'Zavináč: "And he [Pustrpalk] won't be able to carry on [travelling] much longer. He wants his calm! He is going to run away with Missis Professor and send his own wife packing. What shall we do then?"' Translation mine. See also Winckler, *Eisenbart*, p. 122. Elsewhere, Winckler associates Eisenbart's decision to run away with Amarantha with his hope for a sedentary life. See Winckler, *Eisenbart*, p. 178: 'Then he [Eisenbart] swore to run away with her [. . .] and live the comfortable life of a gentleman as a "patented" court doctor; everything would be different in such honourable and noble existence!'

88 Nicholas Royle, *The Uncanny* (New York: Routledge, 2003), p. 1.

89 Sigmund Freud, 'The Uncanny (1919)', in *Fantastic Literature: A Critical Reader*, ed. David Sandner (Westport CT: Praeger, 2004), 74–101 (p. 88).

90 Ibid., p. 87.

91 Ibid., p. 86.

92 Lucie Armitt, *Theorising the Fantastic* (London: Arnold, 1996), pp. 31–2.

93 Haas, *Šarlatán*, autograph score (DMH MM, sign. A 22.687 b), pp. 259–62. Translation by Drábek; additions mine.

94 Ibid., p. 267.

95 Ibid., p. 281. Translation mine.

96 Ibid., pp. 281–2.

97 See Armitt, *Theorising the Fantastic*, p. 50.

98 This scene is based on chapter 10 of Winckler's book, entitled 'In the Metropolis of the Baroque Era' ('In der Metropole des Barock'). Winckler, *Eisenbart*, pp. 179–97.

99 Bourrée is mentioned, along with minuet, gavotte, and rigaudon, on the margin of the second draft of Haas's libretto. Haas, *Návrhy libreta* (DMH MM, sign. B 832), notebook entitled 'Doktor Bledovous/Pustrpalk' and marked 'II. verse', act 2, scene 2, unnumbered first page.

100 Ibid., pp. 381–4.

101 Ibid., pp. 407–15. Translation by Drábek; translation of Haas's stage directions in round brackets mine.

102 Ibid., pp. 415–24.

103 Winckler, *Eisenbart*, pp. 194–5.

104 Haas, *Šarlatán*, autograph score (DMH MM, sign. A 22.687 b), pp. 351–3.

105 Ibid., pp. 364–5.

106 Ibid., pp. 367. Translation mine.

107 Haas, *Šarlatán*, autograph score (DMH MM, sign. A 22.687 b), pp. 398–400. Translation mine.

108 Winckler, *Eisenbart*, p. 386.

109 Haas, *Šarlatán*, autograph score (DMH MM, sign. A 22.687 c), unnumbered first page and p. 426. Translation mine.

110 This scene is based on chapter 26 of Winckler's book: 'Jochimus's Pitiful Fate' ('Jochimus jammervolles Schicksal'). Ibid. pp. 331–45.

111 Ibid., pp. 434–8. Translation by Drábek; translation of Haas's stage directions in round brackets mine.

112 Ibid., pp. 447–50. Translation mine.

113 Ibid., pp. 464–6.

114 Ibid., pp. 475–6. Haas arguably made a symbolic musical reference to the Angel of Death at the very end of the operation: just before Bakalář comes in with his line 'Zde vino!' ('Your wine, sir!'), the orchestra plays a rising succession of falling fourths/fifths, underpinned by a stepwise chromatic ascent in parallels and a static, sustained tone. This, I believe, is an allusion to the opening motive of the second movement of Josef Suk's *Asrael* symphony.

115 Winckler, *Eisenbart*, pp. 338–44.
116 Haas adhered to Winckler's version until very late stages of his work on the opera. It was not until he had finished all versions of his libretto, as well as 26 pages of complete orchestral score (dated 29 December 1936) that he decided to change the ending of the scene. The 26 discarded pages are included in Pavel Haas, *Šarlatán: části opery, skici* (*Charlatan: Parts of the opera, sketches*), Department of Music History of the Moravian Museum, sign. A22 689.
117 Haas, *Šarlatán*, autograph score (DMH MM, sign. A 22.687 c), pp. 501–2. Translation by Drábek; translation of Haas's stage directions in round brackets mine.
118 Ibid., pp. 507–8.
119 Ibid., pp. 548–58. See also Winckler, *Eisenbart*, p. 359.
120 Winckler, *Eisenbart*, p. 364.
121 Haas, *Šarlatán*, autograph score (DMH MM, sign. A 22.687 c), pp. 575–81. Translation by Drábek; translation of Haas's stage directions in round brackets mine.
122 Winckler, *Eisenbart*, pp. 367–8: 'All former patients came to him like spectres in the following nights. Merciful God! [. . .] They came with grinning faces and long teeth, wailing and racketing – ha! Pickelhering was leading them! Scoundrel! [. . .] And once a giant vampire came down from the ceiling . . . "Jochimus?" gasped Eisenbart up into the darkness: "As a pastor, you should know how weak a man is in trying to live up to his principles! You should know!"'
123 Ibid., pp. 394–5.
124 Haas, *Návrhy libreta* (DMH MM, sign. B 832), notebook marked 'Opera: 1. verse', act 4, page 22; notebook entitled 'Doktor Bledovous/Pustrpalk' and marked 'II. verse', p. 94; notebook marked 'III. [verse]', act 3, scene 2, p. 9. Translation mine.
125 Winckler, *Eisenbart*, p. 332: '"And how long does such an operation take?" asked the priest, who was suddenly overcome by anxiety. "I have carried out several within a half of a Paternoster!" Eisenbart reassured him – "one should never spend too much time making presumptions, so let us begin straightaway; come in, Father!"
"Et in puncto ad infernum . . . In a moment to hell!" laughed Jochimus as he bent [passing] under a thick curtain into the booth, which reeked of ointments, vapours, and blood; he was forced to sit down by a sudden rush of sickness.'
126 See the discussion of play with multi-levelled theatrical space in *commedia*-inspired theatre in Green and Swan, *The Triumph of Pierrot*, pp. 111–13.
127 Haas, *Šarlatán*, autograph score (DMH MM, sign. A 22.687 a), p. 57: 'Appears the person of the fat monk Jochimus, who gazes curiously towards Pustrpalk and makes his way [through the crowd] closer to the tribune. His presence draws the attention of the audience. At the same time, one hears the clopping of horses' hooves and the cracking of a whip.' Translation mine.
128 Haas, *Šarlatán*, autograph score (DMH MM, sign. A 22.687 c), p. 449–50.
129 Michael L. Klein: *Intertextuality in Western Art Music* (Bloomington: Indiana University Press, 2005), p. 80.
130 Ibid., p. 87.
131 Watt, *Myths of Modern Individualism*, p. 234.
132 George Pattison, *Kierkegaard and the Crisis of Faith: An Introduction to His Thought* (London: Society for Promoting Christian Knowledge, 1997), p. 79.
133 Ibid., pp. 79–80.
134 Eisenbart's company was partly disbanded as a result of King Friedrich Wilhelm I's 1716 ban of all itinerant performers in Prussia, especially those sponsored by quacks. See M.A. Katritzky, *Women, Medicine and Theatre*, pp. 168–9.
135 Ibid., p. 14.
136 Watt, *Myths of Modern Individualism*, p. 26.
137 Beckerman, 'Haas's *Charlatan* and the Play of Premonitions', p. 38.

138 –el–, 'Sloupek kultury: Šarlatán', *Moravské slovo*, 5 May 1938.
139 Emanuel Ambros, 'Haasova opera "Šarlatán"', *Národní listy*, 5 April 1938.
140 –b–, 'Opera v Brně: Pavel Haas: Šarlatán', *Moravský přítel lidu*, 5 April 1938.
141 –rr., 'Šarlatán', *Moravské noviny*, 5 April 1938.

Bibliography

General bibliography

Armitt, Lucie, *Theorising the Fantastic* (London: Arnold, 1996).
Beckerman, Michael, 'Haas's Charlatan and the Play of Premonitions', *The Opera Quarterly*, 29/1 (2013), 31–40.
Černý, Václav, *Staročeský Mastičkář* (Prague: Československá akademie věd, 1955).
Čurda, Martin, 'Haasův Šarlatán: tragikomedie o starých komediantech, moderních individualistech a podivných dvojnících', *Hudební věda*, 55/3–4 (2018), 391–427.
Freud, Sigmund, 'The Uncanny (1919)', in *Fantastic Literature: A Critical Reader*, ed. David Sandner (Westport CT: Praeger, 2004), 74–101.
Fürst, Ernst, *Doctor Eysenbarth* (Stuttgart and Berlin: Chronos Verlag, 1932).
Green, Martin and John C. Swan, *The Triumph of Pierrot: The Commedia Dell'arte and the Modern Imagination* (University Park: Pennsylvania State University Press, 1993, revised edition).
Katritzky, M.A., *The Art of Commedia: The Study in the Commedia Dell'arte 1560–1620 with Special Reference to the Visual Records* (Amsterdam: Rodopi, 2006).
Katritzky, M.A., *Women, Medicine and Theatre, 1500–1750: Literary Mountebanks and Performing Quacks* (Aldershot: Ashgate, 2007).
Klein, Michael L, *Intertextuality in Western Art Music* (Bloomington: Indiana University Press, 2005).
Mitrychová, Linda, 'Pavel Haas: *Šarlatán*: Kapitoly ke genezi a recepci opery' (unpublished bachelor's thesis, Masaryk University, 2008).
Pattison, George, *Kierkegaard and the Crisis of Faith: An Introduction to His Thought* (London: Society for Promoting Christian Knowledge, 1997).
Pattison, George, *Kirkegaard, Religion and the Nineteenth-century Crisis of Culture* (Cambridge: Cambridge University Press, 2002).
Peduzzi, Lubomír, 'Doktor Eisenbart incognito in einer tschechischen Oper', in *Musik in Theresienstadt: Die Komponisten: Pavel Haas, Gideon Klein, Hans Krasa, Viktor Ullmann, Erwin Schulhoff (gestorben Im Kz Wülzburg) Und Ihre Werke: Die Referate Des Kolloquiums in Dresden Am 4. Mai 1991 Und Ergänzende Studien*, ed. Heidi Tamar Hoffmann and Hans-Günther Klein (Berlin: Musica Reanimata, 1991), 15–20.
Peduzzi, Lubomír, *Haasův Šarlatán: Studie o opeře: Původní nezkrácená verze* (Brno, 1994).
Peduzzi, Lubomír, *Pavel Haas: Život a dílo skladatele* (Brno: Muzejní a vlastivědná společnost, 1993); for German translation see *Pavel Haas: Leben und Werk des Komponisten*, trans. Thomas Mandl (Hamburg: Bockel, 1996).
Royle, Nicholas, *The Uncanny* (New York: Routledge, 2003).
Watt, Ian, *Myths of Modern Individualism* (Cambridge: Cambridge University Press, 1997).
Winckler, Josef, *Wunder-Doktor Johann Andreas Eisenbart* (Berlin: Deutsche Buchgemeinschaft, 1933).

Archival documents

Archival documents deposited in the Department of Music History of the Moravian Museum (Oddělení dějin hudby Moravského zemského muzea)

MUSIC

Šarlatán: Části opery, skici (Parts of the opera, sketches), sign. A 22.689.
Šarlatán: Klavírní výtah (Piano reduction), sign. A 22.688.
Šarlatán: Návrhy libreta (Drafts of libretto), sign. B 832.
Šarlatán: Navrhované změny (Proposed changes), sign. A 22.690.
Šarlatán: Partitura (Score), sign. A 22.687 a, b, c.
Šarlatán: Původní skica opery (Original draft of the opera), sign. A 22.691.
Šarlatán: Skici partitury (Drafts of the score), sign. A 22.689.

OTHER DOCUMENTS

Referáty z novin (Newspaper reviews), sign. J 8.

Archival documents deposited in the Archive of the National Theatre in Brno: Department of Musical Documentation (Archiv Národního divadla Brno: Oddělení hudební dokumentace)

Šarlatán: costume designs by František Muzika, sign. N 275, II–58.

Archival documents in private property of Olga Haasová-Smrčková

'Moje úspěchy a ne-úspěchy' ('My Successes and Non-successes'): a notebook containing newspaper clippings of newspaper articles on and concert reviews of Haas's works.

6 Four Songs on Chinese Poetry

Grief, melancholy, uncanny reflections, and
vicious circles in songs from Terezín

Introduction

> One was confused, one was being confused and brought more confusion into the
> existing confusion. It went so far that the reality was often no longer construed as
> existing and that it decomposed into non-possibility and non-reality. [. . .] One was
> and yet was not. [. . .] One lived on the border between something and nothing.
> Either the reality was different than one thought, or one was different from what
> the reality required one to be, or both. [. . .] One was almost only allowed to be an
> object. One waited and was dependent. One wanted to rebel, but to no effect. [. . .]
> One was oppressed by delusions. They could pass by like a dream. But the moment
> one tried to perceive them as dreams, they became real. And when one wanted to
> consider them real, one saw they were only delusions. Eventually, everything was
> swirling in a ghostly whirl. [. . .] Permanence and transience intermingled. The
> ultimate eschatological questions imposed themselves as they always do when
> man faces the final frontier, the apeiron.[1]
>
> Hans Günther Adler, *Terezín 1941–1945*

In the above-quoted account of his own experience of imprisonment in Terezín,
Hans Günther Adler has painted a disturbingly vivid image of life in the 'schizoid', 'split up and decomposed' reality of the ghetto and its psychological effects.[2]
This quotation provides a suitable epigraph to the discussion of Haas's Four Songs
on Chinese Poetry (composed in Terezín in 1944), which arguably portray a strikingly similar state of human subjectivity, characterised by uncanny ambivalence
between reality and illusion, alienation from reality and from the self, futility of
agency, perception of temporality as static or cyclic, and meditative contemplation of existential questions of life and death.

In his song cycle, Haas set to music four poems from a collection of paraphrases of old Chinese poetry titled *Nové zpěvy staré Číny* (*New Songs of Old
China*, 1940) by Czech poet and translator Bohumil Mathesius (1888–1952).[3]
The composer selected poems which contemplate feelings of loneliness, grief,
and longing for reunion with home and loved ones, thus investing his work
with inescapable autobiographical resonance. While the emotional and psychological states portrayed in the work 'belong' to the protagonist – a character
constructed by the author and encoded in the text – there is no doubt that Haas
experienced such feelings himself.[4] Thus, the author occasionally seems to

cross the boundary and speak through the voice of the protagonist, creating an irreducible element of ambiguity.

In his article entitled 'Exotismus životní absurdity' ('The Exoticism of Existential Absurdity'), Vladimír Karbusický regarded Haas's Four Songs as an expression of the composer's 'sadness' and 'anxiety', resulting from his confinement to the existential 'absurdity of the artificial ghetto of Terezín'.[5] Karbusický further suggested that Haas, like Mahler in *Das Lied von der Erde* (1908), which is also based on paraphrases of Chinese poetry,[6] used the exotic element to set a scene for the contemplation of existential issues of life and death. (In Mahler's case, such thoughts were supposedly inspired by the death of his daughter Maria and the discovery of his own fatal heart condition).[7]

There are some intriguing parallels between the two works. Both present a highly ambiguous portrayal of disturbed human subjectivity, marked by an apparent fixation on an object of loss ('youth' and 'beauty' in Mahler's case;[8] 'home' in Haas's).[9] Mahler and Haas also have in common a strong preoccupation with semantic ambiguity, created by juxtaposition of incongruous moods (what Adorno has described as Mahler's 'charade' of 'unfettered joy and unfettered melancholy').[10] On the other hand, Haas's Four Songs do not feature the elements of nostalgia, stylisation, and chinoiserie found in Mahler.[11] Likewise, Mahler's Romantic, bitter irony ('The Drinking Song of the Misery of the Earth'), and his Decadent invocation of death in 'The Farewell' is very distant from the character of Haas's song cycle.[12] Thus, while *Das Lied von der Erde* provides a useful point of reference, Haas's song cycle needs to be considered on its own merit.

The following reading of Haas's Four Songs is quasi-Symbolist. This approach is informed, on the one hand, by the poetic principle of correspondence between 'external' images of landscape and the protagonist's 'internal' subjectivity, which is common to old Chinese poetry and Symbolist poetry,[13] and, on the other hand, by the apparent focus on minute details of symbolic significance in Haas's music. Particular attention will be paid to Haas's use of uncanny imagery (symmetrical 'mirrors', parallel 'shadows', and enharmonic 'doubles'), some of which has already been observed in the *Charlatan*. On another level, the analysis will explain how psychological phenomena such as trauma, grief, and melancholy are portrayed in Haas's music through patterns of agency and expressive gestures based on ascending/descending linear motion, circular motion, and stasis.[14]

'I Heard Wild Geese'

Table 6.1 First song: text and translation

Zaslech jsem divoké husy . . . *(Wei Jing-wu)*	*I Heard Wild Geese . . .* *(Wei Jing-wu)*
Domov je tam, [daleko, daleko,]	My home is there, Far away, far away,

Zaslech jsem divoké husy . . . (Wei Jing-wu)	*I Heard Wild Geese . . .* (Wei Jing-wu)
daleko tam,	Far away there,
[daleko tam,]	Far away there,
mělo bys domů,	You ought to go home,
zbloudilé srdce!	Lost wand'ring heart!
[Daleko tam, domov, domov.]	So far away, my home, my home.
Za cizí noci,	In foreign darkness, [Lit.: During a foreign / strange night]
v podzimním dešti,	Autumn rain falling,
když nejvíc studil	The coldest moment
smutku chladný van:	Of the sad night wind: [Lit.: the sorrow's cold breeze]
ve vysokém domě svém zaslech jsem	From the height of my strange home I heard [Lit.: in the tall house of mine . . .]
křik divokých husí:	The cry of the wild geese:
právě přilétly.	They've just flown in.
[Domov je daleko tam.]	My home is faraway there.

Source: All of the original Czech poems by Mathesius quoted here and below appear as in Bohumil Mathesius, *Nové zpěvy staré Číny* (Prague: Melantrich, 1940), here p. 33. The composer's additions and alterations are indicated by square brackets. All English translations of Haas's songs here and below appear as in Pavel Haas, *Four Songs for Bass (Baritone) and Piano to the Words of Chinese Poetry* (Prague: Tempo; Berlin: Bote & Bock, 1992). © Copyright Boosey & Hawkes Bote & Bock GmbH, Berlin. Reproduced by permission of Boosey & Hawkes Music Publishers Ltd. Supplementary literal translations in square brackets are my own.

The idée fixe of home, St Wenceslas, and circular motion

The first song begins with a four-note ostinato, which plays a significant role in the cycle as a whole (see Example 6.1). As Viktor Ullmann observed in his review of the piece's premiere in Terezín, the first and the third of these 'sombre songs [which express] yearning for home' are linked by 'an idée fixe of four tones, which keeps returning as an ostinato or a cantus firmus in various metamorphoses'.[15] Karbusický saw in the motive a symbolic reference to the Hymn to St Wenceslas (the patron saint of the Czech nation).[16] Indeed, the motive corresponds with the four notes underpinning the word 'Václave' ('Wenceslas!') in the hymn (see Example 6.2). Moreover, the opening line of the poem ('My home is there'/'Domov je tam') can be seen as a reference to the incipit of the Czech national anthem ('Where is my home?'/'Kde domov můj?').

The ostinato's association with St Wenceslas seems to be confirmed by comparison with a passage from the prayer-like third movement of Haas's 1939 Suite for Oboe and Piano (bb. 51–55), in which the opening three-note motive of the chorale (previously quoted in its entirety) becomes the basis of a delicate two-part

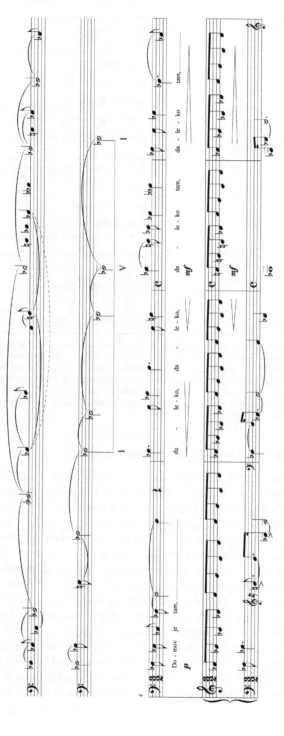

Example 6.1 Agency and voice-leading in the opening vocal phrase. Pavel Haas, *Čtyři písně pro bas (baryton) a klavír na slova čínské poezie v překladu Bohumila Mathesia* (Prague: Panton, 1987), i, bb. 4–7.

Sva - tý Vá - cla - ve, vé - vo - do če - ské ze - mě, knie - že náš,

pros za ny Bo - ha, sva - té - ho Du - cha! Kri - ste le - i - son!

Example 6.2 Hymn to St Wenceslas: the oldest version found in the Latin-Czech Catholic Gradual from 1473.

Source: Transcription from Karel Cikrle, *Nejstarší české písně: melodický vývoj písní Hospodine, pomiluj ny a Svatý Václave* (unpublished master's thesis, Masarykova Universita v Brně, 1959), 72.

counterpoint. There is a similarity with the opening of the Four Songs in textural pattern and modal colour; in fact, the three-note 'svatý' ('saint') motive (D flat – E flat – C flat) and the four-note 'Václave' ('Wenceslas') motive (F flat – E flat – C flat – D flat) belong to the same mode.

Lubomír Peduzzi has used the apparent reference to St Wenceslas in the Four Songs to support his claim that Haas retained during his incarceration the spirit of defiance which he manifested in his pre-Terezín wartime works, namely the Suite for Oboe and Piano and Symphony (1940–41).[17] The Four Songs may contain a Wenceslas reference, but it is rather subdued compared to the full-length quotations found in the previous works, both of which also include allusions to the Hussite chorale ('You Who Are the Warriors of God'). The song cycle also contains none of the topical allusions to religious chant and the military, used in the Symphony to portray (in accord with the popular legend) the twofold role of St Wenceslas as a saint and a warrior. It may be suggested that the patriotic elements were suppressed as a result of censorship in Terezín, but even this explanation is not satisfactory. Given its subtlety, the Wenceslas reference could hardly be regarded as a secret subversive code. The Four Songs are different in essence (qualitatively, not quantitatively) from Haas's earlier patriotic works. They contain an intimately personal and profoundly human reflection on the themes of loss, suffering, and hope. If indeed there is a Wenceslas allusion in this work, it merely specifies (on the level of private association) that the desired home lies 'in the land of Wenceslas'.

Another level of significance arises through an intertextual parallel between the opening of 'I Heard Wild Geese' and the beginning of the Windmill Scene from Haas's pre-war opera *Charlatan* (discussed in Chapter 5). Both begin with a four-note ostinato (albeit of a different kind in each case), from which emerges the voice (baritone) of a protagonist situated in a nocturnal landscape (see Example 5.5). The first words Pustrpalk (the 'charlatan') utters are: 'There, there used to be a village' (compare with 'My home is there, faraway there'). Pustrpalk subsequently tells the story of a village which was 'burnt to the ground' by the Swedes during a recent war.[18] In this intriguing case of intertextuality, the distinction between author and protagonist(s) is hard to sustain against the compulsive analogy between Pustrpalk and composer himself, both of whom find themselves at a place encapsulating the horror of war (a burnt site/a ghetto), haunted by memories of past happiness (the 'village'/'home'). This is one of several uncanny parallels between the Four Songs and *Charlatan* (resulting partly from Haas's continuing preoccupation with the uncanny as a theme) which will be pointed out in this chapter.

Presumably, a number of more or less plausible suggestions could be made about potential thematic or motivic allusions concealed in the four-note ostinato. It has been related to the repetitive quaver motive (F – F – G flat – E) in the duet of Harlequin and Death in Ullmann's opera *Der Kaiser von Atlantis*,[19] to the opening 'cross' motive of Dvořák's *Requiem*,[20] and to the plainchant melody of the *Dies Irae*.[21] Yet another parallel could be suggested with the four-note quaver ostinato (B – C – D – A) underpinning the 'Idylle' from Erik Satie's 1915 *Avant-dernières pensées (Penultimate Thoughts)*. In this piece, there are fragments of an inner monologue (such as 'my heart is cold in the back' and 'the moon is on bad terms with its neighbours') inscribed between the piano staves throughout the piece.[22] However, it would be misleading to assume that the significance of a particular motive necessarily resides in a reference to another piece. Such approach could easily produce simplistic results such as: 'Haas alluded to Satie's "Idylle" in order to communicate the dark, anxious feelings ("my heart is cold") he experienced during what he suspected to be the "penultimate" days of his life.'

The point here is rather to illuminate in more generic terms the significance of particular musical features in the Four Songs by analogy with the functioning of similar features in other works. Karbusický made an interesting point about the circular motion of the four-note ostinato and its implications in terms of the perception of time. He invoked Ullmann's four-note ostinato, associated with the repeated words 'Tage, Tage' ('days, days'), in order to argue that circular motion in both works symbolises the 'hopelessness of life in Terezín, absurdly running in circles'.[23] The comparison with Satie's 'Idylle' suggests that, in other cases, the repetitive, circular movement of an ostinato tends to be associated with contemplation (an inner monologue). The example from Haas's Suite for Oboe and Piano reveals that the composer used a particular kind of contrapuntal texture to convey a meditative, possibly prayer-like character. These nuances of meaning depend not only on the associated literary text and historical context, but also on parameters of tempo, dynamics, level of dissonance, articulation, and so on; Ullmann's ostinato has a more menacing character from those of Satie and Haas partly because it is comparatively faster, louder, more chromatic, and more sharply articulated.

The four-note ostinato in Four Songs is particularly strongly associated with the motive of home. Example 6.1 shows the first entry of the solo voice, which delivers the four syllables of the poem's opening line ('My home is there') on the four notes of the ostinato. The vocal part smoothly joins in the ostinato movement, providing a seamless transition between 'silent rumination' and 'speech'. This suggests that the ostinato, which anticipates this utterance, represents the protagonist's 'inner voice' and that the gesture of 'moving in circles' refers to the quality of the thought process. If the ostinato indeed signifies the idée fixe of home, then the repetitive, circular nature of this rumination could be understood in Julia Kristeva's terms as the 'helpless turning over' of the object of loss in a melancholic mind.[24]

Gestures and agency in voice leading, rhythm, and metre

The opening vocal phrase (bb. 4–7) is highly suggestive of lamentation, owing to the poignant chromatic descent in the latter two bars of the phrase and the 'traumatic' repetition of words in Haas's setting of the line 'far away, there'.[25] As Linda Austin has observed, such 'truncated, repetitive, and recursive' expressions of loss and grief are characteristic of literary laments; like 'sighs and cries of woe' they are the products of emotional states in which 'words become inadequate or unavailable' and the internal turbulence 'erupt[s] in gestures'.[26] Correspondingly, the melodic contour of the phrase displays the conflicting tendency to 'strive' against and succumb to the 'heaviness of descent' which, as Naomi Cumming has argued, is characteristic of gestural expressions of grief.[27] Since the affective significance of such melodic gestures depends on a tonal frame of reference, Example 6.1 includes a voice-leading reduction in order to demonstrate that there is indeed an underlying tonal structure to the phrase, against which the agency of the vocal line can be gauged.

The four-note motive is based on sinusoidal encircling of D flat, which functions as the tonic. The second bar of the vocal phrase (b. 5) is based on a similar four-note template, transposed upwards by a perfect fifth and thus centred 'around' A flat (affirmed by the bass). The absence of A flat from the vocal line, which clings instead to the upper neighbour note B flat, suggests a certain 'striving' against the tonal pull of this relatively stable pitch. The four-note motive is not transposed literally (as C flat – B flat – G flat – A flat); instead, the latter two pitches are 'sharpened' to invest the melody with an ascending tendency. The ascending energy is consummated – and exhausted – with the leap to D flat (the melody therefore traverses the space of an octave). The ensuing chromatic passage descends not only back to A flat but even one tone lower to G flat. Correspondingly, the descent to the 'tonic' D flat is followed by further major-second descent to the neighbouring C flat. Thus, the plaintive chromatic descent thus concludes with two neighbour-note 'sighs'.

Analogous patterns of agency can be observed on the level of rhythm and metre. Here the referential framework is provided by the properties of the underlying ostinato, from which the vocal part becomes progressively differentiated. Beginning with b. 5 (see Example 6.3), the vocal melody is delivered in groups of three crotchets, thus establishing its own metric stratum (3/4 or 6/4), independent from that of the ostinato, which perpetuates the 12/8 (3/2) time signature. The move to longer rhythmic values (crotchets) and metric units (comprising six quavers rather than four quavers) suggests 'striving to transcend' the prescribed boundaries.

The second vocal phrase (bb. 9–12) is based on the same tonal skeleton as the first one (see Example 6.3). B flat functions here as a kind of 'tenor', that is, the scale degree on which most of the text is delivered. The phrase is punctuated by falling melodic skips to the tonic D flat (bb. 10 and 12), which are significant in

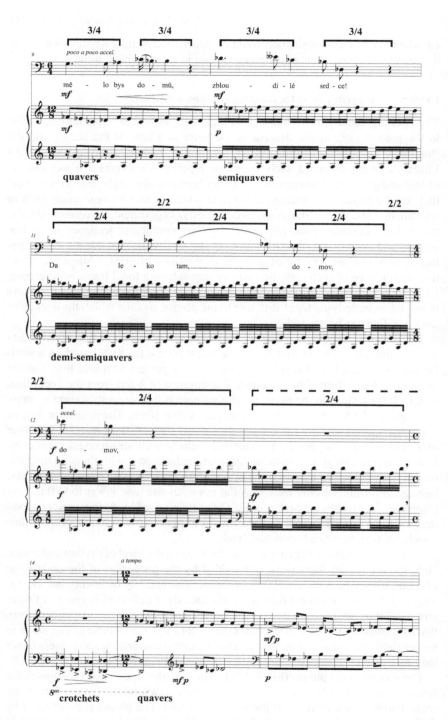

Example 6.3 Agency, rhythmic layers and metric groupings in the second vocal phrase. Haas, Four Songs, i, bb. 9–16.

terms of agency. They suggest a struggle to maintain the tenor and a tendency to fall back to the tonic, as if due to exhaustion or lack of breath. Correspondingly, the units of which the phrase consists become progressively shorter. The final exclamation 'Domov' ('Home'), uttered literally 'with the last breath', rises back to the tenor in a gesture of striving towards the distant place.

Once again, rhythm and metre support this effect. The underlying ostinato undergoes gradual diminution from quavers to semiquavers and even demi-semiquavers. The vocal part remains in the 6/4 stratum, until the exclamations 'Domov, domov', create a hemiola pattern and thus suggest an ascent to a 'higher' rhythmic level: the 'beat' shifts from crotchets to minims. In this sense, both the voice and the piano are pushed to the extremes and the gap between them grows ever wider as a result. While the gradual diminution of the ostinato conveys the sense of agitation and feverish activity, the vocal part's ascent across metro-rhythmic layers is suggestive of 'reaching beyond' the boundaries. The futility of this effort is demonstrated by the return of the four-note ostinato, reinforced by longer rhythmic values and heavy accentuation, which seems to represent the unbreakable cycle in which the subject is trapped.

Uncanny mirror images and shadows in the musical structure

This song (and the cycle as a whole) is characterised by the proliferation of 'mirror images' and 'shadows' in the musical fabric. These features are best regarded as musical signifiers of the uncanny. It is useful to re-introduce here the following lines from Nicholas Royle's definition of the uncanny:

> The uncanny involves feelings of uncertainty, in particular regarding the reality of who one is and what is being experienced. Suddenly, one's sense of oneself [. . .] seems strangely questionable. [. . .] It is a peculiar commingling of the familiar and unfamiliar. It can take the form of something familiar unexpectedly arising in a strange and unfamiliar context, or of something strange and unfamiliar unexpectedly arising in a familiar context.[28]

On the level of pitch structure, mirror images and shadows take the form of symmetrical pitch structures and parallelisms, respectively, giving rise to highly dissonant chromatic structures. These start to appear between bars 20–22 (see Example 6.4). In bar 20, for the first time in the song, the ostinato appears simultaneously in two transpositions. The two tetrachords occupied by the ostinato mirror each other (non-literally) around their common pitch F flat. This principle of mirroring is even more readily apparent in the next bar, where the outer voices of the respective piano parts comprise two perfect fifths (A flat – E flat and E – B), symmetrically arranged around the dyad E flat/F flat (enharmonically E natural). The duality of these adjacent pitches, which continue to be spelled in various enharmonic ways, is also central to the following bar. Here the lower pitch (E flat) is transferred to the higher register; the minor second/augmented unison thus appears in inversion as a major seventh/diminished octave. This becomes

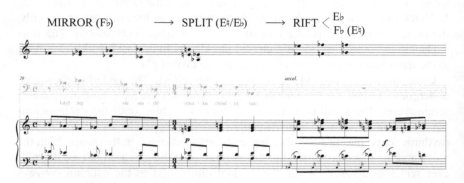

Example 6.4 Signs of the uncanny (mirrors, rifts, and shadows) in voice-leading structure. Haas, *Four Songs*, i, bb. 20–2.

the basis of a highly dissonant sonority pushed around chromatically in parallel motion, in which the movement of each pitch is followed by a shadow from below at the distance of a minor third (right hand) and a tritone (left hand).

The gradual distancing of an object from its mirror image in bb. 20–22 (Example 6.4) may function as a symbolic representation of estrangement from the self: a look in the mirror (the mirroring of tetrachords around the common pitch F flat), the recognition of the self as the other (the splitting of F flat into the dyad E flat/E), and the estrangement of the self from the other (inversion of semitone into diminished octave). The ever-changing enharmonic spelling of E/F flat can be seen as signifying the confusion of the self and the other. It is significant that the symbolic 'rift' in the protagonist's subjectivity should occur in the 'inner voice', below the relatively quiet surface of the vocal part, which only becomes agitated in the following bars (as if the uncanny sensation only gradually ascended into consciousness). The dissonant semitone clashes, rapid increase in dynamics, and chaotic, spasmodic movement in the last bar of the passage (bar 22) can be regarded as gestural representation of the emotional effect of self-alienation: pain, fear, and chaos.[29] The metaphor of shivering is also fitting, considering the reference in the corresponding passage to 'the coldest moment of the sorrow's cold breeze'. A similar character of agitation and confusion is conveyed by the hectic and disordered movement of semiquaver chromatic shadows which underpin the fast-paced declamation (in extreme dynamics and register) of the words 'I've heard the cry of wild geese; they've just flown in' (bb. 25–26).

The 'cry of wild geese' is musically illustrated by a complex demi-semiquaver ostinato pattern asserted in the piano part, which comprises, despite its random appearance, three superimposed layers of the familiar four-note motive (see Example 6.5). This ostinato pattern displays vertical mirroring of tetrachords occupied by the ostinato (D flat – C flat – E flat – F; F – G – A flat – B flat) as well as horizontal refraction of the pattern (phase shift, diminution, reordering of pitches). The left-hand part, too, is symmetrically organised: A flat assumes the central position, with the other two pitch classes located a perfect fourth above and below.

Example 6.5 'Cries of wild geese': self-mirroring and overlapping tetrachords. Haas, Four
Songs, i, bb. 27–8.

The ostinato pattern shown in Example 6.5 can be regarded not only as an
iconic imitation of the geese crying 'over each other' (the superimposition of patterns), but also as a 'mirage' of home (the mirroring and refraction of the 'my-
home-is-there' motive). This uncanny occurrence of 'something familiar [. . .] in
a strange and unfamiliar context' produces a dysphoric, alienating reaction in the
protagonist (hence the mirror image of the self as the other). Indeed, the juxtaposition of the motive of 'strange/foreign night'[30] with that of the protagonist's 'house'
(a familiar place) implies that the protagonist becomes a stranger in his own house
(possibly symbolising his own self).[31]

Tonality, agency, and the subject's 'vicious circle'

Besides its association with uncanny symbolism, symmetry also raises the question of stasis and circularity, which in turn have strong implications in terms of
agency. The ending of the first song, which provides further examples of the
preoccupation with parallel motion and mirroring, suggests that pitch symmetry
may play a significant role in the large-scale tonal design. As the voice enters for
the last time with the four-note motive (again associated with the 'idée fixe' of
'home'), its movement (C flat – B flat – G flat – A flat) parallels from below at
a distance of a perfect fourth the piano right-hand part (F flat – E flat – C flat –
D flat). In the last bar, the upper voices rest on the tonic D flat. That the pedal A flat
does not descend to the tonic could be explained as a gesture suggesting the lack
of tonal resolution. However, the appearance in the last bar of an E flat played *pp*
in an extremely low register suggests that the pedal A flat in fact functions as an
axis of symmetry, a mirror which reflects the vocal D flat (a fourth above) as an
E flat (a fourth below).[32]

The question whether A flat is the tonal dominant, structurally dependent on the
tonic D flat, or an axis of symmetry to which D flat is subordinated, has strong
implications for the issues of agency. It is therefore helpful to give some consideration to the song's large-scale tonal structure with respect to the movement
of the vocal part. In the first half of the song, the vocal part's trajectory can be
reduced to the ascent from the tonic D flat to the dominant A flat (the tenor B flat is
regarded as a neighbour note to the latter); the second half brings the continuation
of this ascent from A flat to E flat (bb. 24–25). This ascending tendency suggests
the effort to move ever higher in register and ever further from the tonic D flat

along the circle of fifths. Indeed, the achievement of the high point E flat coincides with the appearance of the motive of wild geese, which may be seen to represent the idea of literally 'raising above' the present confines and cross the distance that separates the protagonist from home.

However, this interpretation of the subject's agency relies on a tonal frame of reference and linear conception of movement, measured in terms of high/low and near/far (in relation to the tonal centre). In a circular system based on pitch symmetry, these parameters either do not function in the same way (near/far) or they do not exist at all (high/low). If, as the concluding bar suggests, the directional tonal system rooted in D flat yields to non-directional symmetrical arrangement around A flat, then the distinction between high and low disappears and movement in either direction becomes fundamentally futile, however strong the subject's agency might be. If high indeed equals low, then the E flat in bb. 25–26, which constitutes the high point of the tonal trajectory (as well as register, declamatory agitation and rhythmic activity in the vocal part), is inescapably bound to its flip side, the tonic D flat, associated with low register, passivity, and helplessness. In the last two bars, the vocal line traverses the distance between both extremes (descending from the E flat abandoned in bb. 25–26 through A flat to D flat in bb. 35–36) in a single gesture of resignation, as if realising the futility of resistance.

Stasis is not implied solely by pitch symmetries. Static, non-directional repetition is also signified by the circular motion of the ever-present ostinato. Even the most feverish rhythmic activity is ineffectual; one might say that the protagonist is trapped like a hamster in a wheel. The same properties are suggested by the large-scale form (A A'), which consists of two roughly symmetrical halves. It is noteworthy that the symmetry of the musical setting is not implied by the structure of the poem (each half of the song sets four and seven lines of the poem, respectively). Both halves of the song are underpinned by the same dynamic trajectory, resulting from the gradual diminution of the ostinato's rhythmic values, followed by a sudden drop back to long values. In other words, the song consists of two cycles of increasing agitation, followed by resignation. Every attempt on part of the protagonist to execute agency proves to be futile.

'In a Bamboo Grove'

Table 6.2 Second song: text and translation. Mathesius, *Nové zpěvy staré Číny*, p. 16. English translation as in Haas, *Four Songs* (1992).

V bambusovém háji *(Wang Wei)*	In a Bamboo Grove *(Wang Wei)*
V bambusech nejsou lidé,	The bamboos screen no people, [Lit.: Amidst the bamboos, there are no people]
v bambusech sedím sám,	Here I am all alone,
tu na loutnu zahraju tiše,	Now I play a soft tune on my lute,
tu sobě zahvízdám.	Or whistle a quiet tone. [Lit.: Now I whistle to myself]

V bambusovém háji *(Wang Wei)*	*In a Bamboo Grove* *(Wang Wei)*
Kdo, řekněte, lidé, kdo ví,	Who, tell me good people, who knows
že v bambusech sedím sám [, sám]	Where the bamboos hide me, just me, [Lit.: That in bamboos I sit alone, alone]
[že v bambusech sedím sám]	In the bamboos all alone
a na východ srpečku luny	In the east a sickle moon I see [Lit.: And at the rising of a crescent moon]
bambusem pozírám?	Through bamboos overgrown. [Lit.: I gaze through the bamboos]

The second song, entitled 'In a Bamboo Grove', brings a striking contrast to the gloomy character of the previous song through its major modality and dance-like gesture. It can be regarded as a continuation of the topic of 'danse excentrique' (discussed in Chapters 2 and 3), which appears throughout Haas's oeuvre in scherzo-like dance movements of multi-movement works. The character of these movements is always somewhat ambiguous; to a varying degree, darker undertones tend to lurk under the comic surface. Some of the pieces are marked by an innocuous 'clownish' character, while others veer towards the darker pole of the 'grotesque'; in the extreme case, 'danse excentrique' turns into 'danse macabre'.[33]

A common feature of all instances of this topic in Haas's music is the presence of dance-like quaver 'steps', such as those apparent in the ostinato underpinning this song (see Example 6.6). The regularity of such steps is typically disrupted by irregular accentuation, cross-rhythms, and/or other kinds of metric ambiguity. In this particular song, the metrically ambiguous 'whistling' tune (in 3/4 against 2/4 accompaniment) is a case in point (see the last two bars of Example 6.6). The somewhat banal character of the motive is thus combined with the effect of 'awkward hopping' (note the 'bouncy' syncopation on the downbeat), to conjure a caricatural, clownish persona.

There is a hint of semantic ambiguity in the ostinato, marked by semitone oscillation and clashing dissonances; this is not quite congruent with the far more straightforward major-mode character which the vocal line maintains throughout most of the song. It seems as if the protagonist were wearing a cheerful mask over his sad face. The comic mask seems to slip off temporarily in a cadenza-like section located towards the end of the song (see Example 6.6). Based on the prolongation of a flattened sixth degree, the cadenza brings a sudden shift to minor mode. The word 'sám' ('alone') receives special emphasis: it marks the beginning of the cadenza and the assertion of the minor mode; it is also embellished with a mordent, suggestive of 'plaintive' intonation (a 'break in the voice'). The immediately following return of the whistling tune restores the major mode as well as the dance-like rhythmic gesture, but now there is a slight sense of 'laughter through tears'.

Example 6.6 'Cadenza': dysphoric undertones and the rising moon. Haas, *Four Songs*, ii,
bb. 70–8.

It is hardly a coincidence that this moment of reversal coincides with the
appearance of the motive of the rising moon ('at the rising crescent moon
I gaze'), musically depicted by the chromatic ascent in the piano right-hand part
(see Example 6.6). Since moonlight is a mere 'inauthentic' reflection of sunlight,
the moon tends to be associated with the reverse side of all things. It is also
important to bear in mind Haas's association of the moon with dark forces of the
subconscious and uncanny doppelgängers in *Charlatan*.

'The moon is far away from home'

Table 6.3 Third song: text and translation: Mathesius, *Nové zpěvy staré Číny*, p. 39.
English translation as in Haas, *Four Songs* (1992).

Daleko měsíc je od domova *(Čang Čiu-ling)*	*The Moon is Far Away from Home* *(Tchang Tiou-ling)*
Z temného moře	The moon glows from [the] black [Lit.: From a dark sea]
vyrůstá měsíc.	Darkness of the sea, [Lit.: Grows / rises the moon]
V daleké [v daleké] zemi	In that far, in that far land
teď rozkvétá též.	It is blossoming too.

Daleko měsíc je od domova *(Čang Čiu-ling)*	*The Moon is Far Away from Home* *(Tchang Tiou-ling)*
Láska svůj truchlí	Love is lamenting [Lit.: Love is mourning its]
daremný sen –	Its hollow dream,
[láska truchlí svůj sen,]	Love is lamenting its dream,
čeká [čeká] na vzdálený večer.	It waits, it waits for a far-off evening,
[Na vzdálený večer.]	For a far-off evening.
Zhasínám světlo – [this line was left out by Haas]	
Jasněji měsíc	The moon shines ever brighter
svítí v mé hoře.	Through my tears. [Lit.: Into my sorrow]
Noční šat oblékám – [oblékám noční šat]	I put on night-time clothes –
chladné je jíní.	Rime frost chills so much.
Ruce mé, ruce,	Hands of mine, my hands,
kterak jste prázdné	That are so empty
říci to všechno!	To say everything! [Lit.: To say it all]
[Říci to všechno!]	To say everything!
Spánku, sen dej mi	Oh sleep, give me a dream,
[Spánku, sen dej mi]	Oh sleep, give me a dream
o návratu domů!	Of going back home!
[O návratu domů, domů!]	Returning to my home, my home!
Spánku, sen nemůžeš dát:	Sleep, you can give me no dream:
mé toužení stále mě budí.	My yearning keeps me awake.

The motive of the rising moon, which appears at the end of the second and at the beginning of the third song, is more than a 'bridge' between the two. It symbolically represents the transition from (fading) day to (falling) night. Correspondingly, the third song restores the melancholic mood of the first song, bringing back the circular ostinato, the theme of separation from home, the topic of lament, and the profusion of uncanny mirror images.

The opening image of the moon mirrored on the surface of the sea implies the growing distance between the object and its reflection. On another level, this image may represent the subject's own self-reflection and distancing from his own self, which is viewed as other. The next two lines explicitly articulate the idea of the moon facilitating an imaginary connection with 'that far land [in which] it is blossoming too'. As may be expected, symmetrical mirroring abounds in the pitch structure of the vocal line (see Example 6.7). In bb. 3–4, the vocal line is made up of dyads grouped in symmetrically organised pairs. In bb. 5–6, A flat/G sharp functions as an axis of symmetry, around which the melody moves within the interval of a minor third. The idea of mirroring also manifests itself in the enharmonic spelling of pitches B – A – G sharp (b. 6) as C flat – B double flat – A flat (bb. 7–8).

As has been shown in the analysis of the first song, structural symmetry, circularity, and stasis have profound implications for the possibility of musical agency and affective expression. The sense of retardation is even more apparent in the third song, where the vocal line is mostly characterised by circular (rather than linear) motion. Take for example the plaintive chromatic descent on the repeated words 'faraway' and 'in that far [land]' ('daleko, daleko'; 'v daleké, v daleké [zemi]'), which appears near the opening of both songs (compare Examples 6.1 and 6.7). The prominent lament-like descent in the first song contrasts with the much more monotonous delivery in the third one. In the latter case, the chromatic descent is not only shorter but its expressive effect, which relies on a linear,

Example 6.7 Moon in the water: pitch symmetry. Haas, Four Songs, iii, bb. 1–8.

descending gesture, is 'neutralised' by the circular, symmetrical, and therefore static melodic design in which the progression is embedded.

The song's opening vocal phrase (bb. 2–8) is followed by a six-bar piano interlude (bb. 9–14, see Example 6.8). The next vocal entry (bb. 15–18) is, again, rather dispassionate in character, regardless of the emotionally loaded text ('love its lamenting/mourning its hollow dream'). As if to confirm that the mourning is silent, another 'voiceless' piano interlude ensues (bb. 19–24, see Example 6.9). Arguably, the mode of delivery observed here bears strong resemblance to the symptoms of depression which Kristeva subsumed under the term 'psychomotor and affective retardation': slow speech, long and frequent silences, slackened rhythms, monotonous intonation, and the perception of time as slowed down or static.[34]

Lamento bass and the topic of lament

If indeed the expression of grief is frustrated in the protagonist's speech (the vocal part), grief may still manifest itself in another way. What gradually emerges in the 'voiceless' piano interludes is the descending tetrachordal progression suggestive of a *lamento bass*, the emblem of the long-established musical topic of lament.[35] The circular ostinato itself, newly cast in crotchets (as opposed to quavers), transposed to a very low register, and unfolding in a slow tempo (*lento e grave, ma non troppo*), now appears in the guise of a *lamento bass*. Although the ostinato consists of 'wrong' scale degrees in the 'wrong' order (3^ 2^ 7^ 1^ rather than 4^ 3^ 2^ 1^), descending tetrachordal progressions, including 'correct' iterations of the *lamento bass*, permeate the musical texture throughout the song.

The first instance of such saturation with tetrachordal structures appears, significantly, in anticipation of the line 'love is lamenting/mourning its hollow dream' (see Example 6.8). In the first two bars of the first piano interlude (bb. 9–10), the tetrachord occupied by the ostinato (3^ 2^ 1^ 7^ in A flat) is paralleled in the middle voice at the distance of a second (4^ 3^ 2^ 1^ in A flat). Another pair of neighbouring tetrachords appears in a higher register in the following two bars (bb. 11–12). The resulting tetrachordal structure outlines an Aeolian (minor) scale on A flat/G sharp, in which the upper voice (in bb. 11–12) traverses the upper tetrachord (8^ to 5^), whereas the lower voice descends first from 7^ to 4^ and subsequently from 4^ to 1^.

The second piano interlude (bb. 19–24, see Example 6.9) is based on the same template with one significant difference: whereas in the first interlude the pitches belonging to the tetrachords were organised in circular arabesque-like patterns, here they gradually acquire a linear, descending shape. This transformation is complete in bb. 21–24, where the upper voice outlines a diatonic tetrachord (8^ to 5^), embellished with upper neighbour notes, whereas the lower voice contains a diatonic descent (7^ to 4^; 4^ to 1^), filled with chromatic passing notes. It is not until now that the morphological similarity and topical association with *lamento bass* (its diatonic and chromatic types) becomes clearly apparent.

Example 6.8 Tetrachordal structure: the first piano interlude. Haas, Four Songs, iii, bb. 9–14.

Example 6.9 Tetrachordal structure: the second piano interlude. Haas, Four Songs, iii, bb. 19–24.

Trauma surfacing into consciousness

Throughout this song, a subtle, semantically loaded interaction takes place between the piano part (the 'inner voice') and the vocal part. The interplay is suggestive of the gradual 'surfacing' of thoughts into consciousness, correlated with increasing affective response. The return of the four-note ostinato in the third song signifies the return of the 'idée fixe' of home. Subsequently, an oblique reference is made in the

Example 6.10 Affective expression, directionality and agency. Haas, Four Songs, iii, bb. 25–33.

vocal part to a 'far[away] land' without explicitly naming the object of loss. Correspondingly, the emotional response is initially not expressed through affective modulation of the voice; rather, it is symbolically represented by a *lamento bass* progression in the piano part, which, in turn, anticipates the reference to 'mourning' in the vocal part. The fact that the linear, descending shape of the *lamento bass* only gradually emerges from meditative arabesques is thus suggestive of the subject's increasing emotional self-awareness. The reiteration of the line 'love is lamenting/mourning its dream' after the second piano interlude (see Example 6.10) is the first instance in this song of a clear gestural expression of grief and longing: note the mordent figure suggestive of a shaking voice, the expressive inflection of A sharp to A, and the clearly descending lament-like contour of the phrase.

This affective response goes hand in hand with assertion of linear directionality and agency (as opposed to the ostinato's static circularity which previously seemed to engulf the passive subject). After the initial plaintive descent ('love is lamenting its dream') a melodic ascent follows in the bass (bb. 27–30), suggestive of longing ('waiting, waiting for a distant evening'). Besides the ascending gesture, the subject's agency also manifests itself in the prolongation of G (both in the bass and the vocal part), which defies the A flat/G sharp modal centre, implied by the ostinato. However, this gesture of striving is immediately followed by that of succumbing, yielding to the cyclic motion of the ostinato and to the A flat minor modality which it implies (bb. 31–33).

The disturbing effect of moonlight

The reference to the moon in the line 'the moon shines ever brighter into my sorrow' (which might suggest that the protagonist 'sees more clearly' the source of his frustration) coincides with the reappearance of the signifiers of the uncanny in Haas's musical setting (see Example 6.11). The ostinato in the left-hand part is paralleled in the right-hand part in shorter values; the upper tetrachord mirrors the lower one, with which it shares a common pitch. The vocal part repeats in a similarly circular way a chromatic tetrachord (a shadow of the diatonic tetrachord).

As in the first song, the appearance of uncanny mirrors and shadows (accompanied in both cases by references to 'chill' in the text) marks the beginning of a series of musical events suggestive of fragmentation, discord, and emotional turmoil. The beginnings of this process can be observed in the passage shown in Example 6.12. Here, the familiar tetrachordal *lamento* progression takes place in the piano right-hand part. As before, the tetrachordal structure outlines an Aeolian scale on A flat/G sharp; the upper voice is expected to descend from ^8 to ^5 and the lower one from ^7 to ^4 and then from ^4 to ^1. However, the progression concludes instead with an arrival at a dissonant fourth-based sonority (A flat – E flat – B flat), symmetrically organised around the central E flat. As in the analogous passage in the first song (bb. 20–22), a seventh-wide rift is created between neighbouring pitches (B flat – C flat) on the last beat of bar 43. As before, each of the pitches is accompanied by a 'shadow' at the distance of a minor third and a tritone, respectively.

Example 6.11 The uncanny moonlight. Haas, Four Songs, iii, bb. 34–7.

Example 6.12 Subversion of directionality and intervallic rift in the piano right-hand part. Haas, Four Songs, iii, bb. 40–3.

This symbolic perturbation of subjectivity triggers an escalating emotional upheaval in the piano part (bb. 44–48). The sense of unrest and confusion is conveyed by obsessive repetition of two alternating sonorities, rhythmic misalignment of the two hands (syncopation, triplets), and a rapid increase in tempo (*poco a poco accel.*), and dynamics (from *mp* in b. 40 to *ff* in b. 49). This upheaval

Example 6.13 The 'anxiety' motive. Haas, Four Songs, iii, bb. 49–57.

reaches its climax in bb. 49–53 (see Example 6.13) with the appearance of highly dissonant parallelisms based on the familiar chromatic sonority. It is significant that in this manifestation the parallelisms take on the melodic and rhythmic shape of the 'death' motive from *Charlatan* (see Example 5.15). This dramatic and dynamic climax of the song and of the cycle as a whole may therefore be associated with the state of 'mortal anxiety' (the motive shown in Example 6.13 will be referred to as the 'anxiety' motive from here onward). Interestingly, both occurrences of the motive are related to the uncanny. In the opera, Pustrpalk's death coincides with the appearance of the spectre of the monk Jochimus, who is not only Pustrpalk's life-long adversary, but also his alter-ego, a complementary part of his split subjectivity (see Chapter 5).

The text corresponding with the 'anxiety' motive ('Hands of mine, my hands that are so empty to say everything!') comprises several layers of meaning. First, this utterance conveys the impossibility of expressing the ineffable (a characteristic topos of literary laments). Its semantic and grammatical contortion poignantly underscores the insufficiency of language. Second, the image of 'empty hands' symbolises loss and loneliness (having nobody to embrace), as well as powerlessness (given the association of hands with power and agency).[36] Finally, the focus on the hands – the only uncovered part of the body one can see clearly without a mirror when dressed – suggests the focus on the self and perhaps even the sense of alienation.

Symmetry, circularity, and stasis as challenges to agency

The crisis triggered by the uncanny effect of moonlight manifests itself not only by the occurrence of the intervallic rift but also by the subversion of directionality. The latter is apparent from the abortive *lamento* progression in bb. 40–43 (see

Example 6.12). The frustration of the expected descent to ^5 (E flat) by return to ^8 (A flat) in the upper voice (see the top stave of the tetrachordal reduction) indicates that the diatonic system (associated with directed linear motion) is subdued by the principle of symmetry (associated with directionless circular motion). Not only is the *lamento* motive rendered 'circular', but the resulting tetrachord (B flat – A flat – G flat – F flat) is a subset of the (symmetrical and directionless) whole-tone scale.[37]

The conjunction in Example 6.13 of circularity in the music and emphatic expression of powerlessness (the symbol of 'empty hands') in the text underscores the impeding effect of circularity on agency. The vocal line, led in parallel motion with the 'anxiety' motive, is reduced to circling around a single pitch. Increasing emotional intensity is articulated by transposition to a higher register (from A to E). Yet this upheaval is immediately followed (after a moment of silence, tellingly encapsulating the ineffable) by a gesture of 'resignation' (the voice descends back to A in the last two bars of the example), which suggests the futility of agency and the inability 'to say everything'.

An important expressive feature of the song is the paradoxical association of feverish activity and stasis. This conflict between the will to agency and its fundamental impossibility is a major source of the protagonist's frustration. The excess of energy going to waste is clearly depicted in Haas's setting of the last two lines of the poem: 'Sleep, you can give me no dream, my yearning keeps me awake'. The sense of agitation is conveyed musically by a new ostinato pattern (the 'yearning' ostinato, see Example 6.15), based on ceaseless repetition of the 'anxiety' motive (itself a circular version of the *lamento* motive). It is also significant that the chromatic shadows accompanying the 'anxiety' motive are now arpeggiated, thus giving rise to a disquieting demi-semiquaver pulse. A parallel with the 'wild geese' motive from the first song resides in the common principle of horizontal refraction through phase shift.

This movement is only extinguished at the end of the song with the reassertion of the opening crotchet ostinato pattern (see Example 6.14). Instead of tonal resolution, the concluding bar brings the assertion of a static sonority, in which A flat is as much a modal tonic as it is a centre of symmetry (the left hand features

Example 6.14 Ending: enharmonicism, four-note motive, 'anxiety' motive, chromatic shadows, enharmonic doubles, and symmetrical concluding sonority. Haas, Four Songs, iii, bb. 89–92.

a fourth-based chord symmetrically arranged around A flat, while the right hand contains a whole-tone tetrachord).

The song's overall trajectory seems to lead from apathy through a moment of mortal anxiety ('hands, my hands . . .') to agitation ('my longing keeps me awake') and back. The invocation of sleep ('Oh sleep, give me a dream of going back home!'), articulates the protagonist's desire to retreat into a dream world or at least to a sleep-like state of 'anaesthesia' (the state in which he found himself at the beginning of the song, before he started gradually recovering his self-awareness) in order to escape the painful awareness of loss. Another vicious circle thus seems to have come full spin.

Large-scale tonal design: linear, spatial and symbolic explanation

The song's tonal structure is marked by the duality between the modal centres of A flat and A natural.[38] A flat dominates until the onset of the 'anxiety' motive (the transition to A occurs in bb. 46–47). The retransition from the 'natural' region to the 'flat' region takes place in the piano postlude (see Example 6.15). As is apparent from the reduction, the retransition is facilitated by the subdominant transpositional level. The tetrachordal motives (the 'anxiety' motive and later also the four-note motive) appear simultaneously on tonic and subdominant transpositional levels (A and D; A flat and D flat).

The primacy of A flat is asserted in the following cadence (see Example 6.16), which can be regarded in terms of 'balancing out' the significance of D flat (the lower fifth) by emphasising E flat (the upper fifth). Thus, the cadence is rather 'spatial' than 'linear' (in accord with the prevalence of circular repetition over linear progression throughout the song), but nonetheless 'tonal' in terms of the proximity of individual pitch centres on the cycle of fifths.

Of particular interest is the relationship between A and A flat. From the perspective of linear voice leading, A is an upper neighbour note, perhaps a counterbalance to the previous diversion to the lower leading note, G natural (bb. 27–30, see Example 6.10). Thus, if one can speak of a large-scale voice-leading trajectory at all, it is not linear (like the Schenkerian *Urlinie*) but circular, based on the principle of symmetrical chromatic encircling. This would be a 'background' projection of the 'foreground' mirroring pattern observed in the opening bars of the song.

The other way to think about the relationship between A flat and A natural is in terms of the *static* and *spatial* principle of polar opposition (the one discontinuously 'flips into' the other) rather than the *dynamic* and *linear* principle of voice leading (the one continuously 'leads to' the other). The polar opposition manifests itself in the complementarity of pitch content in scales based on the two adjacent pitches. Although the 'perfect' geometrical antipode of A flat on the cycle of fifths is the tritone-related D, A natural is no less remote from A flat than D, as far as pitch content of scales based on the respective tones is concerned (both have two pitches in common).[39]

The preference of A natural is probably motivated by its symbolic relationship with A flat – that of the 'ego' and its 'alter-ego'. The preoccupation with 'uncanny'

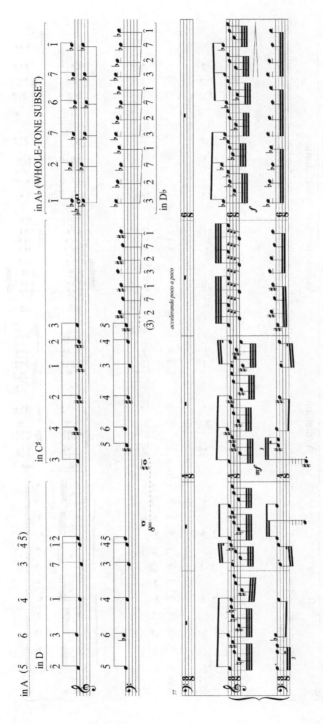

Example 6.15 'Retransition' from A natural to A flat. Haas, Four Songs, bb. 77–81.

Example 6.16 The cadence. Haas, Four Songs, iii, bb. 81–6.

symbolism involving doubles, shadows, and mirror images arguably extends into the realm of large-scale pitch relations. A flat and A natural are two 'facets' of a single entity: 'A'. They are simultaneously identical and different, close (in a linear chromatic scale) and distant (on the spatial circle of fifths). Likewise, the 'twin' scales built on these pitch centres are identical, except that one is all 'natural' and the other is all 'flat'. The same symbolic principle accounts for Haas's play with enharmonic spelling (especially A flat/G sharp). The ostinato (and the rest of the pitch fabric) is notated first with 'flats' (bb. 1–10), then briefly with 'sharps' (bb. 11–26), and then 'flats' again until the 'crisis' in b. 43, which triggers the shift to the 'natural' region of A. Such oscillation between enharmonic variants continues till the very end of the song (see particularly the concluding bars, shown in Example 6.14).

'Sleepless Night'

Table 6.4 Fourth song: text and translation. Mathesius, *Nové zpěvy staré Číny*, p. 37. English translation as in Haas, Four Songs (1992).

Probděná noc *(Han Jü)*	*Sleepless Night* *(Han I)*
Větrem se bambus houpá,	Bamboo swaying in the wind,
na kámen měsíc sed.	The moon sits on hard stone.
Do chvění Mléčné dráhy	[The] shadow of wild ducks flying fast [Lit.: Into the quivering of the Milky Way]
stín divoké kachny v[z]lét.	Across the Milky Way. [Lit.: Shadow of a wild duck flew (up)]
Na naše shledání myslím,	I am thinking of our meeting,
[na naše shledání, shledání myslím,]	Of our meeting, meeting, again,
víčka má míjí sen.	My dream like sun's ray. [Lit.: A dream flickers across my eyelids]
[Víčka má míjí sen.]	Quivering sun's ray.
Zatím co radostí zpívám,	And now while I'm singing for joy,
[zatím co radostí zpívám, zpívám,]	While for joy I'm singing, singing,
strak repot vzbouzí už den.	Magpies' chatter wakes the day.
[Vzbouzí den!]	Wakes the day!
[La, la, la, la, . . .]	La, la, la, la, [. . .]

The last song displays more preoccupation than the others with a literal tone-painting depiction of a nocturnal landscape, which is inseparably entangled with the protagonist's subjective emotional state. The opening motive consisting of descending and ascending chromatic waves illustrates the 'swaying bamboo', moved by gusts of wind. The motive's rocking movement also reflects the protagonist's balancing on the verge of sleep. The 'quivering of the Milky Way' on the dark canopy of the sky is illustrated by a neighbour-note triplet motive, set against a motionless fourth-chord pedal (bb. 21–3). The 'quivering' triplet figure is later juxtaposed with an ascending version of itself, which represents the 'shadow of a wild duck' (bb. 24–25); the ascending gesture corresponds with the composer's creative 'misreading' of 'vlét' ('flew in') as 'vzlét' ('flew up').

If in the first song, the 'cry of wild geese' evoked to the protagonist an uncanny recollection of home, here the sight of the 'shadow of wild ducks' seems to evoke the thought of reunion with (presumably) a friend or lover ('I am thinking of our meeting'). The response to this event is similar as in the first song: an emotional upheaval quickly reaching extreme dynamics and register (see Example 6.17). Familiar signifiers of the uncanny also reappear: note the profusion of clashing chromatic neighbour notes (doubles), the contrary motion (mirroring) between the two piano parts, and the resulting rift in register, splitting the piano part.

Karbusický regarded the short-long rhythmic pattern with off-beat emphasis (see Example 6.17) as a reference to the folklore idiom of the Moravian region of Slovácko.[40] Although such an allusion would be consistent with the theme of longing for home, I would rather draw attention to the gestural and physiological associations of the iambic rhythm (the rhythm of the heartbeat). Its use in this

Example 6.17 'Thinking of our meeting': another uncanny sensation. Haas, Four Songs, iv, bb. 33–42.

particular case brings to mind two commonly used metaphors of grief and anxiety: the sensation of 'heart clenching' (the music's 'spasmodic throbbing') and the turn of phrase 'something may tear one's heart apart' (the rift in register).

The central motive of the poem is the transition from night to day. Just before the break of dawn, the motive of the swaying bamboo returns with the line 'a dream flickers across my eyelids', fittingly illustrating the 'drifting' state of mind and reinforcing the correlation between natural surroundings and subjective experience. It is through a gradual transformation of this motive in the following piano interlude that the song traverses from nocturnal melancholy to the joyful mood of the dawn of a new day. By the end of the interlude, the motive is transformed from its original chromatic and sinusoidal shape into a major-mode diatonic and linearly descending tetrachord. Correspondingly, the sense of timeless drifting gives way to a dance-like gesture induced by the return of the ostinato from the second song (devoid of its dissonant properties). Thus, the last song concludes with a return of the cheerful 'whistling' tune of the second song, which creates a semblance of cyclic closure to the entire work.

Besides this motivic interconnection, the even-numbered songs have in common the motive of the bamboo grove. Considering the life-affirming character shared by these parts of the cycle, the bamboo grove appears as a locus of the pastoral idyll – a safe place in the womb of nature, removed from the pains of the human world ('there are no people amidst the bamboos'). A comparison of the 'whistling' tune with the folk-like tune from Haas's 'Pastorale' (the fourth movement of Haas's 1935 Suite for Piano, discussed in Chapter 3) demonstrates a similarity in textural pattern, 'bouncy' dance-like gesture, articulation, and ornamentation (compare Examples 3.10 and 6.6). Besides, the reference to 'whistling' can be associated with shepherds' 'piping'.

The vocal phrase following the piano interlude ('zatím co radostí zpívám', bb. 65–74) also betrays some morphological similarities with the folk-like tune from the 'Pastorale' (namely large intervallic leaps, staccato articulation, dance-like accompaniment pattern, and mordent-like ornamentation). Furthermore, this is the only section in the whole cycle marked with folk modality, which – precisely because of this singularity – points towards the pastoral. The idyllic image of the awakening of a new day is underscored by musical illustration of 'magpies' chatter' by trills and 'chattering' rhythmic figures. Finally, the sense of spontaneous music-making as a direct expression of joy is effectively conveyed by singing on the repeated syllables 'la, la, la, . . .', accompanied by the 'whistling' tune and the associated dance-like ostinato. The song concludes with an emphatic cadence in C major.

Conclusion: teleology and resolution versus yin/yang perspective

Both Peduzzi and Karbusický regarded the conclusion as unambiguously optimistic. Peduzzi commented on this issue in the following statement:

> These songs, crushingly moving with their deep sorrow, do not, however, lack a spark of an optimistic look into the future [. . .]. [T]he second

song [. . .] is an intermezzo of temporary carefree contentment. The fourth
song [. . .] becomes transformed into joyful singing [. . .] and thus optimisti-
cally concludes the cycle.[41]

Karbuský even associated the ending with the vision of liberation:

> The concluding song offers a suitable opportunity for the [expression of]
> hope for reunion. The vision of freedom transforms the anxious mood into an
> expression of joy. [. . .] The 'la la la la . . .' singing suggests an almost childish
> joy at the prospect of returning home. At the same time, the defiant whistling
> of Mr Wáng Wéi sitting in the bamboos emerges once again, completing [. . .]
> the image of rejoicing in regained freedom [. . .]'.[42]

And yet, the euphoric spirit of the conclusion is hard to reconcile with the melancholic atmosphere which dominates the cycle (with the exception of the second
song). One would almost expect to find some clues in Haas's music suggesting the presence of dark undertones lurking under the joyful surface, but the
search for such subversive hints is inconclusive. Granted, the jubilant singing
and dancing appears somewhat strained, largely as a result of the incongruity of
the juxtaposed moods, but there are no traces of grotesque distortion, and the elements of ambiguity found in the second song (clashing dissonances and major/
minor ambivalence) have been removed in the conclusion. The 'la la la' singing
balances on the verge of exaggeration, but it is not 'childish enough' to create
an ironic distance. The element of the pastoral does not in itself sustain a kind
of Mahlerian interpretation of the ending as a retreat from reality to the illusory
realm of a nostalgic idyll.

What is the significance of the oscillation between contrasting moods
(melancholy – joy – melancholy – melancholy/joy) throughout the cycle? Karbuský's answer to this question is that the 'mutual relationship between Haas's
four songs corresponds with the sonata cycle'.[43] Karbuský claims that Haas
ordered the parts and moods in his song cycle in such a way as to 'create an
up-to-date metamorphosis of the [sonata] archetype', even though 'up-to-date'
actually refers to a nineteenth-century development:

> In the nineteenth century, the second and third acts switched places: the lyri-
> cal movement only came after a scherzo, so that the finale could even more
> dramatically deploy the fanfares of the promised and successfully achieved
> victory.[44]

The model of the sonata cycle comes with hermeneutic assumptions rooted in the
nineteenth-century tradition: the 'heroic' construal of sonata form and the identifi-
cation of the artist with the hero. This paradigm may be appropriate for Smetana's
'autobiographical' quartet 'From My Life' (invoked by Karbuský),[45] which supposedly reflects the composer's struggle with deafness and deteriorating health,
but it cannot be extended to Haas's Four Songs without a considerable degree of
distortion.

Even more importantly, the notion of a linear, teleological narrative leading from conflict to resolution is fundamentally incompatible with the conceptual basis of Haas's song cycle. As has been demonstrated, this work is characterised by circularity and stasis rather than linearity and progression. The succession of the songs portrays the oscillation between mutually correlated polar opposites (darkness/light, night/day, melancholy/joy, death/life, and so on), which seems to have more to do with a natural cycle than the protagonist's agency; indeed, the impossibility of agency is one of the central themes of the work.

The fact that the sequence ends at a life-affirming moment should not be mistaken for any kind of teleological resolution or 'victory'. The semblance of cyclic closure, which results from the return in the fourth song of thematic material from the second song, is 'cancelled out' by an analogous motivic correspondence between the first and the third song. The whole is thus not only balanced, but also potentially open-ended. It is all too easy to imagine a fifth song to follow, opening with the agonisingly repetitive ostinato and throwing the subject back into the state of longing, anxiety, and melancholy. The cycle might go on, endlessly.

Midway through his article, Karbusický briefly deviates from his main line of argumentation predicated on teleology and makes a point in which he recognises the cyclic nature of Haas's piece and interprets it in a positive light. He suggests that Haas's piece conveys the sense of 'consolation in the anthropological constants of existence' and invokes the following passage from the Book of Ecclesiastes to illustrate the idea: 'What has been, is what is meant to be [will be]; what is meant to be, has already been. There is nothing new under the sun, since God renews what has passed.'[46] Karbusický refers to this particular biblical source to forge a link between Haas's Four Songs and the Jewish tradition:

> What is the core of Pavel Haas's personal identity? What is Czech and what is Jewish in his works from Terezín? [. . .] Perhaps the most Jewish thing about Haas's [. . .] Four Songs on exotic texts is the original transformation of the experienced existential absurdity into timeless and supracultural values [which] have nowhere been so profoundly [. . .] captured as in the scriptures born from the nation of Israel. The Book of Ecclesiastes [and] the Book of Job are treasures of the philosophy of existential anxiety, absurdity, but also hope. It is the ultimate absurdity of the anti-Semite ideology [. . .] that a Terezín prisoner could best convey this hope through exotic [Chinese] poetry.[47]

Karbusický seems to suggest that Haas communicated a fundamentally 'Jewish' message through the 'exotic' medium of Chinese poetry, functioning as a kind of (inauthentic?) substitute for the Jewish literary tradition. Nonetheless, Karbusický elsewhere acknowledges that 'old Chinese poetry, too, conveys that which is pan-human, eternally recurring, bridging all differences of races, cultural traditions, nationalities, and social systems'.[48] Although one can but speculate about Haas's familiarity with Chinese philosophy, it is worthwhile to elaborate on the idea that the composer may have reflected in his musical setting some deeper philosophical principles underpinning the Chinese poems. Specifically, the concept of yin and yang provides a useful way to comprehend the interlocking alternation between binary oppositions in the Four Songs.

According to Robin R. Wang, the relationship between yin and yang is characterised by the notions of 'interdependence' ('one side of the opposition cannot exist without the other') and 'mutual inclusion' ('yang always holds some yin and yin holds some yang').[49] These principles are encapsulated in the well-known yin/yang symbol, which 'includes a small circle of yang within the fullest yin and a small circle of yin within the fullest yang'.[50] Furthermore, the relationship between yin and yang is 'fundamentally dynamic and [based] on change'.[51] The two are involved in a constant process of alternation and reversal ('things develop to their extremes and then reverse [. . .] one side becomes the other in an endless cycle').[52] The fundamentally cyclic dynamism of this process is derived from the ceaseless cycles of growth and decline observed in nature (day and night, changing seasons) and, by analogy, in the human world.[53]

These features and processes (interdependence, mutual inclusion, dynamic change, alternation and reversal, and cyclicity) can be observed throughout Haas's song cycle. In the first song, the protagonist laments the loss of home, but in the second song, he finds joy in his loneliness. At the peak of his rejoicing, a germ of sadness appears along with the motive of the moon (the cadenza). This heralds a transition from the activity and brightness (yang) of the second song to the passivity and darkness (yin) of the third song (water and moon are also associated with yin).[54] Finally, the last song is marked by a transformation from night (yin) to day (yang).

Wang further highlights the essential differences between yin/yang thought and Western thought. Whereas the former proposes the dynamic fluctuation of mutually interconnected (or even mutually inclusive) principles, the latter tends to perceive binary oppositions in terms of the conflict of eternally unchanging, distinct (or even mutually exclusive) principles.[55] In contrast to the open-ended, ceaseless rhythm of cyclic change between yin and yang, the Western conception of temporality is typically linear and teleological. Finally, Wang suggests that 'yinyang thinking emerged as a conceptual apparatus to ease the anxiety of lost control', as a means of 'accepting the inevitability of change' in a world which is unpredictable and unstable.

Should one try, in the 'schizoid' reality of Terezín, to retain the Western perspective with its dualism of eternal principles of good and evil, its rigid distinction between life and death or happiness and misery, and its linear concept of time as a trajectory from the past via the present to death in the future, the resulting tension would destroy the human subject from within. Thus, if there is any redemptive message in the concluding section of the Four Songs (beyond the immediate joy of the moment), I believe its core is not the promise of resolution and victory, but the acceptance of a philosophical view (possibly, but not necessarily rooted in a particular cultural tradition) which enables one to embrace reality in all its ambiguity and helps to shift focus from the 'vicious circle' of frustrated individual agency towards the life-affirming cosmic cycle of perpetual transformation. Haas's songs from Terezín convey both the despair of 'death in the middle of life' and the joy of 'life amidst death'.

Notes

1 Hans Günther Adler, *Terezín 1941–1945: Tvář nuceného společenství*, trans. Lenka Šedová, 3 vols. (Brno: Barrister & Principal, 2006–07), iii: Psychologie (2007), p. 50. English translation mine. For German original see *Theresienstadt 1941–1945: Das Antlitz Einer Zwangsgemeinschaft. Geschichte, Soziologie, Psychologie* (Tübingen: Mohr, 1955); for a recent English translation see *Theresienstadt, 1941–1945: the Face of a Coerced Community*, trans. Belinda Cooper (Cambridge: Cambridge University Press, 2016).

2 Ibid., p. 49.

3 Mathesius published four books of paraphrases of Chinese poetry between 1925 and 1949, of which the third became the literary source for Haas's song cycle: *Černá věž a zelený džbán* (Prague: Ot. Štorch-Marien, 1925), *Zpěvy staré Číny* (Prague: Melantrich, 1939), *Nové zpěvy staré Číny* (Prague: Melantrich, 1940), *Třetí zpěvy staré Číny* (Prague: Melantrich, 1949). See Anna Zádrapová, 'Bohumil Mathesius, Jaroslav Průšek a Zpěvy staré Číny', *SOS*, 11/2 (2012), 239–71 (p. 240) [accessed via https://fphil.uniba.sk/fileadmin/fif/katedry_pracoviska/kvas/SOS_11_2/06_14zadrapova-form130130_Kopie.pdf, 7 May 2015].

4 For a discussion of depression, frustration, traumatisation, and psychological deprivation among people in the ghetto see Jiří Diamant, 'Some Comments on the Psychology of Life in the Ghetto Terezín', in *Terezín*, ed. František Ehrmann, Otta Hietlinger, and Rudolf Iltis (Prague: Council of Jewish Communities in the Czech lands, 1965), 124–39.

5 Vladimír Karbusický, 'Exotismus životní absurdity', *Hudební věda*, 34/2 (1997), 147–69 (p. 148). All translations from Czech sources are mine, unless stated otherwise.

6 Mahler used as his source Hans Bethge's 1907 anthology *Die chinesische Flöte*. For more details regarding the literary sources of the work see Fusako Hamao, 'The Sources of the Texts in Mahler's Lied Von der Erde', *Nineteenth-Century Music*, 19/1 (1995), 83–95.

7 Karbusický, 'Exotismus životní absurdity', p. 148. See also Stephen E. Hefling, *Mahler: Das Lied von der Erde (The Song of the Earth)* (New York: Cambridge University Press, 2000), pp. 28–31.

8 Reference is made here to the titles of the two ostensibly joyful (yet nostalgic and wistful) parts of Mahler's song cycle: 'Of Youth' and 'Of Beauty'.

9 The reading of *Das Lied von der Erde* in terms of the irretrievably lost happiness, evoked from the past in memory in order to escape the bleak reality of the present time, has been put forward in Theodor W. Adorno, *Mahler: A Musical Physiognomy* (Chicago: University of Chicago Press, 1992). See particularly p. 145.

10 Ibid., p. 146.

11 Angela Kang, 'Musical Chinoiserie' (unpublished Ph.D. dissertation, University of Nottingham, 2011) [accessed via http://eprints.nottingham.ac.uk/13707/1/575137.pdf, 27 April 2015]. See particularly pp. 31–3.

12 On the symbolism of death in 'The Farewell' see Stephen E. Hefling, *Mahler: Das Lied von der Erde/The Song of the Earth* (Cambridge: Cambridge University Press, 2000), pp. 106, 114.

13 See Paul Groarke, 'Chinese Poetry and Symbolism', *Journal of Chinese Philosophy*, 26/4 (1999), 489–512.

14 Julia Kristeva, *Black Sun: Depression and Melancholia*, trans. Leon S. Roudiez (New York: Columbia University Press, 1989); Naomi Cumming, 'The Subjectivities of "Erbarme Dich"', *Music Analysis*, 16/1 (1997), 5–44.

15 Viktor Ullmann, 'Liederabend Karl Bergmann', in *26 Kritiken über musikalische Veranstaltungen in Theresienstadt*, ed. Ingo Schultz (Hamburg: Bockel Verlag, 1993), 67–8 (p. 67). Translation mine.

16 Karbusický, 'Exotismus životní absurdity', p. 152.
17 Lubomír Peduzzi, 'Terezínské legendy a skutečnosti' ('Legends and Facts about Terezín'), in *O hudbě v terezínském ghettu: Soubor kritických statí* (Brno: Barrister & Principal, 1999), 38–48. See also Lubomír Peduzzi, 'Vlastenecká symbolika posledních děl Pavla Haase', in *Sborník Janáčkovy akademie múzických umění*, 3 (1961; Brno: Státní pedagogické nakladatelství, 1963), 75–97.
18 Pavel Haas, *Šarlatán*, autograph score (Department of Music History of the Moravian Museum, sign. A 22.687 b), p. 186.
19 Karbusický, 'Exotismus životní absurdity', p. 152.
20 Ibid.
21 Jory Debenham, 'Terezín Variations: Codes, Messages, and the Summer of 1944' (unpublished Ph.D. thesis, Lancaster University, 2016), pp. 71–2.
22 Erik Satie, *Klavierwerke* [Piano Works], ed. Eberhardt Klemm, 2 vols. (Leipzig: Edition Peters, 1986–89), ii (1989), p. 76.
23 Karbusický, 'Exotismus životní absurdity', p. 152.
24 Kristeva, *Black Sun: Depression and Melancholia*, p. 46. Kristeva seeks the origins of depression in the realm of symbolic signification through language. She argues that a depressive person's attachment to the object of loss is so strong that it makes the individual unable to substitute it with a set of signs, because this process requires the acceptance of the loss of the 'actual' object. Words therefore lose their meaning and are only capable of 'turning [the object of loss] over, helplessly' (pp. 36–46).
25 The affinity of this plaintive passage to the archaic genre of lament has previously been recognised by Karbusický. See Karbusický, 'Exotismus životní absurdity', p. 151.
26 Linda M. Austin, 'The Lament and the Rhetoric of the Sublime', *Nineteenth-Century Literature*, 53/3 (1998), 279–306 (pp. 279, 282–3, 292).
27 Cumming, 'The Subjectivities of "Erbarme Dich"', 5–44. In her analysis of the aria 'Erbarme dich' from Bach's *St Matthew Passion*, Cumming argues that this piece articulates the conflicting tendencies inherent to grief through 'a unique combination of melodic gestures that contribute to the formation of a complex affective state in which aspects of striving resist the heaviness of descent' (pp. 23–4).
28 Nicholas Royle, *The Uncanny* (New York: Routledge, 2003), p. 1. See also Lucie Armitt, *Theorising the Fantastic* (London: Arnold, 1996), pp. 39–63. See also Sigmund Freud, 'The Uncanny (1919)', in *Fantastic Literature: A Critical Reader*, ed. David Sandner (Westport CT: Praeger, 2004), 74–101.
29 Michael Klein observed that the uncanny is associated with 'terrible recognition, anxiety, dread, death, and the sublime'. See Michael L. Klein, *Intertextuality in Western Art Music* (Bloomington: Indiana University Press, 2005), p. 87.
30 The Czech adjective 'cizí' signifies that something is 'not familiar', 'not one's own' or 'not of the same kind as something or someone else'. The translation 'strange' seems the most appropriate in this context.
31 In fact, much of the characteristic imagery of the uncanny is associated with the topos of the 'gothic mansion', where the positive connotations of home, safety, love and so on are subverted; the mansion is thus perceived as haunted, strange and sinister. Houses are also often viewed as having a soul of their own or reflecting that of their owners. See Armitt, *Theorising the Fantastic*, p. 49.
32 The distance between the pitch-classes should be understood in terms of interval class, which, due to the principle of octave equivalence, renders spatial distribution irrelevant.
33 The reference here is to the second movement (entitled neutrally 'Allegro vivace') of Haas's 1940–41 Symphony.
34 Kristeva, *Black Sun*, p. 34. See also Matthew Ratcliffe, 'Varieties of Temporal Experience in Depression', *Journal of Medicine and Philosophy*, 37 (2012), 114–38 (p. 114).
35 Jory Debenham, who focuses on the form of theme and variations in the works of composers in Terezín, associates this progression with the form of passacaglia. See

Jory Debenham, 'Existential Variations in Terezín', http://orelfoundation.org/index. php/journalArticle/existential_variations_in_terez237n/ [accessed 26 January 2015]. See also William E. Caplin, 'Topics and Formal Functions: The Case of the Lament', in *The Oxford Handbook of Topic Theory*, ed. Danuta Mirka (New York: Oxford University Press, 2014), 415–52.

36 The Czech word 'ruce' refers to 'hands' but also, more broadly, to 'arms'; the latter can be specifically designated by the word 'paže'.

37 This passage anticipates the 'anxiety' motive or, in other words, helps to organically incorporate the quotation of the 'death' motive from *Charlatan*. The motive's contour results from circular rendering of the *lamento* motive and the seventh-wide rift, on which its intervallic structure is based, follows from the mirroring of two fourths (A flat – E flat – B flat) in bar 43.

38 It should be noted that the occurrences of fully formed diatonic modes are relatively rare in this piece. Even in the case of the lament progression in the piano interludes, full diatonic modes arise from the combination of more or less independent tetrachordal units. Most often, such tetrachordal units only have an implicit sense of belonging to a wider modal framework. Bass pedals typically offer the decisive contextual clue determining which scale degrees the specific tetrachords occupy.

39 Since there are only 12 distinct chromatic pitches, clear-cut complementarity is only possible with collections of 6 pitches such as the whole-tone scale. Since diatonic scales contain 7 pitches, even the most distant pair of scales (with 14 pitches among them) will always have at least two pitches in common.

40 Karbusický, 'Exotismus životní absurdity', p. 148.

41 Lubomír Peduzzi, 'Vlastenecká symbolika posledních děl Pavla Haase', p. 85.

42 Karbusický, 'Exotismus životní absurdity', p. 164.

43 Ibid., p. 163.

44 Ibid., p. 164.

45 Ibid.

46 Ibid., p. 153.

47 Ibid., p. 167.

48 Ibid., p. 153.

49 Robin R. Wang, *Yinyang* (Cambridge: Cambridge University Press, 2012), p. 9.

50 Ibid., p. 9.

51 Ibid., p. 11.

52 Ibid.

53 Ibid.

54 Ibid., p. 3: '[T]hings like the earth, the moon, water, the night, the feminine, softness, passivity, and darkness all accord with yin, whereas heaven, the sun, fire, day, masculinity, hardness, activity, and brightness can all be attributed to yang. This division simultaneously emphasizes that these two elements are interrelated and interdependent.'

55 Ibid., p. 5.

Bibliography

General bibliography

Adler, Hans Günther, *Terezín 1941–1945: tvář nuceného společenství*, trans. Lenka Šedová, 3 vols. (Brno: Barrister & Principal, 2006–07), i: Dějiny (2006), ii: Sociologie (2006), iii: Psychologie (2007). For German original see *Theresienstadt 1941–1945: Das Antlitz Einer Zwangsgemeinschaft. Geschichte, Soziologie, Psychologie* (Tübingen: Mohr, 1955). For a recent English translation see *Theresienstadt, 1941–1945: the Face of a Coerced Community*, trans. Belinda Cooper (Cambridge: Cambridge University Press, 2016).

Adorno, Theodor W., *Mahler: A Musical Physiognomy* (Chicago: University of Chicago Press, 1992).

Austin, Linda M., 'The Lament and the Rhetoric of the Sublime', *Nineteenth-Century Literature*, 53/3 (1998), 279–306.

Cumming, Naomi, 'The Subjectivities of "Erbarme Dich"', *Music Analysis*, 16/1 (1997), 5–44.

Debenham, Jory, 'Existential Variations in Terezín', http://orelfoundation.org/index.php/journalArticle/existential_variations_in_terez237n/ [accessed 26 January 2015].

Debenham, Jory, 'Terezín Variations: Codes, Messages, and the Summer of 1944' (unpublished Ph.D. thesis, Lancaster University, 2016).

Diamant, Jiří, 'Some Comments on the Psychology of Life in the Ghetto Terezín', in *Terezín*, ed. František Ehrmann, Otta Hietlinger, and Rudolf Iltis (Prague: Council of Jewish Communities in the Czech lands, 1965), 124–39.

Groarke, Paul, 'Chinese Poetry and Symbolism', *Journal of Chinese Philosophy*, 26/4 (1999), 489–512.

Hamao, Fusako, 'The Sources of the Texts in Mahler's Lied Von der Erde', *Nineteenth-Century Music*, 19/1 (1995), 83–95.

Hatten, Robert S., *Musical Meaning in Beethoven: Markedness, Correlation, and Interpretation* (Bloomington: Indiana University Press, 1994).

Hefling, Stephen E., *Mahler: Das Lied von der Erde* [Mahler: The Song of the Earth] (Cambridge: Cambridge University Press, 2000).

Johnson, Julian, *Mahler's Voices: Expression and Irony in the Songs and Symphonies* (Oxford: Oxford University Press, 2009).

Kang, Angela, 'Musical Chinoiserie' (unpublished Ph.D. dissertation, University of Nottingham, 2011) [accessed via http://eprints.nottingham.ac.uk/13707/1/575137.pdf, 27 April 2015].

Karbusický, Vladimír, 'Exotismus životní absurdity', *Hudební věda*, 34/2 (1997), 147–69.

Karbusický, Vladimír, 'Neukončená historie', *Hudební věda*, 35/4 (1998), 396–405.

Kristeva, Julia, *Black Sun: Depression and Melancholia*, trans. Leon S. Roudiez (New York: Columbia University Press, 1989).

Mathesius, Bohumil, *Nové zpěvy staré Číny* (Prague: Melantrich, 1940).

Mirka, Danuta, ed., *The Oxford Handbook of Topic Theory* (New York: Oxford University Press, 2014).

Monelle, Raymond, *The Musical Topic: Hunt, Military and Pastoral* (Bloomington: Indiana University Press, 2006).

Peduzzi, Lubomír, *O hudbě v terezínském ghettu: Soubor kritických statí* (Brno: Barrister & Principal, 2nd edn, 1999); for German translation see *Musik im Ghetto Theresienstadt: Kritische Studien*, trans. Lenka Šedová (Brno: Barrister & Principal, 2005), 'Terezínské legendy a skutečnosti', 38–48; 'O Gideonu Kleinovi a jeho monografii', 103–13; 'Falešné problémy Haasových Čtyř písní', 79–84.

Peduzzi, Lubomír, *Pavel Haas: Život a dílo skladatele* (Brno: Muzejní a vlastivědná společnost, 1993); for German translation see *Pavel Haas: Leben und Werk des Komponisten*, trans. Thomas Mandl (Hamburg: Bockel, 1996).

Peduzzi, Lubomír, 'Vlastenecká symbolika posledních děl Pavla Haase', *Sborník Janáčkovy akademie múzických umění*, 3 (1961; Prague: Státní pedagogické nakladatelství, 1963), 75–97.

Ratcliffe, Matthew, 'Varieties of Temporal Experience in Depression', *Journal of Medicine and Philosophy*, 37 (2012), 114–38.

Royle, Nicholas, *The Uncanny* (New York: Routledge, 2003).

Sedláčková, Pavlína, 'Čtyři písně na slova čínské poezie: výpověď terezínského vězně' (unpublished bachelor's thesis, Masaryk University, 2011) [accessed via http://is.muni.cz/th/341927/ff_b/bakalarska_prace.pdf?lang=en, 16 October 2012].

Ullmann, Viktor, and Ingo Schultz, *26 Kritiken über musikalische Veranstaltungen in Theresienstadt* (Hamburg: Bockel Verlag, 1993).

Wang, Robin R., *Yinyang* (Cambridge: Cambridge University Press, 2012).

Zádrapová, Anna, 'Bohumil Mathesius, Jaroslav Průšek a *Zpěvy staré Číny*', *SOS*, 11/2 (2012), 239–71 [accessed via https://fphil.uniba.sk/fileadmin/fif/katedry_pracoviska/kvas/SOS_11_2/06_14zadrapova-form130130_Kopie.pdf, 7 May 2015].

Musical editions

Haas, Pavel, *Al S'fod*: Male chorus set to Hebrew words by David Shimoni, 1942 (Prague: Tempo; Berlin: Bote & Bock, 1994).

Haas, Pavel, *Čtyři písně pro bas (baryton) a klavír na slova čínské poezie v překladu Bohumila Mathesia* (Prague: Panton, 1987).

Haas, Pavel, *Čtyři písně pro bas (baryton) a klavír na slova čínské poezie/Four Songs for Bass (Baritone) and Piano to the Words of Chinese Poetry* (Prague: Tempo; Berlin: Bote & Bock, 1992).

Mahler, Gustav, *Das Lied von Der Erde* (Vienna: Universal Edition, 1912).

Satie, Erik, *Klavierwerke (Piano Works)*, ed. Eberhardt Klemm, 2 vols. (Leipzig: Edition Peters, 1986–89), ii (1989).

Ullmann, Viktor, *The Emperor of Atlantis or Death's Refusal*. One-act play by Peter Kien. Op. 49, 1943 (Mainz: Schott, 1993).

Conclusion

Attempts to position the work of Pavel Haas in the history of twentieth-century music almost inevitably invoke the polarity between 'East' and 'West'. This is already present in Peduzzi's claim that the development of Haas's personal style was determined by the dual influence of Janáček and Stravinsky (with the latter standing as a proxy for a complex of avant-garde stimuli flowing in, through Prague, from Paris). The problem of reconciling the local (national/regional/'Eastern') musical tradition with current trends in the international ('universal'/'Western') musical scene is not untypical of Central and East European composers.

However, Haas's situation was different from that of the composers of the older generation, such as Bartók and Szymanowski (born 1881 and 1882, respectively), who carried the responsibility of defining (or re-defining) the national musical tradition, as opposed to the Austro-German tradition, which represented the dominant, international style around 1900. By the time Haas started his compositional career in the 1920s, Janáček had been recognised as the pioneer of Moravian art music, and the tradition of Czech music, handed down from Bedřich Smetana and Antonín Dvořák to Otakar Ostrčil, Otakar Zich, Vítězslav Novák, and Josef Suk, had been firmly established and perhaps even somewhat entrenched.

Haas's generation had a different understanding of the relationship between 'East' and 'West'. In the early 1920s, when Haas faced the challenge of defining his original compositional style, most young Czech composers who sought to align their work with international developments were looking towards France, rather than Austria and Germany, which had previously been the dominant influence upon the Czech musical tradition. Moreover, in the avant-garde circles of Devětsil, this orientation was associated with the spirit of cosmopolitanism, as articulated in Karel Teige's 'Manifesto of Poetism':

> Having observed the fundamentally international nature of modern civilisation, we abandoned provincial and regional horizons [as well as] affiliations with nations and states. [. . .] We joined into the rhythm of collective European [artistic] production, the metronome of which [. . .] was Paris [. . .] not as the centre of French [art], but as the focal point of the international production, its Metropolis and Babylon.[1]

It was largely this cosmopolitan spirit which provoked the criticism of Haas's 'From the Monkey Mountains', regarded by the conservative critics as a modish imitation of alien stimuli from the West.

Indeed, the proclaimed cosmopolitanism of Devětsil is at odds with the reality of Haas's life, considering that the composer never lived permanently outside Brno, and it certainly does not characterise Haas's work as a whole. The experimental era of the 1920s, during which Haas explored a number of diverse kinds of music (Moravian folk music in his study pieces from Janáček's masterclass; exotic modality in *Fata Morgana*; jazz and everyday music in 'From the Monkey Mountains'; and Jewish intonations in the Wind Quintet), was followed by a period of classicising synthesis (rather than increasing eclecticism) in the 1930s. Haas was a Moravian composer inasmuch as he built his original compositional idiom on a Janáčekian basis and remained embedded in the professional musical structures of Brno throughout his life.

In his 1936 study on 'Modern Czech Music', Vladimír Helfert described Haas as an 'avant-gardist in Janáček's school'.[2] Indeed, Haas's engagement with avant-garde ideas sets him apart not only from Janáček, but also from Janáček's older students, such as Václav Kaprál and Vilém Petrželka. At the same time, Haas can also be regarded (to turn Helfert's statement around) as a 'Janáčekian among Czech avant-gardists'. The fact that Haas studied with Janáček and built upon his idiosyncratic compositional idiom sets him apart from composers such as Bohuslav Martinů, Iša Krejčí, Pavel Bořkovec, and Jaroslav Ježek, who followed similar trends but who emerged from the Prague-based compositional tradition.

Haas's musical language

Haas's studies with Janáček played a crucial role in defining the foundations of his compositional language. Unsurprisingly, Janáček's influence is most readily apparent in Haas's early works, such as *Fata Morgana* (1923) and 'From the Monkey Mountains' (1925). However, Haas's encounter with jazz-band music and Poetism made him develop the Janáčekian legacy in radically new ways. Haas's later engagement with Neoclassicism provided a means of following an individual path of stylistic development, while maintaining a degree of continuity with the composer's Janáčekian background. While some aspects of Neoclassicism were in conflict with Janáček's style (especially the preference for objective construction over subjective expression and the revival of old forms and techniques), others were consistent with it (the inclination towards essentially diatonic pitch structures, rhythmic vitality, simplicity of texture, and economy of expression). Besides matters of style, Haas can be distinguished from Janáček by particular features of his individual personality, especially by his distinctive sense of humour with a penchant for irony, caricature, the grotesque, and the conflation of comic and tragic elements.

Haas was arguably more successful than other students of Janáček's in developing a thoroughly original musical language, which nonetheless incorporates and develops salient elements of Janáček's idiosyncratic style. The most immediately apparent Janáčekian feature in Haas's compositional idiom is the use of ostinati and short, repetitive motives, superimposed in layered textures. Haas's music, like that of Janáček, often defies conventional phrase structure, being based on repetition and variation (rather than continuous development) of fragmentary thematic material. The overall form is typically marked by montage-like juxtaposition of contrasting musical materials.

Particularly characteristic of Haas's music is the emphasis on rhythm and metre. Haas was influenced by the rhythmic vitality of jazz and contemporary popular music (as is exemplified by 'Danza' and 'Postludium' from his 1935 Suite for Piano). At the same time, Haas built on Janáček's theory and compositional practice of *sčasování* (a complex of rhythmic and metric phenomena) and on his hierarchical model of metro-rhythmic layers. In some works (such as 'Landscape' and the Four Songs on Chinese Poetry), Haas tends towards Janáček's subjectivist and vitalist conception of *sčasování*, according to which rhythmic elements reflect the changing psychological state of a human subject and/or appear to have a life of their own. In other works, especially in the Study for Strings, Haas adopts (while retaining a strong connection to Janáčekian compositional-technical roots) a more objective, Constructivist approach to composition, using motoric rhythms and their transformations primarily as a means of supporting the formal architecture.

Another characteristic feature of Haas's musical language is the focus on diatonic modality. This, too, is traceable to Janáček, whose legacy provided an alternative for late Romantic harmonic language, on the one hand, and the total chromaticism of the Second Viennese School, on the other. However, apart from pieces that explicitly allude to folk music, such as the 'Pastorale' from the Suite for Piano, and the Seven Songs in Folk Tone (1939–40), Haas's music is generally devoid of Janáčekian folkloric flavour. Haas developed instead a kind of modernist diatonicism, which is typically based on work with repetitive tetrachordal units or other small (three- or four-note) subsets of the diatonic collection; these techniques are exemplified by the 'Praeludium' from the Suite for Piano, the Study for Strings, and the Four Songs on Chinese Poetry.

Haas's diatonicism often has religious undertones: besides explicit quotations of the Wenceslas chorale in the Suite for Oboe and Piano and the Symphony, there are a number of passages throughout Haas's oeuvre marked by a quasi-religious, prayer-like, or meditative character (the examples include 'Pastorale', the last movement of String Quartet No. 3, and the Four Songs on Chinese Poetry). This is sometimes associated with musical features (such as modal inflections, details of ornamentation, and melismatic delivery) that appear to be derived from Jewish musical tradition (this is the case in 'Preghiera' and 'Epilogo' from his Wind Quintet and the first movement of his Symphony).

Haas often used elements of pentatonic modality in his early works, particularly in association with exoticism (*Fata Morgana*) and primitivism ('From the Monkey Mountains'). Blues-scale modal inflections appear in Haas's jazz-inspired works, including 'From the Monkey Mountains' and Suite for Piano. In some of his mature, late works, particularly in his String Quartet No. 3, Haas worked with pitch structures based on inversional symmetry. Haas mirrored Bartók in his pursuit of modernist musical syntax through unconventional use of diatonic material (related more or less directly to folk music) and symmetrical pitch structures.

Haas's work: styles and themes

Some of Haas's song cycles composed around the time of his studies with Janáček (1920–2) reveal a keen interest in exotic subject matter. This tendency is apparent in Haas's *Chinese Songs*, Op. 4 (1919–21)[3] and *Fata Morgana*, Op. 6 (1923). The latter piece, scored for tenor, piano, and string quartet, sets to music five poems from *The Gardener* by Rabindranath Tagore, whose poetry enjoyed great popularity throughout Europe at that time and attracted a number of European composers.[4] Further research would be required to explain how this work fits in the context of early twentieth-century exoticism. Nonetheless, Haas's approach to Tagore's poetry in *Fata Morgana* draws primarily on Janáček's compositional idiom. On the whole, Haas's interest in exotic poetry seems to be confined to the earliest stage of his career, with the significant exception of the Four Songs on Chinese Poetry (1944).

In the 1920s, Haas's music was influenced by the Czech avant-garde movement of Poetism. Throughout his career, Haas alluded to many of the characteristic topoi of Poetism, such as the fairground, carnival, clowns and comedians, everyday art, and jazz. These features coalesce with Haas's lifelong predilection for caricature-like exaggeration and the distortion of physical movement in the recurring topic of 'danse excentrique', which refers to dance movements that typically start on a humorous, clownish note and accelerate into a vertiginous, carnivalesque whirl; examples include the last movement ('The Wild Night') of the quartet 'From the Monkey Mountains', the male chorus *Karneval*, the third movement ('Ballo eccentrico') of Haas's Wind Quintet, and the ragtime-inspired third movement ('Danza') of the Suite for Piano. As another means of portraying musically the carnivalesque view of reality as a whirlwind of incongruous elements, Haas created in 'The Wild Night' a kind of musical collage through cinematic juxtaposition of different kinds of music.

Through these aesthetic affiliations, Haas is related (via the mediating context of Poetism) to Stravinsky, Les Six, and, more broadly, the Parisian avant-garde. Looking to the German context, there are a number of common features shared by Haas and Erwin Schulhoff, whose music was inspired (besides other stimuli) by jazz and folk music (Schulhoff made explicit his admiration for Janáček).[5] Schulhoff also had a strong inclination towards the left-wing avant-garde circles of German Dada,[6] which partly explains why he, like Haas, was interested in caricature and the grotesque.

Neoclassical stylistic tendencies appear in Haas's music from the mid-1930s onwards. The 1935 Suite for Piano marks the shift towards brevity, concision, and economy of means. Besides some earlier instances, such as the 'Pastorale', allusions to music of the past begin to appear in Haas's music in the opera *Charlatan*, situated in a seventeenth-century fairground environment. Haas's Neoclassicism apparently culminated in two instrumental works composed during his incarceration in Terezín: the 1944 Partita in the Old Style, which has unfortunately been lost, and the 1943 Study for Strings, which is characterised by rigorous diatonicism (including 'abstract' tetrachordal structures, folk-like Dorian and Lydian modality, and historicising material reminiscent of *Charlatan*), emphasis on rational construction (apparent from systematic manipulation of metro-rhythmic parameters and tightly controlled overall formal proportion), 'anti-sentimental' motoric drive (resulting from polyrhythmic and polymetric combinations of repetitive motivic fragments), and the use of old-style contrapuntal techniques that hark back to the Baroque tradition (the piece includes fugal sections and passages with a hymn-like cantus firmus).

Arguably, Neoclassicism appealed to Haas because it allowed him to explore the compositional possibilities of working with modal, diatonic musical material related more or less directly to folk music (the kind of material to which he was drawn as a result of his studies with Janáček). However, Haas's approach to Neoclassicism was quite unlike that of Stravinsky. Whereas Stravinsky tended to 'recompose' pieces of older music, employ anachronistic clichés, and maintain a degree of incongruity between traditional (tonal) and modern (post-tonal) syntax, Haas's Neoclassicism (as represented by the Study for Strings) appears much more stylistically and syntactically homogeneous.

The 1930s were a period of Haas's growing artistic maturity, which manifested itself in increased concision in his works. This phase of Haas's individual development went hand in hand with the composer's increased affinity with Neoclassicism. The distance Haas travelled between the mid-1920s and mid-1930s is made apparent when comparing his second and third string quartets. The form of 'Landscape' appears rather loose when compared to the tightly structured, symmetrically organised form of the first movement of the third quartet. The latter work is also representative of Haas's growing interest in the exploration of modernist musical syntax through the combination of diatonic and symmetrical pitch structures. The final movement of the third quartet displays two more features that did not appear in the earlier work: Haas's interest in techniques of counterpoint and imitation (further developed in the Study for Strings) and the quasi-religious character which results from treating modal melodic material in the manner of a cantus firmus.

In some of his works (particularly in *Charlatan*), Haas arguably participated in the wave of interest, apparent in European arts and music from the turn of the century onwards, in the themes of subjectivity, psychology, and the human condition. On the other hand, much of Haas's music displays a considerable degree of distance, associated with reaction against the subjectivism of pre-war art and facilitated by an emphasis on playful, humorous character (Poetism) and/or objective construction (Neoclassicism/Constructivism). Interestingly, these opposing tendencies do not exist separately in different chronological segments of Haas's oeuvre; rather, they tend to appear side by side in contemporaneous works (take for example the strikingly different character of the Four Songs on Chinese Poetry and the Study for Strings) or they even coexist in an ambiguous whole within a single work. In 'The Wild Night', the collective laughter of carnival is juxtaposed, albeit briefly, with a moment of subjective, introspective, and somewhat sorrowful lyricism. In *Charlatan*, the merriment of public fairground productions is contrasted with the main character's increasingly troubled subjectivity. In the Four Songs on Chinese Poetry, the focus is on the protagonist's subjectivity throughout, but the overall image is problematised by the oscillation between melancholy and merriment. Haas's preoccupation with semantic ambiguity and the subtle tension in his music between subjective engagement and distancing strategies is reminiscent of works by Gustav Mahler, although the chronological, cultural, and stylistic distance between the two is considerable.

The beginning of the Second World War provoked the emergence of patriotic symbolism in Haas's music. Although allusions to the Wenceslas chorale may seem to appear in some of Haas's earlier works, unambiguous full-length quotations of the hymn only appear in the Suite for Oboe and Piano (1939) and the unfinished Symphony (1940–41), both of which also include references to the Hussite chorale. Interestingly, the topic of 'danse excentrique', which emerged in Haas's Poetism-inspired works from the 1920s, conveying an innocuous 'clownish' character, becomes transformed into a 'danse macabre' in the second movement of the Symphony, helping to paint a grotesque caricature of Nazism. Haas's use of parody, satire, and the grotesque as a means of political protest in the Symphony brings to mind better-known works by Shostakovich, likewise associated with reaction against totalitarian oppression.

It is noteworthy that Haas did not continue to make overt patriotic and satirical statements during his incarceration in Terezín (at least not in the three surviving works). This is especially striking since works of subversive nature, such as *Der Kaiser von Atlantis* (1943) by Peter Kien and Viktor Ullmann (which would have appealed to Haas by its juxtaposition of satirical and macabre elements, encapsulated in the allegorical duo of Harlequin and Death), are known to have been composed in the ghetto. Moreover, cabaret performances featuring more or less subversive humour were relatively common in Terezín.[7] Instead, Haas's surviving works are associated with community exhortation (*Al S'fod*), private contemplation (Four Songs on Chinese Poetry), and Neoclassical objectivity (Study for Strings).

The turn to compositional craft and 'pure music' in the Study suggests that Haas may have regarded composition as a sovereign domain of meaningful labour, a refuge from the twisted reality of Terezín. Maybe the message of *Al S'fod* – 'Do not lament and do not cry [. . .], but work, work!' – carried particular significance for Haas himself with regard to his own work as a composer. Considering the anecdotal evidence of Haas's debilitating depression and compositional inactivity in the first months of his imprisonment, and the fact that *Al S'fod* is (to the best of current knowledge) the first piece he composed in the camp, it is possible that the exhortation to work was directed, at least partly, at himself. Maybe Viktor Ullmann's spoke for Haas, too, in the following passage from 'Goethe and the Ghetto': 'One has to stress nevertheless that [. . .] in no way whatsoever we sat down to weep on the banks of the waters of Babylon and that our effort to serve the Arts respectfully was proportionate to our will to live, in spite of everything'.[8]

As a Czech composer, a Moravian composer, and (especially) a Terezín composer, Pavel Haas seems bound to occupy a rather marginal position in the history of twentieth-century music. However, as this study hopefully demonstrates, the importance of Haas's work reaches well beyond regional and national boundaries, as well as the walls of the ghetto. Haas engaged with a broad variety of tendencies underpinning the development of Western music, arts, and culture in the first half of the twentieth century. His music belongs to the best of what the inter-war generation of Czech composers had to offer and it presents a valuable contribution to the wealth of twentieth-century European art music.

Notes

1 Karel Teige, 'Manifest poetismu', *ReD*, 1/9 (June 1928), reprinted in *Avantgarda známá a neznámá* [The Known and Unknown Avant-Garde], ed. Štěpán Vlašín, 3 vols. (Prague: Svoboda, 1970–72), ii: *Vrchol a krize Poetismu: 1925–1928* [The Peak and the Crisis of Poetism: 1925–1928] (1972), 557–93 (p. 562).

2 Vladimír Helfert, *Česká moderní hudba: studie o české hudební tvořivosti* [Modern Czech Music: A Study of Czech Musical Creativity] (Olomouc: Index, 1936), reprinted in Vladimír Helfert, *Vybrané studie: O hudební tvořivosti* (Prague: Ed. Supraphon, 1970), 163–312, p. 294. Page references here and below are to the 1970 reprint.

3 See Vladimír Karbusický, 'Neukončená historie', *Hudební věda*, 35/4 (1998), 396–405. Karbusický challenges Peduzzi's claim (*Pavel Haas: Život a dílo skladatele*, pp. 33–4, 130) that all three of Haas's *Chinese Songs* were composed in 1921. According to Karbusický, the first two songs were in fact composed as early as 1919 and the third one was added in 1921. Karbusický (unlike Peduzzi) was also able to identify the literary source: Jaroslav Pšenička, *Ze staré čínské poezie (VII.–IX. stol. po Kr.)* (Prague: J. Otto, 1902). Karbusický further observes that this book (according to Pšenička's own preface) contains Czech translations of selected French poems from *Poésies de l'époque des Thang* by Marquis Leon d'Hervey de Saint Denys.

4 Tagore received the Nobel Prize for Literature in 1913. Janáček set Tagore's poetry to music in *The Wandering Madman* (1922). Two of the poems from Tagore's *The Gardener* which Haas set to music in *Fata Morgana* had previously been set by Zemlinsky ('You Are the Evening Cloud') in his *Lyrische Symphonie* (1922–23) and by Szymanowski ('My Heart, the Bird of the Wilderness') in his Four Songs, Op. 41 (1918). For a detailed overview of the reception of Tagore's poetry by European composers between 1914 and 1925 see Suddhaseel Sen, 'The Art Song and Tagore: Settings by Western Composers', *University of Toronto Quarterly*, 77/4 (2008), 1110–32.

5 Erwin Schulhoff, 'Leoš Janáček: Betrachtungen anläßlich seines siebzigsten Geburtstages', *Musikblätter des Anbruch*, 7/5 (1925), 237–9.

6 See Josef Bek, *Erwin Schulhoff: Leben und Werk* (Hamburg: von Bockel Verlag, 1994), pp. 43–5.

7 See Ulrike Migdal, *Und die Musik spielt dazu: Chansons und Satiren aus dem Kz Theresienstadt* (Munich: Piper, 1986); Rebecca Rovit and Alvin Goldfarb, eds., *Theatrical Performance During the Holocaust: Texts, Documents, Memoirs* (Baltimore MD: Johns Hopkins University Press, 1999); Franz Markus Schneider, 'Terezínský smích', in *Terezínské studie a dokumenty* (Prague: Academia, 1999), pp. 242–50.

8 Viktor Ullmann, 'Goethe and the Ghetto', in Viktor Ullmann, Thomas Mandl, Dževad Karahasan, Jean-Jacques Van Vlasselaer, Herbert Gantschacher, and Ingo Schultz, *Tracks to Viktor Ullmann* (Klagenfurt, Austria: Arbos, Gesellschaft für Musik und Theater, 1998), p. 7.

Bibliography

General bibliography

Adler, Hans Günther, *Terezín 1941–1945: tvář nuceného společenství*, trans. Lenka Šedová, 3 vols. (Brno: Barrister & Principal, 2006–07), I: Dějiny (2006); II: Sociologie (2006); III: Psychologie (2007). For German original see *Theresienstadt 1941–1945: Das Antlitz Einer Zwangsgemeinschaft. Geschichte, Soziologie, Psychologie* (Tübingen: Mohr, 1955). For a recent English translation see *Theresienstadt, 1941–1945: the Face of a Coerced Community*, trans. Belinda Cooper (Cambridge: Cambridge University Press, 2016).

Adorno, Theodor W., *Mahler: A Musical Physiognomy* (Chicago: University of Chicago Press, 1992).

Agawu, Kofi V., 'Stravinsky's "Mass" and Stravinsky Analysis', *Music Theory Spectrum*, 11/2 (Autumn, 1989), 139–63.

Anonymous author (-ak-), 'I. Excentrický karneval umelců v Brně', *Salon*, 3/10 (1925), n. p.

Armitt, Lucie, *Theorising the Fantastic* (London: Arnold, 1996).

Austin, Linda M., 'The Lament and the Rhetoric of the Sublime', *Nineteenth-Century Literature*, 53/3 (1998), 279–306.

Bakhtin, Mikhail, *Rabelais and His World*, trans. Helene Iswolsky (Cambridge MA: MIT Press, 1968).

Beckerman, Michael, 'Haas's Charlatan and the Play of Premonitions', *The Opera Quarterly*, 29/1 (2013), 31–40.

Beckerman, Michael, *Janáček as Theorist* (New York: Pendragon Press, 1994).

Beckerman, Michael, 'Pavel Haas', http://orelfoundation.org/index.php/composers/article/pavel_haas/ [accessed 18 November 2015].

Beckerman, Michael, 'What Kind of Historical Document is a Musical Score? A Meditation in Ten Parts on Klein's Trio', http://orelfoundation.org/index.php/journal/journalArticle/what_kind_of_historical_document_is_a_musical_score/ [accessed 26 January 2015].

Beckerman, Michael and Glen Bauer, eds., *Janáček and Czech Music: Proceedings of the International Conference (Saint Louis, 1988), Studies in Czech Music No. 1* (Stuyvesant NY: Pendragon Press, 1995).

Bek, Josef, *Avantgarda: ke genezi socialistického realismu v české hudbě* (Prague: Panton, 1984).

Bek, Josef, *Erwin Schulhoff: Leben und Werk* (Hamburg: von Bockel Verlag, 1994).

Bek, Josef, *Hudební neoklasicismus* (Prague: Academia, 1982).

Bek, Josef, 'Mezinárodní styky české hudby 1924–1932', *Hudební věda*, 5/1 (1968), 628–48.

Berg, Josef, *K Janáčkovu skladebnému projevu* (Brno: Zprávy společnosti Leoše Janáčka, Vol. 6, 1991).

Berlin, Edward A., 'Ragtime', *Grove Music Online* www.oxfordmusiconline.com [accessed 4 November 2013].

Blažek, Zdeněk, 'Janáček – učitel', *Opus musicum,* 18/3 (1986), 65–71.

Blažek, Zdeněk, 'Leoš Janáček o skladbě a hudebních formách na varhanické škole v Brně', *Opus musicum,* 20/4 (1988), 107–11.

Breton, André, *Manifestoes of Surrealism* (Ann Arbor: University of Michigan Press, 1969).

Brown, Julie, *Bartók and the Grotesque: Studies in Modernity, the Body and Contradiction in Music* (Aldershot: Ashgate, 2007).

Burghauser, Jarmil, 'Hudební metrika v Janáčkově teoretickém díle', in *Sborník prací Filosofické Fakulty Brněnské university,* 32–33 (1984), 137–53.

Burian, Emil František, *Jazz* (Prague: Aventinum, 1928).

Carter, Chandler, 'Stravinsky's "Special Sense": The Rhetorical Use of Tonality in "The Rake's Progress"', *Music Theory Spectrum,* 19/1 (Spring, 1997), 55–80.

Černušák, Gracian, Andrew Lamb and John Tyrrell, 'Polka', *Grove Music Online* www. oxfordmusiconline.com [accessed 2 December 2015].

Černý, Václav, *Staročeský Mastičkář* (Prague: Československá akademie věd, 1955).

Červinková, Blanka, *Hans Krása: Život a dílo skladatele* (Prague: Tempo, 2003).

Chalupa, Dalibor, 'Karneval', *Host,* 4 (1924–25), 166–7.

Cocteau, Jean, 'Cock and Harlequin', in *A Call to Order: Written between the Years 1918 and 1926 and Including Cock and Harlequin, Professional Secrets, and Other Critical Essays,* trans. Rollo H. Myers (New York: Haskell House Publishers, 1974), 8–82.

Code, David J., 'The Synthesis of Rhythms: Form, Ideology, and the "Augurs of Spring"', *The Journal of Musicology,* 24/1 (Winter, 2007), 112–66.

Cohn, Richard, 'Complex Hemiolas, Ski-Hill Graphs, and Metric Spaces', *Music Analysis,* 20/3 (2001), 295–326.

Cohn, Richard, 'Inversional Symmetry and Transpositional Combination in Bartók', *Music Theory Spectrum,* 10 (Spring, 1988), 19–42.

Cone, Edward T., 'Stravinsky: The Progress of a Method', in *Perspectives on Schoenberg and Stravinsky,* ed. Benjamin Boretz and Edward T. Cone (Princeton NJ: Princeton University Press, 1968), 156–64.

Cross, Jonathan, *The Stravinsky Legacy* (Cambridge: Cambridge University Press, 1998).

Cumming, Naomi, 'The Subjectivities of "Erbarme Dich"', *Music Analysis,* 16/1 (1997), 5–44.

Čurda, Martin, 'Druhý smyčcový kvartet Pavla Haase: mezi Janáčkem a Ravelem', *Opus musicum,* 42/4 (2010), 29–46.

Čurda, Martin, '*From the Monkey Mountains*: The Body, the Grotesque and Carnival in the Music of Pavel Haas', *Journal of the Royal Musical Association,* 141/1 (2016), 61–112.

Čurda, Martin, 'Haasův Šarlatán: tragikomedie o starých komediantech, moderních individualistech a podivných dvojnících', *Hudební věda,* 55/3–4 (2018), 391–427.

Čurda, Martin, 'Reading Meaning In and Out of Music from Theresienstadt: the Case of Pavel Haas', in *The Routledge Handbook of Music Signification,* ed. Esti Sheinberg and William Dougherty (Abingdon, New York: Routledge, 2020), 231–242.

Čurda, Martin, 'Religious Patriotism and Grotesque Ridicule: Responses to Nazi Oppression in Pavel Haas's Unfinished Wartime Symphony', in *The Routledge Handbook to Music under German Occupation, 1938–1945,* ed. David Fanning and Erik Levi (Abingdon, New York: Routledge, 2020), 377–98.

Čurda, Martin, 'Smyčcové kvartety Janáčkových žáků z 20. let' (unpublished master's thesis, Masaryk University, 2012).

Čurda, Martin, 'Smyčcové kvartety Pavla Haase z 20. let' (unpublished bachelor's thesis, Masaryk University, 2010).

Danow, David K., *The Spirit of Carnival: Magical Realism and the Grotesque* (Lexington: University Press of Kentucky, 2004).

Debenham, Jory, 'Existential Variations in Terezín', http://orelfoundation.org/index.php/ journalArticle/existential_variations_in_terez237n/ [accessed 26 January 2015].

Debenham, Jory, 'Terezín Variations: Codes, Messages, and the Summer of 1944' (unpublished Ph.D. thesis, Lancaster University, 2016).

Diamant, Jiří, 'Some Comments on the Psychology of Life in the Ghetto Terezín', in *Terezín*, ed. František Ehrmann, Otta Hietlinger and Rudolf Iltis (Prague: Council of Jewish Communities in the Czech lands, 1965), 124–39.

Doležil, Hubert, 'Svatý Václav v české hudbě', *Listy hudební matice*, 9/2 (1929–30), 43–7.

Dřímal, Jaroslav, and Václav Peša, eds., *Dějiny města Brna*, 2 vols. (Brno: Blok, 1969–73).

Drlík, Vojen, 'Tvorba Pavla Haase pro činoherní divadlo', *Opus musicum*, 35/4 (2003), 2–6.

Dulavová, Marie, ed., *Dějiny české hudební kultury*, 2 vols. (Prague: Academia, 1972–81), i: 1890–1918 (1972); ii: 1918–1945 (1981).

Ehrlich-Fantlová, Zdenka, 'The Czech Theater in Terezín', in *Theatrical Performance During the Holocaust: Texts, Documents, Memoirs*, ed. Rebecca Rovit and Alvin Goldfarb (Baltimore MD: Johns Hopkins University Press, 1999), 231–49.

Ehrmann, František, Otta Hietlinger and Rudolf Iltis, eds., *Terezín* (Prague: Council of Jewish Communities in the Czech lands, 1965).

Fer, Briony, David Batchelor, and Paul Wood, eds., *Realism, Rationalism, Surrealism: Art between the Wars* (New Haven CT: Yale University Press in association with the Open University, 1993).

Firkušný, Leoš, *Vilém Petrželka: život a dílo* (Prague: Hudební matice Umělecké besedy, 1946).

Freeman, Robin, 'Excursus: "Nedej Zahynouti Nám Ni Budoucím, Svat[[yacute]] Václave": Klein, Ullmann, and Others in Terezin', *Tempo*, 60/236 (2006), 34–46.

Freeman, Robin, 'Gideon Klein, a Moravian Composer', *Tempo: A Quarterly Review of Modern Music*, 59/234 (October, 2005), 2–18.

Freud, Sigmund, 'The Uncanny (1919)', in *Fantastic Literature: A Critical Reader*, ed. David Sandner (Westport CT: Praeger, 2004), 74–101.

Fukač, Jiří, 'Janáček and the Dance of "Categories"', in *Janáček and Czech Music: Proceedings of the International Conference (Saint Louis, 1988), Studies in Czech Music No. 1*, ed. Michael Beckerman and Glen Bauer (Stuyvesant NY: Pendragon Press, 1995), 371–88.

Fukač, Jiří, Jiří Vysloužil, and Petr Macek, eds., *Slovník české hudební kultury* (Prague: Editio Supraphon, 1997).

Fulcher, Jane F., 'The Composer as Intellectual: Ideological Inscriptions in French Interwar Neoclassicism', *The Journal of Musicology*, 17/2 (1999), 197–230.

Fulcher, Jane F., *The Composer as Intellectual: Music and Ideology in France 1914–1940* (New York: Oxford University Press, 2005).

Fürst, Ernst, *Doctor Eysenbarth* (Stuttgart and Berlin: Chronos Verlag, 1932).

Gabrielová, Bronislava, and Bohumil Marčák, *Kapitoly z dějin brněnských časopisů* (Brno: Masarykova univerzita, 1999).

Gilbert, Shirli, *Music in the Holocaust: Confronting Life in the Nazi Ghettos and Camps* (Oxford: Clarendon Press, 2005).

Götz, František, 'Devětsil v Brně', *Socialistická budoucnost*, 28 May 1921, reprinted in Vlašín, Štěpán, ed., *Avantgarda známá a neznámá*, 3 vols. (Prague: Svoboda, 1970–72), i, 130–3.

Green, Martin, and John C. Swan, *The Triumph of Pierrot: The Commedia Dell'arte and the Modern Imagination* (University Park PA: Pennsylvania State University Press, 1993, revised edition).

Groarke, Paul, 'Chinese Poetry and Symbolism', *Journal of Chinese Philosophy*, 26/4 (1999), 489–512.

Haas, Pavel, 'Haasův kvartet "Z opičích hor": Poprvé proveden v Brně 16. března 1926', *Hudební rozhledy*, 7 (1925–26), 106.

Haas, Pavel, 'O návratu', *Listy Hudební Matice/Tempo*, 5/9–10 (1926), 325–7.

Haas, Pavel, 'O hudbě budoucnosti', *Hudební rozhledy*, 3/3 (1926–27), 58–9.

Haas, Pavel, 'Hudba lehká a vážná', *Tempo*, 15/8 (1936), 90.

Haas, Petr, 'Česká meziválečná hudební avantgarda: pojem "avantgarda" v české hudbě' (unpublished bachelor's thesis, Masaryk University, 2009).

Hasse, John Edward, ed., *Ragtime, Its History, Composers and Music* (New York: Schirmer Books, 1985).

Hasty, Christopher, 'On the Problem of Succession and Continuity in Twentieth-Century Music', *Music Theory Spectrum*, 8 (1986), 58–74.

Hatten, Robert S., *Musical Meaning in Beethoven: Markedness, Correlation, and Interpretation* (Bloomington: Indiana University Press, 1994).

Hefling, Stephen E., *Mahler: Das Lied von der Erde (The Song of the Earth)* (Cambridge: Cambridge University Press, 2000).

Helfert, Vladimír, *Česká moderní hudba: studie o české hudební tvořivosti* (Olomouc: Index, 1936), reprinted in *Vybrané studie: O hudební tvořivosti* (Prague: Ed. Supraphon, 1970), 163–312.

Hinton, Stephen, *The Idea of Gebrauchsmusik: A Study of Musical Aesthetics in the Weimar Republic (1919–1933) with Particular Reference to the Works of Paul Hindemith* (New York: Garland, 1989).

Hinton, Stephen, 'Weill: "Neue Sachlichkeit", Surrealism, and "Gebrauchsmusik"', in *A New Orpheus: Essays on Kurt Weill*, ed. Kim H. Kowalke (New Haven CT and London: Yale University Press, 1986), 61–82.

Hitchcock, H. Wiley, and Pauline Norton, 'Cakewalk', *Grove Music Online* www.oxford musiconline.com [accessed 4 November 2013].

Hodeir, Andre, *Jazz: Its Evolution and Essence* (New York: Grove Press, 1956).

Hoffmeister, Adolf, 'Nesmrtelnost smíchu', *Volné směry*, 26/7–8 (November 1928), reprinted in Vlašín, Štěpán, ed., *Avantgarda známá a neznámá*, 3 vols. (Prague: Svoboda, 1970–72), ii, 628–31.

Holzknecht, Václav, *Hudební skupina Mánesa* (Prague: Panton, 1968).

Holzknecht, Václav, *Mladá Francie a česká hudba* (Prague: Melantrich; Brno: Pazdírek, 1938).

Honzík, Karel, *Ze života avantgardy: zážitky architektovy* (Prague: Československý spisovatel, 1963).

Honzl, Jindřich, 'Státní židovské komorní divadlo v Moskvě', *ReD*, 1/2 (1927–28), 73–6.

Horlacher, Gretchen Grace, *Building Blocks: Repetition and Continuity in the Music of Stravinsky* (New York: Oxford University Press, 2011).

Horlacher, Gretchen Grace, 'The Rhythms of Reiteration: Formal development in Stravinsky's ostinati', *Music Theory Spectrum*, 14/2 (Autumn, 1992), 171–87.

Hyde, Martha M., 'Neoclassic and Anachronistic Impulses in Twentieth-Century Music', *Music Theory Spectrum*, 18 (1996), 200–35.

Janáček, Leoš, 'Úplná nauka o Harmonii', in *Teoretické dílo: Články, studie, přednášky, koncepty, zlomky, skici, svědectví, 1877–1927*, ed. Leoš Faltus, Eva Drlíková, Svatava Přibáňová, and Jiří Zahrádka, 2 vols. (Brno: Editio Janáček, 2007–08), ii/1 (2007), 459–661.

Janáček, Leoš, 'Můj názor o sčasování (rytmu)', in *Teoretické dílo: Články, studie, přednášky, koncepty, zlomky, skici, svědectví, 1877–1927*, ed. Leoš Faltus, Eva Drlíková, Svatava Přibáňová, and Jiří Zahrádka, 2 vols. (Brno: Editio Janáček, 2007–08), ii/1 (2007), 361–421.

Janáček, Leoš, 'Základy hudebního sčasování', in *Teoretické dílo: Články, studie, přednášky, koncepty, zlomky, skici, svědectví, 1877–1927*, ed. Leoš Faltus, Eva Drlíková, Svatava Přibáňová, and Jiří Zahrádka, 2 vols. (Brno: Editio Janáček, 2007–08), ii/2 (2007–08), 13–131.

Jeřábek, Dušan, *Brněnská romance* (Brno: Kulturní a informační centrum, 1997).

Jiránek, Jaroslav, 'The Controversy between Reality and Its Living in the Work of Leoš Janáček', in *Janáček and Czech Music: Proceedings of the International Conference (Saint Louis, 1988), Studies in Czech Music No. 1*, ed. Michael Beckerman and Glen Bauer (Stuyvesant NY: Pendragon Press, 1995), 365–70.

Johnson, Julian, *Mahler's Voices: Expression and Irony in the Songs and Symphonies* (Oxford: Oxford University Press, 2009).

Kang, Angela, 'Musical Chinoiserie' (unpublished Ph.D. dissertation, University of Nottingham, 2011) [accessed via http://eprints.nottingham.ac.uk/13707/1/575137.pdf, 27 April 2015].

Karas, Joža, *Music in Terezín 1941–1945* (New York: Beaufort Books, 1985).

Karbusický, Vladimír, 'Exotismus životní absurdity', *Hudební věda*, 34/2 (1997), 147–69.

Karbusický, Vladimír, 'Neukončená historie', *Hudební věda*, 35/4 (1998), 396–405.

Katritzky, M.A., *The Art of Commedia: The Study in the Commedia Dell'arte 1560–1620 with Special Reference to the Visual Records* (Amsterdam: Rodopi, 2006).

Katritzky, M.A., *Women, Medicine and Theatre, 1500–1750: Literary Mountebanks and Performing Quacks* (Aldershot: Ashgate, 2007).

Kelly, Barbara L., *Music and Ultra-Modernism in France: A Fragile Consensus, 1913–1939* (Woodbridge: Boydell Press, 2013).

Kielian-Gilbert, Marianne, 'The Rhythms of Form: Correspondence and Analogy in Stravinsky's Designs', *Music Theory Spectrum*, 9 (Spring, 1987), 42–66.

Kielian-Gilbert, Marianne, 'Stravinsky's Contrasts: Contradiction and Discontinuity in His Neoclassic Music', *The Journal of Musicology*, 9/4 (Autumn, 1991), 448–80.

Klein, Michael L, *Intertextuality in Western Art Music* (Bloomington: Indiana University Press, 2005).

Kotek, Josef, *Dějiny české populární hudby a zpěvu*, 2 vols. (Prague: Academia, 1994–98), ii: *1918–1968* (1998).

Kotek, Josef, ed., *Kronika české synkopy: půlstoletí českého jazzu a moderní populární hudby v obrazech a svědectví současníků* (Prague: Supraphon, 1975).

Krebs, Harald, 'Some Extensions of the Concepts of Metrical Consonance and Dissonance', *Journal of Music Theory*, 31/1 (Spring, 1987), 99–120.

Krejčí, Iša, 'Ponětí modernosti v dnešní hudbě', *Rozpravy Aventina*, 3 (1927–28), 97.

Kristeva, Julia, *Black Sun: Depression and Melancholia*, trans. Leon S. Roudiez (New York: Columbia University Press, 1989).

Kuna, Milan, *Hudba na hranici života* (Prague: Naše vojsko, 1990).

Kuna, Milan, *Hudba vzdoru a naděje: Terezín 1941–45: O činnosti a tvorbě hudebníků v koncentračním táboře Terezín* (Prague: Editio Bärenreiter, 2000).

Kundera, Ludvík, *Jaroslav Kvapil: život a dílo*, (Prague: Hudební matice Umělecké besedy, 1944).

Kundera, Ludvík, *Václav Kaprál: kapitola z historie české meziválečné hudby* (Brno: Blok, 1968).

Lachmann, Renate, 'Bakhtin and Carnival: Culture and Counter-Culture', in *Mikhail Bakhtin*, ed. Michael E. Gardiner, 4 vols. (London: Sage, 2003), ii, 60–90.

LeBaron, Anne, 'Reflections of Surrealism in Postmodern Musics', in *Postmodern Music/ Postmodern Thought*, ed. Judith Irene Lochhead, and Joseph Henry Auner (New York: Routledge, 2002), 27–73.

Levinger, Esther, 'Czech Avant-Garde Art: Poetry for the Five Senses', *The Art Bulletin*, 81/3 (1999), 513–32.

Levinger, Esther, 'A Life in Nature: Karel Teige's Journey from Poetism to Surrealism', *Zeitschrift für Kunstgeschichte*, 67/3 (2004), 401–20.

Levinger, Esther, 'Karel Teige on Cinema and Utopia', *The Slavic and East European Journal*, 48/2 (Summer, 2004), 247–74.

Lewin, David, 'On Harmony and Meter in Brahms's Opus 76 No. 8', *Nineteenth-Century Music*, 4/3 (1981), 261–5.

Limmer, Martin, 'Studien zur motivischen Arbeit im Werk von Pavel Haas' (unpublished Ph.D. dissertation, Universität Mozarteum Salzburg, 2013).

Locke, Brian S., *Opera and Ideology in Prague* (Rochester NY: University of Rochester Press, 2006).

Locke, Ralph P., 'Cutthroats and Casbah Dancers', in *The Exotic in Western Music*, ed. Jonathan Bellman (Boston: Northeastern University Press, 1998), 104–36.

Losen, Michael, 'Pavel Haas: Die Rezeption seiner Werke bis zum Aufführungsverbot 1939' (unpublished master's thesis, Universität Wien, 2006).

Macharáčková, Marcela, 'Z dějin Brněnského Devětsilu', in *Forum Brunense 2009: Sborník prací Muzea města Brna*, ed. Pavel Ciprian (Brno: Společnost přátel Muzea města Brna: 2009), 79–99.

Martinů, Bohuslav, *Domov, hudba a svět: deníky, zápisky, úvahy a články*, ed. Miloš Šafránek (Prague: Státní hudební vydavatelství, 1966).

Martinů, Bohuslav, 'Igor Stravinskij (1924)' in *Domov, hudba a svět: deníky, zápisky, úvahy a články*, ed. Miloš Šafránek (Prague: Státní hudební vydavatelství, 1966), 31–3, originally in *Listy hudební matice*, 4/3 (1924).

Martinů, Bohuslav, 'Současná hudba ve Francii (1925)', in *Domov, hudba a svět: deníky, zápisky, úvahy a články*, ed. Miloš Šafránek (Prague: Státní hudební vydavatelství, 1966), 46–9, originally in *Listy hudební matice*, 4/9–10 (1925).

Martinů, Bohuslav, 'Half-time', *Anbruch*, 7/5 (1925), 292–3.

Mathesius, Bohumil, *Nové Zpěvy Staré Číny* (Prague: Melantrich, 1940).

Mawer, Deborah, *Darius Milhaud: Modality and Structure in Music of the 1920s* (Aldershot: Scolar Press, Ashgate Publishing, 1997).

Messing, Scott, *Neoclassicism in Music: From the Genesis of the Concept through the Schoenberg/Stravinsky Polemic* (Rochester NY: Rochester University Press, 1996).

Migdal, Ulrike, *Und die Musik spielt dazu: Chansons und Satiren aus dem Kz Theresienstadt* (Munich: Piper, 1986).

Mirka, Danuta, ed., *The Oxford Handbook of Topic Theory* (New York: Oxford University Press, 2014).

Mitrychová, Linda, 'Pavel Haas: *Šarlatán*: Kapitoly ke genezi a recepci opery' (unpublished bachelor's thesis, Masaryk University, 2008).

Monelle, Raymond, *The Musical Topic: Hunt, Military and Pastoral* (Bloomington: Indiana University Press, 2006).

Murphy, Scott, 'On Metre in the Rondo of Brahms's Op. 25', *Music Analysis*, 26/3 (2007), 323–53.

Nemtsov, Jascha, 'Zur Klaviersuite op. 13 von Pavel Haas', *Musica Reanimata Mitteilungen*, 17 (1995), 20–3.

Nemtsov, Jascha and Beate Schröder-Nauenburg, 'Musik im Inferno des Nazi-Terrors: Jüdische Komponisten im "Dritten Reich"', *Acta Musicologica*, 70/1 (1998), 22–44.

Papoušek, Vladimír, *Gravitace avantgard: imaginace a řeč avantgard v českých literárních textech první poloviny dvacátého století* (Prague: Akropolis, 2007).

Pattison, George, *Kierkegaard and the Crisis of Faith: An Introduction to His Thought* (London: Society for Promoting Christian Knowledge, 1997).

Pattison, George, *Kirkegaard, Religion and the Nineteenth-century Crisis of Culture* (Cambridge: Cambridge University Press, 2002).

Peduzzi, Lubomír, 'Doktor Eisenbart incognito in einer tschechischen Oper', in *Musik in Theresienstadt: Die Komponisten: Pavel Haas, Gideon Klein, Hans Krasa, Viktor Ullmann, Erwin Schulhoff (gestorben Im Kz Wülzburg) und ihre Werke: Die Referate des Kolloquiums in Dresden Am 4. Mai 1991 und ergänzende Studien*, ed. Heidi Tamar Hoffmann and Hans-Günther Klein (Berlin: Musica Reanimata, 1991), 15–20.

Peduzzi, Lubomír, 'Haas, Pavel', *Grove Music Online*, www.oxfordmusiconline.com [accessed 18 November 2015].

Peduzzi, Lubomír, 'Haasova "hobojová" suita', *Hudební rozhledy*, 12 (1959), 793–8.

Peduzzi, Lubomír, *Haasův Šarlatán: Studie o opeře: Původní nezkrácená verze* (Brno, 1994).

Peduzzi, Lubomír, 'Janáček, Haas a Divoška', *Opus musicum*, 10/8 (1978), Příloha (Supplement), 1–4.

Peduzzi, Lubomír, 'Jak učil Janáček skládat operu', *Opus musicum*, 12/7 (1980), Příloha (Supplement), 1–8.

Peduzzi, Lubomír, *O hudbě v terezínském ghettu: Soubor kritických statí* (Brno: Barrister a Principal, 2nd edition, 1999); for German translation see *Musik im Ghetto Theresienstadt: Kritische Studien*, trans. Lenka Šedová (Brno: Barrister & Principal, 2005). 'Terezínské legendy a skutečnosti', 38–48. 'O Gideonu Kleinovi a jeho monografii', 103–13. 'Falešné problémy Haasových Čtyř písní', 79–84.

Peduzzi, Lubomír, *Pavel Haas: Život a dílo skladatele* (Brno: Muzejní a vlastivědná společnost, 1993); for German translation see *Pavel Haas: Leben und Werk des Komponisten*, trans. Thomas Mandl (Hamburg: Bockel, 1996).

Peduzzi, Lubomír, 'Představitel Janáčkovy školy', *Hudební rozhledy*, 17 (1964), 785–6.

Peduzzi, Lubomír, 'Vlastenecká symbolika posledních děl Pavla Haase', *Sborník Janáčkovy akademie múzických umění*, 3 (1961; Prague: Státní pedagogické nakladatelství, 1963), 75–97.

Perle, George, 'Symmetrical formations in the String Quartets of Bela Bartók', *Music Review*, 16 (1955), 300–12.

Petrželka, Vilém, and Ivan Petrželka, *Vilém Petrželka: z jeho životních osudů neznámých a zapomínaných* (Brno: Šimon Ryšavý, 2005).

Pivoda, Ondřej, *Pavel Haas: Janáčkův nejnadanější žák* (Brno: Moravské zemské muzeum, 2014).

Pivoda, Ondřej, 'Rozhlasová hudba a Pavel Haas', *Musicologica Brunensia*, 50/2 (2015), 53–67.

Puffett, Derrick, 'Debussy's Ostinato Machine', in *Derrick Puffett on Music*, ed. Kathryn Puffett (Aldershot: Ashgate, 2001), 231–85.

Puri, Michael J. *Ravel the Decadent: Memory, Sublimation, and Desire* (New York: Oxford University Press, 2011).

Racek, Jan, *Leoš Janáček a současní moravští skladatelé: nástin k slohovému vývoji soudobé moravské hudby* (Brno: Unie československých hudebníků z povolání, 1940).

Ratcliffe, Matthew, 'Varieties of Temporal Experience in Depression', *Journal of Medicine and Philosophy*, 37 (2012), 114–38.

Rehding, Alexander, 'Towards a "Logic of Discontinuity" in Stravinsky's "Symphonies of Wind Instruments": Hasty, Kramer and Straus Reconsidered', *Music Analysis*, 17/1 (1998), 39–65.

Rovit, Rebecca and Alvin Goldfarb, eds., *Theatrical Performance During the Holocaust: Texts, Documents, Memoirs* (Baltimore MD: Johns Hopkins University Press, 1999).

Royle, Nicholas, *The Uncanny* (New York: Routledge, 2003).

Schneider, Franz Markus, 'Terezínský smích', in *Terezínské studie a dokumenty* (Prague: Academia, 1999), 242–50.

Schultz, Ingo, *Viktor Ullmann: Leben und Werk* (Kassel: Bärenreiter, 2008).

Schulz, Karel, 'Groteska', *Český filmový svět* 4/2 (March 1926), reprinted in Vlašín, Štěpán, ed., *Avantgarda známá a neznámá*, 3 vols. (Prague: Svoboda, 1970–72), ii, 278–80.

Schwandt, Erich, 'Trio', *Grove Music Online*, www.oxfordmusiconline.com [accessed 2 December 2015].

Sedláčková, Pavlína, 'Čtyři písně na slova čínské poezie: výpověď terezínského vězně' (unpublished bachelor's thesis, Masaryk University, 2011) [accessed via http://is.muni. cz/th/341927/ff_b/bakalarska_prace.pdf?lang=en, 16 October 2012].

Seifert, Jaroslav, and Karel Teige, eds., *Revoluční sborník Devětsil* (Prague: Večernice V. Vortel, 1922; reprinted by Prague: Akropolis ve spolupráci s Centrem výzkumu české umělecké avantgardy, 2010).

Sen, Suddhaseel, 'The Art Song and Tagore: Settings by Western Composers', *University of Toronto Quarterly*, 77/4 (2008), 1110–32.

Shattuck, Roger, *The Banquet Years* (New York: Vintage Books, 1968).

Sheinberg, Esti, *Irony, Satire, Parody, and the Grotesque in the Music of Shostakovich: A Theory of Musical Incongruities* (Aldershot: Ashgate, 2000).

Slavíček, Lubomír, and Jana Vránová, eds., *100 let Domu umění města Brna* (Brno: Dům umění města Brna, 2010).

Slavický, Milan, *Gideon Klein: A Fragment of Life and Work*, trans. Dagmar Steinová (Prague: Helvetica-Tempora, 1996).

Šmejkal, František, and Rostislav Švácha, eds., *Devětsil: Czech Avant-garde Art, Architecture and Design of the 1920s and 30s* (Oxford: Museum of Modern Art, 1990).

Solarová, Truda, 'Gideon Klein', in *Terezín*, ed. František Ehrmann, Otta Hietlinger and Rudolf Iltis (Prague: Council of Jewish Communities in the Czech lands, 1965), 242–5.

Štědroň, Bohumír, 'Česká hudba za nesvobody', *Musikologie*, 2 (1949), 106–46.

Štědroň, Miloš, *Leoš Janáček a hudba 20. století. Paralely, sondy, dokumenty* (Brno: Nadace Universitas Masarykiana, 1998).

Sternstein, Malynne M., *The Will to Chance: Necessity and Arbitrariness in the Czech Avant-Garde from Poetism to Surrealism* (Bloomington: Slavica Publishers, 2007).

Svoboda, Jiří, and Karel Teige, 'Musica a muzika', *Život*, 2 (1922), 86–89, reprinted in Vlašín, Štěpán, ed., *Avantgarda známá a neznámá*, 3 vols. (Prague: Svoboda, 1970–72), i, 405–12.

Teige, Karel, 'Manifest poetismu', *ReD*, 1/9 (June, 1928), reprinted in Vlašín, Štěpán, ed., *Avantgarda známá a neznámá*, 3 vols. (Prague: Svoboda, 1970–72), ii, 557–93.

Teige, Karel, 'O humoru, clownech a dadaistech', *Sršatec*, 4/38–40 (1924), reprinted in Vlašín, Štěpán, ed., *Avantgarda známá a neznámá*, 3 vols. (Prague: Svoboda, 1970–72), i, 571–86.

Teige, Karel, 'Poetismus', *Host*, 3 (July, 1924), 197–204, reprinted in Vlašín, Štěpán, ed., *Avantgarda známá a neznámá*, 3 vols. (Prague: Svoboda, 1970–72), i, 554–61.

Teige, Karel, *Výbor z díla*, ed. Jiří Brabec, Vratislav Effenberger, Květoslav Chvatík, and Robert Kalivoda, 3 vols. (Prague: Československý spisovatel 1966–94), ii: *Zápasy o smysl moderní tvorby, Studie z třicátých let* (1969).

Thomas, Adrian, *Polish Music since Szymanowski* (Cambridge: Cambridge University Press, 2005).

Tyrrell, John, *Janáček: Years of Life*, 2 vols. (London: Faber and Faber, 2006–07), ii: *(1914–1928), Tsar of the Forests* (2007).

Ullmann, Viktor, and Ingo Schultz, *26 Kritiken über musikalische Veranstaltungen in Theresienstadt* (Hamburg: Bockel Verlag, 1993).

Vlašín, Štěpán, ed., *Avantgarda známá a neznámá*, 3 vols. (Prague: Svoboda, 1970–72). i: *Od proletářského umění k poetismu: 1919–1924* (1971). ii: *Vrchol a krize poetismu: 1925–1928* (1972). iii: *Generační diskuse: 1929–1931* (1970).

Vlček, Tomáš, 'Art between Social Crisis and Utopia: The Czech Contribution to the Development of the Avant-Garde Movement in East-Central Europe, 1910–30', *Art Journal*, 49/1 (Spring, 1990), 28–35.

Vohnoutová El Roumhainová, Suzanne, 'Počátky Klubu moravských skladatelů: 1919–1928' (unpublished master's thesis, Masaryk University, 2013) [accessed via http://is.muni.cz/th/64669/ff_m/Diplomova_prace.pdf, 15 November 2015].

Vojvodík, Josef, and Jan Wiendl, eds., *Heslář české avantgardy: estetické koncepty a proměny uměleckých postupů v letech 1908–1958* (Prague: Togga, 2011).

Vysloužil, Jiří, 'Česká meziválečná hudební avantgarda', *Opus musicum*, 7/1 (1975), 1–11.

Wang, Robin R., *Yinyang* (Cambridge: Cambridge University Press, 2012).

Waters, Keith, *Rhythmic and Contrapuntal Structures in the Music of Arthur Honegger* (Aldershot: Ashgate, 2002).

Watkins, Glenn, *Pyramids at the Louvre: Music, Culture, and Collage from Stravinsky to the Postmodernists* (Cambridge MA: Belknap Press of Harvard University Press, 1994).

Watt, Ian, *Myths of Modern Individualism* (Cambridge: Cambridge University Press, 1997).

Winckler, Josef, *Wunder-Doktor Johann Andreas Eisenbart* (Berlin: Deutsche Buchgemeinschaft, 1933).

Wingfield, Paul, 'Janáček, musical analysis, and Debussy's "Jeux de vagues"', in *Janáček Studies*, ed. Paul Wingfield (Cambridge: Cambridge University Press, 1999), 183–280.

Witkovsky, Matthew S., 'Staging Language: Milča Mayerová and the Czech Book "Alphabet"', *The Art Bulletin*, 86/1 (2004), 114–35.

Zádrapová, Anna, 'Bohumil Mathesius, Jaroslav Průšek a *Zpěvy staré Číny*', *SOS*, 11/2 (2012), 239–71 [accessed via https://fphil.uniba.sk/fileadmin/fif/katedry_pracoviska/kvas/SOS_11_2/06_14zadrapova-form130130_Kopie.pdf, 07 May 2015].

Zusi, Peter A., 'The Style of the Present: Karel Teige on Constructivism and Poetism', *Representations*, 88/1 (Fall, 2004), 102–24.

Newspaper reviews and articles

Reviews and articles compiled in Haas's notebook entitled 'Moje úspěchy a ne-úspěchy' ('My Successes and Non-successes'), property of Olga Haasová-Smrčková

–l–, 'Kulturní obzor: V koncertu Klubu moravských skladatelů', *Stráž socialismu*, 18 March 1926.

lk., 'Nová kvarteta', *Moravské noviny*, 19 March 1926.

L. K. [Ludvík Kundera], 'Koncert Klubu moravských skladatelů', *Národní osvobození*, 19 March 1926.
–k–, 'Z brněnských koncertů: Večer kvartetních novinek', *Lidové noviny*, 18 March 1926.
St–, 'Klub moravských skladatelů', *Rovnost*, 18 March 1926.
[unknown], 'Koncerty v Brně', *Tribuna*, 19 March 1926 (cited from Haas's album).
V. H. [Vladimír Helfert], 'Koncerty v Brně: Klub mor. skladatelů', *Ruch*, 20 March 1926.

Archival documents (Pavel Haas)

Archival documents deposited in the Department of Music History of the Moravian Museum (Oddělení dějin hudby Moravského zemského muzea)

Music

Fata morgana, sign. A 22.695 a.
Karneval, sign. A 22.730 b and A 54.252.
Předehra pro rozhlas, Op. 11 (1931), sign. A22.693.
Symfonie: Autografní skica (Autograph sketch), sign. A 22.732 a.
Symfonie: 1. věta (First movement), sign. A 22.732 b.
Šarlatán: Části opery, skici (Parts of the opera, sketches), sign. A 22.689.
Šarlatán: Klavírní výtah (Piano reduction), sign. A 22.688.
Šarlatán: Návrhy libreta (Drafts of libretto), sign. B 832.
Šarlatán: Navrhované změny (Proposed changes), sign. A 22.690.
Šarlatán: Partitura (Score), sign. A 22.687 a, b, c.
Šarlatán: Původní skica opery (Original draft of the opera), sign. A 22.691.
Šarlatán: Skici partitury (Drafts of the score), sign. A 22.689.
Vojcek (Incidental music to play by Georg Büchner), sign. A 29.804.
Z opičích hor, sign. A 29.801 a.

Other documents

Referáty z novin (Newspaper reviews), sign. J 8.

Archival documents deposited in the Archive of the National Theatre in Brno: Department of Musical Documentation (Archiv Národního divadla Brno: Oddělení hudební dokumentace)

R. U. R. (1921): incidental music to a play by Karel Čapek, sign. 168.
Konec Petrovských (1923): incidental music to a play by Quido Maria Vyskočil, sign. 274.
Veselá smrt (1925): incidental music to a play by Nicholas Evreinov, sign. 376.
Černý troubadour (1928): incidental music to a play by Samson Raphaelson, sign. 489.

Archival documents deposited in the Archive of the National Theatre in Brno: Department of Musical Documentation (Archiv Národního divadla Brno: Oddělení hudební dokumentace)

Šarlatán: costume designs by František Muzika, sign. N 275, II–58.

Archival documents in private property of Olga Haasová-Smrčková

'Moje úspěchy a ne-úspěchy' ('My Successes and Non-successes'): a notebook containing newspaper clippings of newspaper articles on and concert reviews of Haas's works.

Musical editions

Haas, Pavel, *Al S'fod*: Male Chorus set to Hebrew words by David Shimoni, 1942 (Prague: Tempo; Berlin: Bote & Bock, 1994).

Haas, Pavel, Čtyři písně pro bas (baryton) a klavír na slova čínské poezie v překladu Bohumila Mathesia (Prague: Panton, 1987).

Haas, Pavel, Čtyři písně pro bas (baryton) a klavír na slova čínské poezie/Four Songs for Bass (Baritone) and piano to the Words of Chinese Poetry (Prague: Tempo; Berlin: Bote & Bock, 1992).

Haas, Pavel, String Quartet No. 2 'From the Monkey Mountains', Op. 7, 1925 (Prague: Tempo; Berlin: Bote & Bock, 1994).

Haas, Pavel, String Quartet No. 3, Op. 15, 1937–38 (Berlin: Bote & Bock; Prague: Tempo Praha, 1991).

Haas, Pavel, Studie pro smyčcový orchestr, 1943 (Berlin: Bote & Bock; Prague: Tempo Praha, completed and revised by Lubomír Peduzzi, 1991).

Haas, Pavel, Suite for Oboe and Piano, Op. 17, 1939 (Prague: Tempo; Berlin: Bote & Bock, 1993, revised by František Suchý).

Haas, Pavel, Suita pro klavír (Suite for Piano) (Prague: Hudební matice, 1937).

Haas, Pavel, Wind Quintet, Op. 10, 1929 (Prague: Tempo Praha; Berlin: Bote & Bock/ Boosey & Hawkes, 2nd rev. edn, 1998).

Haas, Pavel, Žalm 29 (Psalm 29), Op. 12 (Berlin: Boosey & Hawkes/Bote & Bock, n.d.).

Janáček, Leoš, String Quartet No. 1 'Inspired by Tolstoy's Kreutzer Sonata', 1923 (Prague: Supraphon; 2nd edn, revised by Milan Škampa, 1982).

Mahler, Gustav, *Das Lied von der Erde* (Vienna: Universal Edition, 1912).

Satie, Erik, *Klavierwerke* [Piano Works], ed. Eberhardt Klemm, 2 vols. (Leipzig: Edition Peters, 1986–89), ii (1989).

Suk, Josef, *Asrael*: Symfonie Pro Velký Orchestr, Op. 27 (Prague: Státní hudební vydavatelství, 1965).

Ullmann, Viktor, *The Emperor of Atlantis or Death's Refusal*: One-act play by Peter Kien, Op. 49, 1943 (Mainz: Schott, 1993).

Index

agency 3–4, 142, 209–10, 215–20, 224–32, 239–40
Ančerl, Karel 13, 16, 142
Auric, Georges 9, 57
avant-garde: avant-garde innovation vs. Neoclassicism 37; avant-garde vs. modernism 47; Czech inter-war avant-garde 29–30; French avant-garde composers as viewed by K. Teige 35; Parisian avant-garde and its influence on Czech artists and Haas in particular 2, 247, 249; with reference to Haas's 'From the Monkey Mountains' 56, 69, 71, 125; with reference to Haas's *Overture for Radio* 4; with reference to Janáček's compositional school and Haas in particular 11–12, 48; *see also* Devětsil, Neoclassicism, Poetism, Surrealism, *commedia dell'arte*

Bakhtin, Mikhail 69–71, 77, 109, 180; *see also* carnival, grotesque, the
Bartók, Béla 8, 9, 20n43, 43, 69, 93, 246, 248
Berg, Josef 117–21, 124
Berman, Karel 13, 16
block form 116, 119, 140, 157
Bořkovec, Pavel 30, 33, 247
Brno: as home city of Haas and his family 1, 4–5, 7, 13, 16, 19n16, 23n82, 30, 25n114, 58, 247; Devětsil in Brno 30, 48n4; Eccentric Carnival of Artists in Brno 71, 73–4; Janáček's Organ School in Brno 124; musical culture in the inter-war era 7–11; performances of Haas's works 10, 19n24, 21n57, 58, 87n4, 165, 203n45; performances of works by other composers and playwrights 6, 8, 20n34, 20n43, 62, 88n21, 172, 180
Burian, E. F. 30–4, 41

cakewalk 100
caricature 2, 35, 57–8, 62, 86, 180, 247–51
carnival: as a recurring topic in Haas's music 249–50; as a topos of Poetism 2–3, 32, 45, 56; Eccentric Carnival of Artists in Brno 71–3; in Bakhtin's thought 69–71, in Haas's *Charlatan* 170, 187, 189–90; in Haas's 'The Wild Night' 86–7, 109–10; in the poem *Carnival* by D. Chalupa and its setting by Haas 74–7
carnivalesque-grotesque *see* carnival
Chalupa, Dalibor 74–5
Chlubna, Osvald 11–12, 56, 57
circular motion: in Haas's Four Songs on Chinese Poetry 3, 209–10, 214–15, 217, 219–20, 227, 231–5, 239–40; in Haas's *Charlatan* 177–8; in Haas's String Quartet No. 3 145, 155; with reference to fairground imagery 76, 81–2, 182–3, 204n84; with reference to the uncanny 155, 184, 192, 197; *see also* cyclic motion
circus 2, 36, 64, 66, 68–9, 75, 80, 170
Clair, René 68
Club of Moravian Composers 8–10
Cocteau, Jean 30, 34–42, 98
collage: as juxtaposition of incongruous element in Haas's music 45, 47, 94, 108–9, 111n7, 249; in early twentieth-century music 46–7; in the art of Devětsil artists 32, 45–6, 57
Columbine 171–2, 185, 190, 196
commedia dell'arte 36, 167, 170–1, 189, 201, 204n84; *see also* fairground, Columbine, Harlequin, Pierrot, Jean Potage, Pickelhering
Constructivism 12, 29, 31, 36, 71, 250; *see also* Neoclassicism, Poetism
cyclic motion 175–6, 209–210, 239–40; *see also* circular motion